W9-AXE-340

Rick Steves®

BERLIN

Rick Steves
with Cameron Hewitt & Gene Openshaw

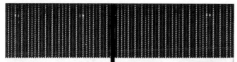

CONTENTS

Post-Pandemic Travels: Expect a Warm Welcome...and a Few Changes
Research for this guidebook was limited by the COVID-19 outbreak, and the long-term impact of the crisis on our recommended destinations is unclear. Some details in this book will change for post-pandemic travelers. Now more than ever, it's smart to reconfirm specifics as you plan and travel. As always, you can find major updates at RickSteves.com/update.

Welcome to Rick Steves' Europe

Travel is intensified living—maximum thrills per minute and one of the last great sources of legal adventure. Travel is freedom. It's recess, and we need it.

I discovered a passion for European travel as a teen and have been sharing it ever since—through my bus tours, public television and radio shows, and travel guidebooks. Over the years, I've taught millions of travelers how to best enjoy Europe's blockbuster sights—and experience "Back Door" discoveries that most tourists miss.

This book offers you a balanced mix of Berlin's serious, historical sights and lively people zones. It's selective: Rather than listing every sight, I recommend only the most important, along with the most interesting neighborhoods to explore— Prenzlauer Berg, Kreuzberg, and the old Jewish quarter. And it's in-depth: My self-guided museum tours  and city walks provide insight into Berlin's vibrant history and today's living, breathing culture.

I advocate traveling simply and smartly. Take advantage of my money- and time-saving tips on sight-seeing, transportation, and more. Try local, characteristic alternatives to expensive hotels and restaurants. In many ways, spending more money only builds a thicker wall between you and what you traveled so far to see.

We visit Berlin to experience it—to become temporary locals. Thoughtful travel engages us with the world, as we learn to appreciate other cultures and new ways to measure quality of life.

Judging by the positive feedback I receive from readers, this book will help you enjoy a fun, affordable, and rewarding vacation—whether it's your first trip or your tenth.

Gute Reise! Happy travels!

Rick Steves

BERLIN

Hip and affordable, Berlin is understandably one of Europe's top travel destinations. It's a city of leafy boulevards, grand Neoclassical buildings, world-class art, and glitzy shopping arcades. Just strolling through its funky neighborhoods gives you a fun glimpse into today's good times. Life here, especially in what was once dreary communist East Berlin, is a poignant, hedonistic—and even jarring—mix of a thriving economy and tragic history.

Berlin played a leading role in Europe's tumultuous 20th century, both in World War I, which led to Hitler's rise to power, and World War II, which ultimately left Berlin (and much of Europe) in ruins.

In the postwar years, Berlin was on the front line of the Cold War between the US and Soviet Union. The division was literally set in stone in 1961, when the communist East German government walled off West Berlin to keep East Germans from escaping to freedom.

Since the fall of the Berlin Wall in 1989, the city has been a constant construction zone of reunification and rebirth. Today Berlin is once again a world capital of a great nation.

Berliners have a remarkable ability to embrace the present while surrounded by sights from their tumultuous past. The city offers thoughtful visitors the opportunity to appreciate and learn from both.

Wander through Berlin's thought-provoking museums and memorials to the millions of victims of World War II. Atop the Reichstag parliament building, tour the modern glass

Clinking mugs at a lively beer hall; cuisine from around the globe to please every palate

dome that promises much-needed transparency in government after the wars of the last century.

Stroll the tree-lined Unter den Linden boulevard, pedal through Tiergarten Park, and take a lazy cruise on the scenic Spree River. Browse the city's many markets and shop for chocolate on bustling Gendarmenmarkt square.

In top-notch museums, cradle a chunk of the concrete-and-rebar Berlin Wall, peruse canvases by Dürer and Rembrandt, and walk through an enormous Babylonian gate amid ancient statuary. Learn about daily life in communist East Berlin and marvel at Easterners' ingenious escapes to the West. Ponder street-art graffiti on your way to the famous bust of Queen Nefertiti. Light a candle at a memorial church and hum "Ode to Joy" at the Brandenburg Gate, Germany's symbol of peace and reconciliation.

Explore vibrant neighborhoods like eclectic Kreuzberg, with Turkish flavor and destination restaurants; lively Prenzlauer Berg, bustling with boutiques, bars, and cafés; and the old Jewish quarter, with delightful courtyard shops and eateries.

Enjoy cosmopolitan cuisine in a melting-pot city known for its gourmet street food. Slurp soup at a foodie hotspot, dive into a cheap *Currywurst*, and munch your way through Kreuzberg's food hall. Wash down hearty sausage with beer in a rollicking beer hall or relaxing beer garden.

The Many Faces of Berlin

Like any cosmopolitan city, Berlin is a melting pot.

Many Berliners are transplants from elsewhere in Germany. Some came to West Berlin back when the Wall was up, lured by draft deferments and tax breaks designed to keep this "outpost of Western freedom" vital. West Berlin became home to a mix of peaceniks, punks, squatters, graffiti artists, and mainstream businesspeople.

After the Wall fell in 1990, East Berlin enjoyed an "anything goes" anarchy that attracted a wave of German artists, students, and young graduates. The 2000s and 2010s drew expats (including Americans, Brits, and Aussies) and more Germans as Berlin blossomed as an exciting, cultural capital.

Berlin is also home to immigrants and refugees from the Middle East and North Africa. In the postwar years, West Germany needed help rebuilding. Throughout the 1960s and 1970s, the government invited guest workers from poorer nations to live and work in Germany. Today, with approximately 200,000 residents of Turkish descent, Berlin is considered the largest "Turkish city" outside of Turkey. Many live and shop in Kreuzberg. These families—some in their third generation— are an integral part of Berlin society.

Recently, Syrian refugees have settled here, opening Middle Eastern bakeries and restaurants, adding spice to the city's rich culinary scene. The Pergamon Museum even recruits Syrians as tour guides to show off the masterpieces of their homeland's ancient culture.

If you really want to understand Berlin...take the time to get to know some Berliners. And be sure to ask about their own personal story. You'll never hear the same one twice. ◼

Graffiti artist in action; students chatting in hip Prenzlauer Berg; Turkish immigrants cooking up tasty fare at a Kreuzberg street market

Berlin's contrasts: Relaxing on the Spree's riverbank; learning about Nazi war crimes at the Topography of Terror

For nightlife, enjoy Berlin's happening music scene, from classical to jazz, cabaret to karaoke, and tango to ballroom dancing. The Friedrichshain neighborhood, east of Alexanderplatz, is a hotspot for nightclubs. Dine at a restaurant, settle in at a rooftop bar, or just grab a drink from a sidewalk vendor, find a riverside bench, and watch boats glide by as the sun sets over a skyline of domes and cranes.

With extra time, take day trips to Potsdam, home to Frederick the Great's palaces; Wittenberg, the theological stomping grounds of Martin Luther; and Sachsenhausen, a former concentration camp that's now a compelling memorial and museum.

Visitors to Berlin are understandably fascinated by the Nazi sights, communism, and the Wall. But for today's young Berliners, that's history. To them, capitalism is the norm, and the Wall is fair game for graffiti. Reflecting on its past while energized by a promising future, today's Berlin is an old city with a new spirit.

Berlin's Top Neighborhoods

Berlin sprawls. Though it's a major metropolis, it doesn't have a single, dense core of skyscrapers. The downtown stretches five miles, following the Spree River, and the city's impressive public-transit system makes it easy to sightsee by neighborhood. This book's coverage is organized by compass direction, radiating out from the center. You'll save lots of time if you thoughtfully group your sightseeing, walks, and dining.

To Sachsenhausen Memorial & Museum

NORTHERN BERLIN
BERLIN WALL SIGHTS
PRENZLAUER BERG
HAUPTBAHNHOF AREA
OLD JEWISH QUARTER

Spree River

HISTORIC CORE
"MITTE"
UNTER DEN LINDEN
MUSEUM ISLAND AREA
REICHSTAG AREA
BRANDENBURG GATE AREA
GENDARMEN-MARKT

ALEXANDER-PLATZ & NEARBY
EASTERN BERLIN
FRIEDRICHS-HAIN

To CHARLOTTENBURG PALACE AREA

TIERGARTEN

CITY WEST
POTSDAMER PLATZ & KULTURFORUM

WESTERN BERLIN

FASCISM & COLD WAR SIGHTS
JEWISH MUSEUM
KREUZ-BERG

SOUTHERN BERLIN

To Potsdam

Not to Scale

TOP NEIGHBORHOODS

Berlin is made up of a series of colorful neighborhoods, with broad boulevards, pleasant parks, long blocks, and low buildings.

Central Berlin (The Historic Core)

Berlin's 1.5-mile sightseeing axis runs along the elegant Unter den Linden boulevard. On the western end are the historic Reichstag (Germany's domed parliament), the iconic Brandenburg Gate, and poignant memorials. To the east is Museum Island, home to a cluster of the city's top museums: the ancient wonders of the Pergamon (Babylonian gate) and Neues (Nefertiti bust) museums, and German paintings in the Old National Gallery.

Also within this core are several grand squares (including Berlin's finest, Gendarmenmarkt), the towering Berlin Cathedral, and museums on German history and the DDR (communist-era artifacts from the former Deutsche Demokratische Republik).

Northern Berlin

North of Unter den Linden near the Hackescher Markt transit hub, the trendy old Jewish quarter is important for its Jewish sights and interesting for its fun-to-explore courtyards. The hip Prenzlauer Berg neighborhood has recommended hotels, restaurants, shopping, and a museum on daily life under communism. The northern zone also contains the Berlin Wall Memorial (the best place to learn more about the Wall), the people-friendly Mauerpark (Wall Park), and the massive Hauptbahnhof (Berlin's huge main train station and shopping mall).

Ishtar Gate (Pergamon Museum); Nefertiti (Neues Museum); an inviting Hackescher Markt café; Mauerpark karaoke

Jewish Museum Berlin; Alexander Platz with "World Time Clock"; world-class art at the Gemälde-galerie; arch at Potsdam

Southern Berlin

South of Unter den Linden are fascism and Cold War sights, anchored by the Museum of the Wall at Checkpoint Charlie (the former border crossing) and the Topography of Terror (which documents Nazi atrocities). Kreuzberg is a fascinating-to-wander neighborhood, with a flourishing Turkish community and colorful market.

Eastern Berlin

East of Museum Island is Alexanderplatz—formerly the hub of communist East Berlin, marked by its stark architecture and impossible-to-miss TV Tower. Farther east sits the gentrifying Friedrichshain neighborhood, with its emerging nightlife scene, sobering Stasi Museum (former communist headquarters), and the East Side Gallery—a graffiti-slathered surviving stretch of the Berlin Wall, popular for an evening stroll along the Spree River.

Western Berlin

This zone hosts glitzy Potsdamer Platz, with malls and sky-scrapers; the nearby Kulturforum, with the art-filled Gemäldegalerie; and the vast park, Tiergarten. To the west is City West, once the heart of communist-era West Berlin and now a classy suburb, home to the upscale Kurfürstendamm boulevard (Ku'damm for short), Kaiser Wilhelm Memorial Church, and several recommended hotels. To the north is the mediocre Charlottenburg Palace, with good art museums nearby.

Day Trips

You have three good—and very different—choices:
The pleasant town of **Potsdam** offers swanky palaces and Cold War sights. The **Sachsenhausen Memorial and Museum** was one of the Nazis' most notorious concentration camps. **Wittenberg** is the hometown of Martin Luther and birthplace of the Protestant Reformation.

Planning and Budgeting

The best trips start with good planning. Here are ideas to help you decide when to go, design a smart itinerary, set a travel budget, and prepare for your trip. For my best general advice on sightseeing, accommodations, restaurants, and more, see the Practicalities chapter.

PLANNING YOUR TIME

As you read this book and learn about your options...

Decide when to go.
May, June, September, and October are my favorite months for Berlin—most likely to be not too hot, not too cold. However, these are also the most crowded months; there can be lines at sights and higher prices at hotels.

July and August are lively—Berliners love to hang out in parks and along riverbanks, as if enjoying a continuous open-air party. Be aware that the city can get unpleasantly hot and humid. If you wilt in the heat, look for the scarce room with air-conditioning.

Berlin is a decent winter getaway: Its museums are ample and offer an escape from bad weather, and a handful of Christmas markets make the city merry and bright. However, many of the important historical sights are outdoors. And in general, Berlin is an exuberantly outdoor-oriented city—a scene that wintertime visitors miss out on. Night draws the shades on your sightseeing early. Dress warmly, with layers. Expect cold (even freezing lows) and rain. For specific temperatures, see the climate chart in the appendix.

Work out a day-by-day itinerary.

The following day plans offer suggestions for how to maximize your sightseeing, depending on how many days you have. You can adapt these itineraries to fit your own interests. To find out what days sights are open, check the "Daily Reminder" in the Orientation chapter. Note major sights where advance reservations are smart. Many of these sights are covered in my free ∩ Berlin City Walk audio tour.

Berlin in One Insane Day

8:30	Ascend the Reichstag dome (reserve in advance).
10:00	Follow my Reichstag & Brandenburg Gate Walk.
11:30	Follow my Unter den Linden Walk (stop for lunch midway in the Galeries Lafayette).
14:00	Do an "express tour" of the German History Museum and/or DDR Museum, or take a one-hour Spree River cruise.
16:00	Follow my Communist East Berlin Walk.
17:00	Taxi or S-Bahn to Nordbahnhof for my Berlin Wall Memorial Tour.
18:30	Taxi to the start of my Prenzlauer Berg Walk, with a break for dinner. (If running late, skip one of the last two.)

Enjoying the view 80 feet above the city from the Reichstag glass dome; stirring photos at the Berlin Wall Memorial

Berlin in Two Days
Day 1

8:30	Ascend the Reichstag dome (reserve in advance).
10:00	Follow my Reichstag & Brandenburg Gate Walk.
11:30	Follow my Unter den Linden Walk (buy a picnic lunch in the Galeries Lafayette).
13:00	Enjoy a Spree River cruise while munching a picnic.
14:30	Choose and visit two Museum Island area sights: Pergamon, Neues Museum, Old National Gallery, German History Museum, or DDR Museum.
17:00	Follow my Communist East Berlin Walk.
18:30	Take the S-Bahn to Hackescher Markt for my Old Jewish Quarter Walk.
20:00	Have dinner in the old Jewish quarter.

Day 2

9:30	Follow my Fascism & Cold War Walk to Potsdamer Platz (touring the Museum of the Wall at Checkpoint Charlie and Topography of Terror along the way).
12:30	Grab lunch and tour the Gemäldegalerie.
15:00	Head to the Berlin Wall Memorial for my tour.
17:00	Follow my Prenzlauer Berg walk.
19:00	Eat dinner in Prenzlauer Berg.

Berlin in Three or More Days
Day 1

8:30	Ascend the Reichstag dome (reserve in advance).
10:00	Follow my Reichstag & Brandenburg Gate Walk.
11:30	Follow my Unter den Linden Walk (buy a picnic lunch in Galeries Lafayette).
13:00	Enjoy a Spree River cruise while munching a picnic.
14:30	Tour Museum Island (Pergamon, Neues Museum, and/or Old National Gallery).
18:30	Follow my Old Jewish Quarter Walk.
20:00	Have dinner in the old Jewish quarter.

Day 2

9:30	Follow my Fascism & Cold War Walk to Potsdamer Platz (touring the Museum of the Wall at Checkpoint Charlie and Topography of Terror along the way).
13:30	Tour the Gemäldegalerie (or another sight of interest).

A Spree River cruise; Berlin's slick main train station (Hauptbahnhof); Museum Island, home to five museums; Anne Frank mural

Atop Berlin's TV Tower for views; shopping at Bikini Berlin concept mall

17:00   Attend the theater, find live music, or take a dance lesson.

Day 3
10:00   Visit the DDR Museum.
11:00   Follow my Communist East Berlin Walk (with Karl-Marx-Allee, East Side Gallery, and Kreuzberg options after).
16:00   Follow my Berlin Wall Memorial Tour.
18:00   Follow my Prenzlauer Berg Walk (with dinner spliced in as you like).

Days 4-7
Explore **City West,** visiting the Kaiser Wilhelm Memorial Church and Käthe Kollwitz Museum, strolling Ku'damm, and browsing KaDeWe and Bikini Berlin stores.

Tour **more museums,** such as the Jewish Museum Berlin, Stasi Museum, and others. Enjoy my **Kreuzberg Walk** through the trendy Turkish quarter.

Join a special-interest **walking tour,** choosing from topics ranging from food to street art to the Third Reich.

Choose from the following day trips: **Sachsenhausen Memorial and Museum,** the city and palaces at **Potsdam,** and the Martin Luther sights at **Wittenberg.**

PLANNING YOUR BUDGET

Run a reality check on your dream trip. You'll have major transportation costs in addition to daily expenses.

Flight: A round-trip flight from the US to Berlin costs about $900-1,500, depending on where you fly from and when.

Public Transportation: For a one-week trip, allow about $40 for transit tickets and a couple of day trips by train. To get between Berlin and the airport, figure around $4 per trip by bus, or closer to $30-45 for a taxi.

Budget Tips: To cut your daily expenses, take advantage of the deals you'll find throughout Berlin and mentioned in this book.

AVERAGE DAILY EXPENSES PER PERSON

$150

Lodging
Based on two people splitting the cost of a $130 double room
$65

Meals
$10 for lunch, $20 for dinner, $5 for beer or ice cream
$35

City Transit
Public transit or taxis/Uber
$10

Sights and Entertainment
This daily average works for most people.
$40

Use Berlin's public transportation (the WelcomeCard transit pass is generally a good bet for busy travelers), and visit sights by neighborhood for efficiency. Enjoy the city's free sights and experiences (people-watching counts).

Some businesses—especially hotels and walking-tour companies—offer discounts to my readers (look for the RS% symbol in the listings in this book).

Reserve your rooms directly with the hotel. Some hotels offer a discount if you pay in cash and/or stay three or more nights (check online or ask). Rooms can cost less outside of peak season (roughly Nov-March). And even seniors can sleep cheap in hostels (most have private rooms) for about $30 per person. Or check Airbnb-type sites for deals.

It's no hardship to eat inexpensively in Berlin. You can get tasty, affordable meals at street stands (selling sausages, falafels, or *döner kebabs*), cafeterias, international eateries, and bakeries. Cultivate the art of picnicking in atmospheric settings.

When you splurge, choose an experience you'll always remember, such as a food-tasting tour or a concert. Minimize souvenir shopping; focus instead on collecting wonderful memories.

Service with a smile at a family-run hotel in Prenzlauer Berg; a one-man stand selling grilled sausages

BEFORE YOU GO

You'll have a smoother trip if you tackle a few things ahead of time. For more information on these topics, see the Practicalities chapter and RickSteves.com, which has helpful travel tips and talks.

Make sure your travel documents are valid. If your passport is due to expire within six months of your ticketed date of return, you need to renew it. Allow up to six weeks to renew or get a passport (www.travel.state.gov). You may also need to register with the European Travel Information and Authorization System (ETIAS).

Arrange your transportation. Book your international flights. Overall, Kayak.com is the best place to start searching for flights. You won't want a car in congested Berlin, but if Berlin is part of a longer trip, figure out your transportation options: You can buy train tickets as you go, get a rail pass, rent a car, or book a cheap flight. (You can wing it in Europe, but it may cost more.)

Book rooms well in advance, especially if your trip falls during peak season or any major holidays or festivals.

Reserve ahead for key sights. To visit the **Reichstag** dome, you must reserve a free entry slot online a week or so in advance. The **Pergamon** and **DDR** museums also accept reservations, which can be a good idea to avoid long ticket-buying lines (for details on all of these, see the Sights in Berlin chapter).

Consider travel insurance. Compare the cost of insurance to the cost of your potential loss. Check whether your existing insurance (health, homeowners, or renters) covers you and your possessions overseas.

Call your bank. Alert your bank that you'll be using your debit and credit cards in Europe. Ask about transaction fees, and get the PIN number for your credit card. You don't need to bring euros along; you can withdraw euros from cash machines in Europe.

Use your smartphone smartly. Sign up for an international service plan to reduce your costs, or rely on Wi-Fi in Europe instead. Download any apps you'll want on the road, such as maps, translators, and Rick Steves Audio Europe (see sidebar).

Pack light. You'll walk with your luggage more than you think. I travel for weeks with a single carry-on bag and a day pack. Use the packing checklist in the appendix as a guide.

Rick's Free Video Clips and Audio Tours

Travel smarter with these free, fun resources:

Rick Steves Classroom Europe, a powerful tool for teachers, is also useful for travelers. This video library contains over 400 short clips excerpted from my public television series. Enjoy these videos as you sort through options for your trip and to better understand what you'll see in Europe. Check it out at Classroom.RickSteves.com (just enter a topic to find everything I've filmed on a subject).

Rick Steves Audio Europe, a free app, makes it easy to download my audio tours and listen to them offline as you travel. For this book (look for the ∩), these audio tours include my Berlin City Walk, which links several key sights through the city center, from the Brandenburg Gate to Alexanderplatz. The app also offers interviews from my public radio show with experts from Europe and around the globe. Find it in your app store or at RickSteves.com/AudioEurope.

Travel Smart

If you have a positive attitude, equip yourself with good information (this book), and expect to travel smart, you will.

Read—and reread—this book. To have an "A" trip, be an "A" student. Note opening hours of sights, closed days, crowd-beating tips, and whether reservations are required or advisable. Check out the latest at RickSteves.com/update.

Be your own tour guide. As you travel, get up-to-date info on sights, reserve tickets and tours, reconfirm hotels and travel arrangements, and check transit connections. Visit the local tourist information office (TI).

Outsmart thieves. Pickpockets abound in crowded places where tourists congregate. Treat commotions as smokescreens for theft. Keep your cash, credit cards, and passport secure in a money belt tucked under your clothes; carry only a day's spending money in your front pocket or wallet. Don't set valuable items down on counters or café tabletops, where they can be quickly stolen or easily forgotten.

Minimize potential loss. Keep expensive gear to a minimum. Bring photocopies or take photos of your important documents (passport and cards) to aid in replacement if they're lost or stolen. Back up photos and files frequently.

Guard your time and energy. Taking a taxi can be a good value if it saves you a long wait for a cheap bus or an exhausting walk across town. To avoid long lines, follow my crowd-beating tips, such as making advance reservations or sightseeing early or late (note that several sights are always open late, and many museums are open late one night a week).

Be flexible. Even if you have a well-planned itinerary, expect changes, strikes, closures, sore feet, bad weather, and so on. Your Plan B could turn out to be even better.

Attempt the language. Many Germans—especially in the tourist trade and in big cities like Berlin—speak English, but if you learn some German, even just a few pleasantries, you'll get more smiles and make more friends. Practice the survival phrases near the end of this book, and even better, bring a phrase book.

Connect with the culture. Interacting with locals carbonates your experience. Enjoy the friendliness of the German people. Ask questions; most locals are happy to point you in their idea of the right direction. Set up your own quest for your favorite jazz club, microbrew, or *Currywurst*. Break out of the tourist track and explore. When an opportunity pops up, make it a habit to say "yes."

Berlin...here you come!

ORIENTATION TO BERLIN

Berlin is a sprawling city (pop. 3.5 million), built on a huge scale. Those who are prepared will be rewarded—that's what this chapter (and the next) is about. You'll learn how to navigate Berlin by subway, tram, bus, taxi, bicycle, or on foot. You'll also find details on Berlin's tourist services, information sources for current events, and recommendations for organized tours. For an overview of the city's neighborhoods and detailed day plans, see the previous chapter. With a smart approach and a measure of patience, you'll have Berlin by the tail.

Overview

TOURIST INFORMATION

Berlin's TIs are for-profit agencies that are only marginally helpful (+49 30 250 025, www.visitberlin.de). You'll find them at the **Hauptbahnhof** (daily 8:00-21:00, by main entrance on Europaplatz) and in City West at **Europa Center** (Mon-Sat 10:00-20:00, closed Sun, hidden inside the shopping mall ground floor at Tauentzienstrasse 9). You'll also find "info box" kiosks at the **Brandenburg Gate** (daily 9:30-19:00, Nov-March until 18:00) and at **Alexanderplatz** in the lobby of the Park Inn hotel (Mon-Sat 7:00-21:00, Sun 8:00-18:00). A separately run TI—focusing on Prenzlauer Berg, and generally more useful—is at the **Kulturbrauerei** (daily 11:00-19:00, ask for the free *Pankow Entdecken* booklet). See the color maps at the back of this book for most locations.

Skip the TI's €1 map, and instead browse the walking tour company brochures—many include nearly-as-good maps for free. Most hotels provide free city maps. If interested in cultural happenings, pick up a copy of the current month's *Exberliner* (in English, €4, free at some hotels, www.exberliner.com).

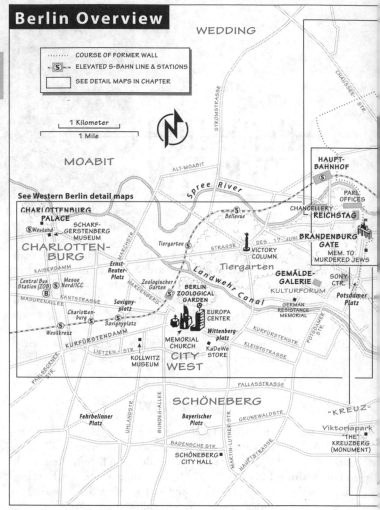

Berlin Overview

WEDDING

.... COURSE OF FORMER WALL

—Ⓢ— ELEVATED S-BAHN LINE & STATIONS

☐ SEE DETAIL MAPS IN CHAPTER

1 Kilometer

1 Mile

MOABIT

ALT-MOABIT

HAUPT-BAHNHOF

PARL. OFFICES

Spree River

CHANCELLERY

See Western Berlin detail maps

CHARLOTTENBURG PALACE

Bellevue

REICHSTAG

BRANDENBURG GATE

SCHARF-GERSTENBERG MUSEUM

Westend

Tiergarten

DES. 17 JUNI STRASSE

VICTORY COLUMN

MEM. TO MURDERED JEWS

CHARLOTTEN-BURG

KAISERDAMM

Ernst-Reuter-Platz

Tiergarten

GEMÄLDE-GALERIE

SONY CTR.

Landwehr Canal

KULTURFORUM

Central Bus Station (ZOB)

Messe Nord/ICC

Zoologischer Garten

BERLIN ZOOLOGICAL GARDEN

Potsdamer Platz

MASURENALLEE

KANTSTRASSE

HARDENBERG

GERMAN RESISTANCE MEMORIAL

Charlotten-burg

Savigny-platz

EUROPA CENTER

Savignyplatz

KURFÜRSTENDAMM

MEMORIAL CHURCH

Wittenberg-platz

KURFÜRSTENSTR.

Westkreuz

LIETZEN-STR.

CITY WEST

KaDeWe STORE

KLEISTSTRASSE

KOLLWITZ MUSEUM

PALLASSTRASSE

SCHÖNEBERG

"KREUZ-

Fehrbelliner Platz

Bayerischer Platz

GRUNEWALDSTR.

Viktoriapark

"THE" KREUZBERG (MONUMENT)

BADENSCHE STR.

SCHÖNEBERG CITY HALL

While the TI sells the three-day Museum Pass Berlin (see the beginning of the next chapter), it's also available at major museums. If you take a walking tour, your guide is likely a better source of nightlife or shopping tips than the TI.

ARRIVAL IN BERLIN

For a detailed rundown of the city's train stations and airports, and for information on parking a car, see the Berlin Connections chapter.

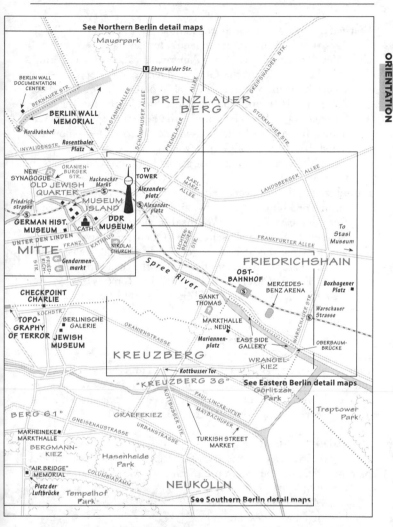

See Northern Berlin detail maps
See Eastern Berlin detail maps
See Southern Berlin detail maps

HELPFUL HINTS

Sightseeing Advice: For tips—including buying advance tickets and sightseeing passes that can save you money—see the Sights in Berlin chapter.

Addresses: Be warned that many Berlin streets are numbered with odd and even numbers on the same side of the street, often with no connection to the other side (for example, Ku'damm #212 can be across the street from #14). Also remember that the *Eszett* symbol (ß) is used in place of "ss" in words like *Straße* (street; sometimes abbreviated as "*Str.*").

Festivals: Berlin hosts a near-constant string of events; see "Holidays and Festivals" in the appendix for key dates.

Cold War Terminology: What Americans called "East Germany" was technically the German Democratic Republic—the Deutsche Demokratische Republik, or DDR. You'll still see those initials around what was once East Germany. The name for what was "West Germany"—the Federal Republic of Germany (Bundesrepublik Deutschland, or BRD)—is now the name shared by all of Germany. Former East or West? Here's a tip: The former communist sector has more tram tracks in the pavement.

Laundry: You'll find several self-service launderettes near my recommended hotels (generally daily 6:00-22:00). In Prenzlauer Berg, try **Eco-Express Waschsalon** (Danziger Strasse 7) or **Schnell & Sauber Waschcenter** (Oderberger Strasse 1); for locations see the map on page 272. In the old Jewish quarter, there are two launderettes around the corner from Rosenthaler Platz: **Waschsalon 115** (Wi-Fi, Torstrasse 115) and **Eco-Express Waschsalon** (Torstrasse 109); for locations see the map on page 276.

GETTING AROUND BERLIN

Berlin's sights spread far and wide. Right from the start, commit yourself to the city's fine public-transit system. Once you do, you'll understand why locals rarely drive in Berlin. This vast city is committed to bikes, and you'll notice smart and efficient bike lanes. This can be very dangerous for pedestrians, so be alert.

By Public Transit

Berlin's transit system uses the same ticket for its many modes of transportation: buses, trams *(Strassenbahn)*, and trains. There are two types of trains: The U-Bahn—like a subway, making lots of short hops around town—is run by the local transit authority (BVG); the S-Bahn, a light rail that goes faster and stops only at major stations, is operated by German Railways (Deutsche Bahn).

For all types of transit, there are three lettered zones: A, B, and C. Most of your sightseeing will be in zones A and B (the city proper); you may enter zone C if you're going to Potsdam, Sachsenhausen, Berlin Brandenburg airport, or other outlying areas.

Sections of the U-Bahn or S-Bahn sometimes close temporarily for repairs, with a bus route replacing the train (*Ersatzverkehr*, or "replacement transportation"; *zwischen* means "between").

Within Berlin, Eurail passes are good on connections from the train station when you arrive and to the station when you depart on counted rail pass days (both S-Bahn and U-Bahn).

Information: Timetables, prices, and trip planning are available on two helpful websites: BVG (www.bvg.de) or VBB (www.vbb.de). Both offer handy, free apps with on-the-go trip routing for U-Bahn, S-Bahn, tram, and bus connections.

For an overview of the transit system, see the color map at the back of this book.

Ticket Options

The €2.90 **basic single** ticket *(Einzelfahrschein)* covers two hours of travel in one direction. It's easy to make this ticket stretch to cover several rides...as long as they're in the same direction.

The €1.90 **short-ride** ticket *(Kurzstrecke Fahrschein)* covers a single ride of up to six bus/tram stops or three subway stations (one transfer allowed on subway). You can save on short-ride tickets by buying them in groups of four (€5.60).

The €9 **four-trip** ticket *(4-Fahrten-Karte)* is the same as four basic single tickets at a good discount.

The **day pass** *(Tageskarte)* is good until 3:00 the morning after you buy it (€8.60 for zones AB, €9.60 for zones ABC). For longer stays, consider a seven-day pass (*Sieben-Tage-Karte;* €34 for zones AB, €41 for zones ABC), or the WelcomeCard (see below). The *Kleingruppenkarte* lets groups of up to five travel all day (€23.50 for zones AB, €24.90 for zones ABC).

If you've already bought a ticket for zones A and B, and later decide to go to zone C (such as to Potsdam), you can buy an "extension ticket" *(Anschlussfahrausweis)* for €1.70, which covers two hours of travel in that zone.

If you plan to cover a lot of ground using public transportation during a two- or three-day visit, the **WelcomeCard** is usually the best deal (available at TIs—including at the airports—and U-Bahn/S-Bahn ticket machines; www.visitberlin.de/welcomecard). It covers all public transportation and gives up to 50 percent discounts off lots of minor and a few major museums, sightseeing tours (including 25 percent off the recommended Original

Berlin Walks and Insider Tour), and music and theater events. It's especially smart for families, as each adult card also covers up to three kids under age 15. The Berlin-only card covers transit zones AB (€23/48 hours, €33/72 hours). For multiple trips beyond the city center, there's a Berlin-with-Potsdam card (zones ABC, €28/48 hours, €38/72 hours; both cards available as 4-, 5-, and 6-day options). If you're a museum junkie, consider the 72-hour **WelcomeCard+Museumsinsel,** which combines transit zones AB (€51) or zones ABC (€55) with unlimited access to the five museums on Museum Island.

Buying Tickets

You can buy U-Bahn/S-Bahn tickets from machines at stations (coins and bills accepted). Tickets are also sold at BVG pavilions at train stations and at TIs, from machines onboard trams (coins only), and on buses from drivers, who give change.

To use a ticket machine, start by pressing the British flag icon for English instructions. Next, select the zone (AB, ABC, or "short trip journey" for a zoneless short-ride ticket) and the type of ticket you want (single, day, or four-trip; for seven-day tickets, select the "other tickets" option), then pay. Most travelers want the AB ticket—either single or all-day ticket. "Adult" *(Erwachsener)* means anyone 14 or older.

Boarding Transit

As you board the bus or tram or enter the subway, validate your ticket in a clock machine (or risk a €60 fine; with a pass, stamp it only the first time you ride). Tickets are checked periodically, often by plainclothes inspectors. You may be asked to show your ticket when boarding the bus. Note that not all tram stops (marked by a sign with a green *H* in a gold circle) have designated platforms on raised sidewalks, and not all trams pull right up to the curb. When the tram arrives, be ready to step into the road to hop aboard.

Useful Transit Lines

Learning a few key transit lines will help shrink this vast city.

U-Bahn: Line **U2** cuts diagonally across the city from Prenzlauer Berg (hotels) to Potsdamer Platz, stopping near Checkpoint Charlie at Stadtmitte. Other handy U-Bahn lines include **U6** (runs north-south through downtown, offering a quick connection to Kreuzberg) and **U1** (cuts east-west through southern Berlin, connecting City West, Kreuzberg, and Friedrichshain). The new line **U5** (some stops open; all may be open in 2021) connects the Hauptbahnhof, Reichstag, and strategic stops along the city's main sightseeing spine: Brandenburger Tor, Unter den Linden (near Bebelplatz), Museumsinsel (Museum Island), Rotes Rathaus (City Hall, near the Nikolai Quarter), and Alexanderplatz.

S-Bahn: Several S-Bahn lines flow like a high-speed river through the heart of Berlin. Lines **S3, S5, S7,** and **S9** zip quickly east-west between key stops: Savignyplatz (hotels in western Berlin), Zoologischer Garten—also known as "Zoo Station" (zoo, City West, Ku'damm), Hauptbahnhof, Friedrichstrasse (near the heart of Unter den Linden), Hackescher Markt (Museum Island, old Jewish quarter, connection to Prenzlauer Berg), and Alexanderplatz (east end of the historic core).

Lines **S1** and **S2** travel north-south between Nordbahnhof (Berlin Wall Memorial), Friedrichstrasse, Brandenburger Tor, and Potsdamer Platz (Kulturforum).

Trams: Trams connect several of my recommended neighborhoods in East Berlin. **#M1** is helpful for getting to and around Prenzlauer Berg—connecting the Hackescher Markt S-Bahn station with key stops along the main drag Kastanienallee; **#12** overlaps with the middle part of #M1; and **#M10** is handy for connecting Cold War sights—it starts at the Hauptbahnhof, goes to Nordbahnhof (Berlin Wall Memorial), connects stops along the Berlin Wall Memorial (Mauerpark, Alexanderplatz, and Frankfurter Tor), and finishes at Warschauer Strasse (for the East Side Gallery).

Buses: Bus **#100** is the handiest for most tourists, traveling east-west along Unter den Linden between the Reichstag/Brandenburg area on one end and Alexanderplatz on the other. Two other helpful lines also travel east-west along Unter den Linden: Bus **#245** connects Alexanderplatz with Zoologischer Garten via Lustgarten (Museum Island), Brandenburger Tor, then angles north to Hauptbahnhof and Tiergarten. Bus **#300** connects Warschauer Strasse with Philharmonie Sud (Kulturforum) via the East Side Gallery, Alexanderplatz, Rotes Rathaus (City Hall), Lustgarten (Museum Island), and Potsdamer Platz. There are stops every few blocks, with buses every 10 minutes or so.

By Taxi and Uber

Cabs are easy to flag down, and taxi stands are common. A typical ride within town costs around €10, and a crosstown trip (for example, Savignyplatz to Alexanderplatz) will run about €25.

Tariff 1 is for a *Kurzstrecke* ticket (short-stretch ride). This ticket can save you several euros for any ride of less than two kilometers (about a mile). To get this rate, you must flag down the cab on the street—not at a taxi stand—and ask for the *Kurzstrecke* rate as soon as you hop in. Confidently say *"Kurzstrecke, bitte"* (KOORTS-shtreh-keh, BIT-teh); your driver will grumble and flip the meter to a fixed €5 rate (for a ride that would otherwise cost €8). If your ride exceeds two kilometers, the meter kicks on and the regular rate takes over.

ORIENTATION

Daily Reminder

Sunday: All sights are open. Many shops are closed, including the Kaufhaus des Westens (KaDeWe) department store. You'll find more shops open in the Hauptbahnhof area.

Many neighborhoods have markets: The Kulturbrauerei (Culture Brewery) has a food market; Mauerpark has an all-day rummage market and community-wide party, including karaoke in the amphitheater; there's a morning flea market near the Ostbahnhof; several blocks on Arkonplatz are filled by a "junk market"; and the Bode Museum hosts an antique-and-book market all weekend.

Monday: Many sights are closed today, including the Berlin Wall Memorial Visitors Center and Documentation Center, Old National Gallery, Bode Museum, Altes Museum, Gemäldegalerie, Palace of Tears, Museum of Decorative Arts, and Charlottenburg Palace.

Tuesday: The Berlinische Galerie and Deutsche Kinemathek Film and TV Museum are closed today.

A huge Turkish street market sprawls along the canalside Maybachufer Street in Kreuzberg. The Berlin Philharmonic offers free lunch concerts at 13:00, except in July and August. The French Cathedral has 30-minute organ concerts at 15:00.

Wednesday: All sights are open except the Boros Collection.

Thursday: Many museums stay open until 20:00, including: everything on Museum Island, the Gemäldegalerie, the Everyday Life in the DDR exhibit, and the Musical Instruments Museum. The Deutsche Kinemathek Film and TV Museum is also open until 20:00 and free from 16:00.

Friday: All sights are open. The Turkish market again sets up in Kreuzberg. The Kaiser Wilhelm Memorial Church holds a "Prayer for Peace" service at 13:00. St. Mary's Church and Nikolaikirche have organ concerts in the afternoon. This is a good night to find live music or check out a concert.

Saturday: All sights are open except the New Synagogue. The DDR Museum stays open until 22:00. Shops typically have shorter hours but some neighborhoods have markets. Live music and concerts abound.

All other rides are tariff 2 (€3.90 drop plus €2/km for the first seven kilometers, then €1.50/km after that). If possible, use cash: Credit card payment comes with a surcharge. If a taxi looks empty but doesn't stop, it's likely on its way to a pick-up requested through one of many ride-sharing apps.

Uber works in Berlin like it does in the US (but rates are tied to taxi fares so you don't really save any money).

Private Car and Driver: Michael Rogowski is a private chauffeur with a very comfortable eight-seat minivan. He speaks decent

English, knows Berlin and environs well, has a knack for finding parking for spontaneous sightseeing, and is a delight to be with (€50/hour, cheaper for longer gigs, m-rogowski@t-online.de).

By Bike

Flat Berlin is a very bike-friendly city, but be careful—motorists don't brake for bicyclists (and bicyclists don't brake for pedestrians). Fortunately, many roads and sidewalks have special red-painted bike lanes. Don't ride on the regular sidewalk—it's *verboten* (though locals do it all the time).

Fat Tire Bikes rents good bikes at the base of the TV Tower near Alexanderplatz (€14/day, cheaper for 2 or more days, trekking bikes available, free luggage storage, daily 9:30-20:00, shorter hours off-season, +49 30 2404 7991, www.fattiretours.com/berlin; for location, see the map on page 286).

Take a Bike—near the Friedrichstrasse S-Bahn station—is owned by a knowledgeable Dutch-German with a huge inventory (3-gear bikes: €8/4 hours, €12.50/day, €19/2 days, slightly cheaper for longer rentals, more for better bikes, includes helmets, daily 9:30-19:00, Nov-March closed Tue-Thu, Neustädtische Kirchstrasse 8—see the map on page 286, +49 30 2065 4730, www.takeabike.de). To find it, leave the S-Bahn station via the Friedrichstrasse exit, turn right, go through a triangle-shaped square, and hang a left on Neustädtische Kirchstrasse.

Bike Rental Berlin is a good option in Prenzlauer Berg (€10/day, helmets-€1, kids' bikes and child seats available, daily 10:00-18:00, often closed off-season—call ahead, Kastanienallee 55—see the map on page 272, +49 30 7153 3020, http://bike-rental-berlin.de).

Simple **Rent a Bike** stands outside Berlin shops, restaurants, and hotels charge €12/day (no maps, no helmets); I prefer the full-service rental shops listed above.

Tours in Berlin

BY BUS

Berlin lends itself to a bus-tour orientation (worth ▲▲). Several companies offer essentially the same circuit of the city with unlimited, all-day hop-on, hop-off privileges for around €25 (two days for a few euros more, check for WelcomeCard discounts). Buses make about a dozen stops at the city's major tourist spots (Potsdamer Platz, Museum Island, Brandenburg Gate, Kaiser Wilhelm Memorial Church, and so on). For specifics, look for brochures in your hotel lobby or at the TI, or check the websites for the dominant outfits: **City-Sightseeing Berlin,** a.k.a. Ber-

lin City Tour, runs red buses and yellow-and-green buses (www. berlin-city-tour.de). **City Circle Sightseeing,** a.k.a. BEX, runs yellow-and-black buses marked with a "Grayline" logo (www. berlinerstadtrundfahrten.de).

Buses come with cursory narration in English and German by a live, sometimes tired guide, or a dry recorded commentary. Try to catch a bus with a live guide (buses generally run daily 10:00-18:00, 4/hour, last departure from all stops around 16:00, 2-hour loop; Nov-March 2/hour, last departure around 15:00). Due to heavy traffic, pick-up times are unreliable; you may find yourself waiting on the curb for a good part of your day.

Before handing over your money, consider following my self-guided "Do-It-Yourself Bus #100 Tour" instead (see the sidebar in this section), which costs only the price of a transit ticket.

BY BOAT
▲▲Spree River Cruises
Several boat companies offer €15 trips up and down the river. In one relaxing hour, you'll listen to an excellent English audioguide, see lots of wonderful new government-commissioned architecture, and enjoy the lively park action fronting the river. Boats leave from docks clustered near the bridge behind the Berlin Cathedral (just off Unter den Linden, near the DDR Museum). For better views, go for a two-story boat with open-deck seating. While you have many interchangeable options, I enjoyed the Historical Sightseeing Cruise from **Stern und Kreisschiffahrt** (departures on the half-hour, mid-March-Nov daily 10:30-17:30, leaves from Nikolaiviertel Dock—cross bridge from Berlin Cathedral toward Alexanderplatz and look right; RS%—show this book for free English audioguide, otherwise €2; +49 30 536 3600, www. sternundkreis.de).

ON FOOT

Berlin's fascinating and complex history can be challenging to appreciate on your own, but a good Berlin tour guide and walking tour makes the city's dynamic story come to life (and can be worth ▲▲▲).

Unlike many European countries, Germany has no regulations controlling who can give city tours. As a result, guide quality is hit-or-miss, ranging from brilliant history buffs who've lived in Berlin for years, to new arrivals who've memorized a script. To improve your odds of landing a great guide, try one of my recommendations.

Most outfits offer walks that are variations on the same themes: general **introductory** walk, **Third Reich** walk (Hitler and Nazi sites), and day trips to **Potsdam** and the **Sachsenhausen Memorial and Museum.** Most tours cost about €12-15 and last 3-4 hours (longer for side-trips to Potsdam and Sachsenhausen); public-transit tickets and entrances to sights are extra. For more details—including prices, schedules, and other themes—see each company's website or pick up brochures at TIs, hotel reception desks, cafés, and shops.

Original Berlin Walks

With a strong commitment to quality guiding, Original Berlin's "Discover Berlin" walk offers a solid overview with a smart itinerary in four hours (€20, RS%—€2 less with this book, daily at 10:30, May-Sept also daily at 14:00). Tours depart from opposite the Hackescher Markt S-Bahn station, outside Starbucks (+49 30 301 9194, www.berlinwalks.de).

Insider Tour

This well-regarded company runs the full gamut of itineraries, as well as a day trip to Dresden. Tours meet outside the Friedrichstrasse train station, on the square beside the Palace of Tears or "Tränenpalast" (+49 30 692 3149, www.insidertour.com).

Berlin Underworlds Association (Berliner Unterwelten Verein)

This group is devoted to Berlin's hidden underground history. Their "Dark Worlds" tour takes you into a WWII air-raid bunker. The "From Flak Towers to Mountains of Debris" tour enters the Humboldthain air defense tower (April-Oct only). The "Cold War Nuclear Bunkers" tour visits a fully functional nuclear emergency bunker in former West Berlin. Meet in the hall of the Gesundbrunnen U-Bahn/S-Bahn station—follow signs to the *Humboldthain/Brunnenstrasse* exit, and find Brunnenstrasse 105 (www.berliner-unterwelten.de).

Do-It-Yourself Bus #100 Tour

Running from the Berlin Zoological Garden to Alexanderplatz, Berlin's city bus #100 laces together the major sights in a kind of poor-man's self-guided bus tour. Since a basic, single bus ticket is good for two hours of travel in one direction and buses leave every 10 minutes or so, hopping on and off works great. Most buses are double decker; ideally, sit on top (up front on the right so you can read the station names easier). Upcoming stops are also indicated on the reader board up front.

Eight stops along the route (out of 16) are near sights you might want to get out and visit. Here's a quick review of the sights within walking distance of each stop, followed by what you'll see as you roll.

Zoologischer Garten: Catch the bus from the second curb. This is the first stop, so any bus #100 is yours. Pulling out, you'll see the bombed-out hulk of the Kaiser Wilhelm Memorial Church, with its jagged spire and postwar sister church.

Breitscheidplatz: This is the stop for Kaiser Wilhelm Memorial Church, Berlin Zoo, and Bikini Berlin shopping mall. As the bus continues, on the left, the elephant gates mark the entrance to the venerable and much-loved Berlin Zoo and aquarium. You'll drive through boring former "West Berlin," filled with hotels and pedestrian-unfriendly intersections. After a left turn, you'll cross the canal and pass Berlin's embassy row. After four stops (Bayreuther Strasse to Nordische Botschaften) you enter the huge Tiergarten Park. The Victory Column (Siegessäule; with its gilded angel) is straight ahead. Circling under the towering column, look right (with the Brandenburg Gate in the distance) and left to appreciate the long axis connecting Central Berlin with Charlottenburg.

Grosser Stern: You'd exit here for the Victory Column. A block beyond the Victory Column (on your left as the bus turns right) is the 18th-century late-Rococo Bellevue Palace, the residence of the federal president (if the flag's out, he's in). Driving along the Spree River (on the left), you'll see several striking national government buildings. A metal Henry Moore sculpture titled *But-*

Alternative Berlin Tours

Specializing in cutting-edge street culture and art, this company emphasizes the bohemian chic that flavors the city's ever-changing urban scene. Their basic three-hour tour (daily at 11:00 and 13:00) is tip-based—you'll be asked to pay what you think it's worth; other tours cost €12-35 (verify meeting point online, mobile +49 162 819 8264, www.alternativeberlin.com).

Food Tours

Many companies offer food tours—a typical offering might start at Hackesche Höfe at 12:00, last 3.5 hours, cost €30, and make five *terfly* (a.k.a. "The Drinker's Liver") floats in front of the slope-roofed House of World Cultures. Through the trees on the left is the Chancellery—Germany's "White House." The big open space is the Platz der Republik, where the Victory Column stood until Hitler moved it. The Hauptbahnhof (Berlin's vast main train station, marked by its tall tower with the *DB* sign) is across the field in the distance between the Chancellery and the Reichstag (Germany's parliament—the old building with the new dome). After two stops (Schloss Bellevue and Haus der Kulturen der Welt), you reach Germany's capital building.

Reichstag/Bundestag: This stop is near the Reichstag, Brandenburg Gate, and the start of my 🕮 Reichstag & Brandenburg Gate Walk (and 🎧 Berlin City Walk audio tour), which covers the next stretch of this bus ride on foot.

Brandenburger Tor: You'd get off here for Unter den Linden, the Memorial to the Murdered Jews of Europe, and the Brandenburg Gate. Back on the bus, you're now on Unter den Linden, the main east-west thoroughfare, which stretches from the Brandenburg Gate through Berlin's historic core to the TV Tower in the distance. You'll pass the Russian Embassy (right) and (at the Friedrichstrasse stop) a Fifth Avenue-style conga line of big, glitzy department stores. This is the touristy heart of Berlin.

Staatsoper: This stop is handy to Bebelplatz and the German History Museum. On the left is Museum Island and the stately Berlin Cathedral. On the right you'll see the Humboldt Forum (former Berlin Palace).

Lustgarten: You'd exit here for Museum Island, Berlin Cathedral, Humboldt Forum, and the Spree River boat tour dock. At the Marienkirche stop, you'll see a statue of Martin Luther and St. Mary's Church on your right, and a line of DDR-era prefab housing blocks on your left as you roll under the TV tower.

Alexanderplatz: Your final stop is this square teeming with people. A transportation hub is one block away.

stops (sampling German ravioli, *Currywurst,* Turkish treats, baked goodies, and some schnapps). Your guide will stoke your appetite with history, jokes, and cultural insights as you walk between stops. A good start is to check Original Berlin Walks' and Insider Tour's websites for the latest offerings.

"Free" Tours
You'll see ads for "free" introductory tours all over town. Popular with students (who've yet to learn you get what you pay for), it's a business model that has spread across Europe: English-speaking students (often Aussies and Americans) deliver a memorized script

---

Extra Credit for "A" Students

Many people who visit Berlin are history buffs in their element. Others are overwhelmed by the city's turbulent past. To help give you a solid background, I've produced lots of free content and made it available on my website (RickSteves.com). Two *Rick Steves' Europe* TV shows worth viewing are my "Berlin" episode and my one-hour special, "The Story of Fascism in Europe." A number of smart Berliners have also helped me with a series of interviews for my *Travel with Rick Steves* public radio show, available on my website or my free Rick Steves' Audio Europe app. Also check out my online "European Art and History" travel talks to better understand the story of Germany.

---

before a huge crowd lured in by the promise of a free tour. The catch: Guides expect to be "tipped in paper" (€5/person minimum is encouraged). While the guides can be entertaining, better ones typically move on to more serious tour companies. These tours are fine for many, but before committing your morning to a free tour, consider: Isn't your valuable time in Berlin worth a few more euros to go with a professional guide?

"Free" tour companies also offer **pub crawls** that are wildly popular with visiting college students (see the Entertainment in Berlin chapter).

Local Guides

Berlin guides are generally independent contractors who can be hired privately but also often work with tour companies (such as those listed here). Most li-censed local guides charge €65/hour or €200-300/day (confirm when booking). Guides can get booked up—especially in summer—so reserve ahead.

Most of these guides belong to a federation called Bündnis Berliner Stadtführer, which is a great source for connecting with even more guides (www.berlinguidesassociation.com).

I've personally worked with and can strongly recommend each of the following guides: Archaeologist **Nick Jackson** (mobile +49 171 537 8768, www.jacksonsberlintours.com); **Lee Evans** (makes 20th-century Germany a thriller, mobile +49 176 6335 5565, lee.evans@berlin.de); **Torben Brown** (a walking Berlin encyclopedia, mobile +49 176 5004 2572, www.berlinperspectives.com); **Holger Zimmer** (a cultural connoisseur and public radio journalist, mobile +49 163 345 4427, explore@berlin.de); **Carlos Meissner** (a historian with a professorial earnestness, mobile +49 175 266 0575, www.berlinperspectives.com); Brit **Maisie Hitchcock** (with a background in journalism and architecture, mobile +49 176 3847 2717, maisiehitchcock@hotmail.com); **Caroline Marburger** (a sharp historian who has lived and studied abroad, mobile +49 176 7677 9920, www.berlinlocals.com); **Bernhard Schlegelmilch** (the only guide listed here who grew up behind the Wall, mobile +49 176 6422 9119, upwards@t-online.de); and **Haşim Anik** (who specializes in Kreuzberg, where he grew up, mobile +49 163 916 2148, hasimanik@hotmail.com).

Be aware that several of these guides (Torben, Holger, Carlos, Maisie, and Caroline) also lead Rick Steves Europe tours, and are often out of town.

ON WHEELS

Fat Tire Bike Tours offers guided bike tours from April through October (around €28, 4-6 hours, 6-10 miles, check schedules at www.fattiretours.com/berlin). Topics include a City Tour, Berlin Wall Tour, Third Reich, evening food tour (€49), Modern Berlin Tour (countercultural, creative aspects of contemporary Berlin), an all-day Potsdam Gardens and Palaces Tour, and private tours for families and small groups. Meet at the TV Tower at Alexanderplatz (reservations smart, +49 30 2404 7991).

Berlin on Bike offers a 3.5-hour introductory tour daily at 11:00. They also offer several themed tours, including Alternative Berlin, Street Art Berlin, and Nightseeing (most €24, 8-12 miles, private tours available, all tours leave from the Kulturbrauerei brewery in Prenzlauer Berg, +49 30 4373 9999, https://berlinonbike.de).

SIGHTS IN BERLIN

Many visitors view Berlin through a Hitler or Berlin Wall lens—fixating on only the 20th century. But there's a lot more to the city: Its sightseeing ranks right up there alongside London, Paris, and Rome in both variety and quality—offering everything from German history, to great works of art by European masters, to world-famous treasures from the ancient world. To help you prioritize, I've chosen what I think are the best of Berlin's many sights, organized geographically for more efficient sightseeing.

Multifaceted Berlin—more than most cities—can be covered with a handful of neighborhood and thematic walks. This book tackles the majority of Berlin's sights in more depth via seven such walks, along with several museum tours, where you'll find crucial information on avoiding lines, saving money, and finding a decent bite to eat nearby. When you see a 📖 in a listing, it means the sight is described in one of my walks or tours. This is why some of Berlin's greatest sights get the least coverage in this chapter.

A 🎧 means that the sight is covered by my free Berlin City Walk audio tour (via my Rick Steves Audio Europe app—see page 22). For these, you can choose whether to read or to listen (though the chapters in this book offer more depth).

For general tips on sightseeing, see the Practicalities chapter. Check RickSteves.com/update for any significant changes that may have occurred since this book was printed.

ADVANCE TICKETS AND SIGHTSEEING PASSES

Consider the following advice and options to make your Berlin sightseeing easier and cheaper.

Advance Tickets: Visiting the Reichstag dome is free, but you must make a reservation in advance. It's also smart to book in advance for several busy Berlin sights, including the Pergamon Museum and DDR Museum. For any sight that interests you, check the website in advance—many are adding timed-entry ticket options.

Museum Passes: Berlin offers several worthwhile sightseeing passes.

The €29 **Museum Pass Berlin** is best for serious museumgoers—it covers nearly all the city sights for three consecutive days (including everything covered by the one-day Museum Island Pass; see details at www.visitberlin.de). It gets you into more than 30 museums, including the national museums and most of the recommended biggies. Covered sights include the five Museum Island museums (Old National Gallery, Neues, Altes, Bode, and Pergamon), German History Museum, and the Gemäldegalerie (and other Kulturforum museums), along with more minor sights. Buy it at any participating museum or a TI. The pass generally lets you skip the line and go directly into the museum—except at the Pergamon, where you should prebook a time slot.

The €18 **Museum Island Pass** (not sold at TIs; see www.smb. museum) covers all sights on Museum Island and is a fine value if you're touring at least two of the collections (though for just €11 more, the three-day Museum Pass Berlin described above gives you triple the days and many more entries). This pass also does not let you skip the line at the Pergamon—book a time slot in advance.

The **WelcomeCard** is a transportation pass that includes discounts for the Berlin Cathedral, DDR Museum, German History Museum, Museum of the Wall at Checkpoint Charlie, Jewish Museum, and others (described on page 29).

Central Berlin (The Historic Core)

Much of Berlin's sightseeing is concentrated in this central strip, stretching over a mile-long corridor from the Tiergarten Park to Museum Island.

REICHSTAG AND BRANDENBURG GATE AREA

This area is covered in detail in the 📖 Reichstag & Brandenburg Gate Walk chapter and my free 🎧 Berlin City Walk audio tour.

▲▲▲Reichstag

Germany's historic parliament building—completed in 1894, burned in 1933, sad and lonely in a no-man's land throughout the Cold War, and finally rebuilt and topped with a glittering glass cupola in 1999—is a symbol of a proudly reunited nation. Visit here to spiral up the remarkable dome and gaze across Berlin's rooftops, and to watch today's parliament in action. Because of security concerns, you'll need a reservation and your passport to enter.

Cost and Hours: Free, reservations required—see next

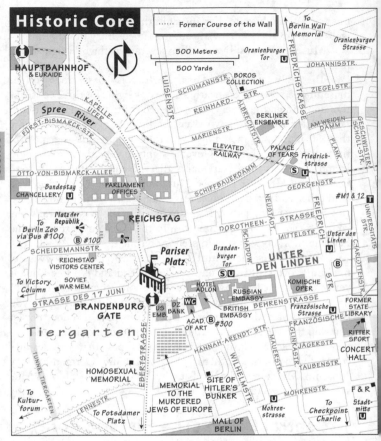

Historic Core

...... Former Course of the Wall

500 Meters
500 Yards

HAUPTBAHNHOF & EURAIDE

Spree River

FÜRST-BISMARCK-STR.

KAPELLE-UFER

OTTO-VON-BISMARCK-ALLEE

Bundestag CHANCELLERY

PARLIAMENT OFFICES

Platz der Republik

To Berlin Zoo via Bus #100

B #100

REICHSTAG

SCHEIDEMANNSTR.

REICHSTAG VISITORS CENTER

To Victory Column

SOVIET WAR MEM.

STRASSE DES 17 JUNI

BRANDENBURG GATE

Pariser Platz

Tiergarten

TUNNEL TIERGARTEN

To Kultur-forum

LENNÉSTR.

To Potsdamer Platz

HOMOSEXUAL MEMORIAL

EBERTSTRASSE

US EMB.

DZ BANK

WC

MEMORIAL TO THE MURDERED JEWS OF EUROPE

SITE OF HITLER'S BUNKER

MALL OF BERLIN

LUISENSTR.

SCHUMANNSTR.

STR.

REINHARD-

MARIENSTR.

ELEVATED RAILWAY

SCHIFFBAUERDAMM

ALBRECHTSTR.

BOROS COLLECTION

BERLINER ENSEMBLE

PALACE OF TEARS

To Berlin Wall Memorial

Oranienburger Strasse

Oranienburger Tor

FRIEDRICHSTRASSE

JOHANNISSTR.

ZIEGELSTR.

AM WEIDEN-DAMM

GESCHWISTER-SCHOLL-STR.

PLANK-

Friedrich-strasse

S U

GEORGENSTR.

DOROTHEEN- STRASSE

NEUSTADT.

SCHADOW-

MITTELSTR.

FRIEDRICH-

#M1 & 12

T

UNIVERSITÄTS-STR.

CHARLOTTENSTR.

Unter den Linden

Branden-burger Tor

S U

UNTER DEN LINDEN

STR.

B

RUSSIAN EMBASSY

HOTEL ADLON

BEHRENSTRASSE

BRITISH EMBASSY

ACAD. OF ART

B #300

HANNAH-ARENDT-STR.

WILHELMSTR.

GLINKASTR.

MAUERSTR.

KOMISCHE OPER

Französische Strasse

FRANZÖSISCHE

JÄGERSTR.

TAUBENSTR.

MOHRENSTR.

Mohren-strasse

U

FORMER STATE LIBRARY

RITTER SPORT

CONCERT HALL

F & R

To Checkpoint Charlie

Stadt-mitte

U

section, daily 8:00-24:00, last entry at 22:00, metal detectors, no big luggage allowed, Platz der Republik 1; S- or U-Bahn: Friedrich-strasse, Brandenburger Tor, or Bundestag; +49 30 2273 2152, www. bundestag.de.

Advance Tickets: You must make a free reservation. It's easy to do online, but book early—spots often fill up several days in advance. Go to www.bundestag.de, and from the "Visit the Bundestag" menu, select "Online registration." You have two choices: "Visit to the dome" includes a good audioguide and is plenty for most; the 90-minute guided tour provides more in-depth information. After choosing your preferred date and time, you'll be sent an

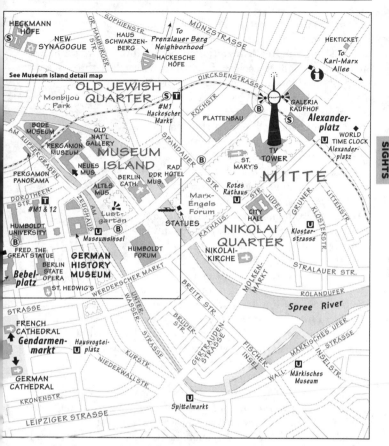

SIGHTS

email link to a website where you'll enter details for each person in your party. A final email will contain your reservation (with a letter you must print out or download to your mobile device).

Without a Reservation: Tickets may be available even when online sales are "sold out"—inquire at the tiny visitors center on the Tiergarten side of Scheidemannstrasse, across from Platz der Republik (daily 8:00-20:00, until 18:00 Nov-March; bookings from 3 hours to 2 days in advance, go early to avoid lines). When booking, the whole party must be present and passports are required.

Another option is to have lunch or dinner at the pricey rooftop restaurant, **$$$$ Käfer Dachgarten** (daily 9:00-16:30 & 18:30-24:00, last access at 22:00, reserve well in advance at +49 30 2262 9933 or www.feinkost-kaefer.de/berlin).

Getting In: Report 15 minutes before your appointed time to the temporary-looking entrance facility in front of the Reichstag, and be ready to show your passport and confirmation letter. After passing through a security check, you'll wait with other visitors for a guard to take you to the Reichstag entrance.

Visiting the Reichstag: The open, airy **lobby** towers 100 feet high, with 65-foot-tall colors of the German flag. See-through glass doors show the central legislative chamber. The message: There will be no secrets in this government. Look inside. Spreading his wings behind the podium is a stylized German eagle, the *Bundestagsadler* (affectionately nicknamed the "Fat Hen"), representing the Bundestag (each branch of government has its own symbolic eagle). Notice the doors marked *Ja* (Yes), *Nein* (No), and *Enthalten* (Abstain)...an homage to the Bundestag's traditional "sheep jump" way of counting votes by exiting the chamber through the corresponding door. (For critical votes, however, they vote with electronic cards.)

Germany's Bundestag (comparable to the US House of Representatives) meets here. Its 631 members are elected to four-year terms. They in turn elect the chancellor. Unlike America's two-party system, Germany has a handful of significant parties, so they must form coalitions to govern effectively. Bundestag members have offices in the building to the left of the Reichstag.

Ride the elevator to the base of the **glass dome** (where you'll pick up the ***Berlin Panorama*** flier and your audioguide). The dome is 80 feet high, 130 feet across, and weighs a quarter of a million pounds. It uses about 33,000 square feet of glass, or nearly enough to cover a football field.

Study the photos and read the circle of captions (around the base of the central funnel) telling the Reichstag story. Then study the surrounding architecture: a broken collage of new on old, torn between antiquity and modernity, like Germany's history. Notice the dome's giant and unobtrusive sunscreen that moves as necessary with the sun. Peer down through the skylight to look over the shoulders of the elected representatives at work.

For Germans, the best view from here is down—keeping a close eye on their government.

Start at the **ramp** nearest the elevator and wind up to the top of the double ramp. Take a 360-degree survey of the city as you hike: The big park is the Tiergarten, the "green lungs of Berlin." Beyond that is the Teufelsberg ("Devil's Hill"). Built of rubble from the destroyed city in the late 1940s, it was famous during the Cold War as a powerful ear of the West—notice the telecommunications tower on top. Knowing the bombed-out and bulldozed story of their city, locals say, "You have to be suspicious when you see the nice, green park."

Find the Victory Column (Siegessäule), glimmering in the middle of the park. Hitler moved it there in the 1930s from in front of the Reichstag as part of his grandiose vision for postwar Berlin. Next, scenes of the new Berlin spiral into view—Potsdamer Platz, marked by the conical glass tower that houses Sony's European headquarters. Continue circling left, and find the green chariot atop the Brandenburg Gate. Just to its left is the curving fish-like roof of the DZ Bank building, designed by the unconventional American architect Frank Gehry. The Memorial to the Murdered Jews of Europe stretches south (to the right) of the Brandenburg Gate. Next, you'll see former East Berlin and the city's next huge construction zone, with a forest of 300-foot-tall skyscrapers in the works. Notice the TV Tower, the Berlin Cathedral's massive dome, and (to the left) the golden dome of the New Synagogue.

Follow the train tracks in the distance from Friedrichstrasse station (on the river beneath the TV tower) to Berlin's huge main train station, the Hauptbahnhof. Complete your spin-tour with the blocky, postmodern Chancellery, the federal government's headquarters. Continue spiraling up. You'll come across all the same sights again, twice, from higher vantage points.

▲▲Memorials near the Reichstag

The area immediately surrounding the Reichstag is rich with memorials. Within a few steps, you'll find monuments to politicians who opposed Hitler; to the many groups targeted by the Nazis (Jews, Roma, homosexuals, and people with disabilities); to victims of the Berlin Wall; and even to the Soviet soldiers who liberated Berlin from Hitler—plunging it into the deep end of the Cold War. For more on these monuments, see the "Nazi and World War II Sites" sidebar.

Most of these memorials are within (or facing) the sprawling park called the Tiergarten, which extends west from the Brandenburg Gate. For more on the Tiergarten, see the listing later in this chapter.

▲▲▲Brandenburg Gate

The icon of Berlin, this majestic gateway has seen more than its share of history. Armies from Napoleon to Hitler have marched under its gilded statues, and for more than 25 years, it sat forlorn

SIGHTS

Berlin at a Glance

▲▲▲**Reichstag** Germany's historic parliament building, topped with a striking modern dome you can climb (reservations required). **Hours:** Daily 8:00-24:00. See page 41.

▲▲▲**Brandenburg Gate** One of Berlin's most famous landmarks, a massive columned gateway, at the former border of East and West. See page 45.

▲▲▲**German History Museum** The ultimate swing through Germany's tumultuous story. **Hours:** Daily 10:00-18:00. See page 55.

▲▲▲**Berlin Wall Memorial** Museums with videos and displays, several outdoor exhibits, and lone surviving stretch of an intact Wall section. **Hours:** Museums open Tue-Sun 10:00-18:00, closed Mon; outdoor areas accessible daily 24 hours. See page 62.

▲▲**Memorials near the Reichstag** Tributes to Nazi victims, including Jews, Roma, homosexuals, opposing politicians, and people with disabilities. See page 45.

▲▲**Memorial to the Murdered Jews of Europe** Holocaust memorial with almost 3,000 symbolic pillars, plus an exhibition about Hitler's Jewish victims. **Hours:** Memorial always open; information center Tue-Sun 10:00-20:00, Oct-March until 19:00, closed Mon year-round. See page 48.

▲▲**Unter den Linden** Leafy boulevard in the heart of former East Berlin, lined with some of the city's top sights. See page 48.

▲▲**Pergamon Museum** World-class museum of classical antiquities on Museum Island (Pergamon Altar closed through 2025). **Hours:** Daily 10:00-18:00, Thu until 20:00. See page 51.

▲▲**Neues Museum** Egyptian antiquities collection and proud home of the exquisite 3,000-year-old bust of Queen Nefertiti. **Hours:** Daily 10:00-18:00, Thu until 20:00. See page 52.

▲▲**Old National Gallery** German paintings, mostly from the Romantic Age. **Hours:** Tue-Sun 10:00-18:00, Thu until 20:00, closed Mon. See page 52.

▲▲**DDR Museum** Quirky collection of communist-era artifacts. **Hours:** Daily 10:00-20:00, Sat until 22:00. See page 56.

▲▲**Courtyards (Höfe)** Interconnected courtyards with shops, eateries, and museums, best explored in the old Jewish quarter. See page 57.

▲▲**Prenzlauer Berg** Lively, colorful neighborhood with hip cafés, restaurants, boutiques, and street life. See page 60.

▲▲**Topography of Terror** Chilling exhibit documenting the Nazi perpetrators, built on the site of the former Gestapo/SS headquarters. **Hours:** Daily 10:00-20:00. See page 66.

▲▲**Kreuzberg** Eclectic, trendy neighborhood with diverse roots, popular eateries, and the Turkish street market. See page 68.

▲▲**Gemäldegalerie** Germany's top collection of 13th- through 18th-century European paintings, featuring Holbein, Dürer, Cranach, Van der Weyden, Rubens, Hals, Rembrandt, Vermeer, Raphael, and more. **Hours:** Tue-Fri 10:00-18:00, Thu until 20:00, Sat-Sun 11:00-18:00, closed Mon. See page 81.

▲**Palace of Tears** Once a border crossing and place of sad goodbyes, now a museum about life in divided Germany. **Hours:** Tue-Fri 9:00-19:00, Sat-Sun 10:00-18:00, closed Mon. See page 59.

▲**Museum of the Wall at Checkpoint Charlie** Stories of brave Cold War escapes, near the site of the famous former East-West border checkpoint; the surrounding street scene is almost as interesting. **Hours:** Daily 9:00-22:00. See page 64.

▲**East Side Gallery** Largest surviving stretch of the Berlin Wall, now covered with murals. See page 74.

▲**Museum of Decorative Arts** Applied arts bric-a-brac from porcelain to fashion, including elaborate reliquaries. **Hours:** Tue-Fri 10:00-18:00, Sat-Sun from 11:00, closed Mon. See page 82.

▲**Kaiser Wilhelm Memorial Church** Bombed-out church ruins from World War II kept as a memorial alongside a meditative modern church. **Hours:** Church open daily 9:00-19:00. See page 83.

▲**Charlottenburg Palace** Baroque former home of the royal family, with large collection of 17th-century French frescoes. **Hours:** Tue-Sun 10:00-17:30, Nov-March until 16:30, closed Mon year-round. See page 89.

in the Berlin Wall's death strip. Today it's a symbol of Berlin's rejuvenated capital.

Just inside (east of) the Brandenburg Gate is the tidy "Parisian Square"—Pariser Platz. This prime real estate is ringed by governmental buildings, banks, historic plush hotels, the Academy of Arts, and the heavily fortified US Embassy.

▲▲Memorial to the Murdered Jews of Europe (Denkmal für die Ermordeten Juden Europas)

This labyrinth of 2,711 irregularly shaped pillars memorializes the six million Jewish people who were executed by the Nazis. Loaded with symbolism, it's designed to encourage a pensive moment in the heart of a big city.

Inside the **information center** (far-left corner), exhibits trace the rise of Nazism and how it led to World War II. Six portraits, representing the six million Jewish victims, put a human face on the numbers, as do diaries, letters, and final farewells penned by Holocaust victims. You'll learn about 15 Jewish families from very different backgrounds, who all met the same fate. A continually running soundtrack recites victims' names. To read them all aloud would take more than six and a half years.

Cost and Hours: Memorial—free and always open; information center—free, open Tue-Sun 10:00-20:00, Oct-March until 19:00, closed Mon year-round, last entry 45 minutes before closing, security screening at entry, audioguide-€3; S-Bahn: Brandenburger Tor or Potsdamer Platz, +49 30 2639 4336, www.stiftung-denkmal.de.

UNTER DEN LINDEN

Berlin's main boulevard—"Under the Linden Trees"—has been the city's artery since the 15th century. Today, it's a well-tended place to stroll. This main drag is covered in detail in the 📖 Unter den Linden Walk chapter and my free 🎧 Berlin City Walk audio tour.

▲▲Strolling Unter den Linden

On this showcase street, you'll sense echoes of the Prussian kings and kaisers who shaped Berlin (and modern Germany). Along the

Nazi and World War II Sites

Sites from World War II fall into two broad categories: Nazi and Hitler sites, and memorials to the Holocaust.

Nazi and Military Sights

Hitler left Berlin in ruins, so there's not much left to see of his capital city. If you're determined, track down these sights.

Hitler's Bunker: The site where Hitler committed suicide is marked by a simple plaque.

Topography of Terror: On the site of the Gestapo and SS headquarters, this has Berlin's best exhibit documenting Nazi crimes.

German History Museum: Exhibits about Hitler and the Nazis.

Former Air Ministry: Once the base for Hermann Göring's Luftwaffe, this is one of only a few still-standing Nazi-built governmental buildings.

Tempelhof Airport: This former airport, now a gigantic park, is another massive, blocky, Nazi-built structure.

German Resistance Memorial: This memorial chronicles Germans who attempted to fight Hitler from within, and houses the Silent Heroes Memorial Center.

Neue Wache: This former guardhouse holds Käthe Kollwitz's pietá, memorializing Germany's victims of tyranny.

Kaiser Wilhelm Memorial Church: In City West, this church has been left in ruins as a reminder of WWII destruction.

Holocaust Sights

Memorials: Groups targeted by the Nazis are honored with memorials, most near Brandenburg Gate.

Stolpersteine (stumbling stones): Small brass plaques embedded in the pavement throughout Berlin identify buildings where Holocaust victims lived.

Old Jewish Quarter Landmarks: The New Synagogue (partially rebuilt after the war) and a Jewish cemetery along Grosse Hamburger Strasse are reminders of the community that once thrived here. Prenzlauer Berg also has a Jewish cemetery and a synagogue that survived Kristallnacht.

Otto Weidt's Workshop for the Blind: This museum in the Haus Schwarzenberg courtyard celebrates a Berliner who employed blind and deaf Jews to save them from the Nazis.

Jewish Museum: While dedicated to the full breadth of Germany's Jewish experience, this museum thoughtfully recalls the Holocaust, both in its modern building's design and in its exhibits (some may be closed when you visit).

Gleis 17: Abandoned train platform in West Berlin that honors the 50,000 Berlin Jews who were deported to concentration camps from this station between 1941 and 1945. Plaques list the destination, number of people, and date of each train.

Sachsenhausen Memorial and Museum: This powerful site outside Berlin remembers the victims who perished at this concentration camp and documents the atrocities that occurred here.

way, you'll discover DDR-era S-Bahn stations, the Russian Embassy, nostalgic *Ampelmann* traffic lights, a futuristic VW showroom, and a statue of Frederick the Great—the 18th-century king who put his hometown on the world map. And you're sure to see lots of construction along this street— which, like Berlin itself, is continually reinventing itself.

Farther east—as you approach Museum Island—are two poignant landmarks. The square called Bebelplatz was designed by Frederick the Great to showcase his idealistic and enlightened vision for Berlin as a cultural capital, with a university library, an opera house, and the first Catholic church built in Prussia after the Reformation. Later, Hitler chose this as the place to torch 20,000 forbidden books in 1933 (look for the glass window in the middle of the square, and peer into a subterranean room of empty bookshelves). Across Unter den Linden and a few steps toward Museum Island, the Neue Wache royal barracks houses a powerful pietà by Berlin sculptor Käthe Kollwitz, honoring the toll Germany's 20th century took on its people.

Gendarmenmarkt

Berlin's finest square sits two blocks south of Unter den Linden (and one block south of Bebelplatz). The square, like its name

("Square of the Gens d'Armes," Frederick the Great's French guard), is a hybrid of Prussia and France. The square is bookended by two matching churches: the German Cathedral (with a free exhibit on the German parliamentary system) and the French Cathedral (dedicated to the French Huguenots who found refuge in Prussia). Gendarmenmarkt's centerpiece is the Concert Hall (Konzerthaus), commissioned by Frederick the Great and built by his favorite architect, Karl Friedrich Schinkel.

MUSEUM ISLAND AREA

Filling a spit of land in the middle of the Spree River, Museum Island has perhaps Berlin's highest concentration of serious sightseeing. The island's centerpiece is the grassy square called Lustgarten, ringed by five museums and the hulking Berlin Cathedral.

This neighborhood is covered in more detail in the 📖 Unter den Linden Walk chapter and my free 🎧 Berlin City Walk audio tour. For cruises on the Spree River from near Museum Island, see the Orientation chapter.

Museum Island (Museumsinsel)

Five of Berlin's top museums—featuring art and artifacts from around the world—are just a few steps apart on Museum Island.

Cost and Hours: Each museum has a separate admission (€10-12, includes audioguide). If you're visiting at least two museums here, get the €18 Museum Island Pass (which covers all 5; also consider the €29 Museum Pass Berlin— see "Advance Tickets and Sightseeing Passes" at the beginning of this chapter for details). The museums are open 10:00-18:00 (Thu until 20:00). The Pergamon and Neues museums are open daily; the Old National Gallery, Bode Museum, and Altes Museum are open Tue-Sun, closed Mon.

Advance Tickets Recommended: To skip ticket-buying lines, purchase a timed ticket for the Pergamon in advance at the museum website. If you have a Museum Island Pass or Museum Pass Berlin, you can book a free timed-entry reservation. The always-busy Pergamon is most crowded in the morning, on weekends, and when it rains; Thursday evenings are the least crowded.

Information: +49 30 266 424 242, www.smb.museum.

Getting There: The Museum Island (Museumsinsel) U-Bahn station on the U5 line is expected to open sometime in 2021. If it's not yet open, the island is a 10-minute walk from the Hackescher Markt or Friedrichstrasse S-Bahn stations. Trams #M1 and #12 connect to Prenzlauer Berg. Buses #100, #245, and #300 run along Unter den Linden, stopping near the museums at the Lustgarten stop.

Expect Construction: A new visitors center will connect the complex with tunnels, possibly by 2024.

📖 These museums are described in more depth in the Museum Island Tour and Pergamon Museum Tour chapters.

▲▲Pergamon Museum (Pergamonmuseum)

This world-class museum contains Berlin's Collection of Classical Antiquities (Antikensammlung)—in other words, full-sized buildings from the most illustrious civilizations of the ancient

world. Its namesake and highlight—the gigantic Pergamon
Altar—is under renovation
and off-limits to visitors until
2025. In the meantime, there's
still plenty to see: the massive
Babylonian Processional Way
and Ishtar Gate (slathered with
glazed blue tiles, from the sixth
century BC); artifacts from
the Assyrians (7th-10th century BC); the full-sized market gate
from the ancient Roman settlement of Miletus (first century BC);
and, upstairs, an extensive collection of treasures from the Islamic
world. Take advantage of the excellent, included audioguide.

▲▲Neues (New) Museum

This beautiful museum, featuring objects from the prehistoric
(i.e., pre-Pergamon) world, contains three collections. Most visitors focus on the Egyptian Collection, with the stunning bust of
Queen Nefertiti. But it's also worth a walk through the Museum of
Prehistory and Early History (see an actual Neanderthal skull and
an exquisitely decorated, nearly three-foot-tall prehistoric hat made
of gold), and some items from the Collection of Classical Antiquities (artifacts from ancient Troy—famously excavated by German
adventurer Heinrich Schliemann—and Cyprus). Everything is
well described in English (fine audioguide included with admission; for more on the museum, see www.smb.museum/museen-
einrichtungen/neues-museum/home).

▲▲Old National Gallery (Alte Nationalgalerie)

Of Berlin's many top-notch art collections, this is the best for *German*
art—mostly paintings from the 19th century, the era in which "German culture" first came to mean
something. For a concise visit,
focus on the Romantic German paintings (top floor), where
Caspar David Friedrich's haunt-
ingly beautiful canvases offer an
insightful glimpse into German
landscapes...and the German
psyche. With more time, peruse
the French and German Impres-

sionists and German Realists on the first and second floors.

Bode Museum

This fine building—at the northern tip of the island—contains a
hodgepodge of collections: Byzantine art, historic coins, ecclesi-

astical art, sculptures, and medals commemorating the fall of the Berlin Wall and German reunification. While this museum may be dull for casual sightseers, avid museumgoers find plenty to excite here—including the stunning Ravenna Mosaic, transplanted here from the Byzantine world of sixth-century Italy. For a free, quick look at its lavish interior, climb the grand staircase under a sweeping dome to the charming café on the first floor.

Altes (Old) Museum

Of the five Museum Island collections, this is the least exciting—unless you're an enthusiast of obscure Etruscan, Roman, and Greek art and artifacts.

Berlin Cathedral (Berliner Dom)

This bulky stone structure, with its rusted-copper dome, looms over Museum Island like the home church of a Prussian kaiser...

because it was. It's a textbook example of Kaiser Wilhelm II's bigger-is-better aesthetic.

While pricey to enter, the lavish interior has some fine details. The great reformers (Luther, Calvin, and company) stand around the brilliant dome like stern saints guarding their theology. King Frederick I rests in an ornate tomb. Those who climb the 270 steps of the dome are rewarded with pleasant, breezy views of the city. The crypt downstairs is not worth your time.

Cost and Hours: €7 includes dome gallery access, not covered by Museum Island Pass, Mon-Sat 9:00-20:00, Sun from 12:00, daily until 19:00 Oct-March, closes around 17:30 on concert days, last entry one hour before closing, audioguide-€4, +49 30 2026 9136, www.berlinerdom.de.

Humboldt Forum (Former Berlin Palace)

Communists replaced the Prussian palace on this site with a giant "brutalist" conference center. Now, that DDR-era building has been replaced with a cultural complex with a main facade that looks just like it did in the time of Frederick the Great.

The new cultural center, called the Humboldt Forum, will be a huge public palace for business, culture, and higher education. The open "piazza" courtyard inside will help give it a community feel. By the time you visit, the forum may be open for business, including concerts under its dome (www.humboldtforum.com).

SIGHTS

Cold War, Berlin Wall, and DDR Sights

When visiting Berlin, it's hard not to get caught up in Cold War intrigue. The city has several quality sights relating to East Berlin from the 1940s to the 1990s; each is covered in depth elsewhere in this book. ▢ To learn more about the Cold War, see the Fascism & Cold War Walk and Communist East Berlin Walk chapters.

Berlin Wall Sights

Berlin Wall Memorial: This is the best all-around place to learn about the Wall; there are two visitors centers and information boards along a mile-long, park-like memorial.

Checkpoint Charlie: While tacky and touristy, the spot where people crossed between West and East is still evocative. The **Museum of the Wall at Checkpoint Charlie** is dated but offers engaging stories of escapes.

Stretch of Wall Along Niederkirchnerstrasse: There's a short stretch of the Wall next to the Topography of Terror and a nearby surviving watchtower.

East Side Gallery: This nearly mile-long stretch of surviving Wall is still painted with vivid graffiti (east of the center, in Friedrichshain).

"Life in the DDR" Sights

Several good, somewhat overlapping museums illuminate various aspects of life in East Germany (a.k.a., the DDR).

DDR Museum: Near Museum Island, this museum's hands-on approach makes East German lifestyles accessible to outsiders.

Everyday Life in the DDR: This free exhibit in Prenzlauer Berg is equally good, though more intellectually rigorous and geared to a German audience.

Palace of Tears: The building where people crossed between East and West (next to Friedrichstrasse Station) has a good exhibit about DDR life.

Stasi Museum: Farther out, in Friedrichshain, this museum fills the former headquarters of the DDR secret police with a dense exhibit about their crimes.

Near Museum Island

The German History Museum is on Unter den Linden, immediately west of Museum Island; and the DDR Museum is (fittingly) just east of Museum Island, on the riverbank facing the back of the Berlin Cathedral. The Nikolai Quarter is a five-minute walk to the south, down the river (facing Museum Island).

Other Cold War Sights

German History Museum: Among its excellent exhibits is one on the Cold War period.

Architecture: The socialist aesthetic is on display around **Alexanderplatz,** the **TV Tower,** and **Karl-Marx-Allee.**

Platz der Luftbrücke: "Air Bridge Square," in front of Tempelhof Field, has a towering monument celebrating the 1948-49 Berlin Airlift.

USSR-Built Memorials: The Russian soldiers who died to free Berlin from Hitler are honored with the **Soviet War Memorial** (in Tiergarten Park) and the much bigger and more dramatic **Treptower Park** (farther out, just east of Kreuzberg).

JFK Sights: The front steps of **Schöneberg City Hall**—where the president famously proclaimed, *"Ich bin ein Berliner"*—is a good stop for JFK fans.

Potsdam: This posh town outside of Berlin holds the **Cecilienhof Palace,** where Truman, Churchill, and Stalin met in the famous 1945 Potsdam Conference; and a **KGB Prison Memorial,** on the site of a Russian "counterintelligence" facility.

Potsdamer Platz, the **Reichstag,** and the **Brandenburg Gate:** These sights were once stranded within or near the Berlin Wall's death strip, and today are some of the city's most vital spaces.

More Cold War

For more in this book, see the sidebars later in this chapter covering the Berlin Airlift and the Stasi. The Berlin Wall Memorial Tour, Communist East Berlin Walk, and Fascism & Cold War Walk chapters also cover various Cold War-related topics.

U6 Cold War Spine: The U6 subway line conveniently links up several powerful Cold War-era sights, in roughly chronological order. For a busy day of Cold War sightseeing, begin at the **Platz der Luftbrücke** to see the monument and Tempelhof Airport where the Berlin Airlift took place. Then ride to the **Checkpoint Charlie** (Kochstrasse) stop to see the most famous border crossing at the Berlin Wall. Next is the **Friedrichstrasse** station, near the Palace of Tears. And finally, the **Nordbahnhof** is at the start of the Berlin Wall Memorial.

▲▲▲German History Museum (Deutsches Historisches Museum)

This impressive museum offers the best look at German history under one roof, anywhere. The permanent collection packs 9,000 artifacts into two huge rectangular floors of the old arsenal building. You'll stroll through insightfully described historical objects, paintings, photographs, and models—all intermingled with multimedia stations. The 20th-century section—on the ground floor—is far better than any of the many price-gouging historical Nazi or Cold War "museums" all over town. A thoughtful visit here provides valuable context for your explorations of Berlin (and Germany).

Cost and Hours: €8, covered by Museum Pass Berlin, daily 10:00-18:00, worthwhile €3 audioguide, Unter den Linden 2, +49 30 2030 4751, www.dhm.de.

☐ See the German History Museum Tour chapter.

▲▲DDR Museum

While overpriced, crammed with school groups, and frustrating to local historians, the DDR Museum has a knack for helping outsiders (rather than "Ost-algic" Germans) understand life in communist East Germany (the *Deutsche Demokratische Republik,* or DDR). The museum is well stocked with kitschy everyday items from the DDR period, plus photos, video clips, and concise English explanations.

Cost and Hours: €9.80, cheaper online; daily 10:00-20:00, Sat until 22:00; just across the Spree from Museum Island at Karl-Liebknecht-Strasse 1, +49 30 847 123 731, www.ddr-museum.de.

Advance Tickets Recommended: While you can get tickets at the museum, you'll save money and avoid the line at the entrance by purchasing them online in advance.

Visiting the Museum: Inside, you can crawl through a Trabant car (known as a "Trabi"; take it for a virtual test drive) and pick up some DDR-era black humor ("East Germany had 39 newspapers, four radio stations, two TV channels...and one opinion"). You'll learn how many East Germans—with limited opportunities to travel abroad—vacationed on Hungary's Lake Balaton or on the Baltic Coast, where nudism was all the rage (as a very revealing display explains). Lounge in DDR cinema chairs as you view a subtitled propaganda film or clips from beloved-in-the-East TV shows, including the popular kids' show *Sandmännchen*—"Little Sandman." The highlight is a tourable reconstructed communist-era home, where you can open drawers and cupboards to find both information panels and the trappings of a typical DDR home. You can even climb into a rickety old "elevator" and get jostled around.

Nikolai Quarter (Nikolaiviertel)

The Nikolai Quarter marks the original medieval settlement of Cölln, which would eventually become Berlin. Huddled around the twin spires of the Nikolaikirche, the area was destroyed during the war, then rebuilt for Berlin's 750th birthday in 1987. It has a cute and cobbled old-town feel...Middle Ages meets Socialist Realism. Today most of the buildings are occupied by touristy shops and restaurants. You can duck into the Nikolaikirche to see its pristinely renovated interior, which now houses a museum (church-free, museum-€5). Nearby are the Knoblauchhaus (18th-century bourgeois mansion; free, daily) and a small, pricey-but-interesting

museum dedicated to local photographer/illustrator Heinrich Zille, who captured engaging slices of Berlin life in the early 20th century (€7, daily 11:00-18:00, http://zillemuseum-berlin.de). Perhaps the best reason to come here is to visit its old-fashioned beer hall—the recommended Brauhaus Georgbräu, with seating along the river.

Northern Berlin

OLD JEWISH QUARTER

Immediately northeast of the Spree River is the old Jewish quarter which, in addition to being packed with intriguing shops and fun eateries, is one of the most important areas for Berlin's historic Jewish community—offering insights into a culture that thrived here until the 1940s.

 📖 For a self-guided walk through this fine area—including the first two sights listed below—see the Old Jewish Quarter Walk chapter.

▲▲Courtyards *(Höfe)*

The old Jewish quarter is a particularly handy place to explore Berlin's unique *Höfe*—interconnected courtyards that burrow through city blocks, today often filled with trendy shops and eateries. Two starkly different examples are nearly next door, and just steps from the Hackescher Markt transit hub: the upscale, *Jugendstil* Hackesche Höfe (Rosenthaler Strasse 40), with

eye-pleasing architectural flourishes and upscale shops; and the funky Haus Schwarzenberg (Rosenthaler Strasse 39), with a museum honoring Otto Weidt—a Berliner who defied the Nazis and saved many lived by employing blind and deaf Jews in his workshop.

New Synagogue (Neue Synagogue)

Marked by its beautiful golden dome, this large, mid-19th-century synagogue is now a museum memorializing the Berlin Jewish community that was decimated by the Nazis. Berlin was long the center of German Jewry and this small but moving exhibit (with good English descriptions) tells the story of this community through the centuries.

You'll enter through a low-profile door in the modern building to the right of the synagogue facade and go through very tight security. A cutaway model shows the entire synagogue. This model, and the view across the vacant lot out back to the iron columns marking where the apse stood, helps you envision this space that once housed 3,200 worshippers. The upper floor personalizes the Nazi terror with individual stories. Skip the climb to the dome; it's unimpressive from the inside and has ho-hum views.

Cost and Hours: €7; Sun-Fri 10:00-18:00, closed Sat; audioguide-€3, Oranienburger Strasse 28, S-Bahn: Oranienburger Strasse, +49 30 8802 8300, www.centrumjudaicum.de.

Boros Collection (Sammlung Boros)

In 1941, Hitler ordered the construction of an aboveground bunker that would shelter citizens during air raids and serve as a future monument for fallen German soldiers. The result, just west of the Oranienburger Tor U-Bahn stop, is a massive structure built to resemble an Italian Renaissance *palazzo* (and to symbolize the grandeur of the Nazi party). Using forced labor, it took just six months to erect. The internal double-helix staircase was equal parts aesthetic and practical for exiting and entering the building efficiently—the building's 120 rooms at one time housed over 4,000 people. After Germany's defeat, the bunker was repurposed as a prison during occupation, as storage for fruits and vegetables in the 1950s, and eventually as a 1990s techno club, before being sold to the Boros family. Since 2007, it's been a venue for their private collection of contemporary art, viewable only on a guided tour (which focuses mainly on the current exhibit rather than the building's history). While visiting the interior is only worthwhile for serious art lovers, the exterior is impressive (and free) to marvel at if you're nearby.

Cost and Hours: €12, reservations required—book on website, English tours Thu-Sun hourly at :30 past each hour 10:00-16:00, closed Mon-Wed, Reinhardstrasse 20, www.sammlung-boros.de.

▲Palace of Tears (Tränenpalast) at Friedrichstrasse Station

Just south of the old Jewish quarter (cross the river on Friedrichstrasse at Weidendammer Brücke and bear right) stands this impactful Cold War site. The Friedrichstrasse train station—situated within East Berlin, but accessible by train from West Berlin—was one of the few places where Westerners were allowed to cross into the East. And when crossing back into the free  world, this was where they'd take leave of their East German loved ones. The scene of so many sad farewells, it earned the nickname "Tränenpalast" (palace of tears). The 1962 building—an unassuming, boxy, bureaucratic structure that was once attached by a corridor to the station—has now been converted into a museum about everyday life in a divided Germany, with a fascinating peek into the paranoid border-control world of the DDR. Ample artifacts—such as suitcases and their contents—illustrate the story. You'll learn about contraband that was smuggled over the border (and the guards who played a constant cat-and-mouse game with the smugglers), and watch archival footage from the era. Of the many "life in the Cold War" sights in Berlin, this is the one most closely linked to a specific location.

Cost and Hours: Free, includes excellent audioguide, Tue-Fri 9:00-19:00, Sat-Sun 10:00-18:00, closed Mon, on the river side of the Friedrichstrasse station—look for the building with large glass windows and blue trim, Reichstagufer 17, +49 30 4677 7790, www. hdg.de/traenenpalast.

PRENZLAUER BERG AND NEARBY

The thriving Prenzlauer Berg district, worth ▲▲, offers an ideal opportunity to see a corner of today's "real Berlin," just beyond the core tourist zone but still easily accessible. Prenzlauer Berg (PRENTS-low-er behrk) was largely untouched by WWII bombs, fell into disrepair during DDR days, and has since been completely rejuvenated. The neighborhood fans out to the north and east from Rosenthaler Platz; the most appealing bit is along Kastanienallee, which connects Rosenthaler Platz to the Eberswalder Strasse U-Bahn tracks (and is served by tram #M1, which begins its run at Hackescher Markt S-Bahn station). The area just to the east, around Kollwitzplatz, is also enjoyable. Key landmarks include the Wasserturm (Industrial Age water tower); trendy Kollwitzplatz (with its upscale playgrounds); the Kulturbrauerei and Everyday Life in the DDR museum; lively Kastanienallee and livable Oderberger Strasse; and the Berlin Wall Memorial sights in and near the Mauerpark. Prenzlauer Berg is also a great place to sleep, eat, shop, and enjoy nightlife.

📖 See the Prenzlauer Berg Walk chapter.

Kulturbrauerei

The "Culture Brewery" is a brewery-turned-cultural center that fills an evocative old industrial space with a handful of interest-

ing shops, breezy restaurants, a movie theater, grocery store, and TI, plus a Sunday food market (12:00-18:00), winter Christmas market, and other outdoor events (Schönhauser Allee 36, +49 30 4435 2170, www.kulturbrauerei.de). Of most interest is the museum described next.

▲Everyday Life in the DDR (Alltag in der DDR)

This museum, tucked in a passage at the northern end of the Kulturbrauerei, recounts the reality of communist East Germany. The thoughtful, well-curated collection—organized by theme—displays original artifacts, videos, photos, art, and mock storefronts that rise above the kitsch factor to give a real sense of the disparity between the socialist ideal and the grinding reality. It's de-

signed not for casual tourists, but for aging Germans eager to teach their kids and grandkids about how they once lived. (The DDR Museum near Museum Island—described earlier—is less substantial, but also more tourist-friendly and therefore more crowded.) Although tricky to appreciate, this museum is free and well worth a visit, particularly if you're well versed in DDR history.

Cost and Hours: Free, Tue-Sun 10:00-18:00, Thu until 20:00, closed Mon; enter at Knaackstrasse 97, +49 30 4677 7790, www.hdg.de.

Visiting the Museum: As you explore, tune into details that offer insight into the DDR daily reality. The rack of magazines—all published to coincide with the big "Workers' Day" May 1 holiday—make it clear that freedom of the press was an illusion. A humble pub's short, handwritten menu demonstrates how limited even basic foodstuffs were—often relying on ersatz, miserable knock-offs (look for the "Kaffee-Mix," containing 51 percent actual coffee...and 49 percent fillers). Better-quality goods were mostly exported to bring in hard Western currency. People with loved ones in the West looked forward to receiving an occasional Westpaket—a care package of Western goods (minus whatever was seized by Stasi mail inspectors). Even the clothing was government-controlled. Peek inside the typical, circa-1979 Datsche—a simple countryside "allotment garden" cottage (owned by one in six East Germans) used for weekend retreats from the grimy city. You'll also learn about vacations (even just visiting Hungary's Lake Balaton—see the big postcards near the Trabi—came with bureaucratic hurdles); the Stasi secret police, who kept a close eye on all citizens; party propaganda, often through organizations like the Free German Youth (FDJ—scouts who were co-opted by communist messaging); and the organization of various workplaces into "collectives" where everyone was supposedly equal, yet somebody was in charge.

SIGHTS

SIGHTS

▲▲▲Berlin Wall Memorial (Gedenkstätte Berliner Mauer)

This is Berlin's most substantial and educational sight relating to its gone-but-not-forgotten Wall. Exhibits line up along several blocks of Bernauer Strasse, stretching more than a mile northeast from the Nordbahnhof S-Bahn station (one of the DDR's "ghost stations") to Schwedter Strasse and the Mauerpark. For a targeted visit, focus on the engaging sights clustered near the Nordbahnhof: two museums (the Visitors Center and the Documentation Center)—with films, photos, and harrowing personal stories; various open-air exhibits and memorials; original Wall fragments; and observation tower views into the only preserved, complete stretch of the Wall system (with a Cold War-era "death strip"). Begin at the Nordbahnhof, pick up an informational pamphlet from the Visitors Center, head up Bernauer Strasse, visit the exhibits and memorials that interest you, then ride home from the Bernauer Strasse U-Bahn station. For a longer visit, walk several more blocks all the way to the Mauerpark. The entire stretch is lined with informational posts (some with video or audio clips) and larger-than-life images from the Wall, painted on the sides of buildings. While you can visit the park at any time, it's best to go when the museums are open, as the videos there are important to see.

Cost and Hours: Free; outdoor areas accessible daily 24 hours; museums (Visitors Center and Documentation Center) both open Tue-Sun 10:00-18:00, closed Mon, memorial chapel closes at 17:00; on Bernauer Strasse at #119 (Visitors Center) and #111 (Documentation Center), +49 30 467 986 666, www.berliner-mauer-gedenkstaette.de.

☐ See the Berlin Wall Memorial Tour chapter.

Mauerpark

Where the eastern reaches of the Berlin Wall Memorial run into the western edge of Prenzlauer Berg, you'll hit the Mauerpark (Wall Park). Once part of the Wall's death strip, today it's a Prenzlauer Berg green space. The park is particularly entertaining on Sundays, when it hosts a rummage market and a giant karaoke party. Along the bluff, below the old DDR soccer stadium, runs a bit of the Wall covered in graffiti art.

HAUPTBAHNHOF AREA
Hauptbahnhof
Berlin's main train station is a sight in itself—a postmodern temple of slick transportation. Even if you're not arriving or departing here, it's worth a quick visit to ogle the soaring main hall, peer down into a canyon of crisscrossing platforms connecting Berlin to the rest of Germany and beyond, and do a little shopping. (On Sundays, this is where you'll find the highest concentration of open shops.) It's also home to the handy, American-run EurAide office—the most user-friendly place in town to book train tickets and reservations. For more on the Hauptbahnhof, see the Berlin Connections chapter.

Natural History Museum (Museum für Naturkunde)
Between the Hauptbahnhof and the Berlin Wall Memorial, this museum is home to "Tristan," one of the best-preserved, most complete T-Rex skeletons ever assembled. While you're there, meet "Bobby" the stuffed ape, and tour shelf after shelf of animals preserved in ethanol (about a million all together). Kid-friendly interactive displays include the "History of the Universe in 120 Seconds" exhibit and virtual-reality "Jurascope" glasses that put meat and skin on the dinosaur skeletons.

Cost and Hours: €8, €5 for kids, timed-entry tickets may be required—check in advance online; open Tue-Fri 9:30-18:00, Sat-Sun from 10:00, closed Mon; Invalidenstrasse 43, U6: Naturkundemuseum, +49 30 2093 8591, www.museumfuernaturkunde.berlin.

Southern Berlin

The following sights are listed roughly north to south (as you'd reach them from Unter den Linden).

FASCISM AND COLD WAR SITES NEAR CHECKPOINT CHARLIE
A variety of fascinating sites relating to Germany's tumultuous 20th century cluster south of Unter den Linden.

📖 For a guided walk connecting these, see the Fascism & Cold War Walk chapter (includes a visit inside the Topography of Terror).

▲Checkpoint Charlie
Famous as the place where many visiting Westerners crossed into East Berlin during the Cold War, the original Checkpoint Charlie is long gone. But today a reconstructed guard station—with big posters of American and Soviet guards, and a chilling "You

SIGHTS

Southern Berlin

To Unter den Linden
Stadtmitte
CHECKPOINT CHARLIE
Potsdamer Platz
Kochstrasse
KOCH.
BERLINISCHE GALERIE
JEWISH MUSEUM
TOPOGRAPHY OF TERROR
FRIEDRICHSTR.
Halleschesches Tor
GITSCHINER STR.
"KREUZBERG 36"
Landwehr Canal
Mehringdamm
ADMIRAL-BRÜCKE
GRAEFEKIEZ
Gneisenaustr. U
GNEISENAUSTR.
URBANSTR.
MITTEN
GRIMM
GRAEFE-STR.
Viktoriapark
"THE KREUZBERG" (MONUMENT)
MARHEINEKE MARKTHALLE
"KREUZBERG Ø1"
BERGMANNKIEZ
Platz der Luftbrücke
TEMPELHOF FIELD & "AIR BRIDGE" MEMORIAL
COLUMBIADAMM
Tempelhof Park
MÜHLENSTR
Spree River
OST-BAHNHOF
MERCEDES-BENZ ARENA
EAST SIDE GALLERY
ORANIENSTRASSE
Mariannenplatz
KREUZBERG
KOTT.-BRÜCKE
Kottbusser Tor
PAUL-LINCKE-UFER
Schönlein. U
MAYBACHUFER
Warschauer Strasse
MARKTHALLE NEUN
Görlitzer Bahnhof
Görlitzer Tor
WRANGELSTR
Schlesisches Tor
OBERBAUM-BRÜCKE
WRANGELKIEZ
Görlitzer Park
TURKISH STREET MARKET
To Treptower Park

1 Kilometer
1 Mile
NEUKÖLLN
·········· COURSE OF FORMER WALL

are leaving the American sector" sign—attracts curious tourists for a photo op. Nothing here is original (except for the nearby

museum—described next), and the whole area feels like a Cold War theme park, with kitschy communist-themed attractions, Trabi rides, hucksters, buskers, and sleazy vendors who charge through the nose for a DDR stamp in your passport. Those nostalgic for the Cold War enjoy seeing this historic site

and visiting the museum, but for a more serious look at the Berlin Wall, visit the official Berlin Wall Memorial (described earlier).

▲Museum of the Wall at Checkpoint Charlie (Mauermuseum Haus am Checkpoint Charlie)

This ragtag but riveting celebration of the many ways desperate East Germans managed to slip through the Wall to freedom has stood here since 1963...taunting DDR authorities. Today East Germany and its Wall are long gone, but the museum is still going strong. Some of the displays have yellowed, the place is cramped and confusing, and the ticket price is way too high, but the museum retains a special sense of history. Visiting here, you'll learn about the creation of the Wall and the many escape attempts (including several of the actual items used by clever escapees). If you're pressed for time, visit after dinner, when most other museums are closed.

Compared to the soberly academic official Berlin Wall Memorial near the Nordbahnhof, this museum has more personality, buoyed by a still-defiant spirit.

Cost and Hours: €14.50, daily 9:00-22:00, last entry one hour before closing, audioguide-€5, U6 to Kochstrasse or U2 to Stadt-mitte, Friedrichstrasse 43, +49 30 253 7250, www.mauermuseum. de.

Visiting the Museum: The first (cramped) room gets you right into it. A VW bug shows how people were smuggled through Check-point Charlie—note the mannequin behind the spare tire.

The **timeline** on the wall behind the car takes you through the events that made Checkpoint Charlie necessary. It's 1946 and the war's over, but the USSR possesses half of Berlin. Churchill warns the world that an Iron Curtain is descending (see the video). In 1949, West Berlin is blockaded (another video), but the city is saved by the US airlift. Still, people are becoming trapped under repressive Soviet rule. The section called "Raoul Wallenberg lives" honors the Swedish diplomat who saved tens of thousands of Jews during World War II, then disappeared under Soviet arrest. Countless others (names in binders) were similarly lost to Soviet work camps.

Upstairs, photos of June 17, 1953 show the brutal suppression of an East German revolt. (The big boulevard through Tiergarten Park is named for this date.)

In the next room, the divide between East and West widens. In 1955, West Germany joined NATO, while the East joined the Warsaw Pact. In 1956, a Hungarian uprising was crushed by Soviet tanks; 1957 saw the arms race and a "Missile Gap." The split between East and West finally hardened into concrete and rebar when the Wall went up in 1961. You'll see a model of the Wall and its fortified and booby-trapped death strip. When the Wall went up, so did the famous Checkpoint Charlie guard station—the first (or last) stop in American territory.

The rest of the museum focuses largely on many ingenious **escape attempts:** A beat-up armor-plated car, suitcases that two women squeezed into, a makeshift zip line for crossing over (rather than through) the border, a gas tank just big enough for one escapee, a wooden cart designed to go through the famous "Tunnel 57" (see page 221), a hot-air balloon that floated two families to safety, a primitive homemade ultralight aircraft, a mini-submarine, a child smuggled in a shopping bag, and many more. Photos show brave escapees and their helpers, such as American John P. Ireland, who posed as an eccentric antiques collector so he could transport refugees in his modified Cadillac.

Other exhibits chronicle the terror of life for those trapped in the East. A list names the 43,000 people who died in "Internal Affairs" internment camps from 1945-1950. Artwork inspired by the Wall includes a large painting of USSR premier Leonid Brezhnev and DDR premier Erich Honecker sharing the traditional "fraternal kiss" between comrades. And you'll see a memorial to Rainer Hildebrandt, who founded this museum shortly after the Wall went up in 1961.

On the **top floor,** you'll find a grab bag of exhibits on freedom movements across the globe: the 1956 Uprising in Hungary, 1968's Prague Spring, the 1980s Solidarity movement in Poland, even Gandhi's protests in India. An extensive exhibit celebrates Pablo Picasso's antiwar painting, *Guernica.* A room honors US President Ronald ("Tear Down This Wall") Reagan, displaying his cowboy hat and boots. A room in the corner of the museum offers a nice view over Checkpoint Charlie.

Finally, on your way out—near the sculpture of a Russian cellist who played at the newly opened Wall—a video captures those heady days when people-power tore down the Wall, and Checkpoint Charlie was history. It's hard not to get a little emotional watching teary-eyed Germans finally embracing their long-lost loved ones.

▲▲Topography of Terror (Topographie des Terrors)

A rare undeveloped patch of land in central Berlin, right next to a surviving stretch of Wall, was once the nerve center for the Gestapo and the SS—the most despi-cable elements of the Nazi government. Today this site hosts a modern documentation center, along with an outdoor exhibit in the Gestapo headquarters' excavated foundations. While there isn't much in the way of original artifacts, the exhibit does a good job of telling this

powerful story, in the place where it happened. The information is a bit dense, but WWII historians (even armchair ones) find it fascinating.

Cost and Hours: Free, includes audioguide, daily 10:00-20:00, outdoor exhibit closes at dusk, Niederkirchnerstrasse 8, U-

Bahn: Potsdamer Platz or Kochstrasse, S-Bahn: Anhalter Bahnhof or Potsdamer Platz, +49 30 254 5090, www.topographie.de.

Nearby: Immediately next door is an unusually long surviving stretch of the Berlin Wall. A block beyond that is the looming, very fascist-style Former Air Ministry—built by Hitler to house his Luftwaffe (Nazi air force), later the DDR's "Hall of Ministries," today the German Finance Ministry, still adorned with cheery 1950s communist propaganda. And a short walk away is a surviving DDR Watchtower, which kept careful vigil over the Wall.

📖 For a self-guided tour of the Topography of Terror exhibit, see the Fascism & Cold War Walk chapter.

MUSEUMS SOUTH OF UNTER DEN LINDEN
▲Jewish Museum Berlin (Jüdisches Museum Berlin)

Combining a remarkable building with a thoughtful permanent exhibit, this is the most educational Jewish-themed sight in Berlin. The exhibit has been undergoing a lengthy renovation but may have reopened by the time you visit. Either way, the building itself is still worth a look—it's packed with symbolism—and the memorials are still open during renovation.

Designed by American architect Daniel Libeskind (the master planner for the redeveloped World Trade Center in New York), the zinc-walled building has a zigzag shape pierced by voids symbolic of the irreplaceable cultural loss caused by the Holocaust. Enter the 18th-century Baroque building next door, then go through an underground tunnel to reach three memorial spaces. Follow the **Axis of Exile**—lined with the names of cities where the Jewish diaspora settled—to a disorienting slanted garden with 49 pillars. Next, the **Axis of Holocaust**—lined with names of concentration camps and artifacts from Jews imprisoned and murdered by the Nazis—leads to an eerily empty tower shut off from the outside world. Finally, the **Axis of Continuity** takes you to stairs and the main exhibit (if open). A detour partway up the long stairway leads (through temporary exhibits) to the Memory Void, a compelling space of "fallen leaves": heavy metal faces that you walk on, making inhuman noises with each step.

Cost and Hours: €8, ask for discount if also going to Berlinische Galerie, daily 10:00-20:00, closed on Jewish holidays;

tight security includes bag check and metal detectors; +49 30 2599 3300, www.jmberlin.de.

Getting There: It's in a nondescript residential neighborhood (halfway between Checkpoint Charlie and the happening Kreuzberg scene). Take the U1/U6 to Hallesches Tor, find the exit marked *Jüdisches Museum*, exit straight ahead, then turn right onto Franz-Klühs-Strasse at the first corner. The museum is a five-minute walk ahead on your left, at Lindenstrasse 9.

Eating: The museum's **$$** restaurant offers good Jewish-style meals, albeit not kosher.

▲Berlinische Galerie

This gorgeous, well-presented museum (with an oversized word-search puzzle out front) showcases modern and contemporary art created in this eclectic city.  The main draw is the permanent exhibit upstairs, offering an intriguing, chronological, and easily digestible look at art generated in Berlin from 1880 to 1980. The collection begins with Conservative (i.e., realistic) art, then gives way to the shimmering Berlin Secession (starting in 1892), and evolves from there. You'll meet Margarette Kubicka (1891-1984), with her colorful, curvy, Cubist-inspired style; and Klimt-like, avant-garde Expressionism, including works by Otto Dix (the biggest name here). You'll get a lesson in the Weimar-era "New Objectivity" (where artists focused on everyday scenes, intentionally objectifying their subjects in response to the abstraction trend). And you'll see how historical events shaped the art: works created under the Nazis (capturing confusion and alienation); scenes of postwar destruction; Cold War-era abstraction; and perspectives on the Wall from West Berlin artists.

Cost and Hours: €8, ask for discount if also visiting the Jewish Museum, Wed-Mon 10:00-18:00, closed Tue, Alte Jakobstrasse 124, +49 30 7890 2600, www.berlinischegalerie.de.

KREUZBERG

Visitors who find downtown Berlin too tame head to Prenzlauer Berg, and those who find Prenzlauer Berg too tame fall in love with Kreuzberg (worth ▲▲). This huge, sprawling neighborhood (pop. 150,000) sits just south of central Berlin.

Kreuzberg's identity was forged during the Cold War, when its Industrial Age apartment blocks were surrounded on three sides by the Berlin Wall. The people who were most willing to live in

Kreuzberg then were Turkish guest workers (trying to make a new life in a new land) and counterculture punks and squatters. For a long time, these two communities coexisted in Kreuzberg. But after the Wall came down, Kreuzberg was prime for redevelopment.

Today, Kreuzberg is in transition: Some areas have long since gentrified, while others are just starting to tidy up. Many areas still have a strong Turkish flavor, but each *Kiez* (smaller sub-neighborhood) has a personality of its own—some are extremely hip and becoming famous for their destination restaurants. (I've listed some street-food choices in the Kreuzberg Walk chapter, and some "destination" restaurants in the Eating in Berlin chapter.)

For a representative look at Kreuzberg, ride the U-Bahn (U1, U3, or U8) to **Kottbusser Tor**—the intersection at the heart of Kreuzberg—and explore. To the north is down-to-earth **Oranienstrasse,** lined with hole-in-the-wall shops and cheap eateries. Or wander south, crossing the Landwehr Canal to the increasingly trendy **Graefekiez** neighborhood. And if it's Tuesday or Friday, don't miss the vivid **Turkish Market,** with bustling street stalls that enliven the Maybachufer embankment near Kottbusser Brücke. All of this is within about a 10-minute walk of Kottbusser Tor.

📖 For more on these sights and a few other fun-to-explore *Kieze,* see the Kreuzberg Walk chapter.

NEAR KREUZBERG
Tempelhof Field
Adolf Hitler built the world's first modern airport terminal here in the late 1930s. After the war, Tempelhof Field was pressed into service 24/7 with airplanes landing, unloading, and taking off again—supplying the blockaded city of West Berlin (see "The Berlin Airlift" sidebar). In 2008—after decades as a commercial airstrip—Tempelhof closed for good. Today, the looming fascist-style terminal stands empty, and the airfield's former runways are a gigantic park—filled with Berliners on a sunny day, enjoying the wide-open spaces and the history.

Visiting the Airfield: Tempelhof is huge and time-consuming to visit—come here only if you're fascinated by the Berlin Airlift or by Nazi-era architecture. First, ride the U6 line to **Platz der Luftbrücke,** a small park where the focal point is a sweeping monument

The Berlin Airlift

The first big post-WWII showdown between the Western Allies and the Soviet Union took place in Berlin, years before the Berlin Wall went up.

On June 24, 1948, the Soviets cut off all land access to West Berlin—which was completely surrounded by East German territory. The Soviets hoped that, through this modern-day siege, West Berliners would come to them for assistance, which would only be given to those who committed to the Soviet cause. The end game was to gradually absorb West Berliners into the East, wiping out the very idea of "West Berlin."

To beat the blockade, the Western Allies dedicated themselves to supplying the two million people of West Berlin—mostly civilians—the only way they could: by air. American, British, Canadian, and other British Commonwealth forces began a yearlong campaign of flying supply sorties back and forth between West Berlin's Tempelhof Field (among others) and big airports in West Germany. They carried not only food, but medicine, fuel, and other critical resources.

In one famous photograph, American airman Gail Halvorsen flies over West Berlin, dropping candy in little parachutes into the outstretched arms of German kids. (Over the course of the airlift, the "Candy Bomber" dropped more than 20 tons of candy on West Berlin.) The photo—and the Berlin Airlift itself—was highly symbolic: The Western Allies, who just a few years prior used their planes to drop bombs, were now using them to keep Germans alive.

At the airlift's peak, a plane landed in West Berlin every 30 seconds, around the clock. Larger planes could carry as much as 8,000 tons per flight. Taking off and landing an overloaded aircraft was dangerous. Over the course of the blockade, 101 people died (in 25 plane crashes and other incidents). And yet, they persevered. Imagine: In a year, there were more than 270,000 flights, delivering a total of 2 million tons of supplies (at a cost, in today's dollars, of between 2.5 and 5 billion).

On May 12, 1949, the USSR lifted the blockade. The Berlin Airlift had succeeded. And it was a turning point in relations between the Western Allies and West Germany: After the Berlin Airlift, it was clear that the Americans and Brits were not here as occupiers, like the Soviets. They were here to help.

honoring the "air bridge" that supplied the city during the Berlin Airlift. (A similar monument—representing the other end of the air bridge—is at the Frankfurt Airport.) The names of those who died in the effort are carved into the base. Nearby is the gigantic **terminal building**—boxy and severe. The head of the Nazi eagle that once topped the airport sits out front.

It's possible to circle all the way around the terminal building to see the runways and park—but it's a long (20-minute) walk. Facing the terminal building, head left, then turn right on Columbiadamm street. You'll walk alongside the massive building, passing (across the street on your left), a small rust-colored **kiosk** at the corner with Golssener Strasse. This is a monument to Columbia Concentration Camp—one of the earliest in the Nazi system. Finally, you reach the entrance to the vast **park,** where people stroll, bike, and picnic on former runways. You'll likely see a few historic airplanes, along with *Biergartens,* softball fields, and (just over the fence) the minaret of one of Berlin's biggest mosques. On a sunny day, the park is packed.

Why has the city preserved this sprawling property—a square mile-and-a-half of prime real estate so close to the city center—as an oversized park? In a 2015 referendum, Berliners (perhaps fatigued by the city's treadmill of construction) jilted would-be developers when they voted decisively to keep this as a park. As for the gigantic building itself, city leaders are still debating what to do with it. Most recently, its hangars were being used to house Syrian refugees.

Treptower Park

For a taste of Moscow-style monumentalism in Berlin, head for Treptower Park. This was one of three major monuments erected in the postwar era to honor the Soviet soldiers who liberated Berlin (the others are in Tiergarten Park and Schönholzer Heide in Pankow, north of Prenzlauer Berg). In the Battle of Berlin (April and May 1945), an estimated 80,000 Soviet troops were killed in the fight to topple Hitler. Opened just four years later, the monument at Treptower Park epitomizes the USSR's bombastic knack for celebrating the fallen heroes of the "Great Patriotic War." Specifically, this monument represents the collective grave of 5,000 unknown soldiers. People who are really into grand Soviet architecture find this worth ▲▲▲; for others, it's simply an oversized curiosity.

Cost and Hours: Free, always open.

Getting There: While Treptower Park has its own S-Bahn station, it's a tedious 15-minute walk from there to the core of the monument itself. Instead, take the U-Bahn to Schlesisches Tor (in Kreuzberg's Wrangelkiez neighborhood), then take bus #165 or #265 to the Herkomerstrasse stop, at the side entrance to the park (along Am Treptower Park road). Enter through the gateway and you'll see the "Motherland" statue.

Visiting the Monument: From the statue of an anguished mother(land), a tree-lined boulevard leads through a ceremonial gateway (shaped like Soviet flags) and past 32 symbolic sarcophagi (carved with reliefs of wartime hardship and courage) to a 40-foot-tall statue of a victorious Soviet soldier. One arm crushes a swastika with a giant sword; the other gently cradles a toddler. In the small memorial room at the statue's base, visitors lay fresh flowers under a mosaic-red-star ceiling. You'll see the monument's theme carved into its stone (in German and in Russian): "The homeland will not forget its heroes."

Notice how well cared-for this monument is. Despite East Berliners' tumultuous relationship with the USSR, the sacrifice of 80,000 soldiers to free Europe from Hitler is still respected. The "Two Plus Four Agreement" (1990)—which relieved Germany of its post-WWII obligations to permit reunification—provided for the preservation of Soviet war monuments in perpetuity. Berlin's large Russian expat community fills this park each year on May 8—the anniversary of the day that the Red Army took Berlin.

Eastern Berlin

ALEXANDERPLATZ AND NEARBY

This area is of interest mostly to those nostalgic for the DDR era.

📖 See the Communist East Berlin Walk chapter.

Karl-Liebknecht-Strasse

This wide boulevard—connecting Alexanderplatz to Museum Island, and named for an early German communist pioneer—is lined with DDR-era landmarks, including the TV Tower, St. Mary's Church (historic church kept open—barely—during communism), Rotes Rathaus ("Red City Hall" of former East Berlin), and the Marx-Engels-Forum, a park with statues of communism founders Karl Marx and Friedrich Engels, who studied in Berlin.

▲Alexanderplatz

Marking the eastern end of the Unter den Linden/Karl-Liebknecht-Strasse thoroughfare, this kitschy-futuristic space was the main square of DDR-era East Berlin. Named (fittingly) for a Russian czar, under communist rule the square was turned into a model of Soviet aesthetics—with stern, blocky facades; a showpiece de-

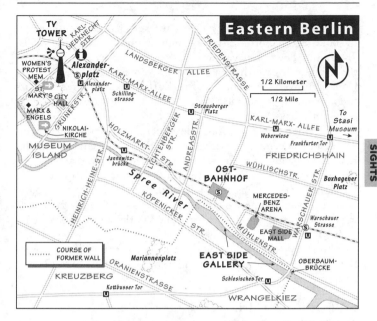

Eastern Berlin

1/2 Kilometer

1/2 Mile

To Stasi Museum

COURSE OF FORMER WALL

partment store; a transit hub for trams and trains; and a trippy "World Time Clock." Nearby is the start of the severely socialist-style Karl-Marx-Allee; originally named Stalinallee, it would have been more at home in Moscow than in Berlin.

TV Tower (Fernsehturm)

One of Berlin's landmarks, this 1,200-foot-tall massive spike is topped by a giant glittering disco ball. You'll see it from just about anywhere in the city, and riding the elevator to the observation deck comes with sweeping

(but almost too-high) views. Various walking and bike tours leave from here.

Cost and Hours: €17.50, daily 9:00-24:00, Nov-Feb from 10:00, Panoramastrasse 1A, www.tv-turm.de.

Karl-Marx-Allee

This socialist-style boulevard was built after the original buildings here were leveled by the Red Army in 1945. As an expression of their adoration to the "great Socialist Father" (Stalin), the DDR government decided to rebuild the street better than ever (the USSR provided generous subsidies). They named it Stalinallee and lined it with apartment blocks ("workers' palaces") designed in the bold "Stalin Gothic" style so common in Moscow in the 1950s. The grand, showy boulevard was built in just four years and startled the West, as it gave them a peek at the potential future of Euro-Communism. Now renamed after Karl Marx, the street and its restored buildings provide a vivid look at architecture from Berlin's communist days.

The boulevard runs from Alexanderplatz to Frankfurter Tor. To see it, you can taxi or ride the U-Bahn to Alexanderplatz and hike east for a mile. Or, for a shorter walk, ride the U-Bahn to Weberwiese and walk to Frankfurter Tor (away from TV Tower, along the right side). Strolling the boulevard, look for information posts along the way, and notice the Social Realism reliefs on the buildings and the lampposts, which incorporate the wings of a phoenix (rising from the ashes) in their design.

From Frankfurter Tor you can ride the tram (#M10, direction: Warschauer Strasse) conveniently to the East Side Gallery described below.

FRIEDRICHSHAIN

This neighborhood—just east of the core "Mitte" area—is quickly transforming, with a sea of construction cranes erecting super-modern buildings (such as the 17,000-seat Mercedes-Benz Arena, and the glitzy East Side Mall). The Warschauer Strasse S- and U-Bahn station area, while gritty, offers a glimpse into this neighborhood. Just uphill is a grungy but gentrifying neighborhood fanning out from Boxhagener Platz—a scruffy square ringed by creative cheap eats. Just downhill from the Warschauer Strasse station is a striking bridge and the start of the East Side Gallery.

▲East Side Gallery

The biggest remaining stretch of the Wall is now the "world's longest outdoor art gallery." This segment of the Wall makes a memorable walk for those interested in street art and/or Berlin Wall history. The gallery stretches for nearly a mile and is covered with murals painted by artists from around the world. The murals (classified as protected monuments) got a facelift in 2009, when the city invited the original artists back to re-create their work for the 20th anniversary of the fall of the Wall. For the history of the East Side Gallery, see www.eastsidegallery-berlin.de.

Getting There: Head for the Oberbaumbrücke (Oberbaum Bridge), which crosses the Spree between Friedrichshain's Warschauer Strasse U-Bahn station and Kreuzberg's Wrangelkiez neighborhood (U1: Schlesisches Tor). From either station, head for the river and look for the long strip of wall, a parallel strip of park-like riverfront, and lots of tourists. Bus #300 stops directly in front of the museum. You could also ride tram #M10 to the last stop and walk downhill until just before the fanciful brick bridge towers.

Visiting the East Side Gallery: From the Oberbaum Bridge, head along the most interesting stretch of the East Side Gallery. Just walking a hundred yards gives you the essence of the gallery and the tourist scene that enlivens it. Walk along as far as you'd like and return, or trek the entire length, nearly a mile, to the Ostbanhof S-Bahn station. Along the way, watch for some iconic scenes:

Dmitri Vrubel's "fraternal kiss" between DDR and USSR leaders (Honecker and Brezhnev), with the message in Russian and German: "Dear God, help me to survive this deadly love." While the painting is based on an actual photograph, this ritual—designed to show the comradeship between leaders of communist countries—is frequently parodied to show other world leaders in cahoots with each other (for example, Donald Trump French-kissing Vladimir Putin).

The black-and-white portrait *Danke, Andrej Sacharow* honors the Soviet dissident and human rights activist. One of the longest works—a row of colorful heads with *Simpsons* overbites—is by French artist Thierry Noir, one of the first street artists who gained fame using the Wall as his canvas. *Test the Rest* shows a Trabi car bursting through the Wall (far down, where the modern apartment high-rise abuts the wall). And Kani Alavi's *It Happened in November* shows the sea of humanity flowing through the wall the night it opened.

Close to the start of the Wall, a gap leads to an overpriced "Wall Museum" (displays in a dozen stuffy rooms—skip it in favor of better museums elsewhere in Berlin).

Strolling along the riverside is a convivial, youthful, and arty scene, especially in the evening. And the whimsical Oberbaum Bridge, a sight in itself, is a marvelous example of Brandenburg Neo-Gothic brickwork.

▲Stasi Museum

This extensive, thoughtfully presented exhibit tells the story of how the communist-era Ministry for State Security (a.k.a. Stasi)—headquartered in these very buildings—infiltrated all aspects of East German life. While the museum is quite dry and out of the way, it's the best place in Berlin to learn about the Stasi.

SIGHTS

The Stasi

Initially formed to investigate and prosecute Nazi crimes, the DDR government's Ministerium für Staatssicherheit (MfS, "Ministry for State Security")—nicknamed the "Stasi" (SHTAH-zee)—quickly became a means of suppressing dissent as civil liberties dwindled in communist Germany. The Stasi considered themselves "the sword and shield of the party."

Modeled after the Soviet Union's secret police, the Stasi recruited informants from every walk of life, often intimidating them into cooperating by threatening their jobs, their children's education, or worse. They eventually gathered an army of some 600,000 "unofficial employees" (inoffizielle Mitarbeiter), nearly 200,000 of whom were still active when communism fell in 1989. At its peak, an estimated one in seven East Germans was cooperating with the Stasi. These "employees" were coerced into reporting on the activities of their coworkers, friends, neighbors, and even immediate family members.

Preoccupied with keeping track of "nonconformist" behavior, the Stasi collected whatever bits of evidence they could—including saliva, handwriting, odors, and voice recordings—and wound up with vast amounts of files.

What was the Stasi's goal? Quite simply, to be in control... of everything. Sometimes they'd pursue criminal prosecution and imprisonment. The worst offenders might be deported. Most often, the Stasi simply harassed. They wanted suspects to *know* they were being watched—to destabilize and marginalize them. Often no formal accusation ever came of these investigations, but lives were ruined nonetheless.

Soon after the Wall fell, DDR authorities scrambled to destroy the illicit information their agents and informants had collected. But the new government mandated that these records be preserved as evidence of DDR crimes, and the documents are now managed by the Federal Commissioner for Stasi Records. These days, German citizens can read the files once kept on them. It's a hard choice: Request their record—and likely find out that friends and loved ones had reported on them—or never know the truth. For a film that brilliantly captures the paranoid Stasi culture, see the 2006 Oscar winner *The Lives of Others*.

Cost and Hours: €6, Mon-Fri 10:00-18:00, Sat-Sun from 11:00, +49 30 553 6854, www.stasimuseum.de.

Getting There: It's a long haul from the center, at Ruschestrasse 103. Take the U5 to Magdalenenstrasse and exit toward *Ruschestrasse*. Up on the street, make a U-turn to the right up Ruschestrasse and look for the yellow sign—the museum is tucked far back in a courtyard.

Visiting the Museum: Exhibits fill three floors of the building where Stasi Minister Erich Mielke had his office. Everything is described in English, with lots of reading and some interesting artifacts.

At the entrance, check out the sprawling **model** of this neighborhood. The Stasi operation filled entire city blocks—essentially creating a city-within-the-city (54 acres, 50 buildings, 7,000 employees) for the sole purpose of surveilling its citizens. On official maps of East Berlin, this area showed up as blank space.

Upstairs, **floor 1** explains the mission and methods of the Stasi—including the "unofficial employees" who were recruited to report on their coworkers, neighbors, and loved ones. Check out the map of *Konspirative Wohnung* in Room 6 showing all the Stasi apartments in Prenzlauer Berg—see if you can spot your hotel's present-day location.

On **floor 2,** you can tour the offices of the Stasi leadership (including Mielke's private study) as it was furnished during its heyday. Seeing these anonymous, bureaucratic spaces, you realize that "the banality of evil" did not end with Hitler. And on **floor 3,** you'll learn more about some of the tools and methods used by the Stasi: Tiny microphones and cameras that could be hidden inside walls, handbags, neckties, watering cans, belts, and buttons. An infrared camera built into the door of a car. X-ray machines for seeing inside care packages sent from the West. In a glass jar, a yellow cloth suffused with the body scent of a suspect—which could be used with trained dogs to track the suspect. And endless stacks of index cards filled with mundane details about the lives of others.

Out in the parking lot is a **photo exhibit** about the events of 1989 that brought this painful chapter to a close: the Peaceful Revolution and the fall of the Berlin Wall.

Other Stasi Sights: If you're particularly keen, you can trek a bit north to the Stasi Prison, where "enemies of the state" served time (€6, visits possible only with tour, often guided by former inmates; English tours daily but call to confirm times before making the trip; Genslerstrasse 66, reachable via tram from downtown—see website for specifics, +49 30 9860 8230, www.stiftung-hsh.de).

SIGHTS

Western Berlin

TIERGARTEN PARK

Berlin's "Central Park" stretches two miles from the Reichstag and Brandenburg Gate to Berlin Zoological Garden. This vast, 500-acre park, once a royal hunting ground, is now packed with cycling paths, joggers, and—on hot days—nude sunbathers.

The main boulevard through its middle—Strasse des 17 Juni—commemorates a bold 1953 uprising in the communist DDR. This series of strikes and protests culminated on June 17, when 40,000 protesters in East Berlin were dispersed by Soviet and East German tanks. Dozens, or possibly hundreds, were killed. While the East brushed the revolt under the rug, June 17 became a national holiday in West Germany—the Day of German Unity.

▲Victory Column (Siegessäule)

The Tiergarten's centerpiece—faintly visible in the distance from the Brandenburg Gate—is the striking Victory Column, built to commemorate the Prussian defeat of Denmark in 1864...then reinterpreted after the defeat of France in 1870. The pointy-helmeted Germans rubbed it in, decorating the tower with French cannons and paying for it all with francs received as war reparations. The three lower rings commemorate Otto von Bismarck's victories (see page 166). I imagine the statues of German military greats—which lurk among the trees nearby—goose-stepping around the floodlit angel at night.

Originally standing at the Reichstag, in 1938 the tower was moved to this position and given a 25-foot lengthening by Hitler's architect, Albert Speer, in anticipation of the planned re-envisioning of Berlin as "Welthauptstadt Germania"—the capital of a worldwide Nazi empire. Streets leading to the circle are flanked by surviving Nazi guardhouses, built in the stern style that fascists loved. At the memorial's first level, notice how WWII bullets chipped the fine marble columns. From 1989 to 2003, the column was the epicenter of the Love Parade (Berlin's citywide techno-hedonist street party), and it was the backdrop for Barack Obama's summer 2008 visit to Germany as a presidential candidate.

Victory Column Climb

Climbing the Victory Column's 270 steps earns you a breathtaking Berlin-wide view and a close-up of the gilded bronze statue of the goddess Victoria. You might recognize Victoria from Wim Wenders' 1987 art-house classic film *Wings of Desire,* or the *Stay (Faraway, So Close!)* video he directed for the rock band U2.

Cost & Hours: €3, daily 9:30-18:30, Sat-Sun until 19:00, Nov-March 10:00-17:00, closes for rain, no elevator, +49 30 391 2961.

SOUTH OF TIERGARTEN PARK

This area, a 15-minute walk from the Brandenburg Gate, is divided into the skyscraper zone of Potsdamer Platz and the arts-and-culture complex called the Kulturforum. For history buffs, the German Resistance Museum and the Silent Heroes Memorial sit just beyond the Kulturforum.

Potsdamer Platz Area

This immense, 150-acre square is home to sleek skyscrapers, shopping malls, a transportation hub, several major corporate headquarters, upscale restaurants, and a few museums.

▲Potsdamer Platz

The architectural face of Potsdamer Platz has changed drastically over time: Berlin's busiest intersection before World War II, it was bombed flat and remained a devastated wasteland until the 1990s, then quickly sprouted a forest of glassy skyscrapers, as if to trumpet the victory of capitalism. Visiting today, you'll see a skyscraper panorama, a replica of Europe's first traffic light, a boldly modern train station, a few chunks of the Berlin Wall, and the Sony Center shopping/entertainment complex. A good place to view it all is from the intersection of Potsdamer Strasse and Ebertstrasse. (From the S-Bahn or U-Bahn, exit following *Leipziger Platz* signs.) The next two sights are also nearby. A quick look at Potsdamer Platz also works well in conjunction with the nearby Kulturforum.

SIGHTS

☐ For more details on Potsdamer Platz and Sony Center, plus a detailed map of the area, see the Fascism & Cold War Walk chapter.

▲Deutsche Kinemathek Film and TV Museum

This exhibit is the most interesting place to visit within the Sony Center. Many early pioneers in filmmaking were German (including Fritz Lang, F. W. Murnau, Ernst Lubitsch, and the Austrian-born Billy Wilder)—and many became influential in Hollywood—making this a fun visit for cinephiles from anywhere. Your admission ticket gets you into several floors of exhibits made meaningful by the essential English audioguide.

Cost and Hours: €8, free Thu 16:00-20:00; open Wed-Mon 10:00-18:00, Thu until 20:00, closed Tue; audioguide-€2, Potsdamer Strasse 2, +49 30 300 9030, www.deutsche-kinemathek.de.

Visiting the Museum: From the ticket desk, ride the elevator up to the third floor, where you can turn left (into the film section, floors 3 and 2) or right (into the TV section, floors 3 and 4).

The film section walks back in time to the German film industry's beginnings, with an emphasis on the Weimar Republic period in the 1920s, when Berlin rivaled Hollywood. Influential films included the early German Expressionist masterpiece *The Cabinet of Dr. Caligari* (1920) and Fritz Lang's seminal *Metropolis* (1927). Three rooms are dedicated to Marlene Dietrich (including one room just for her dresses), who was a huge star both in Germany and, later, in Hollywood.

Another section examines Nazi use of film as propaganda, including Leni Riefenstahl's masterful documentary of the 1936 Berlin Olympics and her earlier, chillingly propagandistic *Triumph des Willens* (*Triumph of the Will*, 1935).

The exhibit's finale highlights today's influential German filmmakers—including Wolfgang Petersen *(Das Boot, Air Force One, The Perfect Storm)* and Werner Herzog (documentaries such as *Grizzly Man* and the drama *Rescue Dawn*). If a visit here gets you curious about German cinema, see the recommendations in the appendix.

The TV section tells the story of *das Idioten Box* from its infancy (when it was primarily used as a Nazi propaganda tool) to today. The 30-minute kaleidoscopic review—kind of a frantic fast-forward montage of greatest hits in German TV history, both East and West—is great fun even if you don't understand a word of it (it plays all day long, with 10-minute breaks). Otherwise, the TV section is a little more challenging for non-German speakers to appreciate. Upstairs (on the fourth floor) is a TV archive where you can dial through a wide range of new and classic German TV standards.

Nearby: The Kino Arsenal theater downstairs shows offbeat art-house films in their original language.

Panoramapunkt

Across Potsdamer Strasse from the Deutsche Kinemathek museum, you can ride what's billed as the "fastest elevator in Europe" to skyscraping rooftop views. You'll travel at nearly 30 feet per second to the top of the 300-foot-tall Kollhoff Tower in the Potsdamer Platz 1 building. Its sheltered-but-open-air view deck provides a fun survey of Berlin's changing skyline.

Cost and Hours: €7.50, €11.50 VIP ticket lets you skip the line, cash only, daily 10:00-20:00, until 18:00 in winter, in red-brick building at Potsdamer Platz 1, +49 30 2593 7080, www.panoramapunkt.de.

Kulturforum

Berlin's *other* ensemble of museums (after Museum Island) fills a purpose-built facility just beyond Potsdamer Platz. Here you'll find a variety of impressive museums and other cultural institutions, including exquisite European Masters at the Gemäldegalerie, musical instruments, and decorative arts. Its New National Gallery (which houses modern art) is closed for renovation.

Combo-Tickets: All Kulturforum sights are covered by a €12 combo-ticket (can cost more if a special exhibit is on, www.kulturforum-berlin.de). They're also covered by the Museum Pass Berlin (explained at the beginning of this chapter).

Getting There: Ride the S-Bahn or U-Bahn to Potsdamer Platz, then walk along Potsdamer Platz.

📖 The Gemäldegalerie and other museums mentioned here are covered by the Gemäldegalerie & Kulturforum Tour chapter.

▲▲Gemäldegalerie

This "Painting Gallery" is one of Germany's top collections of great works by European masters. The Gemäldegalerie shows off fine works from the 13th through 18th century. While there's no one famous piece of art, you'll get an enticing taste of just about all the big names. In the North Wing are painters from Germany (Albrecht Dürer, Hans Holbein, Lucas Cranach), the Low Countries (Jan van Eyck, Pieter Brueghel, Peter Paul Rubens, Anthony van Dyck, Frans Hals, Johannes Vermeer), Britain (Thomas Gainsborough), France (Antoine Watteau), and an impressive hall of Rembrandts. The South Wing is the terrain of Italian greats, including Giotto, Botticelli, Titian, Raphael, and Caravaggio.

Cost and Hours: €14, includes audioguide; Tue-Fri 10:00-18:00, Thu until 20:00, Sat-Sun 11:00-18:00, closed Mon; clever little loaner stools, great salad bar in cafeteria upstairs, Matthäikirchplatz 4, +49 30 266 424 242, www.smb.museum.

▲Musical Instruments Museum (Musikinstrumenten Museum)

Music lovers appreciate this beautifully displayed collection of 600 different items, going back to the 1500s. The included audioguide brings the collection to life and lets you actually hear a few of the instruments in action (€6, Tue-Fri 9:00-17:00, Sat-Sun from 10:00, closed Mon; Tiergartenstrasse 1—easy-to-miss entrance is down Ben-Gurion-Strasse, facing the back of the Sony Center; www.simpk.de).

Nearby: Berlin's yellow **Philharmonic Concert Hall** sits just beyond the Musical Instruments Museum. Appreciate its bold architecture (inspired by a ship at sea, and different from each angle) and step into the lobby to consider a performance during your stay (ticket office open Mon-Fri 15:00-18:00, Sat-Sun 11:00-14:00 except closed July-Aug, +49 30 2548 8999, www.berliner-philharmoniker.de).

▲Museum of Decorative Arts (Kunstgewerbemuseum)

Berlin's answer to London's Victoria and Albert Museum shows off a thousand years of applied arts—from shimmering reliquaries (the Guelph Treasure) and delicate porcelain to Art Deco and *Jugendstil* furnishings, and much more. The highlights are the Dome Reliquary (an elaborately decorated, church-shaped container for saints' bones) and an appealing collection of women's fashions over the centuries (€8, Tue-Fri 10:00-18:00, Sat-Sun from 11:00, closed Mon; Matthäikirchplatz 5, www.smb.museum).

Near the Kulturforum
German Resistance Memorial (Gedenkstätte Deutscher Widerstand)

This memorial and museum, located in the former Bendlerblock military headquarters, tells the story of several organized German resistance movements and the more than 42 separate assassination attempts against Hitler. While the exhibit has no real artifacts, the building itself is important: One of the most thoroughly planned schemes to kill Hitler was plotted here (the actual attempt occurred in Rastenburg, eastern Prussia). That attempt failed, and several leaders of the conspiracy, including Claus Schenk Graf von Stauffenberg, were shot here in the courtyard.

The building also houses the **Silent Heroes Memorial Center**

(Gedenkstätte Stille Helden), a well-presented exhibit celebrating the quietly courageous individuals who resisted the persecution of the Jews from 1933 to 1945. Take some time to learn a few of their stories.

Cost and Hours: Free, includes good English audioguide; Mon-Fri 9:00-18:00, Thu until 20:00, Sat-Sun 10:00-18:00; near Kulturforum at Stauffenbergstrasse 13, enter through courtyard, door on left, main exhibit on second floor up; bus #M29, +49 30 2699 5000, www.gdw-berlin.de.

CITY WEST

The following sights are in the heart of the former "West Berlin" (clustering near Kurfürstendamm boulevard). To get here, ride the S-Bahn to Zoologischer Garten. (For locations, see the "Western Berlin" map, earlier).

▲Kurfürstendamm

Kurfürstendamm boulevard (nicknamed "Ku'damm") starts at Kaiser Wilhelm Memorial Church and does a commercial cancan for two miles. In the 1850s, when Berlin became a wealthy and important capital, her "new rich" chose Kurfürstendamm as their street. In the 1870s, Bismarck made it Berlin's Champs-Elysées. In the 1920s, it was a stylish and fashionable drag of cafés and boutiques. During the Third Reich it was home to an international community of diplomats and journalists, and throughout the Cold War, economic subsidies from the West ensured that capitalism thrived here. Today, Berlin's focus has shifted east and Ku'damm feels more "international-touristy" than "authentic Berlin"—with a Hard Rock Café and a Käthe Wohlfahrt Christmas ornament superstore. But it remains a fine place to enjoy elegant shops (around Fasanenstrasse), department stores, and people-watching.

▲Kaiser Wilhelm Memorial Church (Gedächtniskirche)

This church was originally dedicated to the first emperor of Germany, Wilhelm I. Reliefs and mosaics show great events in the life of Germany's favorite kaiser, from his coronation in 1871 to his death in 1888. The church is actually an ensemble of buildings: a new church, the matching bell tower, a meeting hall, and the ruins of the old church, with its Memorial Hall. The bombed-out ruins of the old church were left standing as a memorial to Berlin's destruction in World War II, with a new church constructed next door.

SIGHTS

Cost and Hours: Church—free, daily 9:00-19:00—or until 18:00 if there's a concert; Memorial Hall—free, Mon-Fri 10:00-18:00, Sat until 20:00, Sun 12:00-17:30. Located on Breitscheidplatz, U2/U9 and S-Bahn: Zoologischer Garten or U1/U9: Kurfürstendamm, www.gedaechtniskirche-berlin.de.

Visiting the Church: Start your visit by picking up the English flier for information on both churches.

Bullet holes dot the exterior of the **ruined church.** After the war, some Berliners wanted to tear down the ruins, but instead they were kept as a Memorial Hall. Inside, under a Neo-Romanesque mosaic ceiling, you'll find a small photo exhibit and before-and-after models of the church.

To replace the ruined church, the authorities held a competition to design a contemporary annex. The winning entry—the short, **modern church** (1961) across from the Memorial Hall—of-

fers a meditative world of 11,000 little blue windows. The blue glass was given to the church by the French as a reconciliation gift. As you enter, turn immediately right to find a simple charcoal sketch of the Virgin Mary wrapped in a shawl. During the Battle of Stalingrad, German combat surgeon Kurt Reuber rendered the Virgin on the back of a stolen Soviet map to comfort the men in his care. On the right are the words "Light, Life, Love" from the gospel of John; on the left, "Christmas in the cauldron 1942"; and at the bottom, "Fortress Stalingrad." Though Reuber died in captivity a year later, his sketch was flown out of Stalingrad on the last medical evacuation flight, and postwar Germany embraced it as a symbol of the wish for peace. Copies of the drawing, now known as the *Stalingrad Madonna,* hang in the Berlin Cathedral, in St. Michael's Cathedral in Coventry, England, and in the Kozan Cathedral in Russia's Volgograd (formerly Stalingrad) as a sign of reconciliation among nations. Every Friday at 13:00 a "Prayers for Peace" service is held simultaneously here and at the cathedral in Coventry.

Outside, a **golden crack** in the sidewalk stretches from the church toward Budapester Strasse, commemorating the December 2016 Christmas Market terrorist attack that took the lives of 12 people here. Look for the names of the victims on the steps.

Nearby: The lively square between the churches and the Europa Center attracts street musicians and performers—especially in the summer. Berliners call the funky fountain the "Wet Meatball." Overlooking the scene is the newly renovated Bikini Berlin

In the West

The area now called City West has seen a lot of history. When Berlin's zoo was built here in the 1840s, this area was farm fields. But as Berlin boomed in the late 19th century, the area developed at a fast clip: In 1882, the Zoologischer Garten (Zoo Station) train station opened, and in 1886, Otto von Bismarck inaugurated the newly broadened and spiffed-up Kurfürstendamm boulevard (known as Ku'damm).

By the 1890s, this area was known as the *Neue Westen*—the "New West." Back then, "West" was associated with modernity. And the *Neue Westen* was where Berlin's famous artistic, alternative, cabaret scene was at its most colorful. It was here that Bertolt Brecht and Marlene Dietrich gained fame; it was here that Christopher Isherwood set many of his *Berlin Stories* (later adapted into the musical and film *Cabaret*); and it was here that influential early filmmakers established the "German Hollywood" in the nascent days of motion pictures. The adjacent Schöneberg district became a popular residential zone for young people eager to be a part of the thriving arts scene. And it was during this era that several "West" landmarks popped up, including the Kaufhaus des Westens (KaDeWe department store) and the Theater des Westens (Theater of the West).

With the advent of the Cold War, this area embraced the "West" in a different sense: capitalism and democracy. Ku'damm became West Berlin's main drag. The West German government poured funds into building Europa Center—glittering skyscrapers to house the headquarters of international businesses, a bold outpost of capitalism. The Schöneberg City Hall became the seat of West Berlin government, and the site of JFK's famous visit.

Thirty years ago, Zoo Station was the first stop for any traveler arriving in Berlin; from here, you'd venture cautiously into the East, before retreating to the safety of Ku'damm. Back then, this guidebook (and every other Berlin guidebook) was entirely West-centric.

With the fall of the Berlin Wall, West Berlin became passé. Investors poured funds into developing previously inaccessible swaths of the East. High-rises on Potsdamer Platz and along Friedrichstrasse eclipsed the ones at Europa Center. Zoo Station—previously the city's de facto main train station—was supplanted by the futuristic new Hauptbahnhof.

Rebranded as City West, this area has bounced back and seems comfortable with its revised identity. No longer the center of the action, City West is content to be an upscale suburb with an illustrious history.

shopping mall, with a mix of local and international shops, pop-up stores, and an upstairs terrace peering down into the zoo.

▲Käthe Kollwitz Museum

This local artist (1867-1945), who experienced much of Berlin's stormiest century, conveyed powerful, deeply felt emotions about motherhood, war, and suffering through the stark faces of her art. This small yet fine collection consists of three floors of charcoal drawings and woodcuts, dotted with a handful of sculptures. The museum may have moved by the time you visit; check the website before you go.

Cost and Hours: €7, daily 11:00-18:00, a block off Ku'damm at Fasanenstrasse 24, U-Bahn: Uhlandstrasse, +49 30 882 5210, www.kaethe-kollwitz.de.

Visiting the Museum: The small **ground floor** gives historical context on Berlin in the early 1900s. Heading up the stairwell, you'll see a timeline of events in Kollwitz's life.

Floor 1 focuses on the relatively happy first half of her life, when she drew from interactions with the poor to create some of her most moving works. You'll see how Kollwitz gained confidence and found her artistic voice in her depictions of the Peasants' Revolt (1520s) and the Weavers' Revolt (1844).

Floor 2 continues the story, with the turning point in her life: 1914, when Kollwitz's first-born son died in battle on Flanders Fields. You'll see her transition to a woodcut technique, focusing on depictions of war colored by her personal loss. Posters from this era show her social conscience—shaming Germans into helping feed their starving compatriots. Her self-portraits from the 1930s are imbued with a world-weariness that will only intensify with the death of her grandson, fighting in Russia, in World War II. (These losses inspired Kollwitz to create her most famous work, the powerful *pietà* inside Germany's war memorial at the Neue Wache—described in the Unter den Linden Walk chapter.)

Kollwitz's sculptures are spread across floors 1 and 2. While best known during her lifetime for her prints, Kollwitz favored sculpting. But lack of access to materials meant that she produced relatively few works. Some that you see here were cast (from her designs) only after her death. Taken together, Kollwitz's evocative oeuvre testifies to her struggle to define the duties of wife, mother, and artist.

Note that Kollwitz didn't live in this building; she and her husband made their home across the city in Prenzlauer Berg (near Kollwitzplatz, the square named in her honor).

Berlin Zoological Garden (Zoologischer Garten) and Aquarium

More than 1,500 kinds of animals call Berlin's famous zoo home... or so the zookeepers like to think. The zoo and the world-class adjacent aquarium draw gaggles of school kids and their frazzled chaperones. For a free look into the monkey enclosure, head inside the nearby Bikini Berlin shopping center, where the ground-floor windows offer an eye-level glimpse at the playful primates (or for a delightful bird's-eye view, head to the mall's rooftop terrace).

Cost and Hours: Zoo and aquarium €15.50 each, €21 for both, kids half-price, daily 9:00-18:30, until 16:30 in winter, aquarium closes at 18:00 year-round; feeding times—*Fütterungszeiten*—posted just inside entrance and listed on the zoo map (best feeding show is the sea lions—generally at 15:15); enter zoo near Europa Center in front of Hotel Palace or opposite Zoologischer Garten station on Hardenbergplatz, Budapester Strasse 34, +49 30 254 010, www.zoo-berlin.de, www.aquarium-berlin.de.

Kaufhaus des Westens (KaDeWe)

The "Department Store of the West" has been a Berlin tradition for more than a century. With a staff of 2,100 to help you sort through its vast selection of 450,000 items, KaDeWe claims to be the biggest department store on the Continent. You can get everything from a haircut (third floor) to souvenirs (fourth floor). The cash-only theater and concert box office on the sixth floor charges an 18 percent booking fee, but they know all your options. The sixth floor is a world of gourmet taste treats. The biggest selection of deli and exotic food in Germany offers plenty of classy opportunities to sit down and eat. Ride the glass elevator to the seventh floor's glass-domed Winter Garden, a self-service cafeteria—fun but pricey.

Hours: Generally Mon-Sat 10:00-20:00, closed Sun, S-Bahn: Zoologischer Garten or U-Bahn: Wittenbergplatz, +49 30 21210, www.kadewe.de.

Nearby: The Wittenbergplatz U-Bahn station (in front of KaDeWe) is a unique opportunity to see an old-time station. The first subway station in Berlin (1902), its interior still has classic advertisements decorating its venerable walls. On the KaDeWe side of the station, a sign lists sites of Nazi concentration camps—one of many examples of present-day Germans ensuring that the crimes of their ancestors are never forgotten.

The Wittenbergplatz station also marks the boundary of the adjacent Schöneberg district.

Schöneberg

Those with an interest in Jewish and Cold War history might enjoy a walk through the Schöneberg district, immediately southeast of the Ku'damm corridor. While largely rebuilt after the war, and therefore less architecturally striking than Ku'damm and Savigny-platz, Schöneberg packs in some powerful history.

Background: Around the turn of the 20th century—when Berlin was booming and the cabaret scene was taking off along the Ku'damm— Schöneberg was *the* place for youthful, alternative flappers to hang their hats. (It was sort of the original "hipster neighborhood," a century before its time.) Many young Jews also moved from the old Jewish quarter in the center to this happening spot; plaques mark the homes of Albert Einstein, filmmaker Billy Wilder, and philosopher/psychologist Erich Fromm, all of whom later fled to the United States to continue their seminal work. Fancy Schöneberg even had its own little neighborhood U-Bahn line (U4). After Hitler's government swept Jews out of this area, several Nazi officials decided to move in—which is why Schöneberg was hammered by World War II bombs.

After the war, the Schöneberg City Hall became the de facto seat of the West Berlin city government. It was on the City Hall's front steps, on June 26, 1963, that John F. Kennedy stood in solidarity with the people of West Berlin: *"Ich bin ein Berliner."* In the 1990s, creative locals erected a series of particularly moving memorials to local residents lost in the Holocaust. And from the 1990s through to today, Schöneberg (especially around Fuggerstasse and Motzstrasse) has been the epicenter of Berlin's thriving gay community—as it was back in cabaret days.

Visiting Schöneberg: While the history is substantial, the sights are subtle. For a quick taste of Schöneberg, ride the U4 or U7 to **Bayerischer Platz,** and explore. This square and the streets around it (with names like Münchener Strasse, Salzburger Strasse, and Innsbrucker Strasse) were inspired by places in Bavaria and the alpine region. The Café Haberland—just above the U-Bahn stop, and named for the urban planner behind this neighborhood—has a fine and free little local history museum. Photos and descriptions inside the U-Bahn station itself add to the story.

On and near Bayerischer Platz, keep an eye out for this neighborhood's unique style of **Holocaust memorials.** Eighty signs feature an image of local life on the front, and on the back, a story (in German only) of how that object was involved in the Holocaust. (For example, near a local bakery, the flipside of a picture of bread recounts how Jews were only allowed to buy groceries between 4 and 5 o'clock in the afternoon—after all the best goods had already been sold.) These signs appeared overnight (thanks to a local artists' collective) in 1993, during a wave of Neo-Nazism and the 60th anniversary of Hitler's rise to power. At first, many residents were offended by these in-your-face reminders of everyday anti-Semitism. But the signs were quickly embraced as people realized... that's exactly the point.

Follow Salzburger Strasse a few blocks southeast of Bayerischer Platz to the **Schöneberg City Hall** (Rathaus)—with a modern, rebuilt tower, holding a "Freedom Bell" that was donated by US forces after World War II. At the front steps where JFK delivered one of his most famous speeches, you'll find a plaque commemorating that day. Just five months later, Berliners flocked here again, this time to mourn the assassinated president. Deep inside City Hall is the "We Were Neighbors" exhibit about the Jewish and Holocaust heritage of Schöneberg (all in German).

Several blocks north, Schöneberg meets the Ku'damm at the historic Wittenbergplatz U-Bahn stop.

CHARLOTTENBURG PALACE AREA

Halfway to the airport, tucked in an upscale residential neighborhood at the northwestern edge of the city, sits Charlottenburg Palace—once a suburban residence of Prussian royalty (including Frederick the Great—see page 114). While there are far better palaces in Germany—including just out of town in Potsdam (see the Day Trips from Berlin chapter)—Charlottenburg offers an easy and accessible look at a royal interior. For art lovers, this area is even more appealing for its cluster of three museums just across the street from the palace, which combine to present a remarkable array of early-20th-century art: Surrealism (Scharf-Gerstenberg Collection); Picasso, Matisse, and Klee (Museum Berggruen); and furniture and decorative arts in the *Jugendstil* and Art Deco styles (Bröhan Museum).

Getting There: Ride U7 to Richard-Wagner Platz or U2 to Sophie-Charlotte Platz and walk 10 minutes up the tree-lined boulevard Schlossstrasse (from either stop, follow signs to *Schloss*), or—much faster—catch bus #M45 (direction: Spandau) direct from Zoologischer Garten or bus #109 from along Ku'damm (direction: Flughafen Tegel). You can also take the S-Bahn to Westend, then ride bus #M45 (or walk 10 minutes). From any bus, you want the Schloss Charlottenburg stop.

Eating: For lunch on Luisenplatz just east of the palace, try the traditional German grub at Brauhaus Lemke brewpub or sample Russian specialties at Samowar (both open daily).

▲Charlottenburg Palace (Schloss Charlottenburg)

Charlottenburg Palace is the largest former residence of the royal Hohenzollern family in Berlin, and contains the biggest collection of 17th-century French fresco painting outside France. If you've seen the great palaces of Europe, this Baroque palace comes in at about number 10. I'd rate it behind Potsdam, too. The palace has several parts: The central "Old Palace" (Altes Schloss) is a mostly reconstructed look at Frederick's wife, Sophie Charlotte, that falls

SIGHTS

Charlottenburg Palace Area

a bit flat on historic interest; the New Wing (Neue Flügel), with background on Frederick the Great, is the better palace experience. You'll also find a variety of other royal pavilions and sprawling gardens.

Cost and Hours: New Wing and Old Palace-€12 each, prices include audioguides, smaller buildings-€3-4 each, combo-ticket for everything-€17; all buildings open Tue-Sun 10:00-17:30, Nov-March until 16:30, closed Mon year-round; +49 331 969 4200, www.spsg.de.

Visiting the Palace: The **New Wing** (Neue Flügel, a.k.a. the Knobelsdorff Wing) features Rococo royal apartments and fine paintings. First you'll head upstairs and walk through the sumptuous, gold-crusted State Rooms of Frederick the Great. The high-

light is the 105-foot-long Golden Gallery, a real-life Cinderella ballroom with rich green walls, faux marble, gold flourishes, and glittering chandeliers. You'll also see Frederick's apartments (the concert chamber where he played the flute, and his study and bedroom). Retracing your steps, you'll enter the cozy Winter Rooms, dating from after Frederick's time. Rooms of royal portraits lead to the old wing, with more apartments and collections of silver, porcelain, and crown treasure. Back downstairs is a painting gallery, with two highlights: In the antechamber, look for the painting of a huge parade in front of Unter den Linden's Neue Wache. Then, at the end of this wing, don't miss the famous *Napoleon Crossing the Alps*—one of five originals of this scene done by Jacques-Louis David.

The **Altes Schloss** showcases Sophie Charlotte's state apartments—her portrait adorns most of the rooms and is the main theme of the audioguide—plus a lavish palace chapel that defied strict Protestant starkness in favor of Baroque supremacy befitting the Prussian Empire (an enormous royal crown sits opposite the altar, watching over the congregation). The highlight is its Porcelain Cabinet with over 2,700 pieces set against mirrored shelves reflecting natural light and a crazy melding of trompe l'oeil painting and 3-D stucco work.

Out back are sprawling **gardens** that are fun and free to wander in good weather, with a few skippable royal pavilions. The one that may be worth considering—past the end of the New Wing—is the **New Pavilion,** offering a concise and accessible look at the two big names of German Romanticism: the paintings of Caspar David Friedrich and Karl Friedrich Schinkel.

▲Scharf-Gerstenberg Collection

This pleasant museum houses more than 250 works of Surrealist and pre-Surrealist art. At the start stands the huge Kalabsha Gate, salvaged from an ancient Egyptian temple before it was moved to make way for the Aswan Dam. The exhibit features big names, including Joan Miró, Salvador Dalí, Paul Klee, Jean Dubuffet, and Francisco de Goya, juxtaposed with lesser-known German artists, such as Otto Dix, Max Ernst, and George Grosz. The *Surreal Worlds* exhibit shows just how freaky the world looks to artists—a jumbled existence of subjects and emotions. The collection is thoughtfully organized by theme, as if these great artists are in conversation. Note that these are "deep cuts" rather than "greatest hits," making this worth ▲▲ for someone with an affinity for this art, but not worth the trip for those with a casual interest.

Cost and Hours: €10 combo-ticket includes audioguide and Museum Berggruen, Tue-Fri 10:00-18:00, Sat-Sun from 11:00, closed Mon, Schlossstrasse 70, +49 30 266 424 242, www.smb. museum.

▲Museum Berggruen

This tidy museum—with lesser-known works by some big-name modern artists (especially Picasso)—is a welcome surprise. The first floor features some of his earlier works: Blue Period, newspaper collages, and early Cubism (including a study for the seminal *Les Demoiselles d'Avignon*). The second (top) floor shows off how the prolific artist dabbled in virtually every medium: ceramic, mixed media, doodles, pencil sketches, and, of course, painting. The ground floor has a fine rotating collection intermixed with more Picasso sculptures. In the annex are notable works by Henri Matisse, Paul Cézanne, and a huge collection of pieces by Paul Klee. Everything is thoughtfully described in English.

Cost and Hours: €10 combo-ticket includes audioguide and Scharf-Gerstenberg Collection, Tue-Fri 10:00-18:00, Sat-Sun from 11:00, closed Mon, Schlossstrasse 1, +49 30 266 424 242, www.smb.museum.

▲Bröhan Museum

This beautifully understated museum displays decorative arts from the early 20th century on three floors (permanent exhibits on ground floor, temporary exhibits upstairs). This collection makes you wish you were furnishing a Berlin apartment in the year 1900. Wander through a dozen *Jugendstil* and Art Deco living rooms, a curvy and eye-pleasing organic world of lamps, glass, silver, and posters. English descriptions are posted in some rooms, and the included audioguide does a fair job describing temporary exhibits, featuring various subjects associated with the design history of the Art Deco and Art Nouveau movements.

Cost and Hours: €8, Tue-Sun 10:00-18:00, closed Mon, Schlossstrasse 1A, +49 30 3269 0600, www.broehan-museum.de.

REICHSTAG & BRANDENBURG GATE WALK

Trace Germany's turbulent 20th-century history on this walk as we weave together a cluster of must-see sights near Berlin's most famous landmark, the Brandenburg Gate. We'll start at the Reichstag—symbol of Germany's nascent turn-of-the-20th-century democracy—and learn how that democracy was toppled by the rise of Nazism. We'll see sites associated with Hitler, remember the destructive consequences of World War II, and ponder a moving memorial to Jewish victims of the Holocaust. We'll remember how postwar Berlin was split in two by the Berlin Wall. And finally, we'll see gleaming new buildings, announcing how Berlin has risen from those difficult years once again.

Orientation

Length of This Walk: Allow about 1.5 hours.

When to Go: Take this walk early in your stay in Berlin to help get your bearings to some key landmarks. It can be done at any time of day, but note open hours for the information center at the Jewish memorial (later). If you'd like to ascend the Reichstag dome, reserve a time in advance, then plan this walk around it. (Without a reservation, try to book a slot while on this walk, and circle back later.)

Getting There: The Reichstag is easiest to reach on bus #100 (Reichstag/Bundestag stop). You can also take the S-Bahn to Brandenburger Tor and walk 10 minutes (through the Brandenburg Gate, then turn right). Or, from the Hauptbahnhof or Brandenburger Tor, ride the U55 line to Bundestag and exit toward *Reichstagsgebäude*.

Reichstag: Free, reservations and passport required—see page 41, daily 8:00-24:00.

Create Your Own Grand Berlin City Intro Walk

If you have limited time in Berlin—or just want to spend your first few hours getting a solid introduction to the sightseeing spine of this sprawling city—consider linking this **Reichstag & Brandenburg Gate Walk** with the 📖 **Unter den Linden Walk,** followed by the 📖 **Communist East Berlin Walk,** to create one big "Berlin City Walk." Following all three walks takes you from the Reichstag to Alexanderplatz and beyond, and can take up to five hours—or fill a whole day if you visit museums along the way.

🎧 I've recorded a condensed version of this whole handy route as a free **Berlin City Walk audio tour** (just under 1.5 hours; see page 22). Whether on paper or in your ear, this Berlin City Walk route sets you up to enjoy a fun and smartly planned visit to Germany's capital.

Memorial to the Murdered Jews of Europe: Memorial free and always open; information center open Tue-Sun 10:00-20:00, Oct-March until 19:00, closed Mon year-round; last entry 45 minutes before closing.

Tours: 🎧 Download my free Berlin City Walk audio tour, which narrates much of the same information covered on this walk.

Services: There are pay WCs in the Berlin Pavillon across the street from the Reichstag, and free WCs in the basement of the Academy of Arts on Pariser Platz.

Eateries: This is not a great area for a satisfying meal.

Starring: Germany's tumultuous 20th century, including its parliament building, its definitive landmark, and its most poignant memorial.

The Walk Begins

• *Start in Platz der Republik and take in your surroundings. Dominating this park is a giant domed building.*

❶ Reichstag

The Reichstag is the heart of Germany's government. It's where the Bundestag—the lower house of parliament—meets to govern the nation (similar to the US House of Representatives).

Berlin has long been a Germanic capital, whatever the form of government: from the first Dukes of Brandenburg in medieval times to the democracy of today. In between, this city was the seat of the kings and emperors of Prussia, the Weimar Republic of the 1920s, Hitler and the Nazis, and communist East Germany.

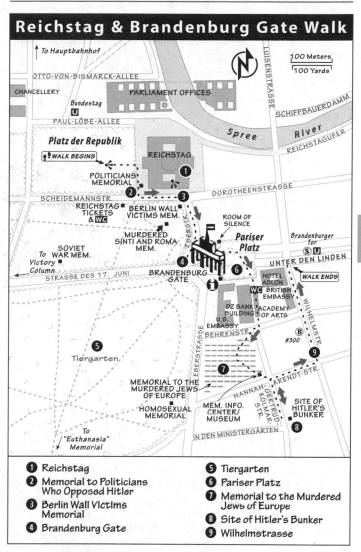

Reichstag & Brandenburg Gate Walk

To Hauptbahnhof

OTTO-VON-BISMARCK-ALLEE

CHANCELLERY

Bundestag U

PARLIAMENT OFFICES

LUISENSTRASSE

SCHIFFBAUERDAMM

PAUL-LÖBE-ALLEE

Spree River

REICHSTAGUFER

Platz der Republik

WALK BEGINS

REICHSTAG ❶

POLITICIANS MEMORIAL ❷

❸

DOROTHEENSTRASSE

SCHEIDEMANNSTR.

REICHSTAG TICKETS & WC

BERLIN WALL VICTIMS MEM.

MURDERED SINTI AND ROMA MEM.

ROOM OF SILENCE

Pariser Platz

Brandenburger Tor S U

SOVIET WAR MEM.

To Victory Column

STRASSE DES 17. JUNI

❹

BRANDENBURG GATE

❻

UNTER DEN LINDEN

WALK ENDS

HOTEL ADLON

WC BRITISH EMBASSY

DZ BANK BUILDING

ACADEMY OF ARTS

WILHELMSTR.

❺ *Tiergarten*

EBERSTRASSE

U.S. EMBASSY

BEHRENSTR.

#300 Ⓑ

❾

❼

MEMORIAL TO THE MURDERED JEWS OF EUROPE

HOMOSEXUAL MEMORIAL

To "Euthanasia" Memorial

MEM. INFO. CENTER/ MUSEUM

HANNAH-ARENDT-STR.

GERTRUD-KOLMAR-STR.

SITE OF HITLER'S BUNKER ❽

IN DEN MINISTERGÄRTEN

100 Meters
100 Yards

❶ Reichstag
❷ Memorial to Politicians Who Opposed Hitler
❸ Berlin Wall Victims Memorial
❹ Brandenburg Gate
❺ Tiergarten
❻ Pariser Platz
❼ Memorial to the Murdered Jews of Europe
❽ Site of Hitler's Bunker
❾ Wilhelmstrasse

REICHSTAG & BRANDENBURG GATE WALK

Think of the history the Reichstag has seen. When the building was inaugurated in 1895, Germany was still a kingdom, ruled by the Hohenzollern family that had reigned here for nearly 500 years. Back then, the real center of power was a mile east of here, at the royal palace. Kaiser Wilhelm II disdainfully called this place the *Reichsaffenhaus*—the "Imperial Monkey House." But after the emperor was deposed in World War I, the German Republic was proclaimed. Look above the columns to see the promise carved into the facade: *Dem Deutschen Volke*—"To the German People."

That first democracy, known as the Weimar Republic, proved weak. Meanwhile, the storm of National Socialism was growing—the Nazis. Soon the Reichstag had dozens of duly elected National Socialists, and Adolf Hitler seized power. In 1933, just weeks after Hitler took power, the Reichstag building nearly burned down. Many believe that Hitler planned the fire as an excuse to frame the communists and grab power for himself.

With Hitler as *Führer* and real democracy a thing of the past, the Reichstag was hardly used. But it remained a powerful symbol and therefore was a prime tar-

get for Allied bombers during World War II. The structure survived, but you can still see evidence of bomb damage: Look closely at the inscription above the door, and notice the telltale lighter repair patches. As World War II wound down, and Soviet troops advanced on the city, it was here at the Reichstag that 1,500 German troops made their last stand. An Iwo Jima-like photograph of Soviet troops raising the hammer-and-sickle on the Reichstag's roof is—at least in the Russian world—an iconic image of that war's end.

After the war, Berlin was divided into East and West. The Berlin Wall ran right behind the Reichstag. Now in a kind of no-man's land, the Reichstag fell into disuse, and the West German capital was moved from Berlin to the remote city of Bonn.

After the Berlin Wall fell, the Reichstag again became the focus of the new nation. It was renovated by British architect Norman Foster, who added the glass dome. In 1999, the new Reichstag reopened, and the parliament reconvened. To many Germans, the proud resurrection of their Reichstag symbolizes the end of a terrible chapter in their country's history.

Look now at the Reichstag's modern **dome.** The cupola rises 155 feet above the ground. Inside the dome, a cone of 360 mirrors reflects natural light into the legislative chamber below, and an opening at the top allows air to circulate. Lit from inside after dark, it gives Berlin a memorable nightlight. If you make a reservation to visit the interior, you can climb the spiral ramp all the way to the top of the dome for a grand city view (for details on visiting, see page 44).

Facing the Reichstag, do a 360-degree spin to find some other big landmarks. To the left of the Reichstag, at the Bundestag U-Bahn stop, the long, partly transparent building houses parliamentary offices. Beyond that, in the distance, is the tower of the huge main train sta-

tion, the Hauptbahnhof (marked *DB* for Deutsche Bahn, the German rail company). Farther left is the mammoth, white, concrete-and-glass Chancellery (nicknamed "the Washing Machine"). This is the office of Germany's most powerful person, the

chancellor. To remind the chancellor who he or she works for, Germany's Reichstag (housing the parliament) is about six feet taller than the Chancellery.

Beyond the Chancellery—and curling behind the Reichstag—is the **Spree River.** When kings ruled Prussia, government buildings crowded right up to its banks. But today, the riverscape is a people-friendly zone.

• *Approach the Reichstag, turn right, walk nearly to the street, and find a small memorial next to the shipping-container-like entrance buildings. It's a row of slate stones sticking out of the ground—it looks like a bike rack. This is the...*

❷ Memorial to Politicians Who Opposed Hitler

These 96 slabs honor the 96 Reichstag members who spoke out against Adolf Hitler and the rising tide of fascism. When Hitler

became chancellor, these critics were persecuted and murdered. On each slab, you'll see a name and political party—most are KPD (Communists) and SPD (Social Democrats)—and the date and location of death (*KZ* denotes those who died in concentration camps). This memorial is the first of several we'll see on this walk (see the sidebar on page 98). Berlin is a city with a troubled past, which its citizens commemorate with moving monuments. Just up ahead is a memorial to the next complex chapter in Berlin's history: communism.

• *Walk east, along the right side of the Reichstag, on busy Scheidemannstrasse, toward the rear of the building. When you reach the intersection at the back of the Reichstag, turn right and cross the street. Once*

Memorials to the Victims of Germany's 20th Century

Modern Germans are painfully aware of the many victims of their forebears. And, particularly in the years since the Berlin Wall came down, the German government has thoughtfully erected monuments to various victims in its capital city. The following memorials, honoring different groups, are within walking distance of the Brandenburg Gate and listed in the order you reach them heading south from the Reichstag.

Memorial to Politicians Who Opposed Hitler: This low-profile memorial, in the paved area immediately in front of the Reichstag, recalls those who dared to defy a rising tyrant (for details, see the description in this walk).

Berlin Wall Victims Memorial: Across the street from the Reichstag is this line of simple white crosses (at the corner of the vast Tiergarten Park; for more, see the description in this walk).

Monument to the Murdered Sinti and Roma of Europe: In the park just behind the Berlin Wall Victims Memorial, an opaque glass wall, with a timeline in  English and German, commemorates the roughly 500,000 Holocaust victims who identified as "Sinti" and "Roma" (the main tribes and politically correct terms for the group often called "Gypsies"). These groups lost the same percentage of their population as the Jews did. A rusty steel portal leads to a circular reflecting pool surrounded by stone slabs, some containing the names of death camps. Along the rim of the pool is the moving poem "Auschwitz," by Santino Spinelli, an Italian Roma.

Soviet War Memorial: Adorned with hammers and sickles, and Cyrillic lettering, this monument honors the Soviet army soldiers who died in the bitter battle for Berlin, which brought World War II

across, on the corner you'll see a humble row of white crosses that predate the fall of the wall.

❸ Berlin Wall Victims Memorial

The Berlin Wall once stood right here, running north-south down what is now busy Ebertstrasse, dividing the city in two. This side (near the crosses) was democratic West Berlin. On the other side was the Soviet-controlled East. The row of white crosses commemorates a few of the many brave East Berliners who died trying to cross the Wall to freedom.

to a decisive conclusion (in the same park as the above memorial, in the opposite direction, toward the Victory Column). Erected by the Soviets in the divided city just months after the war's end, the monument is maintained under the terms of Germany's 1990 reunification treaty. There's a much bigger Soviet war memorial at Treptower Park (see page 71).

Memorial to the Murdered Jews of Europe: This moving memorial is immediately south of the Brandenburg Gate (for more, see the description in this walk).

Memorial to the Homosexuals Persecuted Under the National Socialist Regime: Nazis targeted gay men, and attempted to "cure" homosexuality through hard work, medical experiments, or castration. This stark memorial—a dark-gray concrete box—is tucked into a corner of a park (access it from the Jewish memorial's southwest corner, across Ebertstrasse from Hannah-Arendt-Strasse). Through a small window, you can watch a film loop of same-sex couples kissing—a reminder that life and love are precious.

Memorial to the Victims of Nazi "Euthanasia": Even before the Holocaust began in earnest, as early as 1940, Hitler sought to rid German society of people with physical and mental disabilities. Their deaths are memorialized with a long, transparent blue wall, with info panels and portraits of 10 victims (to the south, in front of the philharmonic, facing the Tiergarten). Over time, the "T4" program—administered from a building that once stood here (Tiergartenstrasse 4)—"euthanized" 300,000 German citizens. While "euthanasia" implies a humane act, this was anything but—many victims died painful deaths, sometimes by starvation.

Think about the events that caused Berlin to become divided: At the end of World War II, Hitler was defeated, and the city was essentially destroyed. In May 1945, Berlin was finally taken by the Soviet army. As had been agreed at the Yalta Conference, the city was split into four sectors, one for each victorious Allied power: the USSR, the USA, Britain, and France.

In short order, it became clear that Berliners preferred the Western Allies to the Soviet sector—and it didn't take long for the paranoid Soviets to begin closing off free passage. Their first bold move came in 1949, when Soviets blockaded road and rail access into West Berlin; the Western Allies responded by supplying the entire city with food, fuel, and medicine by airplane (the Berlin Airlift). Eventually the Soviets relented—and the flow of people from East to West increased. Finally, in 1961, the political division became a physical reality when the East

built an imposing barrier: the Berlin Wall *(Berliner Mauer)*, which encircled West Berlin in concrete, rebar, and barbed wire. (For more, see "The Berlin Wall: The Basics" on page 213.)

During the 28 years the Wall was up, around 5,000 people managed to escape—but an estimated 136 were killed trying to do so. Those are the people honored by this monument. Read some of the crosses. The last person killed was 20-year-old Chris Gueffroy. He died nine months before the Wall fell, shot through the heart just a few steps away from here.

• *Continue south down Ebertstrasse toward the Brandenburg Gate, tracing the former course of the Berlin Wall. A thin strip of memorial bricks embedded in the street pavement indicates where it once stood.*

Ebertstrasse spills into a busy intersection dominated by the imposing Brandenburg Gate. To take in this scene, cross the Berlin Wall bricks to the piazza in front of the...

❹ Brandenburg Gate

This massive classical-looking monument is the grandest—and last survivor—of the 14 original gates in Berlin's old city wall. (This one led to the neighboring city of Brandenburg.)

The majestic four-horse chariot on top is driven by the Goddess of Peace. When Napoleon conquered Prussia in 1806, he took this statue to the Louvre in Paris. Then, after the Prussians defeated Napoleon, they got it back (in 1813)...and the Goddess of Peace was renamed the "Goddess of Victory."

The gate straddles the major east-west axis of the city. The western segment—behind you—stretches four miles, running through Tiergarten Park to the Olympic Stadium. To the east—on the other side of the gate—the street is called Unter den Linden. That's where we're headed. In the distance (if you jockey for position), you can see the red-and-white spire of the TV Tower that marks the end of Berlin's main axis.

Historically, the Brandenburg Gate was just another of this city's many stately Prussian landmarks. But in our lifetime, it became *the* symbol of Berlin—of its Cold War division and its reunification. That's because, from 1961 to 1989, the gate was stranded in the no-man's-land between East and West. For an entire generation, scores of German families were divided—some on this side of the Wall, some on the other. This landmark stood tantalizingly close to both East and West...but was off-limits to all.

By the 1980s, it was becoming clear that the once-mighty Soviet empire was slowly crumbling from within. On June 12, 1987, US President Ronald Reagan stood right here and said, "Mr. Gorbachev, tear down this wall."

Finally, on November 9, 1989, the world rejoiced at the sight of happy Berliners standing atop the Wall. They chipped away at it with hammers, passed beers to their long-lost cousins on the other side, and adorned the Brandenburg Gate with flowers like a parade float. (For more on this story, see "The Wall Comes Down" on page 181.) Six weeks later, on  December 22, West German Chancellor Helmut Kohl led a triumphant procession through the Brandenburg Gate to shake hands with his (soon-to-be-defunct) East German counterpart—the literal opening of a big gateway that marked the symbolic closing of a heinous era. Eventually, the Wall was dismantled, and all Berliners could enjoy total freedom.

• *Turn 180 degrees and take in the vast, green expanse of the park called...*

❺ Tiergarten

Look down the long boulevard (Strasse des 17. Juni) that bisects the 500-acre park called Tiergarten ("Animal Garden"). The boulevard's name comes from the 17th of June, 1953, when brave East Germans rose up against their communist leaders. The rebellion was crushed, and East Berliners had to wait another 36 years for the freedom to walk through the Brandenburg Gate.

In the distance is the 220-foot **Victory Column**, topped with a golden

statue that commemorates the three big military victories that established Prussia as a world power in the late 1800s—over France, Denmark, and Austria—and kicked off Berlin's golden age. (For more on Tiergarten and the Victory Column, see page 78).

• *Walk through the Brandenburg Gate, entering what for years was forbidden territory. Just past the gate, there's a small TI on the right, and on the left is the Room of Silence, dedicated to meditation. As you cross through this historic but long-forbidden gate, you enter a grand square known as...*

❻ Pariser Platz

Pariser Platz marks the start of Unter den Linden, the broad boulevard that stretches before you. "Parisian Square" was so named after the Prussians defeated France and Napoleon in 1813. The square was once filled with important government buildings, but all were bombed to smithereens in World War II. For decades, it was an unrecognizable, deserted no-man's-land, cut off from both East and West by the Wall. But now it's

rebuilt, and the banks and hotels that were here before the bombing have reclaimed their original places, with a few modern additions. And the winners of World War II—the US, France, Great Britain, and Russia—continue to enjoy this prime real estate: Their embassies are all on or near this square.

Take a moment to enjoy this scene. Mindless selfies, stupid promos, scam artists filling petition sheets, pickpockets, Starbucks, and touts hawking free tours. Sure, it's tacky—but it's freedom.

Check out some of the buildings facing the square. The **US Embassy** (on the right as you come through the gate) reopened here in its original location on July 4, 2008. The building has been controversial: For safety's sake, Uncle Sam wanted more of a security zone around the building. But the Germans wanted to keep Pariser Platz a welcoming people zone. The compromise: Extra security is built into the structure itself. Easy-on-the-eyes barriers keep potential car bombs at a distance, and the front door is actually on the back side of the building—farthest from the Brandenburg Gate.

To the left of the US Embassy is the **DZ Bank Building,** built as a conference center in 2001 by Canadian-American architect Frank Gehry. Gehry fans who enjoy his attention-grabbing forms and colors might be surprised at the bank building's low-profile exterior. Structures on Pariser Platz are designed so as not to draw attention away from the Brandenburg Gate. To get your fix of wild and colorful Gehry, step into the building's lobby. The undulating interior is like a big, slithery fish.

Two doors past the bank is the ritzy **Hotel Adlon.** The original hotel was demolished after World War II, and rebuilt in 1997. Over the years, this place has hosted celebrities and VIPs from Charlie Chaplin to Albert Einstein. And, yes, this was where pop star Michael Jackson shocked millions by dangling his infant son over the railing (from the second balcony up). The Hotel Adlon was also the setting for the classic film *Grand Hotel*, in which Greta Garbo uttered the immortal line, "I vant to be alone."

• *And I say, "I vant to move along," because we have a lot more to see. The most direct route to our next stop is by cutting through the **Academy of Arts** (Akademie der Künst) building—it's between Hotel Adlon and the DZ Bank, at Pariser Platz 4. (If the Academy of Arts is closed, loop to the left, circling around the Hotel Adlon to Behrenstrasse.)*

Enter the glassy Academy of Arts (WC in basement) and head toward the back. Just past the ground-floor café (an oasis of calm) is the former office of Albert Speer, Hitler's chosen architect. Continue on, passing Speer's favorite statue, Prometheus *(from around 1900). This is the kind of art that turned on Hitler: a strong, soldierly, vital man, defending the homeland.*

As you exit out the back of the building, veer right on Behrenstrasse and cross the street. You'll wind up at our next stop, a sprawling field of stubby concrete pillars.

❼ Memorial to the Murdered Jews of Europe

This memorial consists of 2,711 coffin-shaped pillars covering an entire city block. More than 160,000 Jewish people lived in Berlin when Hitler took power. Tens of thousands fled, and many more were arrested, sent to nearby Sachsenhausen concentration camp and eventually murdered. The memorial remembers them and the other six million Jews who were killed by  the Nazis during World War II. Completed in 2005 by the Jewish-American architect Peter Eisenman, this was the first formal, German-government-sponsored Holocaust memorial. Using the word "murdered" in the title was intentional, and a big deal. Germany, as a nation, was admitting to a crime. Please be discreet at this powerful sight—this isn't a place for selfies.

The pillars, made of hollow concrete, stand in a gently sunken area that can be entered from any side. Notice that people seem to appear and disappear between the columns. No matter where you are, the exit always seems to be up. The number of pillars isn't symbolic—it's simply how many fit on the provided land. The memorial's location—where the Wall once stood—is also coincidental. Inside the **information center** (in the far-left corner), exhibits trace the rise of Nazism and tell the victims' stories (for details on visiting the information center, see page 48). The memorial is thoughtfully lit at night and guarded.

The meaning of the memorial is open to interpretation. Is it a symbolic cemetery full of gravestones? An intentionally disorienting labyrinth? Perhaps it's meant to reflect how the senseless horror of the Holocaust didn't adhere to rational thought. Like death, you enter it alone. It's up to the visitor to derive the meaning.

• *At the far-left corner, a little beyond the information center, you eventually emerge on the street corner. Our next stop is about a block farther. Carefully jaywalk across Hannah-Arendt-Strasse and continue straight (south) down Gertrud-Kolmar-Strasse. On the left side of the street, you'll reach a rough parking lot. At the far end of the lot is an information plaque labeled* Führerbunker. *This marks the...*

❽ Site of Hitler's Bunker

You're standing atop the buried remains of the *Führerbunker*. In early 1945, as Allied armies advanced on Berlin and Nazi Germany

lay in ruins, Hitler and his staff retreated to this bunker complex behind the former Reich Chancellery. He stayed here for two months. Meanwhile, Berlin was laid to waste by Allied bombing. Tens of thousands of Berliners lost their lives, and hundreds of thousands were forced to evacuate to the countryside.

It was here, on April 30, 1945—as the Soviet army tightened its noose on the Nazi capital—that Hitler and Eva Braun, his wife of less than 48 hours, committed suicide. A week later, the war in Europe was over. The information board here explains the rest of the story. It shows a detailed floorplan of the bunker complex, which stood right about where the plaque is today. A timeline traces the bunker's history and ultimate fate. After the war, the roof was removed, and the bunker was filled with dirt and covered over.

Though the site of Hitler's bunker is part of history, there really isn't much to see here. And that's on purpose. No one wants to turn Hitler's final stronghold into a tourist attraction. Germans still treat the subject of Hitler with extraordinary sensitivity. There's an understandable concern about stoking the fires of neo-Nazism, which never seems to die...in Germany, or around the world. They've been wary of making Hitler's book, *Mein Kampf,* available on a mass level. It took 65 years for the German History Museum to hold its first exhibit on Hitler's life. Schoolkids are taught the hard lessons of history. But when it comes to Hitler memorabilia and Hitler sites, there's a distinct shortage. It's a balancing act—remembering Hitler, without glorifying the memory.

• *Backtrack up Gertrud-Kolmar-Strasse, and turn right on Hannah-Arendt-Strasse. German government administration buildings once lined this street. They were totally destroyed in 1945 and then rebuilt in DDR times as prefab "Plattenbauten" (concrete-slab buildings). Standard during the communist period, they still survive. These housed privileged people in that "classless society," so it was top-end construction—but prefab uniformity nevertheless.*

Take your first left (at the traffic light) on...

❾ Wilhelmstrasse

This street was the traditional center of the German power, beginning back when Germany first became a nation in the 19th century. It was lined with stately palaces housing foreign embassies and government offices. This was the home of the Reich Chancellery, where the nation's chief executive presided. When the Nazis took control, this street was where Hitler waved to his adoring fans, and where Joseph Goebbels had his Ministry of Propaganda.

During World War II, Wilhelmstrasse was the nerve center of the German war command. From here, Hitler directed the war and ordered the Blitz (the air raids that destroyed much of London). As the war turned to the Allies' side, Wilhelmstrasse and the neighborhood around it were heavily bombed. Most of the stately palaces were destroyed, and virtually nothing historic survives today.

Case in point is the **British Embassy** (two blocks up Wilhelmstrasse, on the left, with the smooth, stony facade). When World War II broke out, the British closed their embassy. Then it was bombed by

the Allies. After the war, the West German capital was moved to the city of Bonn...and the British Embassy went with it. But in the 1990s, when the seat of government returned to Berlin, Wilhelmstrasse was completely modernized, and the British Embassy was rebuilt on the same piece of real estate. (The fun, purple wall is the red, white, and blue of the Union Jack mixed together.) This is now just one of nearly 150 embassies in the globalized city that is today's modern capital of Germany.

• *Wilhelmstrasse spills out onto Berlin's main artery, the tree-lined Unter den Linden, next to the Hotel Adlon. Our walk is finished, and you're standing right in front of the Brandenburger Tor S- and U-Bahn station. To continue Berlin's story with a walk down Unter den Linden, turn to the next chapter.*

UNTER DEN LINDEN WALK

From Pariser Platz to Museum Island

Before reunification, before communism, and before Hitler, Berlin was a grandiose imperial capital, a city built to impress world leaders and intimidate would-be enemies. Prussia, founded in the 13th century by the Teutonic Knights, gradually became both a military and a cultural power, and later (in the late 1800s) grew into the "Second German Reich" and the cornerstone of a modern, unified state of Germany.

Berlin's imperial past is often overshadowed by its compelling 20th-century history. But along and near Unter den Linden is where surviving bits of old Berlin best tell the story of the kaisers. This walk, a one-mile stroll from Pariser Platz to Museum Island, takes you through the heart of Berlin's 18th- and 19th-century glory—past Neoclassical remnants of the enlightened Prussian rulers. It also includes three monumental squares—Gendarmenmarkt, Bebelplatz, and Lustgarten—and the Berlin Cathedral, which attests to the over-the-top egotism of the Prussian kaisers who sparked World War I. The walk ends on Museum Island in the Spree River—birthplace of Berlin, home of Prussian princes, and showcase of past rulers' artistic treasures.

Orientation

Length of This Walk: Allow about 1.5 hours. This walk is designed to be done immediately after my 📖 **Reichstag & Brandenburg Gate Walk.** And if you're interested in the communist period, it's easy to continue to the 📖 **Communist East Berlin Walk.** (For more about linking these three walks, see "Create Your Own Grand Berlin City Intro Walk" on page 94.)

When to Go: This walk can be done at any time. Those who plan on touring any of Museum Island's many sights should begin early enough to allow plenty of sightseeing time. You could also use this walk to get your bearings in Berlin, then circle back to the museums on another day.

Getting There: This walk picks up right where my Reichstag & Brandenburg Gate Walk leaves off, near Pariser Platz. To get here directly, take the U-Bahn, S-Bahn, or bus (#100 or #245) to Brandenburger Tor. Buses also follow the route of this walk—handy for skipping ahead or backtracking.

Pickpocket Warning: As Berlin's most touristy gauntlet, Unter den Linden has more than its share of pickpockets (especially around Museum Island). Use caution.

Drive Volkswagen Group Forum: Daily 11:00-18:00, Friedrichstrasse 84, www.drive-volkswagen-group.com.

German Cathedral: Exhibit —free, Tue-Sun 10:00-19:00, Oct-April until 18:00, closed Mon year-round, +49 30 2273 0432.

Berlin Cathedral: €7, includes interior and access to dome gallery, not covered by Museum Island Pass, Mon-Sat 9:00-20:00, Sun from 12:00, daily until 19:00 Oct-March.

Tours: ∩ Download my free Berlin City Walk audio tour, which narrates much of the route of this walk.

Services: You'll find free WCs in the basement of the Academy of Arts (on Pariser Platz, near the beginning of this walk), at Drive Volkswagen Group Forum, and in the basement of the Galeries Lafayette department store on Friedrichstrasse.

Eateries: We'll pass several recommended eateries around Gendarmenmarkt. A favorite for a cheap, fast, and healthy lunch is the basement of the Galeries Lafayette department store.

Expect Construction: The U5 subway extension and the Humboldt Forum on Museum Island may be under construction during your visit.

Starring: Berlin's kaiser-built main boulevard, and a trio of its most impressive squares.

The Walk Begins

• *We'll begin where Pariser Platz (the big square just inside the Brandenburg Gate) meets Unter den Linden. Stand on the sidewalk in front of Hotel Adlon to get a view down this big boulevard.*

❶ Unter den Linden

This boulevard is the heart of imperial Germany. During Berlin's Golden Age in the late 1800s, this was one of Europe's grand boulevards—the Champs-Elysées of Berlin, a city of nearly 2 million people. It was lined with linden trees, so as you promenaded down, you'd be walking *"unter den Linden."* The street got its start in the 15th century as a way to connect the royal palace (a half-mile down

the road, at the end of this walk) with the king's hunting grounds (today's big Tiergarten Park, out past the Brandenburg Gate). Over the centuries, aristocrats moved into this area so their palaces could be close to their king's.

Many of the grandest landmarks we'll pass along here are thanks to Frederick the Great, who ruled from 1740 to 1786, and put his kingdom (Prussia) and his capital (Berlin) on the map. We'll also see a few signs of modern times; after World War II, this part of Berlin fell under Soviet influence, and Unter den Linden was the main street of communist East Berlin.

• *Turn your attention to the subway stop in front of the Hotel Adlon (labeled* Brandenburger Tor). *We'll enter the station and reemerge a block or so farther down the boulevard.*

❷ Brandenburger Tor S-Bahn Station

For a time-travel experience back to DDR days, head down the stairs into this station (no ticket necessary). Keep to the right as you descend (toward the S-Bahn, not the U-Bahn) to the subway tracks. As you walk along the platform about 200 yards, survey the historic, black-and-white photos on the walls and feel the 1950s vibe of the station.

For decades, the Brandenburger Tor S-Bahn station was unused—one of Berlin's "ghost stations." While you're down under, notice how mid-20th-century the station still looks. There's the original 1930s green tile-work on the walls, and harsh fluorescent lighting. Some old signs (on the central kiosks) still have *Unter den Lin-*den (the original name of this stop) written in old Gothic lettering. During the Cold War, the zigzag line dividing East and West Berlin meant that some existing train lines crossed the border underground. To make a little hard Western cash, the East German government allowed a few trains to cut under East Berlin on their way between Western destinations. The only catch: No one could get on or off while the train was in East Berlin. For 28 years, stations like this were unused, as Western trains slowly passed

Unter den Linden Walk

1. Unter den Linden
2. Brandenburger Tor S-Bahn Station
3. Russian Embassy
4. Strolling Unter den Linden
5. Friedrichstrasse
6. Gendarmenmarkt
7. Bebelplatz
8. Statue of Frederick the Great
9. Neue Wache
10. Museum Island
11. Museum Island Sights
12. Spree River

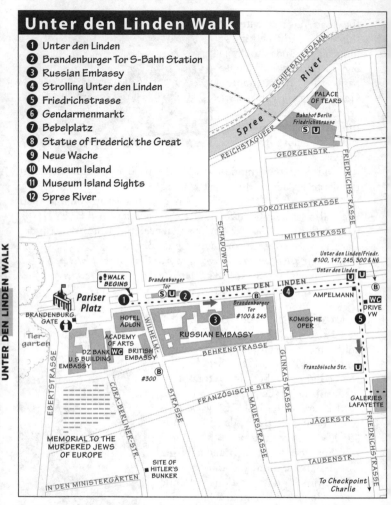

through, and passengers saw only East German guards...and lots of cobwebs. Then, in 1989, within days of the fall of the Wall, these stations were reopened.

• *At the far end of the platform, ascend the escalator, bear right, and head up the stairs to exit. You'll emerge on the right side of Unter den Linden. Belly up to the bars and look in at the...*

❸ Russian Embassy

Built from the ashes of World War II, this imposing building—

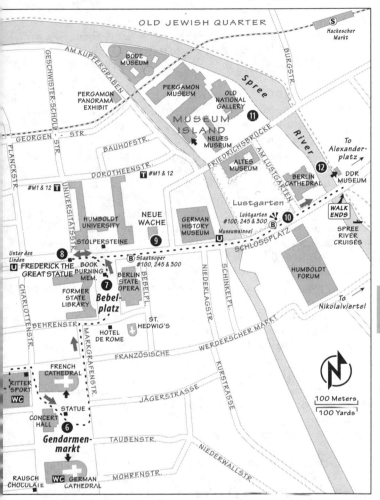

UNTER DEN LINDEN WALK

it's Europe's largest embassy—made it clear to East Berliners who was now in charge: the Soviet Union. It was the first big postwar building project in East Berlin, built in the powerful, simplified Neoclassical style that Stalin liked. Standing here, imagine Unter den Linden as a depressing Cold War era cul-de-sac, dead-ending at the walled-off Brandenburg Gate. After the fall of the Soviet Union in 1991, this building became the

Russian Embassy, flying the white, blue, and red flag. Find the hammer-and-sickle motif decorating the window frames—a reminder of the days when Russia was part of the USSR.

• *Keep walking down the boulevard for two blocks.*

❹ Strolling Unter den Linden

This part of Unter den Linden has traditionally been its business section. And to this day, much of what we'll pass in these early blocks are dull banks, tacky trinket shops, and a few high-end boutiques (Herend and Meissen both sell porcelain here). But as we go along, the scene grows more cultural—the university, the opera, and so on. That's intentional: The Prussian kings wanted to have culture closer to their palace.

As you walk, think of how this boulevard has evolved. In the 19th century, Unter den Linden was a leafy promenade lined with linden trees, which can live for centuries. But most of the trees you see today are not that old. Hitler cut down many of the venerable trees—some of them 250 years old—and replaced them with Nazi flags. Popular discontent among Berliners (even Nazi Berliners) drove him to replant the trees.

Look for big, colorful water pipes running above ground. (If you don't happen to see any along here, you'll see them elsewhere around town.) Berlin's high water table means that anytime foundations are dug into, lots of pumping out is required. And construction is always ongoing in this city, which seems obsessed with reinventing itself. Berliners accept flux as the status quo. As historian Karl Scheffler put it a century ago, "Berlin is a city cursed always to *become*, never to *be*."

• *Pause when you reach the intersection with...*

❺ Friedrichstrasse

You're standing at perhaps the most central crossroads in Berlin—named for, you guessed it, Frederick the Great. Before World War II, Friedrichstrasse was the heart of cultural Berlin. In the Roaring Twenties, it was home to anything-goes nightlife and cabarets where entertainers like Marlene Dietrich, Bertolt Brecht, and Josephine Baker performed. And since the fall of the Wall, it's become home to supersized department stores and big-time hotels. For that reason, the next few blocks of Unter den Linden are pretty dull. So we're taking a detour, following "Frederick's Street" to Frederick's finest square.

On the corner, the **Ampelmann store** celebrates the retro, nostalgic, and strangely beloved communist-era crossing lights that have survived in much of former East Berlin (described on page 303).

Now cross over Friedrichstrasse, turn right, and, within a few steps, duck into #84: the free **Drive Volkswagen Group Forum.** This futuristic, souped-up showroom trumpets the many VW-owned brands: Audi, Bugatti, Bentley, Porsche, Ducati, Lamborghini, and so on. On display are classic models, currently available hot rods, and futuristic prototypes (electric and self-driving cars). As you check your reflection in the chrome, think about Volkswagen's surprisingly dark history. Founded in 1937 and meaning "Car of the People," Volkswagen began as a populist initiative of Adolf Hitler, who sought an affordable automobile for the masses.

Back out on the street, continue down Friedrichstrasse. At the next intersection—with **Behrenstrasse**—notice something strange: No traffic lights. No stop signs. No crosswalks. Studies have shown that when drivers, pedestrians, and cyclists are given no instructions about how to handle an intersection, it forces them all to pay attention and carefully negotiate with each other—and statistically reduces the number of accidents. Berlin is converting some of its intersections to this approach, hoping that a fleeting moment of confusion keeps everyone safer.

Keep heading...carefully...down Friedrichstrasse. After crossing Französische Strasse, duck into the grand **Galeries Lafayette** department store (on your left).
Inside, you can ogle a huge glass-domed atrium—a miniature version of the Reichstag cupola. (It's hard not to drop a coin.) After the fall of the Wall, investors wanted Friedrichstrasse to compete with the glitz of Kurfürstendamm, which—throughout the Cold War—was the main commercial boulevard of West Berlin. But the plan never really took off. Berlin is a neighborhood-oriented city, and sterile Friedrichstrasse isn't appealing to many locals. They'd rather hang out in more colorful neighborhoods

farther out, such as Prenzlauer Berg, Kreuzberg, Friedrichshain, and—yes—Kurfürstendamm. But this area still has some showcase shopping. (Before moving on, note that there's a WC and a handy designer food court in the basement—which you can see below the cupola viewpoint.)

• *From inside Galeries Lafayette, exit onto Französische Strasse, and turn right. You'll pass a shop for* **Ritter Sport***—Germany's favorite mass-market chocolate (which lets fans design their own, personalized candy bars; see page 308)—and then emerge behind a church. Circle around the church to find yourself in a grand square. Let's survey it from in front of the concert hall, with the twin churches left and right.*

Prussian King Frederick the Great
(1712-1786)

Berlin was the capital of Prussia, the large kingdom that became the leading force and cornerstone of German unification in the late 19th century. While Prussia—which no longer exists in any form—can be hard to get your head around, it's easier to understand through the lens of its most influential leader, King Frederick the Great. It was Frederick who largely set forth the ideals that defined Prussia and its successor states.

Frederick the Great's father, the "Soldier King" Frederick William I (1688-1740), believed a strong army was the keystone of a great state. And so—like ancient Sparta—he was preoccupied with the militarization of Prussia. Voltaire famously said, "Whereas some states have an army, the Prussian army has a state."

When Frederick II came to power in 1740, he honored his father's military legacy. He extended Prus-sian territory (taking chunks out of Austria and Poland) and prevailed in the Seven Years' War (1754-1763). But Frederick also wanted Prussia to be a cultural and intellectual leader. As king, he became both a ruthless military tactician and a cultured lover of the arts.

"Old Fritz," as he was nicknamed, was a prodigy on the flute, spoke six languages, and counted Voltaire among his friends. He built over-the-top pleasure palaces at nearby Potsdam. Frederick invited musicians and composers to Berlin. C.P.E. Bach, the son of Johann Sebastian Bach, moved here around 1740 to play harpsichord in a band organized by Frederick—helping to make Berlin Europe's music capital at the time. Under Frederick's rule, Berlin grew wealthy and cosmopolitan.

But Frederick was also enlightened in other, more impactful

❻ Gendarmenmarkt

Berlin's finest square feels like a wonderfully symmetrical stage set—bounded by twin churches, with the Berlin Symphony's Concert Hall and a statue of poet/philosopher Friedrich Schiller in the middle. In summer, Gendarmenmarkt hosts outdoor cafés, *Biergarten*s, and occasional outdoor concerts.

Scanning this grand and cohesive square helps us imagine the elegance of prewar Berlin. And it's a beautiful reminder that Berlin has long been a city made great, in part, by its immigrants. The square's name is part French and part German (after the *Gens d'Armes*, Frederick the Great's royal guard, who were headquartered here). Tolerant Prussia was a magnet for the persecuted (and their ways. The Sun King, Louis XIV of France, famously said, *"L'état, c'est moi"*—I am the state, and all of this is for me. But Frederick had a different spin: *"Ich bin der erste Diener meines Staates"*—I am the first *servant* of my state. Frederick felt an obligation to better the lives of his subjects, through the arts and education.

Frederick wanted Enlightenment ideals to be accessible to all. He believed in social mobility, the rule of law via an independent judiciary, and the Protestant work ethic—by which even the poorest of the poor could improve their lives. The museums and other cultural institutions he built weren't just for his personal pleasure, but to enable the betterment of his subjects.

And that didn't apply only to native-born Protestant Germans. In an age when religious and ethnic minorities were being driven out of many other states, Frederick actively invited talented immigrants to come and contribute to Prussian society. When he annexed Catholic Silesia (from Austria), rather than forcibly convert his new subjects to Protestantism, he integrated them as-is into Prussian life—even allowing them to build churches in the capital.

Frederick was also a practical problem solver. During a famine in the 1760s, it was Frederick who introduced the potato (then virtually unknown in Germany) as a highly nutritious crop. Germans have been potato eaters ever since.

Architecturally, Frederick left his mark all over Berlin (particularly the historic core). The buildings on his custom-built square, today's Bebelplatz, best embody his values: a university library, an opera house, and St. Hedwig's Church (built by those French Catholic émigrés).

In short, many of the characteristics we associate with modern Germans—hardworking, intelligent, well-cultured, effective problem solvers, at times ruthlessly efficient, and, yes, really into potatoes—originated with Frederick the Great.

money). In the 17th century, a fifth of all Berliners were French émigrés. Protestant Huguenots fleeing Catholic France revitalized Berlin with new ideas, practical knowledge, and deep pockets.

The **Concert Hall** (Konzerthaus), one of the city's main classical music venues, was designed by Karl Friedrich Schinkel, the man who put the Neoclassical stamp on Berlin. We'll see more of his works on this walk, and you can view his paintings in the Old National Gallery on Museum Island.

The church to your right is the **French Cathedral** (Französischer Dom). To peek into its austere interior, go inside and head up the stairs (organ concerts advertised at the entrance).

And on the left is the **German Cathedral** (Deutscher Dom).

This church was bombed flat in the war and rebuilt only in the 1980s. Inside, you can peer up into the brick and concrete dome and tour a free exhibit (*Wege, Irrwege, Umwege*—"Milestones, Setbacks, Sidetracks") that traces the history of the German parliamentary system, from the revolutionary days of 1848 through the tumultuous 20th century (it's all in German, but you can borrow the excellent and free English audioguide). The German government invests mightily in educating its populace with initiatives like this. Germany is all too aware that a dumbed-down electorate, manipulated by rabble-rousing politicians who think they get to pick and choose which "facts" are real, can be a very dangerous thing.

By the way, neither of these churches is a true "cathedral"—because neither was the seat of a bishop. Frederick the Great enjoyed mixing German and French.

The German name *Dom* (cathedral) is simply a play on the French word *dôme* (cupola).

Before leaving the square, check out the elite **Rausch** chocolate shop (behind the German Cathedral, with the green awnings). And for a classy lunch here, consider the recommended Lutter & Wegner restaurant.

• *Get ready for a few more "free flow" intersections. Facing the churches, head right up Markgrafenstrasse. Turn right on Behrenstrasse, and in a half-block, you'll emerge at another dramatic square, Bebelplatz. Head for the center of the square (to a glass window set into the pavement), and survey the impressive buildings around you (noticing that you're back at Unter den Linden, which runs along the top of the square).*

❼ Bebelplatz: Square of the Books

Frederick the Great built this square to show off Prussian ideals: education, the arts, improvement of the individual, and a tolerance for different groups—provided they're committed to the betterment of society. This square was the cultural center of Frederick's capital. In many ways, it still is. Spin counterclockwise to take in the cultural sights, some of which date back to Frederick's time.

Start by looking across Unter den Linden. That's **Humboldt University,** one of Europe's greatest. Marx and Engels both studied here before going on to start the communist movement. Other distinguished alums include the Brothers Grimm and more than two dozen Nobel Prize winners. Albert Einstein taught here until he fled Germany to join the faculty at Princeton in 1932. Today, it has more than 100,000 students.

Continue panning left. Fronting Bebelplatz is the **former state library**—which was funded by Frederick the Great. After the library was damaged in World War II, communist authorities decided to rebuild it in the original style...but only because Lenin studied here during much of his exile from Russia. Inside, on the second floor, is a 1968 vintage stained-glass window that depicts Lenin's life's work with almost biblical reverence.

As you continue your spin, the square's far end is marked by one of Berlin's swankiest lodgings—**Hotel de Rome,** housed in a historic bank building. Their trendy rooftop bar is a treat in good weather.

Next, the green-domed structure is **St. Hedwig's Church** (nicknamed the "Upside-Down Teacup"). It stands as a symbol of Frederick the Great's reli-

gious and cultural tolerance. The pragmatic king wanted to encourage the integration of Catholic Silesians into Protestant Prussia after he annexed their region in 1742. And so this—the first Catholic church in Berlin since the Reformation—was built. It's dedicated to St. Hedwig, the patron saint of Silesia (a region now shared by Germany, Poland, and the Czech Republic).

Up next is the **Berlin State Opera** *(Staatsoper)*—originally established in Frederick the Great's time. Frederick believed that the arts were essential to having a well-rounded populace. He moved the opera house from inside the castle to this showcase square. To make it even more accessible, the king set aside a few budget-priced tickets for every performance. Over the centuries, the opera has survived, but the building has been repeatedly damaged and rebuilt. It was bombed in 1941, rebuilt to bolster German morale and to celebrate its centennial two years later in 1943, and bombed again in 1945. Its latest reconstruction—a top-to-bottom remodel—was recently completed.

Look down through the glass window in the pavement at what appears to be a room of empty bookshelves. This **book-burning memorial** commemorates a notorious event that took place here during the Nazi years. It was on this square in 1933 that staff and students

from the university built a bonfire. Into the flames they threw 20,000 newly forbidden books—books authored by the likes of Einstein, Hemingway, Freud, and T.S. Eliot. Overseeing it all was the Nazi propaganda minister, Joseph Goebbels, who also tossed books onto the fire. As the flames rose up, he declared, "The era of extreme Jewish intellectualism has come to an end, and the German revolution has again opened the way for the true essence of being German." Hitler purposely chose this square—built by Frederick the Great to embody culture and enlightenment—to symbolically demonstrate that the era of tolerance and openness was over.

A plaque nearby has a quote by the 19th-century German poet Heinrich Heine. The Nazis despised Heine because—even though he converted to Christianity—he was born a Jew. His books were among those that went up in flames on this spot. Read Heine's prophetic quote, written in 1820: "Where they burn books, in the end they will also burn people." Put in other words (by Voltaire, a friend of Frederick the Great's): "Those who can make you believe absurdities can make you commit atrocities."

• *Leave Bebelplatz toward Unter den Linden, angling left to reach an equestrian statue, in the median of the boulevard.*

❽ Statue of Frederick the Great

This statue honors the one man from Berlin's early history who matters most: Frederick the Great. Frederick ruled as king of Prussia in the mid-1700s. He turned his capital, Berlin, into a world-class city. (For more on Frederick, see the sidebar, earlier.)

Notice which way the statue of Frederick is pointing: east. He's riding toward the epicenter of Prussian imperial power, where his royal palace once stood. We're now entering the stretch of Unter den Linden that best represents Frederick's legacy.

• *Cross to the university side, and continue heading east down Unter den Linden. You'll pass in front of Humboldt University's main gate, where sellers of used books set up their tables. Immediately in front of the gate, embedded in the cobbles, notice the row of square, bronze plaques—each one bearing the name of a university student who was executed by the Nazis.*

You'll see similar **Stolpersteine** *("stumbling stones") all over Berlin (for more, see page 188).*

Just beyond the university on the left, head for a building that looks like a Greek temple set in a small park filled with chestnut trees.

❾ Neue Wache

The "New Guardhouse" was built in 1816 as just that—a fancy barracks for the bodyguards assigned to the Hohenzollern palace just ahead (it's the Neoclas-

sical building across the street, with four tall columns marking the doorway). Over the years, the Neue Wache has beenw transformed into a memorial for fallen warriors. Check out the pediment over the doorway: The goddess of Victory stands in the center amid the chaos of war, as soldiers fall.

The Neue Wache represents the strong, united, rising Prussian state Frederick created. It was just one of the grand new buildings built to line this stretch of Unter den Linden. The style was Neoclassical—structures that looked like Greek temples, with columns and triangular pediments. Each successive German regime has used the Neue Wache to honor its soldiers. The Nazis memorialized their war dead here, and in 1960, the communists rededicated it to the victims of fascism. After the Wall fell in 1989, the structure was transformed again, into a national memorial.

Step inside. In 1993, the austere interior was fitted with the statue we see today—a replica of *Mother with Her Dead Son*, by

Käthe Kollwitz, a Berlin artist who lived through both world wars. It marks the tombs of Germany's unknown soldier and an unknown concentration camp victim. The inscription reads, "To the victims of war and tyranny." (It's complicated to honor your war dead when you started and lost a great war...or two. But you can honor the victims of your tyrant—both foreign and domestic.) The memorial, open to the sky, incorporates the elements—sunshine, rain, snow—falling on this modern-day *pietà*.

Back outside, notice the flagpoles flying the German flag and

the red and white Berlin flag, with the city's symbol—a black bear—in the center.

• *Continue down Unter den Linden, passing by the pink yet formidable Zeughaus (early 1700s), the oldest building on the boulevard. Built in the Baroque style as the royal arsenal, it later became a military museum, and today houses the excellent* **German History Museum**.

When you reach the bridge, cross the Spree and step onto Museum Island.

⓾ Museum Island and Former City Palace

This island, sitting in the middle of the Spree River, is Berlin's historic birthplace. Take in the scene: the lazy river, the statues along the bridge, and the impressive buildings all around you.

Berlin was born on this marshy island around the year 1200. In fact, the name "Berlin" may be derived from an old Slavic word for "swamp." (Others theorize the city's name derives from the German word for a female bear, "Bärin," an animal found on the medieval coat of arms and today's city flag.) The location was ideal: the river brought commerce, and the island provided protection.

As the city grew, this island remained the site of the ruler's castle and residence—from Brandenburg dukes and Hohenzollern prince-electors, to the kings of Prussia and the kaisers of the German Empire. Berlin was always the leading city of the northern Germanic world, even long before there was a united "Germany."

Over the centuries, the royal palace grew in magnificence to match the growing empire. At its peak under Prussian rulers (1701-1918), it was a splendid and sprawling Baroque palace called the Stadtschloss, topped at one end with a dome (as you see on the right side of Unter den Linden). It was considered the most important secular Baroque building north of the Alps.

The royal palace site has long been the heart of the city. It began as a fortified castle in the 1400s and morphed through the ages until it became the imposing home of Prussian rulers in the 19th century.

After World War I, the last Prussian ruler was deposed, and

Why Does Berlin Smell?

At some point during your visit to Berlin, it's bound to happen: You'll step into a shop, or a museum, or a restaurant...and walk into a puff of pungent air. Giving the clerk a dirty look, you'll mutter under your breath, "Jeez, open a window!"

Don't blame them. Blame the swampy soil upon which Berlin sits. Simply put, the air here can smell—particularly on a warm, moist, stale day, when swamp gas bubbles up from deep below, entering buildings through the plumbing. This phenomenon, called *Berliner Luft* ("Berlin Air"), has confused and offended visitors ever since there was a Berlin. Adolf Hitler (Austrian by birth, proudly Bavarian by choice) once sniffed that Berlin was "unfit to be German."

As for Berliners, they're used to their aromatic air...and some have even grown to love it. The unofficial city anthem is a jaunty tune called "Berliner Luft," which celebrates the sweet fragrance of Berlin.

the palace was gutted in a 1945 air raid in the last days of World War II. In 1950, the East Germans erected in its place the Palace of the Republic—a massive, blocky parliament building. In the early 21st century, that communist building was demolished, and for years this entire city block was a vacant lot—just a big grassy park.

Now, at great expense, Germany has rebuilt a palace on the site, called the **Humboldt Forum.** This "palace for all" (which should be open by the time you visit) comple- ments the cultural offer- ings on Museum Island, with space for businesses, restaurants, and a muse- um of art and culture.

The main facade fits beautifully with the Neoclassical architecture along Unter den Linden. The side facing the Spree River, how- ever—in a nod to those feeling a little "Ost-algia"—has the stern functionalism of the Palace of the Republic from DDR days. On the back side, a round turret harkens back to the original medi- eval fortress. Along the river a Monument to Freedom and Unity (scheduled for completion in 2021) will include a 164-foot-long bowl (which can be walked in) and two inscriptions: *"Wir sind das Volk!"* (We are the People), chanted by Communist protesters in 1989, and *"Wir sind ein Volk!"* (We are one People), which grew out of the first slogan when focus turned to reunification.

• Now, turn your attention to the left side of Unter den Linden. There's a spacious garden, bordered on two sides by impressive buildings.

⓫ Museum Island Sights

First, get oriented: The island's big, central square is called the Lustgarten. At the far end is the Altes Museum—marking the start of a cluster of Neoclassical museum buildings. And to the right is the imposing Berlin Cathedral, with its green domes.

For 300 years, the **Lustgarten** has flip-flopped between being a military parade ground and a people-friendly park, depending on the political tenor of the time. In the Nazi era, Hitler enjoyed giving speeches here—from the top of the museum steps overlooking this square. In 1999, the Lustgarten was made into a pleasant park, one of Berlin's most enjoyable public spaces.

At the far end of the Lustgarten is a cache of grandiose **museum buildings** that represent the can-do German spirit of the 1800s. Before the 19th century, there was no "Germany"—just a collection of 39 little German-speaking countries: Bavaria, Saxony, the lands along the Rhine, and so on. The mightiest of these ministates was Prussia, with its capital right here on this island. What united the "German" people was their common language and historic roots. In the 1800s, a movement was coalescing. Its goal: to unite all those little German-speaking states into a single modern nation. Economically, German iron and coal output multiplied, and trade was booming. Finally, in 1871, Germany was united—creating overnight an industrial powerhouse with Europe's largest economy. Berlin, the new country's new capital, was filled with optimism, energy, and visions of greatness. (Ironically, Germany's sudden emergence among Europe's economic powers destabilized the Continent, helping lead it into World War I.)

These Neoclassical buildings represented the goal of creating a New Germanic Athens. The earliest building—the one you see from here, with the long colonnade—was the Altes Museum, which went up in the 1820s. It was designed by Karl Friedrich

Schinkel, the architect who remade Berlin in the Neoclassical style. (Schinkel also designed the Concert Hall on Gendarmenmarkt, the Neue Wache, the bridge we just crossed, and even the warrior statues on the bridge.) The rest of the Museum Island complex began taking shape in the 1840s, when city leaders envisioned the island as an oasis of culture and learning. Today, these impressive buildings host five grand museums. The **Altes Museum** houses classical antiquities. Just beyond are the **Neues Museum** (Egyptian, prehistoric, and classical antiquities), the **Pergamon Museum** (classical antiquities), the **Old National Gallery** (German Romantic painting), and the **Bode Museum** (Byzantine art and mosaics).

Dominating the island is the towering, green-domed **Berlin Cathedral** (Berliner Dom). This is only a century old, built during the reign of Kaiser Wilhelm II—that jingoistic emperor in the spiked helmet who led Europe into World War I. He considered himself not merely a king but a *kaiser*—a Caesar. The church's bombastic Wilhelmian architecture is a Protestant assertion of strength. It seems to proclaim, "A mighty fortress is our God...and he speaks German."

The years of Kaiser Wilhelm's rule, from 1888 to 1918, were a busy age of building. Germany had recently been united, and the emperor wanted to give his capital stature and legitimacy (it was Kaiser Wilhelm who built the Reichstag). The Wilhelmian style is over the top: a garish mix of Neoclassical, Neo-Baroque, and Neo-Renaissance, with rippling stucco and gold-tiled mosaics. This cathedral, while Protestant, is as ornate as if it were Catholic.

The church is at its most impressive from the outside. To see the extravagant interior and climb the dome (270 steps, sweeping views), you can pay the pricey admission (for details on visiting, see page 53).

• *Continue down Unter den Linden past the cathedral, and pause on the bridge over the Spree. Look left, past the cathedral.*

⓬ Spree River

The Spree River is people-friendly and welcoming. A parklike promenade leads all the way from here to the Hauptbahnhof. Along it, you'll find impromptu "beachside" beer gardens with imported sand, BBQs in pocket parks, and lots of locals walking their dogs, taking a lazy bike ride, or jogging. Spree River boat tours depart from near here (for details, see page 34).

You may notice *"don't drop anchor"* signs. Believe it or not, there are still unexploded WWII bombs around town, and many are in this river. Every month, several bombs are found at construction sites.

• *Our Unter Den Linden walk is finished. From here, you have lots of options:*

To finish up your orientation stroll through the heart of Berlin, see the ▢ Communist East Berlin Walk, which begins nearby at the Marx-Engels-Forum park (cross the bridge and veer right into the park).

To tour Museum Island's sights, see the ▢ Museum Island Tour and ▢ Pergamon Museum Tour chapters.

Other options include the ▢ German History Museum Tour (just a short backtrack across the Spree), the DDR Museum (across the river from the cathedral—see listing on page 56), or the ▢ Old Jewish Quarter Walk—in a trendy neighborhood with plenty of restaurants, fun-to-explore courtyards, and artifacts of Berlin's Jewish history (begins a short walk away, at the Hackescher Markt S-Bahn station). To get there, cross the bridge behind the Berlin Cathedral, turn left, and follow the riverbank north for a couple of blocks. Bear right under the rail tracks, and you're in the heart of Hackescher Markt. The Hackescher Markt S-Bahn station is a handy hub for getting to other points in the city.

Or you can hop on bus #100, #245, or #300 at the Lustgarten stop (along Unter den Linden, right in the middle of Museum Island), which can take you in either direction—east to Alexanderplatz (behind the TV Tower), or west to the Brandenburg Gate area and beyond.

MUSEUM ISLAND TOUR

Neues Museum • Old National Gallery • Bode Museum

One of Berlin's most ambitious urban renewal projects is taking place in the cultural park of Museum Island, which sits right in the middle of the Spree. The 19th-century Prussian king Friedrich Wilhelm IV, who imagined this island as a place of art and learning, masterminded the construction of what would eventually become five separate museums. WWII bombs and communist-era neglect left the buildings and their collections in shambles. Now, each of these world-class galleries (proud home to the Greek Pergamon Altar and the exquisite Queen Nefertiti bust) is being renovated in turn. When it's finally done, a grand visitors center will link the museum campus together.

Museum lovers could spend all day here. The Pergamon Museum is covered in depth in the next chapter, and the other four museums are covered here. Use this rundown to help you choose:

The **Pergamon Museum** is the most famous of the five, renowned for its treasures from ancient Babylon, Assyria, Rome, and the Islamic world. (Think of it as the "German British Museum.") Its massive-scale artifacts are thrilling, but its star attraction—the Pergamon Altar—is undergoing a years-long renovation. For complete orientation details and a self-guided tour, see the next chapter.

The **Neues Museum** rolls back in time to the prehistoric world. Among its highlights are a toothy Neanderthal skull, a remarkably crafted Golden Hat belonging to early Celtic people, and—most important—the bust of Nefertiti, arguably *the* most famous artifact from ancient Egypt. Nefertiti—a bigger crowd-pleaser than anything in the Pergamon—makes the Neues perhaps even more purely enjoyable for a casual visitor.

The **Old National Gallery** focuses on German Romantic painting from the 19th century (especially Caspar David Fried-

Planning Your Visit to Museum Island

Use the tours in this and the following chapter to frame your time on Museum Island. If you have a half-day, spend about an hour apiece in the Pergamon, Neues, and Old National Gallery—hitting only the top pieces in each one. If you have a full day, dive deeper into those three. For most, the Bode and the Altes museums are skippable.

At each museum, pick up a floor plan when you enter, and use it to find the rooms I highlight on each tour. And, remember, the audioguides included in your admission are excellent.

rich's moody landscapes). This is the best museum in town for *German* art.

The **Bode Museum** is, frankly, more about its striking museum building (with its grand domed entryway) than its collection of Byzantine art, sculptures, and coins. It's worth a visit for numismatists and those who appreciate Byzantine mosaics.

The **Altes (Old) Museum** is the least interesting of the bunch. Unless you're looking for more classical antiquities, skip it (I did).

Orientation to Museum Island

Cost: Individual admission to the Pergamon or the Neues is €12; it's €10 for the Old National Gallery, Bode, or Altes; if you're visiting at least two museums consider getting the Museum Island Pass or Museum Pass Berlin.

Hours: Museum hours are 10:00-18:00, Thursdays until 20:00. The Pergamon and Neues museums are open daily; the Old National Gallery, Bode Museum, and Altes Museum are open Tue-Sun, closed Mon.

Information: All five museums are managed by the Staatliche Museen zu Berlin (SMB; +49 30 266 424 242, www.smb. museum).

Reservations and Ticketing Tips: To skip ticket-buying lines at the Pergamon Museum, purchase a timed ticket in advance at the museum website.

If you have a Museum Island Pass or Museum Pass Berlin, it's recommended to book a free timed-entry reservation at the Pergamon, as the passes don't provide line-skipping privileges. To do that, go to the museum website (in German), click the link to buy tickets, pick the date you want to visit, then scroll down to find the option marked "*frei: übrige*" and select the number of people. Next, choose the time you want, add the reservation to your cart, and complete your checkout.

The popular Pergamon and the Neues are typically busiest in the morning, on weekends, and when it rains. Crowds aren't a problem at the Old National Gallery or the Bode.

Renovation: A formidable renovation is underway on Museum Island. When complete (2024 at the earliest), a new visitors center will link the Pergamon Museum with the Altes Museum, the Pergamon will get a fourth wing, tunnels will lace the complex together, and this will become one of the grandest museum zones in Europe. In the meantime, pardon their dust.

Getting There: The nearest S-Bahn stations are Hackescher Markt and Friedrichstrasse, each about a 10-minute walk away. The Am Kupfergraben tram stop (#M1 or #12) is just across the river from the Pergamon. Or ride bus #100, #245, or #300 along Unter den Linden to the Lustgarten stop. The new U5 Museum Island (Museumsinsel) U-Bahn stop may be open by the time you visit.

Getting In: The new riverside entrance pavilion called the James-Simon-Galerie is now open on the west bank of Museum Island. Eventually it will provide underground connections to all the island's museums. For now, you'll find separate, well-signed entrances to the Pergamon, Neues Museum, and Old National Gallery facing a leafy courtyard behind the colonnade on Bodestrasse.

Tours: Each museum has its own excellent audioguide (included in admission). Ask for these when you enter, and use them to supplement the selective information given here.

Services: Each museum has free (often obligatory) coat-check desks and lockers.

Eateries: You'll find basic cafés in the Altes, Neues, and Bode (the Bode's is beautifully set in its free-to-enter domed lobby).

Starring: The bust of Nefertiti (in the Neues Museum) and German Romantic paintings (in the Old National Gallery).

Neues (New) Museum

After being damaged in World War II and sitting in ruins for some 40 years, the Neues Museum has been gorgeously rebuilt. Oddly, this so-called "new" museum features the oldest stuff around. The star attraction is the famously beautiful bust of Egypt's Queen Nefertiti. You have permission to make a beeline for her and call it a museum. But with more time, the Neues offers much more: ancient statues, a vivid papyrus collection, slice-of-life artifacts, and dreamy wax portraits decorating mummy cases.

↻ SELF-GUIDED TOUR

This one-hour tour, covering the museum from top to bottom, takes you on a roughly chronological journey through time—from a 45,000-year-old skull, to a prognosticating prehistoric hat, to portraits of that ancient Egyptian power couple, Nefertiti and Akhenaton.

• *The Neues Museum ticket desk is across the courtyard from the entrance. Ticket in hand, enter and pick up the floor plan.*

*Head up the central staircase to the top floor, level 3. At the top of the stairs, turn left, entering Room 311. Pass through three rooms, to **Room 309**. You run into a glass display case with a skull, a few bones, and a bust of a human head. Welcome to prehistory.*

LEVEL 3
Neanderthal Skull from Le Moustier

This skull with impressive dentition comes from a teenage Neanderthal boy who lived 45,000 years ago in central France. A bust displayed next to the skull re-creates what archaeologists think he might have looked like. (A Neanderthal Michael Cera?)

The Neanderthal people (scholars surmise) lived alongside our Homosapiens ancestors. Humans and Neanderthals occasionally even interbred, but their offspring never flourished, so the two remained separate species. Around 30,000 BC, the Neanderthals mysteriously died out. The skeleton of this teenage boy was discovered—in a fetal position, accompanied by a few crude stone-cutting tools—in 1908, in a cave in France's Dordogne River Valley. The boy's Homo-sapiens neighbors, the Cro-Magnons, would go on to create the wondrous cave paintings in nearby Lascaux.

Also displayed in Room 309 are the ancient bones of the animals these early people hunted—mammoths, moose, and so on—along with human tools, spearheads, and pottery.

• *Exit at the far end of the room, cross the landing, and pass through Room 306. You'll go from the Stone Age to the Ice Age to our next stop— one of the treasures of the Bronze Age. You'll find it in the dimly lit corner Room 305.*

Golden Hat

The tall, conehead-like Golden Hat—made of paper-thin gold leaf—was likely worn by the priest of a sun cult popular among the Celtic people of central Europe around 1,000 BC. It's stamped with symbols of the heavens—mostly sun-like circles, plus a few crescent moons, and stars on the top.

Admire the incredible workmanship of these prehistoric people. The hat, 30 inches tall, was hammered from a pound of gold into a single sheet of gold leaf less than a millimeter thick. (Originally, the gold hat probably had an inner support structure of cloth or

MUSEUM ISLAND

wood.) To make the hat, these early Celtic peoples fired up a charcoal furnace stoked with a bellows that could heat things to 1500 degrees F. To strengthen the finished hat and keep it from cracking, they mixed silver and copper into the pure gold. To make the decorations, they used a dozen individual tools with sun-, moon-, and star-shaped stamps.

This weird hat could be used to predict full moons or solstices up to five years in advance. Here's how it worked: There are 21 horizontal bands, each containing a number of symbols. You'd add up the symbols within each band—e.g., a row of 20 suns, each with five concentric circles, totals up to 100 symbols. You'd add that to neighboring bands to calculate the various months, seasons, and years. Note that the fourth band from the top (with the crescent moons and eyes) is special: Its 38 symbols calculated oddities like leap years.

The hat could be used as either a solar calendar (a year of 365 sunrises) or lunar calendar (a year of 12 full moons, totaling 354 days). It could even demonstrate how those two counting methods sync up every 19 years. This "lunisolar" calendar (linking the moon and the sun) preceded the ancient Greek calendar by 500 years.

For superstitious Celtic people, this hat must have seemed supernatural. It endowed the druid who wore it with almost magical powers. He could predict upcoming events with eerie accuracy. It told the tribe when to plant and when to harvest, when to worship which gods, and when to throw the next New Year's Eve bash.

• *If you hear some strange sounds as you view the Golden Hat, they're coming from right outside the room—where you'll find a display of slinky, golden **lur horns** from northern Europe. Press the button to hear their haunting tone.*

Next up, ancient Egypt. Continue circling the top floor counterclockwise. You'll pass through exhibits on the Iron Age. (Europeans began forging iron around 1000 BC—by which time the overachieving Egyptians had already been doing it for 400 years.)

*When you reach the stairwell, descend to the next floor and turn right, entering **Room 208**—the Egyptian Collection.*

Browse through the large Room 208, full of statues in glass cases. The poses are stiff—seated or standing, with few details that mark these as individual people. Make your way through Egyptian history. There's the so-called Old Kingdom (c. 2500-2000 BC), when the pyramids were built. The Middle Period (c. 2000-1500 BC) was a turbulent time marked by foreign invasions. The New Kingdom (c. 1500-1000 BC) saw Egypt rise to its pinnacle of power, overseen by the husband-and-wife team we are about to meet—Akhenaton and Nefertiti.

• *Continue into **Room 209**, which features objects from the reign of the pharaoh Akhenaton.*

LEVEL 2
Bust, Relief, and Stele of Akhenaton

The bust and relief on display capture the distinctive likeness of the pharaoh who transformed Egypt. Both show his narrow face, prominent chin, sensual features, and Mick Jagger lips. The bust, unfinished and badly damaged, was once painted and held a crown covered with gold leaf. Note the uraeus on Akhenaton's forehead; worn by pharaohs, this symbol of supreme authority shows a cobra rearing to strike.

When Akhenaton took the throne in 1380 BC, he rocked conservative Egypt by promoting monotheism to his polytheistic subjects. He lumped the countless gods of the Egyptian pantheon into one all-powerful being, Aton the sun god. Akhenaton's reign was a striking exception to Egypt's 2,000 years of political, religious, and artistic rigidity.

Akhenaton married Nefertiti—a commoner, whose name meant "the beautiful one has come." They moved into a new palace and started a family. In the small adjoining room to the left, look for the happy couple in the carved-relief stele. Wearing their royal crowns, they relax under the shining rays of the sun god. At the tips of the rays, a few cross-shaped ankh hieroglyphs— the symbol of life—represent Akhenaton's new deity sending  life to his subjects. The royal children frolic on the laps of their regal mummy and daddy. This relief, softened by its human touch, has a naturalness that's quite different from the stiffness of most traditional Egyptian art.

Postscript: Akhenaton's daughter married a teenage pharaoh, Tutankhamen—"King Tut." It was the unearthing of Tut's mummy in 1922 that helped stoke Europe's interest in Egyptology.

• *Before leaving, take a last glance at the bust of Akhenaton from the side. Notice the V-shaped tilt of the neck—we'll see it mirrored in the next room. Now let's meet Akhenaton's wife (and Tut's mother-in-law), the "beautiful one" named Nefertiti. She has a room all her own—***Room 210.** *(Note that she's had it with the paparazzi—photos of Nefertiti are strictly* verboten.*)*

Bust of Nefertiti

The 3,000-year-old bust of Queen Nefertiti, wife of Akhenaton, is the most famous piece of Egyptian art in Europe.

Nefertiti has all the right beauty marks: long slender neck,

perfect lips, almond eyes, symmetrical eyebrows, pronounced cheekbones, and a perfect spray-on tan.

Nefertiti's pose is perfectly symmetrical from every angle—front, back and side. From the side, her V-shaped profile creates a dynamic effect: she leans forward, gazing intently, while her funnel-shaped hat swoops up and back. Her colorful hat is a geometrically flawless, tapered cylinder.

And yet, despite her seemingly perfect beauty, Nefertiti has a touch of humanity. Notice the fine wrinkles around the eyes—these only enhance her beauty. She has a slight Mona Lisa smile, pursed at the corners. Her eyebrows are so delicately detailed, you can make out each single hair. From the back, the perfection of her neck is marked with a bump of reality—a protruding vertebra. Her look is meditative, intelligent, lost in thought. Like a movie star discreetly sipping a glass of wine at a sidewalk café, Nefertiti seems somehow more dignified in person.

In real life, Nefertiti, though born a commoner, was much honored. As the pharaoh's wife, she was also recognized as a god on earth, part of the trinity of Akhenaton, Nefertiti, and the sun god Aton. Nefertiti had six children—all daughters.

The bust is made of limestone, with a stucco surface. It may have been meant as a companion piece to the bust of Akhenaton in the previous room. But this bust never left its studio. It served as a master model for all other portraits of the queen. (That's probably why the artist didn't bother putting the quartz inlay in the left eye.) Stare at her long enough, and you may get the sensation that she's winking at you.

How the queen arrived in Germany is a tale out of *Indiana Jones*. The German archaeologist Ludwig Borchardt uncovered her in the Egyptian desert in 1912. The Egyptian Department of Antiquities had first pick of all the artifacts uncovered on their territory. After the first takings, they divided the rest 50/50 with the excavators. When Borchardt presented Nefertiti to the Egyptians, they passed her over, never bothering to examine her closely. (Unsubstantiated rumors persist that Borchardt misled the Egyptians in order to keep the bust for himself—prompting some Egyptians to call for Nefertiti's return, just as the Greeks are lobbying the British to return the Parthenon frieze currently housed in the British Museum.)

Although this bust is not particularly representative of Egyptian art in general—and despite increasing claims that her long neck suggests she's a Neoclassical fake—Nefertiti has become a symbol of Egyptian art by popular acclaim. And since her arrival in Berlin, she's also become something of a symbol of Germany itself—Germany's "queen." Hitler promoted her as a pagan symbol of his new non-Christian Reich. When Germany was split in the Cold War, both sides fought to claim her. Today Nefertiti's timeless beauty has come to represent the aspirations of the German people.

• *The Egyptian Collection continues in* **Room 211**—*the "Library of Antiquity."*

Papyrus Collection

This large room is filled with what looks like empty display cases. Press a button to watch a 3,000-year-old document trundle out of its protective home. You'll see ancient texts in many languages—Egyptian hieroglyphs, Greek, Latin, and so on. They're written on everything from paper to cloth, wood, pottery, stone tablets, and parchment—but the most prevalent material is papyrus. The collection here contains thousands of examples of this most classically Egyptian material, made from the fibrous pith of a common marsh reed. Perusing these documents is a fascinating look at the ancient world's laws, business transactions, plays, and even early fiction.

• *Exiting Room 211, you'll pass through more rooms with exhibits on migrations, barbarians, and ancient Rome (including larger-than-life Roman statues), plaster casts of Ghiberti's famous bronze doors on the Florence Baptistry, coins, and displays about medieval times after the fall of the classical world.*

Then head downstairs to level 1, and turn left, entering **Room 111.**

LEVEL 1
More Egypt

There's much more of Egypt in this and the next rooms—statues of pharaohs, wall paintings, reliefs from tombs, even a reconstructed burial chapel. In Room 109, the glass cases of **"30 Centuries of Sculpture,"** filled with the sculpted heads of pharaohs, priests, and scribes, trace concepts of portraiture over the millennia.

In the center of Room 109, find the **Berlin Green Head,** from around 350 BC. No one knows who this bald, smooth-skinned man was, but his knitted-brow look makes him come to life. (Some think his shaved head indicates he was a priest.) Sculpted even as Egypt was being conquered by Greece, this combines Greek realism with timeless Egyptian features. This Green Man's determined look is a thought-provoking glimpse into Egypt's future.

If you want still more Egypt, you'll find it downstairs on level 0, where you can see small-scale statuettes and models as well as a sea of large sarcophagi.

• *But we'll finish our tour here on level 1. Back-track the way you came, cross the stairwell, and make your way to* **Rooms 103-104.**

Schliemann's Troy

There's not much to see in these rooms—a few gold necklaces and old pots—but the text panels help explain the craze for antiquities that brought us the Neues Museum.

Much of it can be traced to the man featured in these rooms: Heinrich Schliemann (1822-1890) was the real-life Indiana Johann of his era. Having read Homer's accounts of the Trojan War, Schliemann set out on a quest to find the long-lost ruins of the city of Troy. He (probably) found the capital of the Trojans (in Turkey), as well as the capital of the Greeks (Mycenae, in the Greek Peloponnese).

Displays tell the fascinating story of how Schliemann smuggled the treasures out in fruit baskets, then their long journey until they were donated to the German government. (Unfortunately, Schliemann's treasure trove was looted when the Soviets invaded Berlin during World War II, which is why so few artifacts remain here.) Schliemann's derring-do sparked the imagination of all Europe. Soon, other archaeologists were traveling to Egypt, Greece, and Rome, and returning with the artifacts that fill this grand museum. *Danke,* Herr Schliemann, for bringing the ancient world back to life.

• *Our next museum is the one that resembles a Greek temple (behind the Neues and Altes museums).*

Old National Gallery (Alte Nationalgalerie)

Dramatic, colorful, Romantic landscapes are the star of this gallery of 19th-century art. The most famous of the German Romantics is Caspar David Friedrich, and we'll see his moody painting *Monk By the Sea.* The museum also features a few choice works from well-known French Impressionists Manet, Monet, Renoir, and company. True art lovers will enjoy the German Realists, with their slice-of-life scenes from the Industrial Age. You probably won't recognize any of the paintings. But it's still an enjoyable 45-minute stroll through German culture from the 1800s—the century when Germany came of age and found its cultural identity.

⊘ SELF-GUIDED TOUR

Start on the **third floor**—the main focus of the collection—and work your way down. You can take the stairs, or look for the elevator by the ticket desk.

LEVEL 3
Romantic Paintings

• *The first stop is in the small, standalone **Room 3.02** just off the landing (straight ahead as you come up the stairs; from the elevator, you'll have to backtrack to the landing).*

Casa Bartholdy Murals

Use this room's colorful paintings as an introduction to the Romantic art we'll see next. These frescoes, originally painted on the

walls of a villa in Rome, tell the biblical story of Joseph. They were done by idealistic artists of the artistic brotherhood called the Nazarenes.

It was the early 1800s, and the German people were searching for their unique national identity. In art, the Nazarenes were breaking free from the Italian and French styles that had dominated Germany's academies for centuries. For inspiration, they returned to Germany's cultural roots—the Middle Ages.

As a result, the Bible story of Joseph looks strangely medieval: medieval-looking kings, peasants in tunics, rustic castles, and Germanic landscapes. The Nazarenes were seeking a purer form of expression that was uniquely German. This almost religious fervor would inspire the next generation of German artists—the Romantics.

• *Make your way through some of the smaller side-rooms to reach the large* **Room 3.05**—*in the very center of the building (flanked with white columns).*

Karl Friedrich Schinkel

Schinkel is best known as the architect who remade Berlin in the 1820s. He designed buildings all around the city, including the Neue Wache, the Concert Hall on Gendarmenmarkt, the Altes Museum—and even a section of the museum you're in. With Greek columns, clean lines, and mathematical symmetry, Schinkel's buildings epitomized the then-popular Neoclassical style.

But as a painter, Schinkel took a totally different path—toward Romanticism. His haunting landscapes clearly show his fascination with architecture. Gothic cathedrals and castles dominate his scenes. These buildings are clearly fantasies: They're impossibly tall, perched dramatically on cliffs, overlooking distant vistas, and engulfed in clouds. Foliage grows over the buildings, and animals wander through. Nature rules. Where puny humans do appear, they are dwarfed

by the landscape and buildings. Scenes are lit by a dramatic, eerie light, as though the world is charged from within by the power of God. Welcome to Romanticism.

• *Head back to one of the side corridors. Next, continue to the large* **Room 3.06.**

Caspar David Friedrich Room

The greatest German artist of the Romantic era was Caspar David Friedrich (1774-1840). A quick glance around this room gives you a sense of Friedrich's subjects: craggy mountains, twisted trees, ominous clouds, burning sunsets, and lone figures in the gloom.

Rather than painting placid, pretty scenes as other landscape artists might, Friedrich celebrated Nature's awesome power. The few people he painted are tiny and solitary, standing with their backs to us. As they ponder the vastness of their surroundings, we're invited to see the world through their eyes, and to contemplate humankind's minuscule place in the grand scheme of things.

• *Hey, this is "Romantic" painting, so my descriptions have to be equally melodramatic. Now, let's see a few of Friedrich's paintings—in chronological order, as we trace the sometimes turbulent arc of his life.*

Monk by the Sea, 1808-1810: A lone figure stands on a sand dune, pondering a vast, turbulent expanse of sea and sky. Scholars have suggested that the monk—slender, with long blond hair—is Friedrich himself.

This painting made Friedrich instantly famous. It was exhib-

MUSEUM ISLAND

Romanticism

The movement known as Romanticism, popular in the early 1800s, emphasized the heart over the head. Romantics questioned the clinical detachment of science, industrial pollution, and the personal restrictions of modern life. Instead, they reveled in strong emotions, personal freedom, and the beauties of nature.

Romantics worshipped nature's awe-inspiring splendor. Walking through forests, along rivers, and up mountainsides, Romantics communed with their true self: namely, the primitive, "noble savage" beneath the intellectual crust. Romantic painters tried to capture the beauty of nature, but especially its drama. Ominous clouds, rainbows, distant horizons, eerie lighting effects—all these suggested not just what the eye saw but what the heart felt.

The German Romantic movement was closely tied with German national identity. Remember, as late as the mid-1800s, there was no German "nation." What tied the German people together was their indigenous roots, language, folklore, and common myths. These dated back centuries, to medieval times. So German Romantics glorified these medieval roots. The old folklore was resurrected and popularized by the Brothers Grimm. Painters depicted unspoiled German landscapes and dreamy German villages. Portraits of the German people showed them as rugged and proud. These were themes that would strum the heartstrings of anyone with Teutonic blood. So inspired, the German people would unite and form the modern nation of Germany in 1871.

ited here in Berlin, in 1810, and was bought by none other than the king of Prussia. By then, Friedrich was in his mid-30s. He'd honed his craft at a stuffy painting academy, but his true passion was roaming Germany's rugged countryside and sketching with pencil and paper, directly from nature. Then he returned to the studio to meticulously compose the final work in oils.

This beach scene is laid out in three horizontal layers: land, sea, and sky. This horizontal axis is offset by a single

vertical line—the lone monk. You'll see this same horizontal/vertical technique in other Friedrich canvases.

Landscapes by Friedrich might better be called "skyscapes." In this painting, the sky taking up the majority of the canvas is a murky mix of black clouds, grey wisps, and ambiguous lighting. The scene has no obvious "frame," and seems to bleed off the edges of the canvas to infinity. This vague atmosphere mirrors the ambiguous emotions of the monk.

And what exactly is the monk thinking? Friedrich gave us a clue: When this painting was first exhibited, it had a companion piece, which we'll see next.

• *That companion piece now hangs alongside* Monk by the Sea.

Abbey Among Oak Trees, 1809-1810: It's an incredibly bleak scene—a ruined Gothic church, bare trees, and desolate tombstones. Almost unnoticed among the graves is a sad parade of tombstone-like monks bearing a coffin.

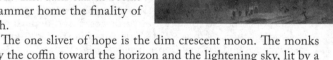

Death is a common theme in Friedrich's work. Between the ages of 7 and 13, Friedrich saw his mother and two sisters die, and he watched his brother drown. This dark canvas seems to hammer home the finality of death.

The one sliver of hope is the dim crescent moon. The monks carry the coffin toward the horizon and the lightening sky, lit by a new moon. Might there be some hope beyond the grave?

Hmmm...

Friedrich lets that thought drift upward above the trees, into the sky, and out the top of the canvas...where it bleeds up until it would have reached that companion painting *Monk by the Sea,* which originally hung directly above this one. There, one of the monks has wandered off, alone, to a desolate beach. He ponders the death of his fallen brother and the vast unknown that lies beyond this mortal existence.

• *You know, I think we could all use something a little cheerier. So find the next painting...*

Woman at a Window, 1822: In 1818, the renowned 44-year-old artist married 25-year-old Caroline—the woman in this painting. She leans out the window of Friedrich's studio. As with so many of Friedrich's

paintings, his subject has her back to us, so we see what she sees: a blue sky and a row of colorful poplar trees.

With his marriage and the birth of three kids, Friedrich's dark life brightened. His colors get lighter and more vibrant, and he begins adding more flesh-and-blood people to his minimal landscapes.

This painting's composition is another carefully planned grid. Its strong three-dimensionality sucks you right into the scene. Notice how the floorboards direct your eye from where we stand to the woman at the window. Your attention soars out the dark studio, past the mast of a moored ship, across the river, to the distant trees and the sunny skies beyond.

• *Next up, look for...*

Man and Woman Contemplating the Moon, 1818-1825: A couple emerges from a dark forest onto a hillside. They stand and gaze into the deep night sky, lit by a hazy moon. The woman places her hand gently on the man's shoulder as they pause to contemplate. (By the way, Samuel Beckett said this painting was the inspiration for his play, "Waiting for Godot.")

• *The next two paintings were also intended as companion pieces.*

Moonrise over the Sea, 1822: It's evening, and two women and a man perch atop a rock and watch as ships return to the harbor. As the moon rises through a layer of clouds, it casts a shimmering light across the wide sea and even wider sky.

Although Friedrich rarely talked about the symbolism of his work, he often added intriguing elements that invite interpretation. To some, these ships suggest how we all "sail" through the journey of our lives like ships across the sea, hoping to return to a safe harbor where loved ones await.

The Solitary Tree, 1822: An aging but still-strong tree rises up stoically from a stark landscape. The composition of this work is classic Friedrich—a vertical tree silhouetted against a horizontal landscape, splitting a V-shaped valley in a triangular mountain range.

Notice the tiny shepherd leaning

against the tree. It's as if the presence of man hardly makes a mark on the wide world of nature.

• *The biggest painting in the room is...*

The Watzmann, 1824-1825: Friedrich often painted actual locations in Germany, like this mountain in Bavaria. A strong proponent of German identity, Friedrich celebrated German topography—which he viewed as being as rugged and fierce as the German people. He was part of the rising movement that would later flower into an independent German nation.

This view looks across a craggy mountain meadow to snow-capped mountains rising beyond. Romantics like Friedrich got high on what they called the "sublime," a mystical ecstasy inspired by the power of nature. Here, we feel Friedrich's experience of having his spirit soar upward in its presence.

• *Let's see one last painting as we conclude Friedrich's life story.*

Ruins of Eldena, c. 1824-1825: Friedrich loved to wander through this ruined monastery near his home. The trees overgrowing the eroding arches suggest how nature overtakes civilization, and how time overtakes us all.

Friedrich himself was feeling the effects of time. As he aged, his already eccentric personality settled into extended bouts of depression. He spent more and more time alone, wandering the fields and woods. As a Romantic, he tried to learn the timeless spiritual truths that nature can teach. But just a few years after finishing this painting, Friedrich suffered a stroke. His health declined, and his ability to paint went downhill. At the same time, his style went out of fashion. He died poor, forgotten, and—like the solitary figures in so many of his paintings—alone.

Friedrich's work languished in obscurity for two generations. When it was finally rediscovered, it had an enormous impact. His hazy atmospherics and light effects would inspire Monet, Whistler, and Turner. His lone figures against bleak backdrops were copied by Expressionists—imagine Munch's "The Scream." His meticulously composed patterns of pure color would evolve into purely abstract art—think Mark Rothko.

More than anything, it was Friedrich's spirit that lived on. His antimaterialism inspired many others who would choose art as a spiritual path. His works celebrate the brave individuals who thumb their nose at society's expectations and forge their own path through life.

• *Whew! Let's take a break from all that drama. For a complete change of pace, check out nearby* **Rooms 3.08–3.13,** *which are arranged in a semicircle at the end of this wing.*

Biedermeier Style

These rooms feature paintings in the so-called Biedermeier style (c. 1815-1848), the conservative flip side to Romanticism's individualism, turbulence, and political radicalism. The adjective *bieder* means "solid" and "plain," words that could describe the prosperous and morally upright middle class seen in these canvases, dressed up in their Sunday best. Eduard Gaertner's *Unter den Linden* (1852-1853) shows happy Berliners promenading down the boulevard, past the Frederick the Great statue to the Stadtschloss (the now-gone city palace). Biedermeier landscapes are pretty, not dramatic. The style is soft-focus, hypersensitive, super-sweet, and sentimental. The poor are happy, the middle class are happy, and the world they inhabit is perfectly lit.

• *Then came the democratic revolutions of 1848, the invention of the camera, Realism, and Impressionism...and all hell broke loose. For a quick look at some of the other trends in Europe of the 1800s, head downstairs to level 2. Walk straight through two big halls into* **Room 2.03.**

LEVEL 2
French Impressionists
This one big room is lined with minor works by big-name French artists. Unlike the carefully composed, turbulent, and highly symbolic paintings of the German Romantics, these scenes appear like simple unposed "snapshots" of everyday life.

Pan the room to see works that, even if not masterpieces, are typical of the Impressionist and Post-Impressionist masters. There are Renoir's pink-cheeked girls, Degas' working girls, Cézanne's fruit bowls, and Gauguin's Tahitian girls. Monet's church scene (*View of Vétheuil-sur-Seine,* 1880) uses messy blobs of paint to create the effect of shimmering sunlight. In Manet's *In the Conservatory* (1879), a woman relaxes on a park bench while a man leans in with a comment. At first, they seem to be strangers. But look at the center of the composition: their

two hands, with wedding rings. They're husband and wife, secure enough in their relationship that they are intimately connected without an outward show of devotion.

• *Our tour is over. But if you still want more, it's easy to find a few other highlights on your map.*

REST OF THE MUSEUM

In Room 2.14 are two well-known **portraits by Franz von Lenbach** of world-changing Germans: Otto von Bismarck (Germany's first prime minister) and the composer Richard Wagner.

Downstairs on level 1, 19th-century Realism reigns, with room after room of small brown canvases of everyday German life in the 1800s. **Adolph Menzel** made his name painting elegant (non-Realist) scenes of royal gatherings and historical

events. But it's his Realist scenes that lived on. *Iron Rolling Mill* (Room 1.13) captures the gritty side of the Industrial Age with a warts-and-all look at steelworkers toiling in a hellish factory.

The **sculpture collection** (Room 1.01—at the entrance to this wing) features classical-looking works by the Danish Thorvaldsen and the Italian Canova. The highlight is the German sculptor Johann Gottfried Schadow's delightful *Die Prinzessinnen,* showing the dynamic duo of Prussian princesses, Louise and Frederike.

There. You've toured the 1800s—from spiritual Nazerenes to emotional Romantics, from stuffy Biedermeiers to elegant Neoclassicism, from gritty Realists to the Impressionists and the dawn of the 20th century.

• *If you still have an appetite for more museums—and a combo-ticket burning a hole in your pocket—the next best stop is the Bode Museum, a 10-minute walk away at the northern tip of Museum Island.*

MUSEUM ISLAND

Other Museums

BODE MUSEUM

Connoisseurs (but not most people) will love this classy, uncrowded, eclectic museum of B-list sculpture, painting, and precious objects. You can browse its highlights—a Byzantine mosaic and one of the world's best coin collections—in 30 minutes.

The museum is perched at the "prow" of Museum Island, as if rising up from the river. Even if you're not visiting the galleries, it's free to step into the lavish lobby, under a great dome, where a statue of Frederick William of Brandenburg on horseback welcomes you. With his curly locks blowing in the wind and wielding his general's baton, Frederick put Prussia on the map in the 1600s, setting the stage for his great-grandson Frederick the Great a century later. (It's also free to climb the grand lobby staircase to the charming museum café.)

Visiting the Bode: Cross through the entry lobby, walk straight through the first hall, and step into the "Basilica" hall. From there, go through the door on the left, then work your way back (bearing left) to the corner **Room 115,** with a glittering mosaic.

Ravenna Mosaic: The Byzantine Empire was Europe's beacon of light during the dark centuries after the Fall of Rome, when barbarians roamed the land. Fortunately, the empire had secured the outpost of Ravenna, on Italy's Adriatic coast, offering a vision of strength, stability, and hope.

Imagine seeing this brilliant mosaic in a church apse back then (AD 550). It shows a serene Jesus, who is the very image of youthful vigor. He stands holding a cross in one hand and a book in the other, opened to a comforting message: "Qui Vi Dit Me..." (Whoever has seen me has seen the Father, John 14:9) and "Ego et Pater..." (I and the Father are one; John 10:30).

Flanking Christ are two handsome angels, Michael and Gabriel. All three stand in a flowery meadow, suggesting that they bring a bit of heaven down to troubled mortals on earth. Notice that Christ wears the cross-shaped halo reserved for the Trinity. Above him, in the arch, are 12 doves—a joyous representation of the 12 apostles. Above that we see Christ again, this time in the traditional pose seen in so many Byzantine churches. He's the "Pantocrator," the Ruler of All, seated on a throne, holding a book, and raising his right hand to bless the whole world. He's flanked by a heavenly host of angels, standing in a sea of fire. The angels blow their horns to announce the Apocalypse—when the old age will be destroyed so a new one can emerge.

• To find the coin collection, retrace your steps to the "Basilica" room, cross to the far end, and take the stairs up under the "Small Dome." At the top of the stairs, take the left door and circulate around the wing, finding the smaller rooms on the outside of the building. Begin in Room 241.

Coins and Medals: Browse Room 241 clockwise to get an overview of the collection, which spans 2,700 years of coinage. The "Electrum" from ancient Greece (c. 600 BC) is surprisingly sophisticated—a gold-silver alloy coin depicting sphinxes, Pegasuses, and masks. The chronological history starts in Room 242. There are ancient Greek drachmas (c. 500 BC) adorned with chariots, bulls, warriors, and rulers. The ancient Romans featured their Caesars. The medieval collection is especially strong in German coins, medals, and document seals.

Room 243 picks up the timeline, going from crude 12th-century coins all the way to 20th-century Deutsche Marks, Berlin Wall medallions, and the 21st-century euro. If you haven't had enough, hunker down at a computer terminal to explore the rest of the museum's 500,000 coins. One thing you won't see is the giant, 100-kilogram gold coin from Canada (worth $1 million Canadian)—known as the "Big Maple Leaf." It was stolen in a high-profile heist in 2017.

ALTES (OLD) MUSEUM

For museum completists, there's one more to consider—but if you're museumed out, it's definitely skippable. At the south end of the complex, facing Lustgarten, is the Altes (Old Museum), featuring the rest of Berlin's Collection of Classical Antiquities: Etruscan, Roman, and Greek art.

PERGAMON MUSEUM TOUR

Pergamonmuseum

Of the five museums concentrated on the aptly named Museum Island, the Pergamon is most deserving of your time and attention. In the late 19th century, German archaeologists scoured the Eastern Mediterranean region, unearthing remarkable artifacts of the earliest human civilizations. Indiana Jones-like adventurers like Heinrich Schliemann brought their oversized findings home to Berlin. The best of these are on display in the Pergamon Museum—Germany's answer to the British Museum.

The manageably sized Pergamon lets you peruse impressive treasures from four different civilizations in a couple dozen well-laid-out rooms. Although the museum's star attraction—the gigantic Pergamon Altar—is undergoing a years-long renovation, there are plenty of other jaw-dropping monuments displayed here. You can traverse a long, glazed-tiled hallway, past roaring lions, to the gargantuan Ishtar Gate. There's the hall-sized Gate of Miletus and a floor-sized mosaic from the Roman world. And there's the Islamic collection, culminating in the elaborately painted Aleppo Room, a 400-year-old testament to multiculturalism.

If you're planning to visit the Pergamon and one or more additional Museum Island sights, get a pass and set aside a good part of the day. For more details about Museum Island and the other sights here, see the previous chapter.

Orientation

Cost: €12, covered by Museum Island Pass and Museum Pass Berlin.

Hours: Daily 10:00-18:00, Thu until 20:00.

Information: +49 30 266 424 242, www.smb.museum.

Pergamon Altar Closed: The museum's namesake Pergamon Altar is undergoing conservation and won't be on view for years. In the meantime, the rest of the museum is still impressive.

Reservations and Ticketing Tips: To skip ticket-buying lines, purchase a timed ticket in advance at the museum website. If you have a Museum Island Pass or Museum Pass Berlin, it's smart to book a free timed-entry reservation in advance, as there are no line-skipping privileges with passes.

Mornings are busiest at the Pergamon, and you're likely to find long lines any time on Saturday or Sunday. Bad weather also brings crowds. The least-busy time is Thursday evening, when it's open late.

Getting There: The nearest S-Bahn stations, Hackescher Markt and Friedrichstrasse, are a 10-minute walk away. The Am Kupfergraben tram (#M1, #12) stops are closer—just across the river from the museum. Or ride bus #100, #245, or #300 along Under den Linden to the Lustgarten stop, and walk through Lustgarten park and around the Altes Museum to reach the Pergamon entrance. The new U5 Museum Island (Museumsinsel) U-Bahn stop is scheduled to open sometime in 2021.

Getting In: Part of a multiyear renovation of Museum Island, a new entrance pavilion called the James-Simon-Galerie is now open on the west bank of the island. From street level, standing on Bodestrasse between the Neues Museum and Altes Museum, take the staircase to the left of the Neues Museum.

Tours: The superb audioguide (included) helps broaden your experience.

Length of This Tour: Allow about 1.5 hours for the Pergamon—less if you skip the Museum of Islamic Art.

Special Exhibit: During the Pergamon restoration, a nearby pavilion is hosting an exhibit on the altar called *Pergamonmuseum—Das Panorama* (€19 combo-ticket with Pergamon Museum, €6 with the Museum Island Pass or Museum Pass Berlin, open same hours as the museum, on Am Kupfergraben—directly across from Museum Island; exhibit described at the end of this tour).

Services: Baggage check is next to the ticket desk.

Merkel Sightings: Germany's formidable leader, Angela Merkel, could live in the expansive digs at the Chancellery. But she and her husband (who's a professor at Humboldt University) have long lived in an apartment overlooking Museum Island. You'll see a couple of policemen providing modest protection in front of her place on Am Kupfergraben, directly across the bridge from the Pergamon Museum.

Eateries: Renovation has closed this museum's on-site café. You'll

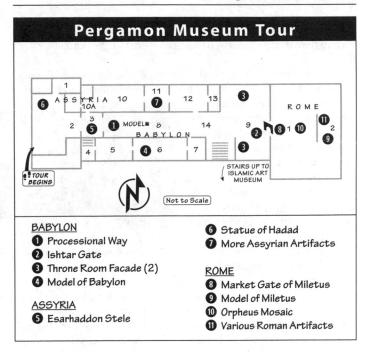

Pergamon Museum Tour

BABYLON
❶ Processional Way
❷ Ishtar Gate
❸ Throne Room Facade (2)
❹ Model of Babylon

ASSYRIA
❺ Esarhaddon Stele

❻ Statue of Hadad
❼ More Assyrian Artifacts

ROME
❽ Market Gate of Miletus
❾ Model of Miletus
❿ Orpheus Mosaic
⓫ Various Roman Artifacts

find basic cafés at the Neues or Bode museums (the Bode's is beautifully set in its free-to-enter domed lobby).

Starring: Ancient wonders, from Babylon and Assyria to ancient Rome and medieval Islam.

The Tour Begins

We'll start on the first floor with the Babylonians and their predecessors, the Assyrians. Next come several over-the-top monuments from the ancient Roman world. Finally, we'll head up to the second floor to see impressive artifacts from the Islamic world, which carried the torch of civilization through medieval darkness.

• *From the ticket desk, enter through a large doorway into a room of statues and turn right to find **Room 8**—a long hallway lined with blue tiles.*

BABYLON, 609-539 BC
❶ Processional Way

You've entered the city of Babylon, circa 575 BC, under the reign of King Nebuchadnezzar II.

Babylon (50 miles from modern-day Baghdad) was the capital of Nebuchadnezzar's vast empire and the world's most glorious city. Rooms 8 and 9 re-create one of Babylon's architectural wonders: a ceremonial highway called the Processional Way that led into the walled city through its main entrance—the Ishtar Gate. To picture how it all may have looked, peruse the model in the center of Room 8.

Now stand at the far end of Room 8 (facing the Ishtar Gate, in the next room), look down the lion-lined hallway, and imagine walking down the Processional Way in all its glory. Trumpets blare, drums pound, and the procession begins. Following a yellow-brick road that was 200 yards long and 30 yards wide, you'd pass fierce lions depicted in colorful glazed tile on your way to the Ishtar Gate. The walls to either side rose

50 feet—if you look up, you can see the blue ramparts that once topped the gate's original height.

The roaring lions symbolize Ishtar, the fierce goddess of love (i.e., sex and fertility) and war. The lions walk against the flow, warning us of the awe-inspiring sanctuary we're approaching. Above and below the lions are rows of daisy-like flowers. The colorful tiles—arranged in bands of blue, turquoise, yellow, black, white—accentuate the horizontal flow of this impressive promenade.

The Processional Way was central to an annual 11-day festival giving thanks to the benevolent gods for the return of spring. King Nebuchadnezzar rode in his chariot down the long passageway, dressed in his finest robes. His entourage and priests carried statues of the deities from their winter hibernation back into the city. Passing through the Ishtar Gate, they would arrive at the temple dedicated to Marduk, king of the gods and patron of the city. There, the statues would be returned to their sanctuary. And Nebuchadnezzar—Marduk's mortal counterpart—would ceremonially "marry" a temple priestess who represented Ishtar, thus uniting heaven and earth and restoring harmony to the world.

• *Promenade past the gauntlet of lions, into* **Room 9,** *for a closer look at the...*

❷ Ishtar Gate

Nebuchadnezzar II made sure that all who approached his city got a grand first impression. His massive blue Ishtar Gate inspired awe and obedience. The gate stands 46 feet tall and 100 feet wide (counting its jutting facets).

This was the grandest of Babylon's gates, one of eight in the 11-mile wall that encompassed this city of 200,000. It was a double wall—the outer wall was 10 feet thick, the inner 20 feet. The Ishtar Gate we see today was the smaller gate for that smaller outer wall. Looming behind it was its counterpart—nearly twice as tall, a third wider, and much more massive. (The museum has the larger gate, but it's too big to display.) In its day, the Ishtar Gate was famous—one of the original Seven Wonders of the World.

Zero in on the decoration. Though the gate was dedicated to Ishtar, it has symbols of other gods as well. The yellow-black horned bulls (specifically the aurochs, a species now extinct) symbolize Adad, the god who brought sun and rain to provide a bountiful harvest. The skinnier animals are mythical dragons, with scaly bodies, curled horns, forked tongues, and fire breath. They combine body parts of the lion, cobra, eagle, and scorpion, and thus symbolize both Marduk and his son Nabu, god of wisdom and writing.

Check out the inscription on the left side of the gate rising halfway up the wall, which (among other things) reads: "I Nebuchadnezzar laid the cornerstone of this gate and had them built out of pure blue stone. Upon the walls are bulls and dragons—magnificently adorned with luxurious splendor for all mankind to behold and wonder."

• *On the walls to either side of the gate are two similar-looking tiled panels. These were part of the...*

❸ Facade of Nebuchadnezzar's Throne Room

Nebuchadnezzar lived near the Ishtar Gate, and these colorful panels once decorated the facade of his Royal Palace, specifically the Throne Room. This is just a slice of the original facade that once stretched 58 yards. The panels fit nicely into the whole architectural ensemble we've seen, with similar-looking glazed tiles in the same colorful palette. They depict palm trees, plus lions and daisies, all framed with elaborate garlands and patterns.

All the pieces in this hall—the Ishtar Gate, Processional Way, and Throne Room panels—are made of decorative brick, glazed and fired in the ancient Egyptian faience technique. Decorations like the lions, which project outward from the surface, were carved or molded before the painted glaze went on.

The colors—yellow, green, and blue (from rare lapis lazuli)—

The World of Nebuchadnezzar II

Nebuchadnezzar II (r. 605-562) was one of history's most notorious fiends, at least according to the Bible. He ransacked the temple of Jerusalem. He carried off many Israelites into decades of captivity in Babylon. He threw three Hebrews into a fiery furnace, forced Daniel to psychoanalyze his weird dreams, built a hubristic Tower of Babel, and became the fallen "morning star"—the metaphor for evil tyrants whom God must punish.

In fact, Nebuchadnezzar II was the ruler whose empire was—for a brief moment in the sweep of history—the queen of the civilized world. His Babylonian kingdom stretched across the Middle East, from Egypt to the Persian Gulf.

Babylonia had only recently thrown off the yoke of the Assyrians. Those wars had left the country devastated. Babylon was ransacked and burned, the temple to Marduk was desecrated, and sacred statues were stolen.

Nebuchadnezzar rebuilt. He was determined to make his capital of Babylon the world's richest, most sophisticated city. He reconstructed the temples and restored all the old gods. Marduk, the city's patron deity, was honored with an enormous ziggurat—a seven-story step-pyramid, 100 yards tall (the Bible's Tower of Babel). Nebuchadnezzar built a grand royal palace, faced with colorful tiles and fitted with a secret underground passageway through town. The city walls were impregnable. Most famously, he built (or maybe merely rebuilt) the awe-inspiring Hanging Gardens, a series of stone terraces landscaped with trees, vines, and waterfalls—one of the Seven Wonders of the World. And, for a ceremonial entryway into this amazing city, he built the marvelous Processional Way, lined with tiled lions, leading to the Ishtar Gate.

Babylon rose quickly, and would fall just as fast. Nebuchadnezzar reigned for 43 years—the brief Golden Age of Babylon. Two decades later, Babylonia was overrun by Persians.

PERGAMON

come from natural pigments, ground to a powder and mixed with melted silica (quartz). The chemicals bonded in the kiln fires, creating a sheen that's luminous, shiny, and even weather-resistant.

The museum's Babylonian treasures are meticulous reconstructions. After a Berlin archaeologist discovered the ruins in modern-day Iraq in 1900, the Prussian government financed their excavation. What was recovered was little more than piles of shattered shards of brick. It's since been augmented with modern tilework and pieced together like a 2,500-year-old Babylonian jigsaw puzzle.

• *You might peek into Room 6 (if it's open) to see the* ❹ *Model of Baby-*

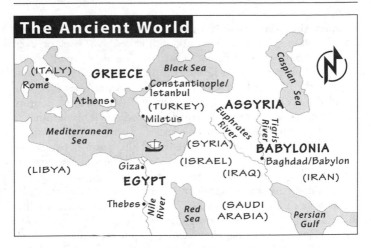

The Ancient World

(ITALY) Rome • **GREECE** • Athens • Black Sea • Constantinople/Istanbul • (TURKEY) • Miletus • Mediterranean Sea • Caspian Sea • **ASSYRIA** • Euphrates River • Tigris River • (SYRIA) • **BABYLONIA** • Baghdad/Babylon • (ISRAEL) • (IRAQ) • (IRAN) • (LIBYA) • Giza • **EGYPT** • Thebes • Nile River • Red Sea • (SAUDI ARABIA) • Persian Gulf

Ion, which shows the temple complex of Marduk (the end point of the Processional Way) and Nebuchadnezzar's ziggurat.

*But our tour is moving on to the next civilization. Start in **Room 3**, with a tall artifact that marks the link between the Babylonians and their northern cousins, the Assyrians.*

ASSYRIA, 900-670 BC
❺ Esarhaddon Stele

This stele, or ceremonial column, commemorates the historical high point of Assyrian civilization, which dominated the Middle East a century before Babylon.

It's the year 670 BC, and King Esarhaddon is celebrating his victory over Egypt. The king is huge, lording it over the two puny Egyptian captives kneeling humbly at his feet—the pharaoh's son (with crown) and another man. Esarhaddon is adorned with his royal fez crown, elaborately braided hair, and ZZ Top beard. He raises his right hand to present a thank-you offering to the gods. In his left hand he holds a scepter, as well as two leashes, to lead his two captives by the neck.

The inscription written across the entire lower half (in cuneiform script) tells of Esarhaddon's cruel conquest: "I wrought a mighty bloodbath," it says. Esarhaddon loved to boast of leveling whole villages, kidnapping the pharaoh's wife and family, plundering Egypt's wealth, and leaving behind pyramids of severed heads. Even the Bible chronicled Esarhaddon's conquest (in Isaiah 20:4): "So shall the king of Assyria lead away the Egyptian prisoners, young and old, naked and barefoot, even with their buttocks uncovered, to their everlasting shame."

With his victory over Egypt, Esarhaddon completed the conquest of the Middle East begun by his grandfather Sargon II (who invaded Palestine) and father Sennacherib (who sacked Babylon and kidnapped their gods). Esarhaddon proclaimed his dominance by erecting steles like this one in southern Turkey.

This stele also marks the passing of the baton between two great Mesopotamian powers, Assyria (in the north, near modern-day Mosul) and Babylon (in the south, near Baghdad). You see, Esarhaddon had taken control of Assyria after his brothers assassinated their father (II Kings 19:37). Esarhaddon began rebuilding Babylon, which his father had plundered. Ironically, within a few generations, a rebuilt Babylon become so powerful that the locals drove out their Assyrian overlords and soon dominated the Middle East.

• For an even grander look at Assyria, step into **Room 2**, where it's not hard to locate the...

❻ Colossal Statue of the Weather God Hadad

The 10-foot-tall basalt statue (c. 775 BC) depicts the popular Assyrian god Hadad (or Adad). He wears a thick beard and a helmet with curly horns (tucked close on either side), indicating his godly power. His (missing) hands likely held his symbol, the lightning bolt.

Hadad was the bringer of rain in the arid Middle East, and this statue was erected as an offering to gain the favor of this all-important god. It was Hadad's storms that fed the Tigris and Euphrates rivers, which irrigated the fields—putting the fertility in the Fertile Crescent. The inscription covering his long skirt is in Aramaic (not cuneiform), as Hadad was a popular god throughout the vast Assyrian empire.

• Backtrack to Esarhaddon's stele and veer left to find **Rooms 10-13**, containing...

❼ More Assyrian Artifacts

Browsing through these rooms, you'll get a sense of Assyrian grandeur. Assyrians were great warriors and ruthless conquerors. But they were also efficient administrators of the lands they controlled. As empire builders who dominated the Middle East for three centuries, they have been called the "Romans of the East."

PERGAMON

You'll see artifacts from several royal palaces, as the Assyrian kings liked to make their mark by building new palaces in new capital cities along the Tigris. There are ruins from Ashur (the oldest capital, midway between modern Baghdad and Mosul), Nimrud (farther north), Nineveh (near Mosul), and Dur-Shurrakin (also near Mosul).

In Room 10, you'll see 3,500-year-old objects from the capital at Ashur, including its Temple of Ishtar. In Rooms 10-12, huge statues of winged bulls (these are casts, not originals) demonstrate the colossal scale and wealth of the Assyrians. There are also wall panels depicting the Assyrian king (with his traditional fez and beard) alongside winged spirits who spritz him with a pine-cone censer. You'll also see panels of the king in his chariot, hunting lions (the royal sport). The cuneiform inscriptions brag.

Room 12 has the basalt water basin of the Temple of Ashur. It's decorated with gods, who wear their obligatory horned crowns.

This reservoir distributed water to the priests for their sacred ablutions. It was built to celebrate the king's new system of irrigation canals.

In Room 13 you'll see examples of cuneiform script—the first system of writing. It was invented around 3500 BC by the Sumerians, who predated the Assyrians and Babylonians in Iraq. The script is called cuneiform, or "wedge-shaped," because it was made not with pen on paper but with a wedge-shaped tool pressed into a soft clay tablet.

By the seventh century BC, Assyria was declining and Babylonia was on the rise. When King Esarhaddon (whose stele we saw) divided his kingdom between his two feuding sons, chaos ensued, Egypt rebelled, invaders poured in, and Nineveh was sacked. Nebuchadnezzar II of Babylon became the new master of the Middle East. Then Babylon fell to Persia (539 BC), which in turn was conquered by the Greek Alexander the Great (c. 333 BC). By 150 BC, Alexander's empire was coming under the sway of the next great civilization—Rome.

• *Return to the Ishtar Gate and pass through it, into a large hall* **(Rooms 1-2)** *with supersized monuments from ancient Rome. Climb up the balcony opposite the gate and take it all in.*

ROME, AD 100-200
❽ Market Gate of Miletus

Flash-forward 700 years to ancient Miletus—the wealthy, cosmo-

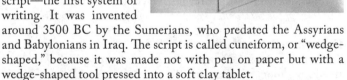

politan, Roman-ruled, and Greek-speaking city on the southwest coast of Asia Minor (modern Turkey).

Dominating this room is the huge Market Gate of Miletus. This served as the entrance to the town's agora, or marketplace. Traders from across the Mediterranean and Middle East passed through the three arched doorways into a football-field-sized courtyard surrounded by arcades, where business was conducted.

The gate certainly makes for a grand entryway. It's two stories tall, with niches where statues were once displayed. The sides project outward 20 feet, framing the gate. Overall, it's a typically Hellenistic style that mixes Greek and Roman features popular around the Mediterranean.

The gate was built around AD 100, likely during the reign of Trajan or Hadrian, whose statues may have stood in the upper story. Peruse a ❾ **scale model of Miletus** atop the balcony. Find the gate on the model: It's the small white part of the wall farthest from the harbor, standing at the entrance to the town's agora.

Miletus was destroyed by an earthquake centuries ago. Around 1900, German archaeologists unearthed the rubble, and the gate was painstakingly reconstructed here in Berlin.

• *In front of the gate, on the floor, are two large Roman mosaics.*

❿ Orpheus Mosaic

The exquisite mosaic floor of colored stone and glass comes from the dining room of a Roman villa in Miletus, c. AD 200. Part of the mosaic features the mythical Greek musician Orpheus. Inside a square panel in the middle, Orpheus sits, playing his lyre, enchanting the animals who come to listen—a crow and a dog, as well as other wild beasts in the frames around him. In stark contrast, in the rectangular mosaic (from an adjacent room in the villa), the animals are wild, and winged hunters track them down. The size and workmanship of these mosaics is a testament to the wealth and sophistication of the people in Miletus, an important seaport as far back as 1900 BC.

• *Opposite the Gate of Miletus is a mish-mosh of...*

PERGAMON

Pondering Pergamon

As the collections of the museum demonstrate, each civilization topples the next. But, in the process, they also learn from and build on the previous one.

The Ishtar Gate of Babylon witnessed the rise and fall of the great Assyrians and Babylonians. Then Babylon fell to the Greco-Romans, who built the glorious Gate of Miletus. When Rome fell, the Middle East rose again under Islam, with caliphate capitals in Damascus, Baghdad, and Constantinople/Istanbul. When the Muslim Ottomans were toppled after World War I, Europe became dominant once again.

In the late 20th century, the Islamic world began to assert itself. The Iraqi dictator Saddam Hussein proclaimed himself the "son of Nebuchadnezzar" and started rebuilding the ancient Processional Way and Ishtar Gate in former Babylon. But, in 2003, Saddam's statue fell to US forces under George W. Bush—"Mission Accomplished." But as Iraq disintegrated, embittered Sunni rebels rearmed under the banner of ISIS, vowing to establish a new Islamic caliphate. To purge the land of pagan idols, ISIS thugs destroyed priceless ancient Assyrian ruins near Mosul and a Roman temple in Syria.

The systematic destruction and iconoclasm of one civilization's cultural treasures by the next wave of invaders makes the Pergamon's collection even more precious.

⓫ Various Roman Artifacts

The curved marble balcony is part of the **Tomb of Cartinia,** an ancient priestess in the cult of Juno, who died near Rome around the time of Julius Caesar (c. 50 BC). The 4-foot-tall segment you see was part of a cylindrical tomb that rose nearly 40 feet. The facade is carved with a frieze of vines, garlands, pitchers, and bowls.

This room also displays interesting exhibits on various places and eras of Roman history.

• *By AD 500, Rome's vast empire had fallen. Europe settled into 500 years of relative darkness and decline. Meanwhile, a new civilization was rising in the Middle East—Islam. Over the next centuries, Islamic culture would take over the territories of the former Assyria and Babylonia, and many parts of the Roman Empire.*

To complete your tour of civilizations, find the stairs in front of the Ishtar Gate and head up to floor 2, which is dedicated to art and artifacts from the world of Islam. (While interesting, if you're short on time this part of the museum is skippable.)

MUSEUM OF ISLAMIC ART

The Museum of Islamic Art contains ceramic tile work, bowls, jugs, carved ivory horns, metal-worked necklaces, mosque lamps, and

PERGAMON

carpets, carpets, carpets. Most of these fine objects are decorated in the distinctive Islamic style: elaborate patterns of intertwined lines, vines, and calligraphy, with only the occasional image of a person or animal. Muslim artists avoided depicting living creatures for fear of creating what the Quran and Bible call idols of false gods. The workmanship is exquisite. It demonstrates how—after Rome fell and Europe was mired in medievalism—the Islamic world carried the torch of civilization.

• *For most, a quick breeze through these rooms is enough. Some may wish to skip ahead to the impressive Aleppo Room (at the start of floor 2, to the right, in Room 15). But if you're up for more, here are a few highlights, placed into the sweep of Islamic history. Work clockwise through floor 2, and watch Islamic history unfold (roughly) chronologically. From the first room (with the map of the Islamic world), turn left.*

Islam's Beginnings (Room 2): Shown here are a few humble but rare objects from Islam's origins in the seventh century. After Muhammed died (AD 632), his teachings spread rapidly throughout the Middle East, thanks to his cousins (from the same hometown of Mecca) of the Umayyad family. At its peak (c. 700), the Umayyad empire encompassed nearly a third of the world's population and stretched into North Africa and Spain. Both secular and religious leaders, the Umayyads (661-750) ruled their caliphate from their capital in Damascus.

The rectangular stone fragment on display comes from a palace the Umayyads built in one of their holdings, Palestine. Its intertwined vines, leaves, scrolls, and stylized pomegranates are typical of Umayyad decoration.

In the year 750, the Umayyad caliph was assassinated, his surviving family members fled to Spain, and the Islamic world had a new ruling order.

Abbasid Period (Room 3): The displayed art of the Abbasid period (750-1258) focuses on the palace-city of Samarra. Various ceramics, carved ivory, and ornate prayer niches (mihrabs) attest to the enlightenment of this so-called Islamic Golden Age. The Abbasids, who made their capital in Baghdad, vowed to make their rule tolerant to non-Arabs and non-Muslims, reflecting the diversity of their vast caliphate. While Europe fumbled in the darkness, the Islamic world flourished, enriched by its mathematicians, astronomers, doctors, and thinkers. Thanks to the Abbasids, we have the works of ancient philosophers such as Plato and Aristotle, whose writings were preserved in Arabic and Persian translations. The Abba-

sids were sensitive to the needs of their own people and the cultures on their frontiers—Egyptian, North African, European, Greek, Byzantine, and Indian.

Art of the Seljuks (Rooms 4-5): The Seljuks (c. 1050-1150) wrested temporary control of the Abbasid empire and moved the capital to Iran. In fact, the Seljuks were responsible for the conquest of Miletus, whose city gate we saw earlier. On display in Room 5 is a blue mihrab, the prayer niche found in every mosque around the world. This ceremonial alcove shows worshippers which direction to face to pray toward Mecca. This one has typical Abbasid faience tiles, decorated with vines, calligraphy of Quran verses (especially along the top), and a geometrical maze (below, with 12-pointed stars).

Alhambra Cupola (Room 6): This room is topped with an awesome domed ceiling, brought here from the Alhambra palace in Granada, Spain. In 711 the Umayyads had expanded their caliphate as far as Spain, making that country Islamic for the next seven centuries. Moorish Muslims ruled from the glorious Alhambra palace, surrounded by lush gardens and bubbling

fountains. This dome is only a tiny slice of the opulence still on display in Granada.

The cupola, carved in cedar and cottonwood, once topped a square room—as it rises, the ceiling morphs into an octagon, then a circle, which breaks up into a kaleidoscope of trapezoids and triangles, with a circular rosette in the center. The incredibly complex geometrical pattern is meant to replicate a starry sky, blended with Arabic letters boasting the Spanish Muslim motto: "There is no victor but Allah."

The Alhambra palace in Granada—the last outpost of Muslim rule in western Europe—finally fell to the Christian monarchs Ferdinand and Isabel in 1492.

Mshatta Facade (Room 9): These monumental walls and towers—120 feet long and 15 feet high—were part of an Umayyad desert castle, one of many that dotted the Middle East (especially in present-day

Jordan, where this one stood). These castles were both imposing fortresses, to assert control of the locals, as well as luxury palaces.

The castle's walls are decorated in a zigzag pattern with rosettes and elaborately lacy designs. Look closely (especially in the left part) to make out a filigreed forest of intertwining trees, vines, and flowers peopled with animals both real and imagined. The design reflects elements borrowed from Sasanian art, the last great Middle Eastern empire before Islam.

Ottoman Empire (Rooms 12-14): You'll see lots of carpets, but no "ottomans"—the upholstered benches popularized by these

Turkish rulers. The Ottomans (1299-1922) rose to power after Abbasid Baghdad was sacked by Genghis Khan's followers, ending the Islamic Golden Age. The Ottomans conquered Constantinople/Istanbul and established their capital there. At their peak (c. 1650), they ruled an empire that included both the Middle East and eastern Europe—even Vienna. Under the Ottomans, carpet weaving became high art. Ottoman rulers often employed Greek (Christian) artists to craft their carpets, jewelry, and fine manuscript illustrations.

• *The grand finale is tucked off in a little glassed-in side room of its own...*

Aleppo Room (Rooms 15-16): The walls of this ornately painted room come from a 400-year-old home in today's Syria.

The owner—a Christian living in the Ottoman-dominated city of Aleppo—was a wealthy trader. He wanted his home to have an impressive entrance hall that would make his guests and clients feel at home. The man did business with people from all faiths and cultures in cosmopolitan Aleppo, circa 1600.

This room is illustrated with motifs from Christian, Arabic, Persian, and Jewish traditions. It was a big paint job—covering almost a thousand square feet of surface area, painted on wood panels. It's impeccably preserved—a rare example of an Ottoman-era home.

The result is a happy mix that suggests diverse cultures living in harmony. The artists painted Islamic motifs, like intertwined vines, geometric designs, and calligraphic quotes from Arabic proverbs. They drew from the Jewish tradition, with scenes of Abraham sacrificing Isaac and quotes from the Psalms. There are Christian scenes—Mary with Child, Salome's Dance, the Last Supper, and St. George. There are secular scenes from Persia—of pashas with their harems or on royal hunts, and even episodes from a famous Persian love story.

• *The Aleppo Room is a good place to end this tour of the Pergamon Museum. The museum offers a once-over of many civilizations across several millennia. For me, it's a reminder that many different peoples—often at war—can also live in peace.*

WHAT ABOUT THE PERGAMON ALTAR?

The museum's namesake and most famous piece—the Pergamon Altar—is being stored out of view while the hall that houses it is slowly modernized. The altar likely won't be back until around 2025.

The "altar" is actually a temple, a masterpiece of Hellenistic art from the second century BC. Modeled after the Acropolis in Athens, it was just one component of a spectacular hilltop ensemble of temples, sanctuaries, and theaters in the Greek city-state of Pergamon (near the west coast of today's Turkey).

When Pergamon was excavated in the late 19th century, bits and pieces of the temple were brought to Berlin and reassembled to re-create the western third of the original temple building. Enormous and nearly intact, stairs lead up to a chamber with a small sacrificial altar where priests and priestesses sacrificed and burned animals, while toga-clad Greeks assembled in awe below. Wrapped around the entire temple was the Gigantomachy Frieze, a 269-foot-long dramatic pig pile of mythological mayhem, showing the Greek gods under Zeus and Athena doing battle with a race of giants. (Naturally, the gods win.)

If visiting the **Pergamon-museum—Das Panorama** special exhibit, it's at a pavilion on Am Kupfergraben (directly across from Museum Island). The main attraction here is a huge, wraparound panorama painting of the city of Pergamon in AD 129 (by Berlin artist Yadegar Asisi). Some of

the original sculpture from the altar, the largest piece of the altar frieze, and digital 3D models help visitors fill in the details.

GERMAN HISTORY MUSEUM TOUR

Deutsches Historisches Museum

While this city has more than its share of hokey "museums" that slap together WWII and Cold War bric-a-brac, then charge too much for admission, this thoughtfully presented facility is clearly the top history museum in Berlin. With 9,000 artifacts, exhibits, documents, paintings, and photographs—filling the kaiser's old armory and spread across dozens of rooms on two floors—the German History Museum offers a sweeping look at 1,500 years of German history.

That's a lot. But with the help of this chapter, you'll breeze through it quickly and painlessly. For a general overview, read this chapter (as well as the Germany: Past & Present chapter, near the end of this book), then browse at will. By the end, you'll have gone from Charlemagne to "Mr. Gorbachev, tear down this wall" and gained a better understanding of Germany's amazing story. Don't get bogged down in the Middle Ages; be sure to reserve time and energy for the fascinating 20th century.

Orientation

Cost: €8, covered by Museum Pass Berlin.

Hours: Daily 10:00-18:00.

Information: +49 30 2030 4751, www.dhm.de.

Getting There: It's immediately west of Museum Island (just across the river) at Unter den Linden 2. Buses #100, #245, and #300 stop right in front (Staatsoper stop). By tram, the Am Kupfergraben stop (for trams #M1 and #12) is a block behind the museum. The nearest S-Bahn stops are Friedrichstrasse and Hackescher Markt, each about a 10-minute walk away. The new U5 Museum Island (Museumsinsel) U-Bahn stop, which may have opened by the time you visit, is a short walk to the east.

Tours: Many of the exhibits are described only in German. Invest in the excellent €3 audioguide. Then, as you wander, dial in the number of any object that piques your curiosity to learn about it.

Length of This Tour: Allow at least two hours for the entire museum; for a shorter visit, focus on the 20th century on the main floor.

Special Exhibits: The museum often has excellent temporary exhibits in the annex behind the main building; these are included in your ticket price—ask when you arrive.

Baggage Check: A cloakroom and lockers are just off the main lobby, to the left of the ticket desk.

Eating: A restful café/restaurant with fine indoor and terrace seating offers a pleasant break.

Starring: The full span of German history, from the remnants of the Roman Empire to today.

The Tour Begins

The entrance lobby is flanked by statues of a professorial Vladimir Lenin and, from the 1930s, the ideal Aryan man—illustrating how a good Nazi should at least feel if not look.

From the lobby, turn left and head upstairs to the first floor, then work your way down. As you tour the collection, stay on track by locating the museum's historic chapters (pillars along the way marked with a date span—for example, "500-900"); these match my headers below. Read my summaries, then browse the exhibits nearby. At the top of the stairs, consider taking 30 minutes for the dry but informative video on German history (with English subtitles).

• *Start your tour by finding the first info pillar—"500-900."*

FIRST FLOOR
From the Beginning until 1918
500-900

"Germany" began circa AD 500, as the Roman Empire was falling apart. Western Europe became a land of ethnic Romans and Celts, speaking Latin and worshipping Christ. But the Germanic tribes to the East *(Ost)* remained *Deutsch*-speaking and pagan for centuries. On display from this era, you may see a medieval Saxon

GERMAN HISTORY MUSEUM

manuscript, and a famous portrait along the right wall (by Albrecht Dürer) of the man who would finally bring Germany into the European fold: Charlemagne.

• *A few steps farther along, the collection continues with...*

900-1500

When Charlemagne was crowned "Holy Roman Emperor" in the year 800, it united much of Europe into a Kingdom of the Franks—and marked the conversion of the Germans to Christianity (see the ecclesiastical art). Charlemagne's symbol, the eagle (see the old wooden statue), became the symbol of Germany on today's coat of arms.

Charlemagne's successors as "Emperor" were essentially kings of Germany, creating the nucleus of the unified German state. The "Golden Bull of 1356" (a copy of which is on display—by the windows) made sure that the Emperors were chosen by certain "electors"—mostly Germans. The Bull also dictated that one of the electors be from far-off Brandenburg—putting Berlin on the map.

1500-1600

The most powerful Holy Roman Emperor was Charles V—see his portrait. He ruled much of Europe during the Renaissance and Age of Discovery. On display is (a copy of) the 1492 globe Columbus used to plot his voyage—round and pretty accurate, except there's no America yet.

Meanwhile, the German monk Martin Luther was shocking Europe with new and radical ideas, sparking the Protestant Reformation. You'll find a number of Luther artifacts, including the Edict of Worms (next to the portrait of Charles V), where Charles V condemned the Protestant heretic, and a Bible translated by Luther into everyday German. Luther's Bible helped to establish the "modern" German language spoken today. There are portraits by Lucas Cranach of his good friend Martin, portraits of other Reformation players, and

even of Katherina von Bora—the ex-nun that the ex-monk Luther would marry. And you'll find some crude political cartoons insulting the Roman Church. What Luther started spiraled into a Europe-wide movement—Protestantism—that led to centuries of turmoil (for more on Luther and his life, see page 351). With Martin Luther, Germany stepped out of the medieval shadows and onto the European stage.

1600-1650

Germany's rise from feudal backwater to modern nation was swift. In the left corner of this section, next to the tapestry, find the small

room with four big paintings called the "Augsburger Labours" (c. 1520s). They give a fascinating glimpse at four seasons of bustling city life in an era when German trade and industry were flourishing. It's a surprisingly cosmopolitan world of burghers and beggars, women and children, Italian dandies, Jews, and turbaned Turks. Germany was thriving, but it still remained decentralized and under the shadow of its larger neighbor, France.

1650-1740

A portrait of King Louis XIV at his peak radiates the power and sophistication of France. Meanwhile, the German-speaking peoples had to deal with an invasion from the east by the Muslim Turks (see the Ottoman tent). When Vienna was besieged in 1683, the city had to be rescued by (among others) an army from far-off northern Germany—Prussia.

1740-1789

You'll see portraits of various aristocrats who jockeyed for dominance in Germany (see Empress Maria-Theresa Habsburg in a blue dress). When Prussia's Frederick the Great reluctantly agreed to an arranged marriage with Elisabeth Christine of the Habsburg clan (see their portraits hanging side-by-side), Prussia's prestige grew. (For more about Frederick, see the sidebar on page 114).

Find Frederick the Great's military uniform—it's a few steps farther along, on the left. Though it looks dressy, this was actually the casual-Friday uniform that this man-of-the-people king usually wore instead of royal regalia. Notice the cut-fingered gloves, so he could pinch snuff. On his chest is the medallion of the Order of the Black Eagle, an honor bestowed on nobles, generals, artists, politicians, and foreign dignitaries into the 20th century.

Browse the nearby displays to understand why Frederick was so Great. He made Prussia a European power and Berlin a cultural capital. He brought the Age of Enlightenment to Germany. He met with the writer Goethe (see his bust) and published Immanuel Kant's "Inquiry" (on display). Science flourished (see scientific instruments) as did music (see early keyboards and a picture of the Mozart family). As new ideas raced across Europe, it came to a violent eruption in France—the Revolution.

1789-1815
Spanning the next couple of rooms are scenes of the French Revolution and the rise of Napoleon. Napoleon conquered the Austrian Habsburgs (see the captured flag), leaving the German-speaking people with one great power—Prussia.

1815-1848
Find Napoleon's hat and sword. In 1815, these objects were captured when Napoleon was defeated at Waterloo by Europe's two new powers: England and Prussia.

Browsing these rooms, you can trace the rise of German nationalism. There are medallions marking Luther's 300th anniversary, a great source of national pride. You'll see machinery (thread-weavers, steam-powered contraptions) from the Industrial Revolution that was fueling Germany. Farther along you'll see a model of an early train—the invention that would soon lace the scattered German people together.

• *Arc to the right to stay on chronological course.*

1848-1849
In 1848, revolutions broke out across Europe (you'll see turbulent scenes from cities like Paris and Berlin). Progressive Germans wanted a modern nation, ruled by the "Constitution of 1849" (on display), but the movement failed. It seemed that Germany could only be united by force, under a dominant power: Prussia.

1850-1871
Prussia took over Germany's destiny when Wilhelm I and his shrewd prime minister, Otto von Bismarck (see their busts), used political wheeling-and-dealing and outright force to try to forge Germany's principalities and dukedoms together. They even

The Kaiser Whisperer:
Otto von Bismarck (1815-1898)

The person who shaped modern Germany more than any other was not a king or a kaiser, but the walrus-mustachioed advisor whispering in the kaiser's ear: Otto von Bismarck. Bismarck held various titles over the course of 30 years (and three kaisers)—from foreign minister of Prussia to the first chancellor of Germany. But sometimes titles are meaningless; Bismarck, who never wore a crown, was one of the greatest political geniuses of all time.

In 1850, Germany was 39 little countries. But then, German industry boomed. In 20 years, German iron and coal output multiplied sixfold, surpassing that of France. German unification seemed inevitable. The big question was: Which of the two largest Germanic states—Prussia or Austria—would take the lead in a united Germany?

Otto von Bismarck, who had served as ambassador to Russia and France, had a plan. And Kaiser Wilhelm I of Prussia (r. 1861-1888) listened to him. The original master of "realpolitik," Bismarck said, "Not by speeches and majority votes are the great questions of the day decided, but by blood and iron." He united Germany as if reading from a great political recipe book.

Bismarck cozied up to Prussia's liberals to win support in parliament. He amassed Prussia's mighty army using unconstitutional taxes. He leaked classified documents to the press to twist public opinion into just the political pretzel he needed.

In his foreign policy, Bismarck mixed brutal warfare and back-slapping diplomacy. He made alliances simply to break them, thereby creating a handy excuse to fight. He started wars with Austria and Denmark to acquire more territory and knock the competition down a peg. Once victorious, he generously made them his friends. He winked at Europe's great leaders, gained their confidence, and proceeded to make them history's fools.

The final step was to acquire the small German-speaking states on the border with France. The resulting Franco-Prussian War lasted only a few weeks, with Prussia winning easily.

Bismarck's recipe for success had created the dish nobody in Europe wanted: a united Germany. By 1871, once-fragmented Germany had become a Prussian-dominated, conservative, and militaristic German empire. The balance of power had been disturbed. And the rest of Europe hoped the unification of Germany would not lead to a large war...or two.

invaded France in the Franco-Prussian War to rally the German people together in a cause. The Germans won, and you'll see paintings of their triumph and the spiked military helmets they proudly wore. In 1871, the German people united, and they waved an eagle flag (on display) of a new nation: Germany.

1871-1890

A huge painting radiates the optimism and glory of the new nation. Dignitaries gather in Berlin's royal palace (which once stood on Museum Island) to announce the opening of the Reichstag. Presiding on the dais (with red robe, crown, and document) is the handsome young ruler, Wilhelm II. He wears the Order of the Black Eagle and bears

the title of not merely king, but emperor *(Kaiser)*. This was, after the medieval Holy Roman Empire, the "Second German *Reich*."

Kaiser Wilhelm II reigned over a period of unprecedented wealth and prosperity. Germany was an industrial powerhouse, acquiring rich colonies in Africa and expanding its military might. Berlin's population surged, and the capital rivaled Paris and London as a cultural center. Find the *Kaiser Panorama* display, with old photos of turn-of-the-century Berlin in its glory, as couples and carriages promenade down Unter den Linden.

1890-1914

Europe seems happy-go-lucky on the surface (with newfangled automobiles and sewing machines to make life easier). But deep-seated political problems are threatening that peace. The elite seems oblivious to the struggles of the working class. By 1914, Germany was a powerhouse, destined for a glorious future.

1914-1918

Germany leaps enthusiastically into the Great War. You'll see the propaganda view and the reality.

1918-1919

The war is over, and revolution and the proclamation of the republic follow. It's a showdown between the far left and the far right as the devastated country is in turmoil.

• *To see how it all played out, head downstairs to the ground floor, cross directly across the lobby, pass the café, and enter the exhibit rooms marked* German History 1918 to 1994.

GROUND FLOOR
20th Century
1918-1925

World War I pitted Germany against France, England, and others. Photos show the grim reality of a war fought from defensive

trenches, where a machine gun (on display) could do the killing of 500 soldiers with rifles. Posters (and a poignant woodcut by Berlin artist Käthe Kollwitz) capture the bitter and cynical mood that descended over Germany. By war's end, Germany had lost 1.7 million men, and 4 million came home wounded.

Europe's victors dealt harshly with Germany, sowing enormous resentment. The Weimar Republic was doomed to fail. The German economy was in shambles (see the pile of ridiculously inflated currency).

And yet, the side room (on the right) shows how, even in these tough times, booming Berlin (whose population doubled in the postwar years) flourished: the cabaret scene (flapper dresses); the development of motion pictures (Berlin was the original "Hollywood"); Bauhaus (the stripped-down architectural style that's still influential today); and impressive ocean liners.

1925-1933

Dueling displays show off propaganda and uniforms from the two poles of Germany's political spectrum: National Socialists (Nazis) and Communists.

Ultimately the Nazi Party prevailed. Their propaganda convinced the German people that they were strong and good, but had been betrayed by a rigged system. In 1933, the Nazis took control of Germany under Adolf Hitler.

1933-1939

Hitler narrowly became chancellor. But within weeks, the Reichstag burned in a shocking fire (see photo)—giving him an opening to consolidate power.

At first, Germany seemed to prosper under the Nazis. They recruited supporters from all walks of life (see Hitler Youth posters, and the closet of Nazi uniforms).

GERMAN HISTORY MUSEUM

The German National Anthem

"Deutschland, Deutschland über alles..." The song first became popular during World War I. In the 1920s it was adopted as Germany's national anthem, along with the colors of the national flag—black, red, and gold.

When Hitler took power, he loved hearing the powerful words of the song's opening verse: *"Deutschland, Deutschland über alles, über alles in der Welt."* The words proclaimed: "Germany, Germany above all, above all the world." But after Hitler's defeat, no one wanted to hear those Nazi-tinged sentiments anymore. They switched the official anthem to just the third verse: *"Einigkeit und Recht und Freiheit, für das deutsche Vaterland!"* Those lyrics celebrated "Unity, justice, and freedom..."

Meanwhile, the country was divided into communist East and democratic West. East Germany had its own national anthem, a completely different song. Then in 1990 came unity, and they all sang the same song once again. A united Germany proudly sings the anthem that ends with the words "Bloom, you German Fatherland." *"Blüh' im Glanze dieses Glückes, blühe, deutsches Vaterland!"*

But under the surface, dissent simmered, and was brutally suppressed—find the footage of Nazis burning books on Bebelplatz, just across the street from this museum. In the smaller rooms beneath the mezzanine, view the propaganda posters designed to train the German people to identify—and hate—Jews and other minorities on sight. These demonstrate how, even early in his reign, Hitler's strategy to scapegoat these groups for Germany's problems was embraced by many of his subjects. The Nazis escalated their atrocities against Jews—the 1935 Nürnberg Laws, the 1938 destruction of synagogues (Kristallnacht)—eventually culminating in the "Final Solution" and the Holocaust. (More on that later.)

To shore up support, Hitler appealed to Germans' sense of national and ethnic pride. He preached about the *Volksgemeinschaft*—a "people's community" of purely Germanic, Aryan ideals. Find the large, wall-sized church tapestry of cutesy German-style houses and common people marching in lock-(goose) step with Nazi-uniformed troops.

The Nazis set Germany on a path of global domination. They were determined to prove Germany's might, hosting the

GERMAN HISTORY MUSEUM

Olympics in 1936 (see poster). Nearby, find the model of the domed building by architect Albert Speer, and ponder Hitler's megalomania. Hitler made plans to turn Berlin into "Welthaupstadt Germania," the "world capital" of his far-reaching Third Reich. The centerpiece would be this impossibly huge domed Volkshalle—950 feet high and able to accommodate 180,000 people. It would squat over the Spree River, just north of the Reichstag, as the anchor of a grandiose north-south axis called the Avenue of Splendors. Hitler's grand plans were put on hold as Germany once again went to war.

1939-1941

At the start of World War II, Germany's Blitzkrieg ("Lightning War") demolished its enemies. But then came several devastating, watershed battles, such as Stalingrad. A small theater shows the propaganda newsreels both sides produced and consumed each week, twisting understanding of what was actually happening.

1941-1943

As the tide turned against Germany, the destruction began creeping back into the Fatherland. The Allies (the US and Britain) began aerial bombardment of German cities, especially Berlin (see the bomb casings and the fragments of a downed RAF bomber, dredged from a German lake).

1943-1945

It became total war, including genocide. Exhibits document the atrocities at Hitler's concentration camps, including registration photos of prisoners. In a powerful room on the right, a model shows the reality of Hitler's grandiosity: a crematorium at Auschwitz (in Nazi-occupied Poland) designed to exterminate Jews. Incoming prisoners were tricked into disrobing and entering a huge, underground "shower room," only to be killed by Zyklon-B gas. Then workers (most of them inmates hoping to postpone their own demise) would pile the bodies into four huge crematoria, which blazed 24/7 to burn the evidence of Nazi crimes. (This same model appears at the Holocaust museums at Auschwitz, in Washington, DC, and at Israel's Yad Vashem.)

1945-1949

Finally, the Nazis are defeated and Hitler shoots himself. Troops from the US and USSR shake hands at the Elbe River, while newspaper headlines trumpet an Allied victory. But more than 60 million were dead worldwide, including 6 million Jews and 6 million non-Jewish Germans. A video shows how totally demolished many German cities were by war's end.

Even before the last shots were fired, Allied leaders had already met at the Potsdam Conference to divvy up a defeated Germany (see the photo of Churchill, Truman, and Stalin). Berlin and

Germany were divided between the Soviet-leaning East and the US-leaning West. Right then, World War II became a protracted Cold War.

1949-1989

A border post marks the "inner German border" between West and East. Exhibits juxtapose slices of life in the two Germanys. The West's economy recovered (see the smart VW bug), while the East's languished (the clunky DDR-era Trabant cars known as Trabi). East Germany remained under the oppressive thumb of the Soviet communist government for decades. But by the 1980s, the Soviet empire was cracking, and the German people longed to reunite.

1989-1994

In 1989, the Berlin Wall—the most iconic symbol of division and oppression—began crumbling. You'll see videos of the celebrations, preserved sections of the wall, and clips of US president Ronald Reagan demanding they "tear down this wall." The Wall came down, Germany was reunited, and the homemade banners of freedom were raised.

REST OF THE MUSEUM

For architecture buffs, the big attraction is the modern annex behind the history museum, designed by American architect I. M. Pei, who is famous for his glass pyramid at Paris' Louvre. (To get there from the old building, cross through the courtyard, admiring the Pei glass canopy overhead.) This annex complements the museum with temporary, often-fascinating exhibits. A striking glassed-in spiral staircase unites four floors with surprising views and lots of light. It's here that you'll experience why Pei is called the "perfector of classical modernism," "master of light," and a magician at uniting historical buildings with new ones.

COMMUNIST EAST BERLIN WALK

From Museum Island to Alexanderplatz

From 1949 to 1990, East Germans had it tough. On this mile-long walk, we'll focus on sights associated with communist East Germany—also known as the DDR *(Deutsche Demokratische Republik).*

We'll start at the statues of Marx and Engels, the founders of communism who had roots here in Berlin, and then walk along a boulevard named after Karl Liebknecht, the founder of Germany's communist party. We'll see St. Mary's Church, which carried the Christian torch through the atheistic communist era. And we'll pass by the skyscraping TV Tower, built by the communists as an exclamation point for their ideology. This walk ends just off Alexanderplatz—once the symbol of communist modernity, now a thriving commercial zone.

Let's embark on a stroll through what was the showcase "downtown" of communist East Berlin.

Orientation

Length of This Walk: Allow about 45 minutes.

When to Go: This walk picks up where the ⌑ Unter den Linden Walk ends. Because this walk has no sights that are important to enter, it can be done anytime and makes for a nice evening stroll.

Getting There: We'll begin at the Marx-Engels-Forum—the park across the bridge from the Berlin Cathedral and Museum Island. It's easy to reach on bus #100, #245, or #300 (Lustgarten stop); these buses basically follow the course of this walk, making it easy to skip ahead or backtrack. The Hackescher Markt S-Bahn station is a 10-minute walk from the start of the walk, while the new U5 Museum Island (Museumsinsel)

U-bahn stop, which may be open by the time you visit, is a five-minute walk.

St. Mary's Church: Free, daily 10:00-18:00, Karl-Liebknecht-Strasse 8.

TV Tower: €17.50, daily 9:00-24:00, Nov-Feb from 10:00.

Eateries: You'll pass plenty of tourist-oriented fast-food joints along this walk. A recommended brewery—Brauhaus Lemke (across the street from the TV Tower)—is handy. And the walk ends at Alexanderplatz, with plenty of bratwurst vendors and other casual eateries.

Starring: Landmarks, legacies, and the severe communist aesthetic of East Berlin.

The Walk Begins

• *To start, find the* **statues of Marx and Engels,** *at the river-end of the big park across the bridge from the massive Berlin Cathedral. The recommended DDR Museum, where everyday artifacts paint a vivid picture of life in Cold War-era East Germany, is immediately across the river from the cathedral (related to but not included in this walk). And around the corner from there (on the left side of Karl-Liebknecht-Strasse, next to the extremely capitalistic Radisson Hotel) is the fun Ampelmann store, dedicated to the beloved symbol of the DDR—its iconic, retro street light. Note that as the boulevard crosses the river, Unter den Linden becomes Karl-Liebknecht-Strasse.*

❶ Statues of Karl Marx and Friedrich Engels

These statues of the founders of Communism mark the Marx-Engels-Forum, a park dedicated in 1986 by the East German government. During the

heady days before the Berlin Wall and the Iron Curtain fell, a half-million Berliners gathered here to call for freedom and an end to the economic and social experiment preached by these two philosophers.

The statues are part of an ensemble of sculptures that tell a story. Follow the plot: Behind Marx and Engels, a relief shows the Industrial Age reality of a cold and heartless world of exploitation. Then came Marx and Engels. But progress toward workers' rights had to be earned—photos on pillars show images from around the world as workers struggle against the forces of capitalism. The happy ending that comes with all social realism is de-

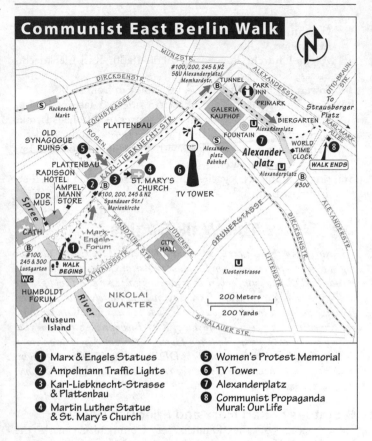

Communist East Berlin Walk

1. Marx & Engels Statues
2. Ampelmann Traffic Lights
3. Karl-Liebknecht-Strasse & Plattenbau
4. Martin Luther Statue & St. Mary's Church
5. Women's Protest Memorial
6. TV Tower
7. Alexanderplatz
8. Communist Propaganda Mural: Our Life

picted in a bronze relief of free-flowing images: a utopian workers' paradise with thankful mothers hugging their children.

Marx and Engels were economists who studied at Berlin's Humboldt University in the early 1800s. They co-authored the landmark *Communist Manifesto* (1948), which ends with the famous line, "Workers of the world, unite!"

Preoccupied with the "class struggle" through history—between the haves (bourgeoisie) and the have-nots (proletariat)—Marx and Engels believed that everyday working people should take control of the means of production. Over the next decades, Marx and Engel's ideas proved enormously influential. They caught on with a Russian named Vladimir Lenin. In 1917, Lenin led the Bolshevik Revolution that toppled the Russian czar and established the communist Soviet Union (USSR). Their motto? "Workers of the world, unite!" Three decades later, Lenin's successor Josef Stalin sent the Red Army into Germany to defeat Hitler and the Nazis.

Life in the DDR

Throughout the Cold War, East Germans had basic security but no freedom. When the DDR was established in 1949, the

Socialist Unity Party of Germany (SED) held all the power. East Germany had no president, chancellor, or prime minister—just the SED general secretary, a reigning puppet whose strings were pulled from Moscow.

The DDR economy became increasingly centralized. The government produced all goods, forcing East Germans to lead cookie-cutter lives: wearing identical wardrobes while eating off identical dishes in identical apartments. DDR tourists all toted the same cameras. The best goods were made in the West—and were smuggled in and sold on the black market. Things that couldn't be smuggled in were usually cheap knock-offs.

Travel was severely restricted. If you were lucky, your family had a *Datsche*—a humble, shack-like holiday house in the countryside. Trips to Hungary's Lake Balaton or Baltic Sea beaches were as exotic as you could hope for.

Movies and TV shows were more propaganda than entertainment, though most East Germans could (illegally) receive Western broadcasts. They'd watch with the volume turned down and hope nobody was listening.

But someone *was* always listening. The DDR had spies everywhere, including tens of thousands of everyday people induced to inform on their neighbors. The Stasi security force read people's mail and observed the most intimate details of their lives using hidden cameras. Public life was filled with suspicion, fear, and paranoia. (For more on the Stasi, see the sidebar on page 76.)

All of this amounted to a life of constant contradiction: A system claiming to be "for the common person" actually did everything it could to make people's lives more difficult.

And yet, when communism ended, the transition wasn't easy. For years, many former East Germans remained "Ostalgic". What they missed was the relaxed pace of life: With no real advancement opportunities, people had ample time to spend with family and friends. Some also pined for the security of knowing they'd always be provided for...albeit humbly.

Today's thirtysomethings and fortysomethings—who were too young to really suffer under communism—embrace symbols of the era, like the *Ampelmann* traffic lights, more out of nostalgia than a desire to return to life behind the Iron Curtain. For most Berliners, the East-West stuff is a distant memory. It may be fascinating among tourists, but locals tend to think about communism or the Berlin Wall only when visitors bring it up.

After the war, the USSR occupied the eastern half of Germany and established a communist state: the DDR.

The statues of Marx and Engels don't look particularly fierce. Locals have nicknamed these two grandfatherly guys "The Old Pensioners," and young people enjoy posing with the duo. Notice Marx's shiny lap, and Engels' well-worn finger.

• *From here, with your back to the river, angle through the park veering left, in the direction of the TV Tower. As you emerge from the park and hit Spandauer Strasse, look right to see the red-brick* **city hall**, *where Berlin's mayor has an office. It was built after the revolutions of 1848 and was arguably the first democratic building in the city. Later it became the city hall of communist East Berlin—giving its nickname, "Rotes Rathaus" (Red City Hall), a dual meaning.*

At the intersection, a cute DDR-era street light will tell you to stop or walk.

❷ Ampelmann: Jaunty DDR Traffic Lights

All over what was East Berlin, keep an eye out for these—affectionately called *Ampelmann* ("traffic-light man"). Even after the fall of the Wall, the figures proved so popular that residents waged a 10-year court battle to keep them from being replaced. And now, they're even beginning to show up in the former West Berlin—perhaps the only East German symbol to gain popularity in the West. The mania for *Ampelmann* is a good example of what's known as "Ost-algia"— a play-on-words describing nostalgia toward the *Ost,* or East.

• *Cross Spandauer Strasse. To your left is...*

❸ Karl-Liebknecht-Strasse and *Plattenbau*

This street is named for a founder of Germany's communist party: Karl Liebknecht, a martyr to the Marxist cause, and reminder of the communist regime.

As you continue walking toward the TV Tower, notice the uniformity of the high-rise concrete buildings lining the boulevard to your left. These are ***Plattenbau*** ("panel buildings"). While the DDR government maintained a few token historic landmarks (like the Rotes Rathaus), their real architectural forte was pre-fabricated, high-capacity, low-aesthetics housing.

These apartment blocks may seem undesirable, but they were fairly popular places to live. Although cheaply constructed, they came with modern amenities like central heating and real plumbing (for example, each unit had its own bathroom), and many even had elevators that occasionally worked. For many, these were far preferable to the much older, more primitive flats in historic districts like Prenzlauer Berg (today renovated and trendy).

While the buildings' exteriors and public spaces are frightfully gloomy, residents prided themselves on creating cozy and welcoming little nests inside. Being invited to dinner at one of these apartments in DDR times showed you the stark contrast between cold, paranoid public life and colorful, gregarious private life. In their own homes, people could pursue hobbies and spend time with family.

• *Head for the old church up on the right.*

❹ Martin Luther Statue and St. Mary's Church

Approaching the church, you see a bold statue of **Martin Luther.**
St. Mary's Church, like the rest of Europe, was Roman Catholic

until about 500 years ago when this solitary German monk rocked European history by kicking off the Protestant Reformation. As he's usually portrayed, Luther stands here boldly looking skyward, with his hand on the word of God.

Luther caused such a stir by simply translating the Bible from Latin into German so regular people could study its message themselves—without the oversight of the Catholic Church.

This statue dates from 1895. Though it survived World War II, it was damaged by shrapnel. Feeling Luther's pierced, dented body and ripped off heel, ponder the deadly power of shrapnel.

St. Mary's Church (Marienkirche), with its prominent steeple, dates from 1270. Under communist rule, religion was frowned upon, as the state was officially atheist. (Many Berlin churches, miraculously spared destruction by Allied bombs, were unceremoniously torn down by the new regime—but this one was left standing.) East Berliners could still worship at the St. Mary's Church, but being openly Christian was never a good career move.

Just inside the church, an artist's rendering helps you follow the interesting but very faded old "Dance of Death" mural that wraps around the narthex (dating from about 1470, the generation before Luther). The message: Death is the great equalizer. And no one—not kings, nor bishops, nor peasants—gets out of here alive.

The church's whitewashed interior is austere, with heavy oak pews. While originally Roman Catholic (like all churches in Eu-

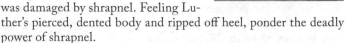

COMMUNIST WALK

rope before the Reformation), St. Mary's Church has been Lutheran for about 500 years. In true Protestant style, the interior is dominated by the pulpit (for Protestants, it's all about the word of God) and the pipe organ (Luther said, "To sing is to pray double."). To learn more, buy the little pamphlet for an interesting self-guided tour.

• *From the church, cross the boulevard and detour a half-block down little Rosenstrasse to find a beautiful memorial set in a park. We'll take a break from communist East Berlin to ponder this poignant monument from Nazi times.*

❺ Women's Protest Memorial

This memorial (built in 1990, when speaking out against tyranny was once again permitted) is a reminder of a courageous and unusually successful protest against Nazi policies. In 1943, when "privileged Jews" (men married to Gentile women) were arrested, their wives demonstrated en masse on this street—the famous "Rosenstrasse Protest." The location was fitting, as this was also the site of Berlin's oldest synagogue (you can see the faint footprint of that old building in the field just behind the monument). Remarkably, these brave women won their husbands' freedom. Note the Berliner on the bench nearby, looking indifferent. Those who understand the value of history are fond of saying, "The road to Auschwitz was built with hatred but paved with indifference." As most Berliners did, he looks the other way, even when these bold women demonstrated that you could speak up and be heard—even under the Nazis.

• *Return to Karl-Liebknecht-Strasse, and gaze up at the 1,200-foot-tall...*

❻ TV Tower (Fernsehturm)

The communist regime is long gone, but it left this enduring legacy. The TV Tower—built in 1969 to celebrate the 20th anniversary of communist East Germany—was meant to show the power of the atheistic state at a time when DDR leaders were removing crosses from the country's church domes and spires. But when the sun hit the tower, the reflected light created a huge, bright cross on the mirrored ball. Cynics called it "The

Pope's Revenge." East Berliners joked that if the TV Tower fell over, they'd have an elevator to freedom in the West. (For a steep price you can ride to the top for a grand view.)

• *Return to the church side of the boulevard and continue walking east down Karl-Liebknecht-Strasse, passing the TV Tower on your right. You'll cross under a railway overpass, then walk alongside a mall called Galeria Kaufhof. Just past the mall, turn right onto a broad pedestrian street. It leads through a low tunnel and into a big square, surrounded by modern buildings. The blue U-Bahn station signs announce you've arrived at...*

❼ Alexanderplatz

Alexanderplatz was built in 1805, during the Prussian Golden Age. Because this was a gateway for trade to Eastern Europe, it

was named for a Russian czar, Alexander. In the Industrial Age, it became a transportation hub. In the roaring 1920s, it was a center of cabaret nightlife to rival Friedrichstrasse. And under the DDR, it was transformed into a commercial center. This was the pride and joy of East Berlin shoppers.

And then, on November 4, 1989, more than a half-million East Berliners gathered on Alexanderplatz to demand their freedom. Protesters chanted, *"Wir wollen raus!* We want out!" The winds of change were in the air; a week later, the Berlin Wall was history.

Today's square is a mix of old and new. Stand just beyond the first U-Bahn station entrance for the best view. Take a 360-degree,

clockwise spin-tour—starting with Galeria Kaufhof, to the right of the TV Tower. In communist times, the Kaufhof department store was the ultimate shopping mecca...which wasn't saying much. In front is an abstract-sculpture fountain ringed with a colorful base that attracts sitters. Next, the tall, glassy skyscraper is a DDR-era hotel, now called the Park Inn. Primark, next door, is a major European discount clothing chain. If you see lots of young shoppers here, it's because of Primark.

Continuing clockwise past the Saturn electronics store and the colorful Kandinsky-esque Alexa building, notice the once-futuristic **World Time Clock,** a nostalgic favorite installed in 1969 that remains a popular meeting point. The clock—topped with a slowly spinning model of the solar system—can tell you the time anywhere in the world. In front of the World Time Clock is a small, recently built police station (the square can be dodgy late at night).

Behind the clock sits the first of two big buildings that pre-date the Nazis and the communists. These are built in the Bauhaus architectural style (circa 1930), with the stern and blocky aesthetic of "form follows function."

You may see **human hot dog stands.** These hot dog hawkers wear ingenious harnesses that let them walk around while they cook and sell tasty, cheap German sausages.

Today, Alexanderplatz is a popular landmark—locals call it "Alex-platz." Trams and trains come and go, dueling drummers and buskers vie for attention, and people crisscross the square on their way to wherever. Alexanderplatz remains a people place.

• *From here, follow the tram tracks, walking out the far end of Alexanderplatz to the left of Saturn. Then hook right and pause at the busy intersection, from where you can see the...*

❾ Communist Propaganda Mural: *Our Life*

You can't miss the Haus des Lehrers ("House of the Teacher"), the communist-era Ministry of Education. It's the tall, glassy building wrapped with a colorful mosaic. The mural, titled *Our Life,* was created in 1964 with 800,000 tiles. Locals have nicknamed it "the abdominal bandage," and some say it's the biggest piece of art in Europe.

Our Life trumpets the accomplishments of the DDR's education system. East Germany, like all communist states, believed strongly in a well-educated populace...at least, about topics it deemed appropriate. The mosaic wraps entirely around the building, covering two floors (22 feet tall). Inspired by Mexican muralists but serving as propaganda for the state, it's a parade of idealist scenes celebrating the occupations and

accomplishments of a peaceful and modern socialist state. It shows a youthful and industrious world, happily conformist to assure a promising future.

The House of the Teacher is at the corner of Karl-Marx-Allee—a grand boulevard that, during communist times, was

The Wall Comes Down

The collapse of the Soviet Union and the DDR was less about pressure from the West and more about the internal failings within the communist system. The world was rapidly globalizing. Isolation was no longer an option. By the mid-1980s, Moscow was warming to the West. Soviet leader Mikhail Gorbachev declared that he would no longer use force to keep Eastern European satellite states under Soviet rule.

In the summer of 1989, Hungary opened its borders to the West—making it impossible for DDR authorities to keep their people in. In October, a series of anti-regime protests swept the East German city of Leipzig, attracting thousands of supporters. Then, on November 4, East Berliners held a rally on Alexanderplatz, with more than a half-million protesters.

All of this persuaded the East German Politbüro to begin relaxing travel restrictions. In back-room meetings early on Thursday, November 9, officials decided they would allow a few more Easterners to cross into the West. The Politbüro members then left town early for a long weekend.

The announcement of the new policy was left to a spokesman, Günter Schabowski, who knew only what was on a piece of paper handed to him moments before he went on TV for a routine press conference. At 18:54, Schabowski read the statement dutifully, with little emotion: "Exit via border crossings...possible for every citizen." Reporters, unable to believe what they were hearing, prodded him about when the borders would open. Schabowski looked with puzzlement at the brief statement, shrugged, and offered his best guess: *"Ab sofort, unverzüglich."* ("Immediately, without delay.")

Schabowski's words spread like wildfire through the streets of both Berlins, its flames fanned by West German TV broadcasts. East Berliners began to show up at Wall checkpoints in droves, demanding that border guards let them pass. But the guards could not reach anyone who could issue official orders. (It later became clear that Politbüro members, who had also seen the announcement, were hiding out.)

Finally, around 23:30, a border guard named Harald Jäger at the Bornholmer Strasse crossing decided to simply open the gates. In a giddy pandemonium, East Berliners rushed into the West, reuniting with family and friends. Once open, the Wall could never be closed again.

named after Stalin. On October 7, 1989, the DDR celebrated its 40th anniversary with a massive military parade along this route. At a podium, under bright-red *40 Jahre DDR* banners, Mikhail Gorbachev stood alongside East German premier Erich Honecker and watched an endless stream of soldiers goose-step by. Surveying the pageantry, Honecker declared, "The Wall will be standing even in 100 years." About a month later, Honecker was removed from power; the Wall opened, then fell; and the stage was set for the reunification of a fully democratic and capitalistic Germany— leaving communist artifacts like the massive *Our Life* mural as a reminder of a failed system.

• *Our walk is over. Karl-Marx-Allee (formerly Stalinallee) continues east toward the fountain in the distance. It's worth strolling along this grand Soviet funded-and-designed showcase if you want to see more DDR Berlin (for details, see page 73).*

Alexanderplatz is a convenient transportation hub to the rest of Berlin. Or you can take bus #100, #245, or #300 back along Karl-Lieb-knecht-Strasse and on to Unter den Linden.

OLD JEWISH QUARTER WALK

From Hackescher Markt to Monbijoupark

Berlin's former Jewish quarter once centered in the area around Hackesche Höfe. This area, with a big synagogue and several smaller, easy-to-miss landmarks, evokes a complicated and moving history. Today, this part of Berlin is also a great place in which to get a taste of the city's thriving foodie, cultural, and arts scene.

This walk combines these two themes—trendy Berlin and Jewish Berlin. We'll also duck into several quintessentially Berliner *Höfe*—interconnected courtyards that burrow deep into city blocks, where much of Berlin life plays out. Perhaps most of all, I enjoy this area as an opportunity to connect with a real-life Berlin neighborhood that's conveniently close to—yet apart from—the touristy historic core.

Orientation

Length of This Walk: Allow about 45 minutes (a bit more if lingering in the New Synagogue).

When to Go: This walk works well anytime—and may be even better in the evening, after you've wrapped up your Museum Island sightseeing, and when restaurants and bars are lively. The downside of an evening walk: The New Synagogue is closed.

Getting There: It's simple—just ride the S-Bahn (or tram #M1) to Hackescher Markt. If you're walking from Museum Island, follow the riverbank behind and across from the Berlin Cathedral, then angle right under the train tracks (takes less than 10 minutes).

Otto Weidt's Workshop for the Blind: Free, daily 10:00-20:00, in Haus Schwarzenberg at Rosenthaler Strasse 39, www.museum-blindenwerkstatt.de.

1. Hackescher Markt
2. Hackesche Höfe
3. Haus Schwarzenberg
4. Oranienburger Strasse
5. Grosse Hamburger Strasse
6. Sophienkirche
7. Auguststrasse
8. Heckmann Höfe
9. New Synagogue
10. Monbijoupark

New Synagogue: €7, Sun-Fri 10:00-18:00, closed Sat.

Services: Otto Weidt's Workshop has a free WC, as do area cafés and fast-food restaurants.

Eateries: You'll pass plenty of options; for recommendations, see the Eating in Berlin chapter.

Starring: Bustling local life, characteristic courtyards *(Höfe)*, and poignant reminders of Berlin's Jewish heritage.

The Walk Begins

• *Begin in the bustling square next to the Hackescher Markt S-Bahn station.*

❶ Hackescher Markt

This delightful people zone—tucked up against the train station trestle—is a lively place to simply hang out. It has ample al fresco cafés and restaurants, and on Thursday and Saturday mornings, it's further enlivened by a modest open-air market, with food stalls, clothes, and touristy items.

The handsome old S-Bahn station is a classic example of

Old Jewish Quarter Walk

the 19th-century city's Neo-Gothic brickwork, called *Backstein* ("baked stone"). It frames off a beautiful space, with artful iron window frames and benches with built-in chessboards—inviting Berliners to linger. Most of the brick archways are filled with restaurants.

Hackescher Markt marks the boundary between the touristy hotels-and-museums zone of the historic core and the more

characteristic neighborhoods of residential Berlin. This is the gateway to the historic working-class quarters, which sits just across the river from the city center, to the northeast. In German cities (with prevailing southerly and westerly winds), the northern and eastern parts of town—downwind of industry—were historically considered undesirable, but they were affordable for the lowliest workers.

Starting in the late 1600s, this district became the core of

Berlin's Jewish community, after Berlin was hit particularly hard by the devastating Thirty Years' War (1618-1648)—sometimes called the "first world war" because of the many nations involved and its high number of casualties. The Prussian rulers needed help rebuilding and repopulating. Their pragmatic brainstorm was to import wealthy minorities who had been expelled from other countries. They allowed 50 Jewish families from Vienna—escaping pogroms in Austria—to resettle in this part of town. Beliefs at the time forbade Christians from engaging in moneylending, a service that Jews could provide. Based here, the Jews were close to the city's commercial center and their customers.

Hackescher Markt got its current shape thanks to Hans Christoph Friedrich Graf von Hacke, a military hero who was promoted to Berlin City Commandant under Frederick the Great. In 1750, Hacke turned the smelly barns and swamplands of this area into a fine market square, similar to what you see today. The king was so pleased, he named the new space after Hacke.

From Hackescher Markt, walk with the train station on your right to the busy cross-street with **tram tracks.** In Berlin, it's easy to lose track of whether you're in the "former West" or the "former East." Here's a tip: Trams were abundant in the East, while the West favored buses and subway lines. Usually, if you see tram tracks, you're in the former East Berlin.

• *Cross the street, turn left, and carry on straight across Rosenthaler Strasse, past the tram stop. You're headed for the entrance to that stately yellow-and-blue building (at Rosenthaler Strasse 40), the...*

❷ Hackesche Höfe

Step inside and explore this series of eight courtyards bunny-hopping through a wonderfully restored *Jugendstil* (German Art Nouveau) building. From the street, courtyard after courtyard unfolds in the typical design of a standard Berlin apartment complex. The Hackesche Höfe is an unusually pristine—and unusually commercialized—example of a *Höfe* complex. This genteel space was built during a genteel age (1907), with artful details and spacious courtyards that were a reaction against the overcrowded, hastily built apartment blocks of nearby Prenzlauer Berg. We'll see other, much simpler examples of Berlin *Höfe* on this walk, revealing that much of Berlin's charm hides behind the street front.

Hackesche Höfe is a fun place to browse. Wander, explore, and do a little window-shopping. Courtyard #3 is a tranquil garden, while courtyard #5 is particularly charming, with outdoor benches.

When you're done exploring, backtrack to the entrance. Standing in the doorway, look down at your feet, where you'll find four brass plaques embedded in the cobbles. These are *Stolpersteine* ("stumbling stones"): small monuments to everyday people who were murdered in the Holocaust. Each little plaque tells a story—in this case, of the Salinger family, who lived at this address. In 1942, daughter Ursula was deported to Riga, where she was killed. In 1943, dad Georg, mom Rosa, and son Gerd were deported to Auschwitz, where they were executed. If you keep an eye on the ground, you'll see many *Stolpersteine* around Berlin—but particularly in this neighborhood, the former Jewish quarter.

• *With your back to the Hackesche Höfe entrance, turn left. Just two doors down (at Rosenthaler Strasse 39) is the funky, ramshackle entrance to another courtyard, with a totally different feel.*

❸ Haus Schwarzenberg

Owned by an artists' collective, this *Hof* comes with a bar, cinema, graffiti-slathered open-air art space (reminiscent of mid-1990s

Berlin), and the basement-level Monsterkabinett gallery (with far-out hydro-powered art). Its Café Cinema is one of the last surviving '90s bohemian-chic bars. In keeping with its anarchistic spirit, the courtyard is named after the self-proclaimed "Free Republic of Schwarzenberg," which tried to carve out its own little statelet between the US and Soviet sectors at the end of World War II. (It lasted about six weeks.)

This courtyard holds an inspirational museum as well. **Otto Weidt's Workshop for the Blind** (Museum Blindenwerkstatt

Otto Weidt) vividly tells the amazing story of a Berliner who heroically protected blind and deaf Jews during World War II. Otto Weidt employed them to produce brooms and brushes, and because that was useful for the Nazi war machine, he managed to finagle a special status for his workers. You can see the actual brush factory with pedal-powered machines still lined up.

Stolpersteine (Stumbling Stones)

As you wander through the former Jewish quarter, you might stumble over small brass plaques in the sidewalk called *Stolp-ersteine. Stolpern* means "to stumble," which is what you are meant to do. These plaques mark the former homes of Jewish and other WWII victims of the Nazis. The *Stolpersteine* are meant not only to honor and personalize the victims, but also to stimulate thought and discussion. In addition, they're a meaningful rebuke to a prewar slur: When

non-Jews tripped on a protruding rock or cobble, it was the custom among some Germans to say, "A Jew must be buried here." The *Stolpersteine* turn this idiom around, creating individual monuments to those who have no graves to mark their unjust deaths.

More than 50,000 of these plaques have been installed across Europe, mostly in Germany. They're made of brass so they stay polished as you walk over them. On each plaque is the name of the victim who lived in that spot, and how and where that person died. While some Holocaust memorials formerly used neutral terminology like "perished," now they use words like "murdered" *(ermordet)*—part of the very honest way in which today's Germany deals with its past. (The word *versteckete* means the person hid for a time.) Installation of a *Stolperstein* can be sponsored for €120; you can learn more about each person's story at www.stolpersteine-berlin.de.

The exhibits are described well (in English and Braille), and there's a good intro video and free audioguide.

A second museum here, the pricey Anne Frank Center, is geared toward visiting school groups and offers almost no history on Berlin itself.

• *Exiting Haus Schwarzenberg, backtrack past the entrance to Hacke-sche Höfe and hook right around the corner, then keep right at the fork to walk along...*

➍ Oranienburger Strasse

This street leads straight to the New Synagogue, but we'll take a more roundabout route to uncover some hidden gems. Oranienburger Strasse is an eclectic mix of local and touristy. You'll pass (on the left) a Beata Uhse sex shop, part of a German chain owned by a Luftwaffe pilot-turned-businesswoman who opened what's considered "the world's first sex shop" in 1962—helping to normalize a healthy attitude about sexuality in postwar Germany. You'll see popular street-food stands slinging Berlin's favorite quick and cheap meals: falafel, shawarma, and *Currywurst*. (The Curry 61 shop is a local favorite.) You'll pass a variety of other everyday shops, including a costume superstore. And, at the next corner, you reach The Sixties Diner, popular for locals who want to "eat American" in a swirl of red vinyl and shiny chrome.

• *With amazing foresight, the street at the corner was named long before the arrival of the American diner. Turn right on Grosse Hamburger.*

❺ Grosse Hamburger Strasse

For 200 years, Grosse Hamburger Strasse was known as the "street of tolerance" because the Jewish community here donated land to Protestants so they could build a church. Hitler turned it into the "street of death" *(Todesstrasse),* bulldozing 12,000 graves in the city's oldest Jewish cemetery and turning a Jewish nursing home into a deportation center.

A few steps up Grosse Hamburger Strasse, on the right, pause at the small fenced park that marks the oldest **Jewish cemetery** in the city. Defiled by the Nazis, there are almost no headstones left, but through the gate, you can see a few tombstones with Hebrew carvings.

In front of the fence is a small evocative **memorial,** honoring the 55,000 Berlin Jews who were murdered in the Holocaust. The

monument is piled with small stones, following the Jewish tradition of placing a stone on a grave as a sign of remembrance, and to prevent the body from being disturbed.

The memorial dates from DDR times. In the waning years of communist East Germany, the failing government grew desperate for international support. Following the USSR's lead, the DDR made overtures to Israel, including the creation of this monument (which originally was intended for a memorial at the Ravensbrück concentration camp in northern Germany, but was installed in this more high-profile location instead).

Berlin has a Jewish population of about 30,000, though few are descended from the city's pre-WWII German-Jewish community. Most are immigrants, including Polish Jews who passed through here after World War II and decided to stay, and Russian-speaking Jews who came after the fall of the Soviet Union. More recently, young Jews from Israel and the US have been drawn to the city.

Just beyond the cemetery (on the right, behind the fence) is a **Jewish high school.** At the end of the fence, over the arched entry, you can still faintly read its name: *Knabenschule für Jüdischen Gemeinde.* This school—like all important Jewish locations in Berlin—is heavily fortified and guarded by police (and monitored by security cameras). The stout protection is also symbolic: Germany, conscious of its history, is determined to protect today's Jewish people.

Across the street, notice the big gap between the two yellow buildings. **"Missing buildings"**—bombed out in World War II and never rebuilt—are not rare in Berlin, but this one has been turned into a thought-provoking memorial: High up on the white walls facing into the courtyard, notice the names of the people who once lived here.

A few steps farther, on the right, a courtyard leads to the ❻ **Sophienkirche**—a Protestant church built on land that the Jewish community voluntarily donated for that purpose in the 1690s, giving this "Street of Tolerance" its nickname. See the info plaque of Martin Luther King, Jr., who delivered a sermon here in 1964.

Just past the church, at the intersection with Krausnickstrasse, look left to see the gilded dome of the New Synagogue, where we'll head soon. But for now, continue straight one more block, passing the St. Hedwig Catholic Hospital (the huge red-brick complex covered in ivy) on your left—further showing this street's historic intermingling of faiths (Jewish, Protestant, Catholic).

• At the end of the block, turn left onto...

❼ Auguststrasse

While outwardly nondescript, Auguststrasse hides beautiful little pockets of Berlin's uniquely artistic sensibility. This is *the* place in town to go gallery-hopping. Head down the street, passing the fun Do You Read

Me? bookstore (on the left at #28) and the first of many galleries (on the right at #61).

A few doors down, the crumbling building set back from the street on your left (at #24) is **Clärchens Ballhaus.** This old/

new, traditionalist/hipster venue has been a Berlin institution since 1913. In the evenings, it hosts ballroom dancing, dance lessons, and a lively courtyard restaurant under twinkly lights. You can peek upstairs into the Spiegelsaal—the Mirror Room—a grand but faded tearoom with dingy-chic decor and crystal chandeliers. For a fun and accessible taste of Berlin nightlife, head back here in the evening: The ground-floor dance hall swings and cha-chas each night after 21:00 (for more, see page 313).

Continue down Auguststrasse, dipping into the galleries and enjoying the quiet, untouristy pace of life. After passing a couple of crumbling facades on your left, you reach a big, red-brick building that once housed a Jewish girls' school and more recently the Kennedys Museum (now closed). This is the spot where **President Kennedy** uttered his most famous quote in Berlin, and of the recommended **Mogg Deli** (the best place in Berlin for a Brooklyn-style Reuben).

• *Just after the former Jewish girls' school, also on the left, is the entrance to the...*

❽ Heckmann Höfe

This classic Berlin courtyard complex is a pleasing mix of residential and commercial. Enter through the door marked *Zur Oranien-*

burger Strasse, then keep going all the way to the opposite end of the block. As you pass through, think about how these *Höfe* were organized, socially. Notice that not all apartments were created equal: The units at the back of the complex (where you entered) are small, with relatively small windows and not much natural light. As you move through the courtyards to the main entrance at the far end, the apartments get bigger and more light-filled. Clearly, these *Höfe* were designed to house different socioeconomic classes in the same residential complex.

· It was believed that, by mingling with wealthy and cultured people from the front, the poorer people at the back would be inspired and empowered to improve their lot in life. The idea was for a family to gradually work their way ever closer to the apartments in the front as they became more educated and found more lucrative work.

This unusually "progressive" attitude—which was fundamental to Prussian society—originated with Frederick the Great, the ultimate enlightened despot. Unlike his contemporary, the French Louis XVI, Frederick believed he had a duty to better his commoners' lot in life. Perhaps not coincidentally, Prussia managed to avoid the ugliness of a homegrown, barricades-and-guillotines revolution. (For more on Frederick, see page 114.)

Enough history. It's time for candy. Working your way through the courtyard, you'll pass a fine inner square (with leafy trees, public seating, a sweet teahouse, and a small theater). From here, you can see the back of the New Synagogue—its dome, and the glass structure that stands where part of the original building stood. Keep going, pausing (just before reaching Oranienburger Strasse) at the **Bonbonmacherei,** where you can watch traditional candy being made the old-fashioned way (Wed-Sat 12:00-19:00, closed Sun-Tue).

Exit the Heckmann Höfe onto Oranienburger Strasse.

· *Our next stop is left, a few doors up Oranienburger Strasse. You can't miss the glittering dome of the...*

❾ New Synagogue (Neue Synagoge)

Consecrated in 1866, the original synagogue that stood here was the biggest and finest in Germany, with seating for 3,200 worshippers and a sumptuous Moorish-style interior modeled after Spain's Alhambra palace. Services were held here until 1940, when the Nazis confiscated the building. It had escaped significant damage on Kristallnacht ("Crystal Night") in 1938, but was bombed in 1943 and partially rebuilt in 1990.

Only the dome and facade have been restored—a window overlooks the vast vacant field marking what used to be the sanctuary. On its facade, a small plaque—added by East Berlin Jews in 1966—reads "Never forget" *(Vergesst es nie).* Today the former synagogue is a museum and cultural center. (For what you'll see inside, see page 58.)

• *The main part of our walk is finished. But if you'd like to unwind, a fine park is just a few minutes away. With the New Synagogue at your back, turn left and walk along Oranienburger Strasse (toward the TV Tower). At the corner, veer right across the street to reach...*

⑩ Monbijoupark

Convivial spaces like this one—busy with locals on a warm summer day—are the essence of today's Berlin. Everybody's out, meeting up with friends and

enjoying a green space in a busy city: sunbathing, grilling, splashing in the children's swimming pool, shooting hoops, or having a drink at the bar along the balustrade facing the Spree River.

This was the site of the opulent, Rococo-style Monbijou Palace, which was battered by World War II, demolished in 1959, and replaced by this park in the 1960s. Notice the suspiciously symmetrical bulge in the park (at the corner nearest the synagogue)—in Berlin, a likely sign that wartime rubble is buried beneath.

Also deep in the park is a popular amphitheater for summer performances. Monbijoupark is the centerpiece of Berlin's thriving tango scene. In keeping with its youthful and international bent, Berlin brags it has the world's second-best tango culture after Buenos Aires.

Take a seat. Relax. Grab a drink and settle in to enjoy it—like a real Berliner—looking out over the Spree and Museum Island. And think about all we've seen on this walk: trendy hangouts, fun-to-explore courtyards, and thought-provoking echoes of Berlin's Jewish past. In a city like Berlin—and a neighborhood like the former Jewish quarter—it just makes sense that all those things can coexist so naturally.

• *From Monbijoupark, with your back to the river, turn left and walk back about five minutes along Oranienburger Strasse. Here you'll find the #M1 tram (which zips up to the Prenzlauer Berg neighborhood) and the Oranienburger Strasse S-Bahn station. Or, from Monbijoupark, you can cross the bridge to the Bode Museum and start exploring Museum Island.*

PRENZLAUER BERG WALK

You can't just see the big sights and say you've been to Berlin. This is a city of neighborhoods—of fierce local pride and funky one-off businesses. And to experience that essence of Berlin, one of the best neighborhoods to visit is Prenzlauer Berg (PRENTS-low-er behrk), just north of the historic core.

Prenzlauer Berg is Berlin's Brooklyn. It has its own proud identity as a huge and fascinating city-within-a-city (pop. 165,000). It grew like crazy in the late 19th century, when newly unified Germany was on the rise, Berlin was industrializing, and housing was needed for the influx of labor from the countryside. It was spared the worst of WWII devastation, but grew dilapidated under the communists. After the fall of the Wall, many locals fled to a better life in the West—vacating their flats and opening the door (literally) to a generation of squatters, students, artists, tree huggers, and alternative-lifestyle idealists who remade the neighborhood in their own image. Years of rent control kept things affordable for its bohemian inhabitants and its remaining working-class residents.

And more recently, Prenzlauer Berg has continued to evolve. Landlords are now free to charge what the market will bear, and the vibe is changing. As hipsters grow up and get real jobs, many are staying put—happy to push their designer baby carriages through Prenzlauer Berg's inviting parks. Other longtime residents, who cling to their bohemian ways, are finding themselves priced out.

This walk isn't about sightseeing. There's barely a museum or a landmark here worth going out of your way for. Rather, it's about the past, present, and future of this quintessentially Berlin neighborhood. Prenzlauer Berg is a great place to spend the night, to have a meal, to go shopping, or simply to explore.

Orientation

Length of This Walk: Allow 1.5 hours, or more if you plan to visit the Everyday Life in the DDR museum.

When to Go: This walk works anytime. It could be especially pleasant on a warm evening, when locals are out enjoying their neighborhood.

Getting There: Ride the U2 to Senefelderplatz.

Everyday Life in the DDR: Free, Tue-Sun 10:00-18:00, Thu until 20:00, closed Mon.

Berlin Wall Memorial: Free; outdoor areas accessible 24 hours daily; Visitors Center and Documentation Center open Tue-Sun 10:00-18:00, closed Mon, memorial chapel closes at 17:00.

Services: You'll find free WCs at the Kulturbrauerei, Everyday Life in the DDR museum, and Prater beer garden.

Eateries: Prenzlauer Berg is packed with eateries; for my recommendations—most of which are on or near this walk—see the Eating in Berlin chapter.

Starring: Historic apartment blocks, leafy squares, pierced and tattooed parents, and hipster cafés and boutiques in Berlin's most inviting residential neighborhood.

PRENZLAUER BERG WALK

The Walk Begins

• *Our walk begins near the boundary between Prenzlauer Berg and the central Mitte district, at the Senefelderplatz U-Bahn stop. Exit the U-Bahn toward* Schönhauser Allee/Schwedter Strasse/Metzer Strasse. *At the top of the stairs, turn right, cross the street, walk toward the TV Tower, and pause at the corner. You're in the area called...*

❶ Senefelderplatz

Welcome to Prenzlauer Berg. This sprawling neighborhood has several smaller sub-areas (like Senefelderplatz), each with its own character. On this walk, we'll hopscotch around Prenzlauer Berg, checking out landmarks and sampling various slices of Berlin life.

Looking downhill, it's clear that Prenzlauer Berg really is a *Berg* ("mountain"—er, maybe just a hill). While the city center of Berlin is flat, Prenzlauer Berg was a forested hill on the outskirts. Today, part of Prenzlauer Berg's appeal is how well preserved it is—just beyond the core, and therefore largely untouched by WWII bombs or heavy-handed DDR developers.

As we explore this neighborhood, keep an eye out for the easy-to-miss bike lanes—sometimes painted red or simply brick lined—which are heavily used. Be warned: Pedestrians reading

PRENZLAUER BERG WALK

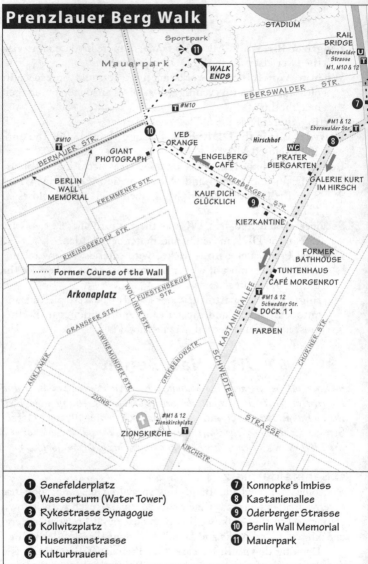

Prenzlauer Berg Walk

STADIUM

RAIL BRIDGE

Eberswalder Strasse
M1, M10 & 12

Sportpark

Mauerpark

WALK ENDS

EBERSWALDER STR.

T #M10

#M1 & 12
Eberswalder Str.

VEB ORANGE

Hirschhof

WC

PRATER BIERGARTEN

ENGELBERG CAFÉ

GALERIE KURT IM HIRSCH

BERNAUER STR.

T #M10

GIANT PHOTOGRAPH

ODERBERGER STR.

KAUF DICH GLÜCKLICH

BERLIN WALL MEMORIAL

KREMMENER STR.

KIEZKANTINE

RHEINSBERGER STR.

······ Former Course of the Wall

Arkonaplatz

WÖLLINER STR.

FÜRSTENBERGER STR.

FORMER BATHHOUSE

TUNTENHAUS

CAFÉ MORGENROT

KASTANIENALLEE

T #M1 & 12
Schwedter Str.

DOCK 11

FARBEN

GRANSEER STR.

SWINEMÜNDER STR.

GRIEBENOWSTR.

CHORINER STR.

ANKLAMER STR.

ZIONS-

SCHWEDTER

#M1 & 12
Zionskirchplatz

ZIONSKIRCHE T

STRASSE

KIRCHSTR.

① Senefelderplatz
② Wasserturm (Water Tower)
③ Rykestrasse Synagogue
④ Kollwitzplatz
⑤ Husemannstrasse
⑥ Kulturbrauerei
⑦ Konnopke's Imbiss
⑧ Kastanienallee
⑨ Oderberger Strasse
⑩ Berlin Wall Memorial
⑪ Mauerpark

their guidebooks who absentmindedly wander into these lanes are given no quarter.

• *Turn with your back to busy Schönhauser Allee and walk two blocks along Metzer Strasse through a sleepy residential area. At Strassburger Strasse, turn left and walk toward the park with a big mound in the middle. As you walk, notice the original Prenzlauer Berg homes on the right side of the street, and the modern-style building on the left.*

Soon you'll reach the park known as...

PRENZLAUER BERG WALK

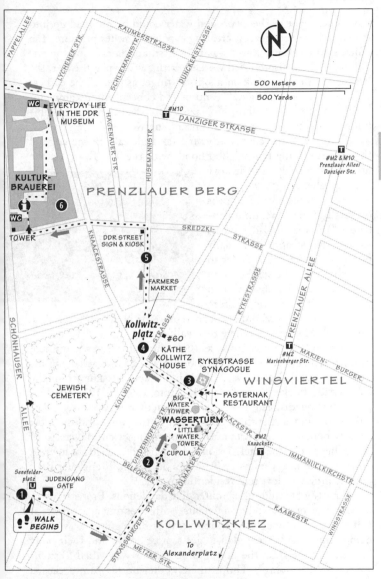

❷ Wasserturm (Water Tower)

This mound covers a series of large reservoirs that provided water to the fast-growing district of Prenzlauer Berg in the late 19th century. Jog left to find the staircase that takes you all the way to the top of the mound. Up top, the red-brick structure in the middle of the mound is the cupola of a huge, earthenware dome that covers the subterranean reservoirs. This waterworks intentionally sits on the highest spot in the city—and water could be pumped up into the two big towers nearby, creating even more water pressure. The taller, skinnier water tower was built first, and later came the fatter one—which also housed workers at this water plant. Later, the Wasserturm cellars took on a sinister tinge, as one of the earliest sites of Hitler's *"Wildes-KZ"* (improvised concentration camps for political enemies)—before the Nazis established their more ambitious and organized concentration camp network.

Stand with the cupola at your back and walk to the edge of the hill, surveying the neighborhood (with the TV Tower on the horizon). Consider the history of Prenzlauer Berg:

This forested area was originally called Windmühlenberg—"Windmill Hill." Later, it was the location for many breweries, since it was easier to dig cellars into the solid ground here than in the shallow and mucky Mitte district. From here, barrels of beer would be loaded onto the Nordbahn train line (in today's Mauerpark, where this walk ends).

By the late 19th century, as the capital of the newly unified, modern state of Germany (1871), Berlin was an industrial engine. Factories and railroads were being built, and peasants from the countryside flocked here for work. From 1860 to 1910, Berlin's population quadrupled from a half-million to over two million. For a time, Berlin was the third-largest city in the world and the most densely populated in Europe. In Germany, most cities' version of "the other side of the tracks" is on the north and east side of town—downwind of heavy industry. And here in Berlin, Prenzlauer Berg quickly grew as a low-rent residential quarter.

Apartment buildings sprouted like dandelions. Property owners were in a hurry to take on tenants—often renting apartments at a discount even though the extremely slow-drying mortar was still damp. The tenants were glad to get a price break, and their body heat helped speed up the drying process (this was called *Trockenwohnen*—"dry living"). Unfortunately, the mortar fumes caused severe health problems.

Prenzlauer Berg quickly became congested. People lived in almost Dickensian conditions, with many residents crowded into each apartment. To save money, tenants might take on a *Schlafbursche*—someone who worked the night shift and would sublet your bed to sleep in during the day ("the sharing economy," Airbnb-style, well before its time).

With so many people living in such close quarters, fire was a big threat. Looking out over the skyline, notice the uniformity of building heights—they rarely exceed 70 feet, because that's how high the fire department's ladders could reach (the Berlin government decreed this maximum height in the 1860s).

• *Now that you have the big picture, head to the taller, skinnier water tower, go down the stairs, and pass a playground where you may see children from a nearby "children's garden" (kindergarten). At the curb, bear left and carry on past the big water tower, to the far end of the park. Across the way, walk 30 yards or so up the pretty, broad street called Rykestrasse. On the left side of this street is the...*

❸ Rykestrasse Synagogue

Notice the substantial barriers jutting out in front of a red-brick building. This is a synagogue—built in 1904, and one of a hand-ful that still exist in Ber-lin. While it looks small from the outside, this is Germany's largest sur-viving synagogue—with an original capacity for 2,000 worshippers. Step up to the black gate and see the front door with the glittering Ten Command-ments above it.

It's typical for synagogues to be set back from the street like this—hiding in a big courtyard and camouflaged to blend in with the other houses on the street. As it turns out, this is what helped save this synagogue. On Kristallnacht ("Crystal Night," November 9, 1938), in a modern-day pogrom, anti-Semitic government agents and civilians smashed and set fire to synagogues all over Germany. In most cases, fire departments simply let them burn to the ground. But here at Rykestrasse, the burning synagogue put the surrounding non-Jewish homes in jeopardy, so the fires were extinguished. The synagogue remains a place for worship, an active cultural center, and school. Like all Jewish sites in Berlin, it has a strong police presence.

• *Head back out toward the Wasserturm and turn right, passing Paster-nak Restaurant. Continue roughly straight along Knaackstrasse. After one short block, you emerge at...*

❹ Kollwitzplatz

This square is named for the artist **Käthe Kollwitz** (1867-1945), who lived in a building that stood on your right (currently #56A, with the wide blue stripe). Kollwitz—a printer and sculptor—lived through tumultuous times. She lost a son in World War I and a grandson in World War II. Her husband ran a medical office, where Käthe witnessed an almost constant wartime stream of sick and downtrodden citizens. Her work is, understandably, reflective of the trauma of her era. Kollwitz's most famous work is the *pietà* she sculpted for the Neue Wache on Unter den Linden, Germany's primary monument to lives lost to fascism. For a more intimate look at Kollwitz's work and life, visit the small but excellent museum (described on page 86) devoted to her near the Ku'damm, in Western Berlin (notice the ad for this with her self-portrait on the street corner).

A few doors down from Kollwitz's former house, at **#60,** you can read some of this building's history into its current state. First, notice the two little doors flanking the main entrance—still marked with the names of the businesses that once occupied them (*H. Weigand* and *Restauration*). Finely crafted medallions are still visible over those doors. At the base of the arch, notice the bulbous barriers protecting the corners—designed to prevent horse carriages from scuffing the walls when they came and went out of the courtyard. But like much of Prenzlauer Berg, this house has clearly been renovated quite recently. Looking up, you can see the date *9 Nov 1989* and the word *Freiheit* (freedom), commemorating the fall of the Berlin Wall.

Despite its cramped heyday in the late 19th and early 20th centuries, and its post-DDR stint as the domain of squatters (more on that later), Prenzlauer Berg has become one of Berlin's vibrant and youthful neighborhoods.

Cross the street into the park, turn right, and hang out for a moment by the big, seated sculpture of Käthe Kollwitz and (just to

the right) the lively playground. Berlin is a city of small sub-neighborhoods called *Kieze*. Each *Kiez* ("keets") is just a few square blocks, named for a nearby landmark (for more on *Kieze,* see the sidebar on page 245). In this case, you're in the heart of the Kollwitzkiez—the poster child for the pros and cons of gentrification. Look around. Do you see lots of designer strollers? Well-coiffed, latte-sipping young parents? Dapperly dressed toddlers? Kollwitzplatz is the epicenter of Prenzlauer Berg's über-wealthy yuppie scene. A popular satirical cartoon strip—*Die Müt-ter vom Kollwitzplatz*—lampoons exactly this scene. (Prenzlauer Berg is also ground zero for a major baby boom. Count how many strollers you see on the rest of this walk—I'm betting on double digits.)

Class stratification is a huge preoccupation among Ber-liners. Over the last decade, several neighborhoods—like the Kollwitzkiez—have swung from seedy-but-affordable to gentri-fied-and-overpriced...sometimes in a matter of months. Today, a small apartment in this area will cost up to €2,000 per month—if you can find one. While that may seem cheap by London or Paris standards, keep in mind that a decade ago, Prenzlauer Berg was a bohemian paradise, where creative free spirits could afford to live dirt cheap while pursuing their interests and maybe working a little on the side. Now these people are being priced out by *die Mütter vom Kollwitzplatz* and being forced to move farther and farther into the suburbs—bringing with them lots of resentment about the changing face of Berlin.

• *Exit the park to Käthe Kollwitz's left, cross the street, and jog left. Go down...*

❺ Husemannstrasse

While Prenzlauer Berg largely survived World War II, it fell into disrepair under the communists. (Cynical East Berliners would joke, "The DDR is really civilized—they create ruins without using weapons.") In 1987, East and West Berlin both celebrated the 750th anniversary of the city's founding, and the DDR government had the street spruced up—restoring it to its original, circa-1900 glory.

Stroll along the left side of the street, enjoying the fine little details. At #9, decorative heads look down—facing a green well-head. This dates from before there was indoor plumbing. See the glass in the street? That gar-goyle spout makes this a nasty spot to park. Look for flagpole holders by some doors—dating from a time when you were re-quired to fly the commu-

nist DDR flag for holidays like the First of May.

Also along here, notice the typical arrangement of Prenzlauer Berg homes: The ground floor was generally for shops and work-shops (often tucked far back in courtyards—we'll see good exam-ples of these later). Notice that the first floor up has much higher ceilings and bigger windows—this *belle-etage* (also called *piano nobile*—"beautiful" or "noble" floor) was by far the most desirable and expensive. The higher up, and the farther back in the building, the smaller the windows—servants often lived in the top-back parts of the courtyards, with the most stairs and lowest ceilings.

Near the end of the block (at #15, on the left), you'll see where those 1987 DDR restorers cheaped out. Looking up, notice that only the first story was painted, while the rest was left dilapidated.

At the intersection with Sredzkistrasse, notice the old-timey street signs, with the Berlin bear—also dating from that 1987 remodel. On the round poster kiosk (invented in Berlin for posting ads), notice the emergency telephone numbers for police, fire department, and Red Cross.

• *Turn left on Sredzkistrasse and walk to the big, yellow, castle-like building.*

❻ Kulturbrauerei

Remember that Prenzlauer Berg was once a wooded hill with dozens of breweries—including this one, the Schultheiss-Brauerei. By the 1920s, this was one of the largest breweries in the world. World War II put an end to that, as Nazis confiscated the brewery, turned it into a factory for the Wehrmacht (armed forces), and, in the closing days of war, barricaded themselves within the brewery grounds. Today the entire site has been renovated to maintain its historic buildings and to provide a venue for the cultural transformation of Prenzlauer Berg.

Head up the stairs just past the smokestack, step through a round gate into the main courtyard, and stroll all the way through

to the far end. You'll see a cinema, several small theater and music venues (Frannz Club and Alte Kantine are local favorites; the Haus für Poesie has poetry readings), and various shops, cafés, and restaurants—all wrapped in a 19th-century, brick-industrial shell, with much of the original signage  intact. On Sundays, you'll find a trendy street-food market here (12:00-18:00), and in December, it plays host to a Christmas market. On the left, notice the Ramba Zamba theater—an acclaimed venue, with productions (in German) performed by people with and without disabilities.

Opposite Ramba Zamba, in the corner passage of the courtyard, is the entrance to the **Everyday Life in the DDR** museum—a concise look at East German lifestyles. For more on this museum, see page 61.

• *Continue through the passage past the museum. Turn left, then left again around the corner onto Danziger Strasse, toward the green rail bridge. Cross the street, hook left, and walk directly under the bridge to reach...*

❼ Konnopke's Imbiss

If you have yet to try Berlin's most famous dish—*Currywurst* (sausage smothered in curry ketchup)—now's your chance. Konnopke's

is a local favorite, not just because they grill up a mean *Currywurst*, but also because of their long heritage. Konnopke's has been around since 1930 and remained family operated even through DDR times...a rare feat. Back then, opportunities to eat out were rare, so people would enjoy gathering here, under the railroad tracks, to down a sausage and meet up with friends. And they still do. In fact, after the stand was demolished in 2010 during roadwork, Berliners rioted—and Konnopke's was rebuilt in this slick, glass-and-steel hut.

Their window display offers a handy visual orientation to a variety of German meats: *Krautwurst, Knacker, Bockwurst,* and *Bratwurst* (subtle variations on grilled sausages); *Paar Wiener* (a pair of weenies); *Chili Krakauer* (spicy sausage); *Geflügelspiess* (chicken skewers); and *Bulette* (a classic Berlin dish—basically a huge meatball, like a round hamburger). They even have a vegan *Currywurst...* this *is* Prenzlauer Berg, after all.

• *With your back to Konnopke's, cross the street and proceed to the smaller street, which angles to the left. This is...*

❽ Kastanienallee

This delightful drag is the essence of today's Prenzlauer Berg—with a fun and lively variety of restaurants, shops, and residences. Lo-

cals have nicknamed this "Casting Alley"—this is where Prenzlauer Berg's fashionable residents go to see and be seen. We'll stroll the most colorful stretch of Kastanienallee, then double back to another fine street that leads to the end of our walk.

Along here, notice the abundance of tempting eateries, dishing up every type of cuisine. While I've recommended some specific restaurants in the Eating in Berlin chapter, you almost can't go wrong getting a bite or drink along this stretch.

A few steps down Kastanienallee on the right, notice **Prater Biergarten**—Berlin's oldest beer garden. Step under the gate and explore, passing a huge bicycle parking lot (a must in this bike-happy city). Deep in the beer garden, amid the trees and the tables, you get the feeling of what this place must have been like when it opened in 1837—back when it was in the middle of a forest. Workers, soldiers, and servants would escape the city to drink, hang out, and fool around in the woods. Prater Biergarten is such a treasured landmark that the surrounding apartment blocks were built around it rather than disturb it.

Back out on Kastanienallee, keep heading down the street. At #12, on the right, see if **Galerie Kurt im Hirsch** is open (it has very short hours—usually Sat-Sun 14:00-17:00). This is the most venerable of Prenzlauer Berg's funky art collectives. Venturing back through a series of dilapidated old courtyards takes you back to the bohemian vibe of the 1990s.

Cross to the left side of Kastanienallee. At Oderberger Strasse, look left to see a fine old Neo-Renaissance building with pretty gables. This was built in 1902 as a **public bathhouse** *(Volksbadeanstalt)*. Remember how crowded Prenzlauer Berg apartments were back then? On top of the tight conditions, most people didn't even have private bathrooms. Buildings came equipped with an *Etagenklo*—a shared toilet on the stairwell connecting floors. And if you wanted to bathe, you had to go to a public bathhouse, such as this one. Like much of Prenzlauer Berg, it fell into disrepair, and for decades it was used only as an occasional venue for concerts. But the building was recently completely restored and now houses the recommended Hotel Oderberger, a restaurant, and—as in the old days—a shallow swimming pool in a beautiful hall (you can step into the reception and peek into the pool).

Continue down Kastanienallee. A half-block farther, on the left at #86, you can't miss the **Tuntenhaus** ("Drag Queen House")—with a ramshackle exterior and provocative, old-school-Prenzlauer Berg messages spelled out in big silver letters: *Kapitalismus zerstört tötet* ("Capitalism destroys and kills"). During the post-DDR but pregentrification period—in the 1990s—Prenzlauer Berg was a hotbed for squatters, including the drag queens *(Tunten)* who lived at this address. (For more on the squatting lifestyle, see the sidebar.) Now legal, the Tuntenhaus maintains its creative and collective vibe. Next door, the **Café Morgenrot** ("Red Dawn") is also operated by an artists' collective, with coffee, cocktails, vegan goodies, and weekend punk concerts in the cellar.

Continuing down Kastanienallee, you'll pass **Dock 11**—a renowned modern-dance school and studio, which attracts performers from all over Germany. They're very active in the community (offering, for example, children's dance classes) and often present high-quality, cutting-edge dance performances (look for these advertised at the entrance, or check www.dock11-berlin.de). Step into the graffitied, ramshackle courtyard, and poke around.

Next door, at #77, is a green building marked **Farben.** Its short stature (just three stories) is a sign that this is one of Prenzlauer

Berg's oldest surviving buildings (dating from the 1850s). Today it houses the tiny Lichtblick art house cinema. Being discreet—people live here—walk deep back into this building's courtyard to see how Prenzlauer Berg housing complexes are designed: a series of courtyards broken up by high-density housing. At the far end is a little *Keramik Werkstatt*—evocative of the busy little workshops that would traditionally be buried far from the street.

In the late 1980s, these courtyards became a cradle of anti-DDR sentiment. Prenzlauer Berg was run down, and the authorities proposed tearing the neighborhood down and replacing it with more efficient and modern concrete block housing instead. But locals had a respect for this area's history and fought to keep the original architecture. They'd take ownership of courtyards like this one, chipping away at the concrete and planting grass and gardens—a process called *Hofbegrünung* ("courtyard greening-up"...urban gardening before it was hip). It was a literal "grassroots movement" of opposition to the centrally planned communist aesthetic (which hated the idea of people making their own decisions)—people were reclaiming their "shared property" from a government they didn't trust. As the DDR's grip slipped, courtyards became gathering places for artists, musicians,

Squatters

When the Wall came down in 1989, many East Berliners packed up and set out to create a new life in the West—leaving behind deserted apartments. Meanwhile, students and artistic types flocked the other way, coming from all over Germany to live in an exciting and creative city in transition.

For a year or two after 1989, it was pretty much anything-goes in East Berlin. People would arrive in Prenzlauer Berg, choose a building, go door to door, find an apartment that appeared empty, move in, change the locks...and it was theirs. If you wanted to make it official (rather than be a "squatter"), after a certain time had passed you could offer to pay rent at the local housing authority. They'd write up a contract and you'd be legal.

This wasn't easy living: Prenzlauer Berg was a shamble, and the apartments were old. For heat, you'd have to haul coal up several flights of stairs, passing the building's shared toilet on the stairwell. It was rare to have a telephone—most people waited in line to use the corner pay phone. (One Prenzlauer Berg resident from that time told me his apartment not only had a phone, but one that allowed free long-distance calls to anywhere in the world. He never got a bill, so he just kept on calling—until the day the phone simply stopped working.)

Over time, you could make small improvements to "your" property and really make it your own. There's even a special expression in German—*instand besetzen*—that means, essentially, "squatting in a house while you repair it." To further incentivize people to fix up these desperately dilapidated buildings, for a brief period in the early 1990s the city offered *Selbsthilfe* ("self-help"). That is, if you did the work yourself, the city would pay about half for the materials.

And so, while squatting is conventionally thought of as a social evil, in post-DDR Berlin, it was an essential component of the city's recovery. It's one of those "social ills"—like graffiti—that just seems to fit Berlin to a T.

and rabble-rousing neighbors. (Another such gathering place was churches. For more on the role of churches—especially the nearby Zionskirche—in providing a haven for free speech under a dictatorship, see the sidebar.)

• *Exiting the Farben courtyard, cross the street to the Künstler Magazin art-supply store (at #33), turn right, and head back up the other side of Kastanienallee. Enjoy browsing the businesses on this side of the street, and when you get back to Oderberger Strasse, turn left.*

❾ Oderberger Strasse

This unusually wide and inviting street is a favorite of Prenzlauer Berg residents. Its width suggests that, during the neighborhood's industrial heyday, this was a main artery for deliveries to the Nordbahn (where we're headed now).

Window-shop the funky bars and cafés along here. But choose wisely. You'll spot many tacky, interchangeable "tropical cocktail" bars, with hanging lanterns out front and menus of forgettable Asian dishes, falafel, and Mexican food. These places—mostly catering to tourists—are disdained by many locals as not being authentically Berlin.

Instead, as you stroll, keep an eye out for these favorites: **Kiezkantine** (on the left at #50) is a cheap lunch spot run as a charity for

the mentally disabled. At #44, **Kauf Dich Glücklich** ("Shop Yourself Happy") is another neighborhood classic—a ramshackle bar known for its tasty waffles and ice cream.

Across the street from Kauf Dich Glücklich (just past #18), notice the big gap in the buildings—a sure sign that one of Prenzlauer Berg's few random casualties from WWII bombs once stood here. This gap in particular leads to a historic courtyard: the **Hirschhof** ("Deer Courtyard"), now a community park with kids playing nearby...under the gaze of a graffiti deer *(Hirsch)*.

Continue along Oderberger Strasse. You'll pass the recommended **Engelberg** café (on the right at #21, with Bavarian food in a trendy Berlin setting), then Berlin's oldest red-brick fire station, and then another gap (WWII destroyed building).

Just past the gap, peruse the window displays at **VEB Orange** (#29, with the East German hammer-and-compass insignia)—a tongue-in-cheek antique store specializing in DDR-era items. If it's cheaply made of bright-colored plastic, you'll find it here. The little cups shaped like chickens—for eating a hard-boiled egg— were standard-issue throughout the DDR and remain a kitschy symbol of those times. The name *VEB (Volkseigener Betrieb)* means "people's own company"—the main way of doing business in communist times, when private property was frowned upon (as opposed to West Germany's standard, the GmbH—a privately owned "business with limited liability").

• *Soon you'll reach a point where the road takes a dramatic bend to the*

"Church from Below": Church-Based Resistance and the Zionskirche

A couple of blocks from this walk (down Kastanienallee) stands the Zionskirche. While there's little to see there, inside or out, it's an important landmark of the neighborhood—and Prenzlauer Berg's history of resistance.

In the Depression-era 1930s, a wealthy young man named Dietrich Bonhoeffer (1906-1945) chose the simple life of a priest and worked with disadvantaged children here at the Zionskirche. Later he spoke out boldly against the rise of Nazism, conspired against the Hitler regime, was sent to a concentration camp, and was hanged just weeks before the end of the war.

In the 1980s, the Zionskirche hosted the "Environmental Library" *(Umweltbibliothek)*—an underground resource for the anti-DDR, pro-environment crew that took root in dilapidated Prenzlauer Berg courtyards. In a sign of the DDR's waning power, the government's attempts to shut down the library failed.

This is a good example of the role that the Church played throughout DDR times: While the atheistic regime formally stripped the Church of its power, individual churches provided a safe place for like-minded people to gather and organize. This phenomenon—called *Kirche von unten* ("Church from below")—was one of the most significant footholds of anti-DDR resistance. To attract participants, many DDR churches had *Bluesmesse*—church services combined with popular musical acts. In October of 1987, the Zionskirche famously hosted a rock concert by a West Berlin band, who screamed into their microphones from the pulpit. Later that night, concertgoers were attacked by East Berlin skinheads—a PR black eye for the proudly "antifascist" DDR government, just when it least needed one.

And it wasn't just in East Berlin. In nearby Leipzig, Monday evening "prayer for peace" gatherings began in 1982 and later became the nucleus of citywide protests in September and October of 1989—which proved instrumental in the collapse of the DDR.

These days, churches are considered conservative and old-fashioned. The Zionskirche offers an intriguing lesson that, back in DDR times, it was exactly the opposite.

left—as if to avoid the busier road (Bernauer Strasse) just beyond. You're approaching a portion of the...

❿ Berlin Wall Memorial

The Berlin Wall came over the hill on the horizon, then took a sharp turn along Bernauer Strasse. You're standing in what was the East. Just across busy Bernauer Strasse was the West. That's why, rather than flowing logically into the main road, the lane you're on takes a hard left.

Follow it around the corner and then, facing away from the busy street, locate the blown-up photograph on the side of the building above on the right (with info posts in the lot below it). Hundreds of people gathered right here. It's 1989, and the Berlin Wall has just (finally) cracked open. You come here, with everyone else in the neighborhood, in hopes of setting foot in West Berlin for the first time since 1961. And then—unbelievably—it actually happens. The Wall falls.

That giant photograph—and the rust-colored pillars just below it—are the last stop of the more than one-mile-long Berlin Wall Memorial. You could follow informational pillars like this one all the way to the beginning—or, at the end of this walk, you can hop on a tram to Nordbahnhof and follow those sights in order. (More on that in a moment.) But, to finish this walk, follow those crowds across what was the Wall.

• *Cross busy Bernauer Strasse and head into the...*

⓫ Mauerpark

This "Wall Park" fills an area that used to be the deadly no-man's-land between East and West. Today it's known as a lively gathering place where locals now exercise their freedom with gusto.

Head up the hill to the graffitied wall of the sports stadium to get the big picture. Have a seat (or go for a swing) and survey the valley below you.

The brick path is where the Wall once ran. The vast field beyond (now under development) was, before that, the site of the Nordbahn train line—  once the economic lifeline of Prenzlauer Berg. The big wall behind you—now a favorite canvas for local graffiti artists—strategically blocked the view of the West for people attending an event at the DDR soccer stadium, the Friedrich-Ludwig-Jahn-Sportpark. This was built to host the

World Youth Festival in 1951 and is still marked by its original bombastic light towers (even light towers were designed to stir young communist souls).

While this park is usually quiet, it's packed on Sundays, when it hosts a lively outdoor market and a big karaoke sing-off on the outdoor stage...a celebration of life, as Berliners literally dance on the grave of the Wall that divided their city. In Prenzlauer Berg, the future is very bright indeed.

• *Our walk is finished. If you head back to Bernauer Strasse, you'll find a stop for tram #M10. If you'd like to see more of the Berlin Wall, you can take this to the right, to the Berlin Nordbahnhof stop, at the start of the* 📖 ***Berlin Wall Memorial Tour.***

Alternatively, you can take tram #M10 to the left one stop (or simply walk a few minutes) to reach the Eberswalder Strasse U-Bahn station—with Konnopke's (if you're ready for a Currywurst) and several other great restaurants; the start of Kastanienallee (for more browsing); tram #M1 back down along Kastanienallee, and eventually to Hackescher Markt; and the U2 subway line to anywhere in Berlin. The Kulturbraueri and Everyday Life in the DDR museum are a short walk just beyond the U-Bahn station.

BERLIN WALL MEMORIAL TOUR

Gedenkstätte Berliner Mauer

Nowhere in Berlin is the Cold War division between East and West clearer than at the Berlin Wall Memorial. The Memorial is located along the former "death strip"—the no-man's-land between East and West. For decades, it was strewn with barbed wire and patrolled by guards with itchy trigger fingers. Today it's a long, narrow, and poignant park, running for nearly a mile alongside the most complete surviving stretch of the Wall in Berlin. The park is dotted with thought-provoking memorials and information-packed displays. There's even a small stretch of Wall that's been preserved with its original double-walled construction, heavy fortifications, and an intimidating guard tower. Along the way, you can visit two different museums (the Visitors Center and Documentation Center) with excellent films, photos, and exhibits on this turbulent chapter of human history.

Orientation

Cost: Free.

Hours: Outdoor areas accessible 24 hours daily; Visitors Center and Documentation Center open Tue-Sun 10:00-18:00, closed Mon, memorial chapel closes at 17:00.

Information: +49 30 467 986 666, www.berliner-mauer-gedenkstaette.de.

When to Go: The outdoor part of this tour can be done in the evening, but it would be a shame to miss the two indoor exhibits, which close at 18:00.

Getting There: Our tour begins next to the Nordbahnhof S-Bahn station. In fact, the station itself is a Cold War sight (see "The Nordbahnhof 'Ghost' Station" sidebar, later). Take the S-Bahn (line S1, S2, or S25) to Nordbahnhof. Exit by following

BERLIN WALL

signs for *Bernauer Strasse*—you'll pop out at the memorial. You can also get there on tram #12 or #M10 (from near Prenzlauer Berg hotels).

Getting Oriented: The Visitors Center hands out free brochures with maps and information on the Memorial. These point out many "incident markers" of events that occurred here, such as escape attempts. Note that there are different brochures for the four sections—A, B, C, D—be sure to pick up all you'll need. My tour covers Sections A and B in depth, with a basic overview of the rest.

Length of This Tour: Allow about two hours for the full experience (including an hour in the two exhibits with their powerful videos). Add another hour if walking all the way to the Mauerpark.

Services: The Visitors Center and Documentation Center both have free **WCs.**

Eateries: There's a small **bakery/café** at the Documentation Center. The **Factory Kitchen** (at the start of Section C on the east side of the park) is a cheap and stylish cafeteria. Though it caters to a business club for start-ups in the area, it also welcomes the public (Mon-Fri 9:00-17:00, closed Sat-Sun, +49 30 4431 0950).

Starring: The Berlin Wall, the "death strip," and the irrepressible human spirit.

The Berlin Wall: The Basics

West Berlin was a 185-square-mile island of capitalism surrounded by East Germany. Between establishment of the DDR (East Germany) in 1949 and construction of the Berlin Wall in 1961, an estimated three million East Germans emigrated (fled) to freedom. To stanch their population loss, the DDR erected the 96-mile-long "Anti-Fascist Protective Rampart" almost overnight, beginning on August 13, 1961. They claimed the Wall was to keep bourgeois West Berliners safely at bay. Of course, its real purpose was the opposite: to keep East Berliners from leaving.

The Berlin Wall *(Berliner Mauer)* was actually two walls. The outer was a 12-foot-high concrete barrier topped with barbed wire and a rounded, pipe-like surface to discourage grappling hooks. The inner wall was lower-profile. Sandwiched between was a no-man's-land ("death strip") between 30 and 160 feet wide.

There were eight points where you could legally cross between West and East Berlin, the most famous of which were Checkpoint Charlie (see page 225) and the Friedrichstrasse train station, with its so-called "Palace of Tears" (see page 59). In general, Westerners could temporarily enter the East, but not vice-versa.

Even after the Wall went up, people continued to try to escape. During the Wall's 28 years, there were about 5,000 documented successful escapes—and 565 of those were East German guards. An estimated 136 people were killed at the Wall while trying to escape. Meanwhile, living in West Berlin—

surrounded by concrete, barbed wire, and enemy soldiers armed to the teeth—was no picnic. The West German government offered generous tax incentives to encourage people to live here. It also waived compulsory military service for men—which is partly why West Berlin attracted many draft-dodging, alternative-lifestyle punks and hippies.

The Berlin Wall came to symbolize the larger Cold War between East and West. President John F. Kennedy gave a speech of solidarity in West Berlin, declaring, *"Ich bin ein Berliner"*—I am a Berliner. A generation later, President Ronald Reagan stood in front of the Brandenburg Gate and demanded of his Soviet counterpart, "Mr. Gorbachev, tear down this wall."

Finally, one November night in 1989, the Berlin Wall came down, as suddenly as it went up. For that story, see page 181.

BACKGROUND

This particular stretch of the Wall (running right along Bernauer Strasse) was long the center of the world's attention: It was the poster child for Berlin's division, and for the Cold War in general. That's because, in a grotesquely literal symbol for a divided city, apartment buildings were incorporated into the structure of the Wall itself. Film footage and photographs from the early 1960s show concerned Berliners watching workmen seal off these buildings from the West, brick by brick. Some people attempted to leap to freedom from upper-story windows, with mixed results. It was here that international news crews came to document the dramatic escape attempts, the bleak no-man's-land, the anti-Soviet protests, and the makeshift memorials to fallen victims. As you visit the park, you'll learn about how the Wall went up, the brutal methods used to keep Easterners in, and the stories of brave people who risked everything to be free.

The Tour Begins

Our walk laces together several scattered sights associated with the Memorial. First stop: the Visitors Center, with its introductory films. Then comes the Memorial park. Along the way, we'll stop into the Documentation Center, a museum about the Wall's history.

• *Start your visit at the Visitors Center, the rust-colored, blocky building located kitty-corner from the Nordbahnhof (at the far west end of the long Memorial park, at Bernauer Strasse 119).*

❶ Visitors Center (Bezucherzentrum)

At this modern, cube-shaped building, you'll find a helpful staff, an inviting gift shop, a rack of maps and info brochures, a handy WC, and a few vending machines. Check the next show-times for the two 15-minute introductory films in English (which run once an hour in succession). If you don't have time to wait for the English versions, the German versions have English subtitles.

The film titled *The Berlin Wall* covers the four-decade history of the Wall. First, it shows the events leading up to the Wall, as the Cold War gradually turned Berlin into a flashpoint between communism and the West. It chronicles the postwar division into Allied and Soviet sectors (1945), the Soviet Blockade and Allied Airlift (1949), and the

Berlin Wall Memorial

Berlin Wall Memorial
...... Former Course of the Wall

To Sections C & D,
U Bernauer Strasse,
T #M10 to Prenzlauer Berg
& Mauerpark

TOUR ENDS

FACTORY KITCHEN

STRELITZER STR.

HUSSITENSTRASSE

BERNAUER STRASSE

ACKERSTRASSE

9

OPEN-AIR DISPLAY

ESCAPE ATTEMPTS

CHAPEL OF RECONCILIATION

SECTION B

#M10 T

7

8

DOCUMENTATION CENTER

WC

6

GUARD TOWER

ACKERSTRASSE

PRESERVED PART OF WALL

5

100 Meters

100 Yards

CEMETERY CROSS

WINDOW OF REMEMBRANCE

TOUR BEGINS

VISITORS CENTER

WC

4

WALL FRAGMENTS

Sophien Parish Cemetery

1

3

"DEATH STRIP"

SECTION A

2

3-D MAP

#M10 T & #12

BERGSTRASSE

NORDBAHNHOF EXIT

GARTENSTRASSE

Nordbahnhof S

INVALIDENSTRASSE

1 Visitors Center
2 3-D Map of the Former Neighborhood
3 "Death Strip"
4 Window of Remembrance
5 The Wall
6 Documentation Center
7 Escapes from Border Strip Buildings
8 Chapel of Reconciliation
9 Tunnel 57

BERLIN WALL

democratic uprising crushed by Soviet tanks (1953). Then, in 1961, the Soviets told the East Germans to close the border entirely and erect the Wall. You'll hear about frantic escape attempts. Finally, there's the gradual thawing of the Cold War, and the eventual tearing down of the Wall in 1989.

The other film, ***Walled In!***, features a 3-D re-creation of the former death strip, helping you visualize what it is you're about to walk through.

• *Exit the Visitors Center, cross Bernauer Strasse, and enter the Memorial park. You're leaving former West Berlin and entering the no-man's-land that stood between East and West Berlin. Once in the park, find the rusty rectangular monument with a 3-D map.*

❷ 3-D Map of the Former Neighborhood

The map shows what this neighborhood looked like back in the Wall's heyday. The shiny metal dot on the left marks where you're

standing. Fifty years ago, you'd be right at the division between East and West Berlin—specifically, in the narrow strip between two sets of walls. One of those walls is still standing—there it is, stretching along Bernauer Strasse. As you gaze down the long park, West Berlin would be to your left (on the north side of Bernauer Strasse), and East Berlin to your right.

Now find the Nordbahnhof, both on the map and in real life—the entrance is across the street on your left. While the Wall stood, the Nordbahnhof station straddled both East and West. (For more on this, see the sidebar.)

• *Stroll along the path through this first section of the park ("Section A"). Along the way are small sights, remembrances, and exhibits. As you stroll, you're walking through the...*

❸ "Death Strip" (Section A)

Today's grassy park, with a pleasant path through it, was once the notorious "death strip" *(Todesstreifen)*. If someone was trying to es-

cape from the East, they'd have to scale one wall (a smaller one, to your right), cross this narrow strip of land, and climb the main Wall (to your left, along Bernauer Strasse). The death strip was an obstacle course of barbed wire, tire-spike strips to stop cars, and other diabolical devices. It was continually

patrolled by East German soldiers leading German Shepherds. Armed guards looked down from watchtowers, with orders to shoot to kill. At night, the area was harshly lit by streetlamps—four originals remain standing (just up ahead). Before it was the no-man's-land between the walls, this area was the parish graveyard for a nearby church; ironically, DDR workers had to move a thousand graves from here to create a "death strip."

• *About midway through this section of the park, find the freestanding rusted-iron wall filled with photos.*

❹ Window of Remembrance

The semitransparent photos are of people who died trying to escape East Berlin. You'll see their faces, names, and dates of death (displayed chronologically).

Find **Otfried Reck,** just 17 years old (eighth from the left, top row). On November 27, 1962, he and a friend pried open a ventilation shaft at the boarded-up Nordbahnhof, and descended to the tracks, where they hoped to flag down a passing westbound train. The police discovered them, and Reck was shot in the back. There's a memorial to him now directly across from the Visitors Center.

Ernst Mundt (just left of Otfried) died directly behind you, at the cemetery wall. On September 4, 1962, he rode his bike to the cemetery, which—because of its location near the Wall—was constantly patrolled by guards. He climbed the death strip's inner wall and ran across the top, headed in the direction of the Nordbahnhof and freedom. He was shot in the head, and his hat (the one in the picture) flew off. He died, age 40. (The brochure from the Visitors Center describes dozens of similar stories and pinpoints each victim's memorial plaque in the park.)

Across the path from the Window of Remembrance is a row of overgrown, graffiti-covered, discarded Wall panels. We'll see an intact version soon.

Continue walking through Section A. You're now walking along the original, preserved asphalt patrol path, passing by the four original streetlamps and a cross marking the Sophien Parish Cemetery. The church cemetery still exists (it's to your right), but the cross marks a section of graves they had to dig up in 1961 to build the death strip.

• *Now, walk across the grass and find a place to get a good close-up look at...*

❺ The Wall

The Wall here is typical of the whole system: about 12 feet tall, made of concrete and rebar, and capped by a rounded pipe that made it tough for escapees to get a grip. The top would have been further outfitted with coils of barbed wire.

This was part of a 96-mile-long Wall that encircled West Berlin, making it an island of democracy in communist East Germany. The West Berlin side of the Wall was typically covered with color-

The Nordbahnhof "Ghost" Station

This S-Bahn station was one of the "ghost stations" of Cold War Berlin. It was built in 1926, closed in 1961 (although trains kept passing through), and opened again in 1989. When the Wall went up, the station was boarded up by East Germany. West Berlin subway trains had permission to zip through on the underground tracks, but they couldn't stop here, and no one was allowed to get on or off.

Today, the station keeps reminders of its haunted past. Inside, photos posted on the walls compare 1989 with 2009. As the displays explain, East German border guards, who were stationed here to ensure that nobody got on or off those trains, were themselves locked into their surveillance rooms to prevent their escape.

At the station's exit to Bernauer Strasse, note the plaques (at the top and bottom of the stairs) that say *Sperrmauer 1961-1989*—"Barrier wall." Back in the 20th century, this exit was blocked—a bricked-off no-man's-land.

ful graffiti by free-spirited West Berliners. A few bits of graffiti remain here.

Reach out and touch the Wall. Feel an exposed bit of rebar. Think of the lives lost. You're touching history.

• *Now, exit the park through the hole in the Wall, turn right along Bernauer Strasse, and make your way a short distance to the crosswalk. Across Bernauer Strasse is a modern gray building with a view terrace, located at #119 (labeled* Gedenkstätte Berliner Mauer*). This is the...*

❻ Documentation Center (Dokumentationszentrum Berliner Mauer)

This excellent museum is geared to a new generation of Berliners who can hardly imagine their hometown split so brutally in two. The two floors of exhibits have photos and displays to explain the logistics of the city's division and its effects. Listen to the riveting personal accounts of

escapees—and of the border guards armed with machine guns and tasked with stopping them.

On the second floor, at the back of the room, be sure to watch the poignant seven-minute film, *Peaceful Revolution.* The video highlights the power of the people and traces the events that led to the Wall's collapse: the 1989 protests in Hungary, Leipzig, Prague, Berlin, and Dresden; the press conference where a bumbling bureaucrat accidentally announced the opening of the Wall "immediately"; the massing of desperate East Berliners at the Bornholmer Strasse crossing of the Wall that very night—and the guards finally shrugging at each other and simply opening the checkpoint; crowds rushing through the Wall, embracing loved ones, climbing up top, and chipping off a chunk; and an awe-filled, wide-eyed East Berliner wandering along the Ku'damm, saying, "Me! In West Berlin!"

From this floor, stairs lead to the rooftop **Tower** *(Turm)* where you're rewarded with a view. You can look across Bernauer Strasse

and down at Berlin's last preserved stretch of the death strip with an original guard tower. More than 100 sentry towers like this one kept a close eye on the Wall. In the far distance, the communist-built TV Tower overlooks the scene.

• *Exit and continue on. Cross Bernauer Strasse (where it intersects with Ackerstrasse) and enter the next section of the Memorial park.*

❼ Escapes from Border Strip Buildings (Section B)

Ahead, you'll see a group of information panels—some with text and photos, others with audio and video clips. These are a few of many such information points, which stretch the entire length of the Memorial.

The panels tell the story of what happened here: On August 13, 1961, the East German government officially closed the border. A sense of dread spread among East Germans, as they feared being permanently trapped under Soviet control. People began fleeing to the parts of Berlin controlled by other European powers—like the French, who held the neighborhood on the north side of Bernauer Strasse.

Over the next few weeks and months, bit by bit, the border hardened. Ackerstrasse was closed to traffic as East German soldiers laid down rows of barbed wire. They began to evacuate the residents living on the border strip. They bricked up the buildings' street-side entrances so no one could flee. People were suddenly separated from their West Berlin neighbors just across the street.

During this brief window of time (summer of '61 to early '62), there were many escape attempts, and the residents of West Berlin did all they could to help. West German first responders were at the ready. A woman called out of the window for the fire department, which came with a ladder to bring her down to freedom. A man jumped down into the waiting rescue net of firefighters. A desperate man simply fell three stories from the rooftop onto the pavement of Bernauer Strasse. He was badly injured, but a West Berlin ambulance was there to whisk him to the hospital...and freedom. Another man slid down a rope to safety as West Berlin police blinded the East German guards with their floodlights. More people escaped as the West Berlin police brandished their weapons while the fire department raised their ladders.

Most of these escape attempts were in those first few months. By 1962, the residents had been evicted, the buildings demolished, and the formidable Wall was going up. People kept trying to flee, but most later attempts from here ended in arrests. Not everyone survived. On August 22, 1961, Ida Siekmann died as she jumped from her third-floor apartment at Bernauer Strasse 48. She became the first casualty of the Berlin Wall.

• *Keep going up the path through Section B, to the round building up ahead.*

❽ Chapel of Reconciliation (Kapelle der Versöhnung)

This modern chapel stands on the site of the old Church of Reconciliation. Built in 1894, the old Gothic-style church served the neighborhood parish. When the Wall went up, the church found itself stranded in the death strip. The congregation had to find another place to worship, and the church was abandoned. Border guards used the steeple as a watchtower. The church became famous in the West as a symbol of how the godless commies had driven out religion and turned a once-great culture into a bleak wasteland. The church itself was finally blown up by the East Germans in 1985, ostensibly because it got in the way of the border guards' sight lines. (In fact, it was one of several churches demolished around this time, to send a message to troublesome Christian protestors.) Little remains of the original church. You can see its footprint traced in the ground around the chapel and a bit of the foundations. The church bells and twisted iron cross are displayed a few paces away. The church was gone, but people on both sides of the Wall continued praying that someday there'd be a "reconciliation" between East and West.

After the Wall came down, this chapel was built to remember the troubled past and to try to heal the memory. Inside the church, the carved wooden altarpiece was saved from the original structure. The chapel hosts daily prayer services for the victims of the Wall.

• *Continue past the chapel into the second portion of Section B.*

Tunnels and More

Walk uphill then bear left to a large **open-air display** under a canopy (amid the ruins of a destroyed Bernauer Strasse home). Photos, info boards, and press-the-button audio clips explain what it was like to live here, so close to the front line of the Cold War. They paint a stark picture of daily life under oppressive communist rule.

Head back up to the main path, turn left, and continue. You'll pass two parallel rows of metal slabs, labeled *Fluchttunnel 1964.*

This marks the route of the most famous tunnel of all: ❾ **Tunnel 57** (named after the 57 people who escaped through it). Its location is marked by rows of metal plates embedded in the ground.

In the spring of 1963, a group of grad students in West Berlin hatched a wild plot to free their friends in the East. They set up their operation in an abandoned West Berlin bakery north of Bernauer Strasse. There, they cut a hole in the floor and started tunneling toward the East. They went down 35 feet, then across—under Bernauer Strasse, under the Wall, and under the death strip. After five months of hard labor, they'd hollowed out a tunnel stretching more than 150 yards. Fortunately, when they surfaced, they found themselves safely behind a nondescript building on Streitzler Strasse—about 75 yards south of today's park. The students alerted their friends in the East to get ready to escape.

On Sunday evening, October 3, 1964, the East Berliners began making their way to the address they'd been given. They gave the password—"Tokyo"—and were ushered inside by the West Berliners, who led them to the tunnel entrance. One by one they went into the narrow, dark tunnel, crawling on their hands and knees. As the night wore on, suspicions were aroused. East German police descended on Streitzler Strasse. Shots were fired. An East German guard was killed. The West German helpers beat a hasty retreat through the tunnel to safety.

The tunnel was immediately destroyed by the communist authorities. But it had served its purpose—saving 57 lives. Years later, one of the helpers, Reinhard Furrer, looked back and reflected on the whole experience. He could view it from a unique perspective—200 miles up, as he orbited the earth as an astronaut on Spacelab.

A few steps beyond the tunnel are information posts with more details and photos of tunnel escapes.

At the end of this stretch of the Wall Memorial, stand inside the rusty metal posts rising 50 feet high. These mark the spot of a long-gone watchtower. From here, look back over the death strip and imagine the view of a DDR guard. Then turn 90 degrees left and look down the lane (with the TV Tower in the distance). Consider the block of once dreary flats now enjoying peace and freedom.

• *The main part of our walk is done. To experience more of the Memorial, you could continue through Sections C and D, where you'll find more open-air exhibits similar to what we've already seen (explained next).*

But if you're ready to leave the area, the Bernauer Strasse U-Bahn station is just a block farther up Bernauer Strasse. Or you can backtrack to the Nordbahnhof. And tram #M10 follows Bernauer Strasse all the way to Eberswalder Strasse, in the heart of Prenzlauer Berg.

Rest of the Memorial

The last two sections of the Berlin Wall Memorial—with periodic information points—stretch along Bernauer Strasse another two-thirds of a mile all the way to the Mauerpark. While still interesting, it's really more of the same. You can easily skip ahead to the Mauerpark by hopping on tram #M10 (which runs along Bernauer Strasse, tracing the path of the Memorial; the Friedrich-Ludwig-Jahn-Sport-park stop is right at the Mauer-park).

If you walk, here's what you'll see:

Section C focuses on the building of the Wall: the gradual beefing up of the fortifications; surveillance over the death strip; and metal markings showing the path of two additional escape tunnels. At the end of this section (at the intersection with Brun-nenstrasse, and the Bernauer Strasse U-Bahn stop), one of the most iconic Berlin Wall escape photographs fills the entire wall of a building: teenaged DDR border guard Conrad Schumann, in full uniform and carrying his weapon, running full-tilt and leaping over barbed wire to freedom in the West.

Finally, **Section D** is nearly as long as the first three sections combined. Here the path cuts a half-block inland, to a strip between buildings that mostly follows an old patrol road (jog right as you cross Brunnenstrasse and look for signs). The theme of this area is everyday life in the shadow of the Berlin Wall, including exhibits about how West Berlin was affected; those who dug tunnels and carried out other activities to help escapees; the soldiers who guarded the Wall; the politics of the Wall; and how the media were used as a tool and a weapon during the Cold War. You'll emerge at Schwedter Strasse, where a building-size photograph shows the people who amassed here on the night of November 9, 1989, eagerly anticipating the opening of the Wall.

• *From Mauerpark, you can walk two blocks (or ride tram #M10 one stop) to the Eberswalder Strasse U-Bahn stop. Or, if you're in the mood for even more Berlin Wall sights, you could continue riding the #M10 all the way to Warschauer Strasse and the start of the East Side Gallery (see page 74). In the opposite direction, tram #M10 goes all the way back the way you came, to the Nordbahnhof S-Bahn station.*

BERLIN WALL

FASCISM & COLD WAR WALK

From Checkpoint Charlie to Potsdamer Platz

Several fascinating sites relating to Germany's tumultuous 20th century are south of Unter den Linden. Starting at Checkpoint Charlie, the most famous Cold War border crossing, we'll walk several blocks to the Topography of Terror and former Air Ministry (both rare surviving Nazi artifacts), and end at Potsdamer Platz, a skyscraper jungle representing Berlin's late-20th-century reconciliation, reunification, and rejuvenation. This area is beloved by armchair historians, including people who never cared about history before coming to Berlin (a common affliction).

As you stroll, keep in mind that we're hopping back and forth between two distinct periods of Germany history: First, the 1930s and early 1940s, when fascism was on the rise—ultimately resulting in Adolf Hitler taking power as führer, his National Socialism (Nazism) becoming the law of the land, and his brutal SS fighting force terrifying Germans and enemies alike. And second, the mid-1940s through 1989: the Cold War period that kicked off as Hitler was defeated, dividing a battle-wracked Berlin down the middle into capitalist West and communist East.

Orientation

Length of This Walk: Allow about an hour for the walk itself; if also entering the Museum of the Wall at Checkpoint Charlie or the Topography of Terror, add an hour apiece.

When to Go: The walk can be done at any time. If you're pressed for time, you can squeeze this walk in later in the day, as the two museums stay open a bit later (see hours later).

Getting There: Ride the U-Bahn to Kochstrasse/Checkpoint Charlie (U6); exit toward *Haus am Checkpoint Charlie*. You'll emerge across the street from the Museum of the Wall, a block from this walk's starting point. It's also a short walk from Stadtmitte (U2 or U6), or about a 15-minute walk south of Unter den Linden (down Friedrichstrasse).

Museum of the Wall at Checkpoint Charlie: €14.50, daily 9:00-22:00, last entry one hour before closing.

Topography of Terror: Free, daily 10:00-20:00, outdoor exhibit closes at dusk.

Services: There are free WCs at both the Museum of the Wall and the Topography of Terror as well as in the basement of the Sony Center near the Film and TV museum.

Eateries: Several tourist-oriented eateries (e.g., sausage stands, American fast-food chains) cluster around Checkpoint Charlie and along Zimmerstrasse. The Sony Center, where this walk ends, also has plenty of food options.

Starring: The Berlin Wall (intact fragments, and a reconstruction of its most famous crossing) and Hitler's crimes (documented on the site where they took place).

The Walk Begins

• *Find a spot on a corner at the crowded intersection facing Checkpoint Charlie. Ideally, stand under the* "You are leaving the American sector" *sign (by the KFC).*

❶ Checkpoint Charlie

For nearly three decades (1961-1989), this was a border crossing between East and West Berlin. It became known worldwide and stood as a symbol of the Cold War itself. Today, the checkpoint and associated buildings are long gone, but a re-creation gives you a sense of what it was like.

The name "Charlie" came about because it was the third checkpoint in a series. Checkpoint A (Alpha) was at the East-West German border, a hundred miles west of here. Checkpoint B (Bravo) was where people left East Germany and entered the Allied sector of Berlin. This was Checkpoint C (Charlie). Its roots lie in the days immediately after World War II, when this intersection was the border between the US-occupied neighborhood and the Soviet zone. In 1952, the Soviets officially closed the border between East and West Germany with a fence, blocking East Germans from leaving. But West Berlin was still open until the Wall went

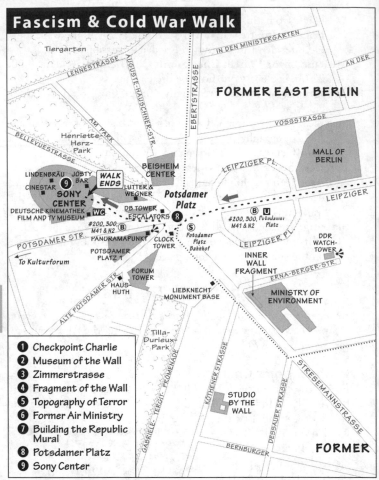

Fascism & Cold War Walk

Tiergarten

IN DEN MINISTERGÄRTEN

LENNESTRASSE

AUGUSTE-HAUSCHNER-STR.

AM PARK

EBERTSTRASSE

AN DER

FORMER EAST BERLIN

VOSSSTRASSE

BELLEVUESTRASSE

Henriette Herz-Park

MALL OF BERLIN

LEIPZIGER PL.

LINDENBRÄU   JOSTY BAR
CINESTAR
SONY CENTER   ⑨
DEUTSCHE KINEMATHEK FILM AND TV MUSEUM

BEISHEIM CENTER

WALK ENDS

LUTTER & WEGNER

DB TOWER ESCALATORS

Potsdamer Platz

LEIPZIGER

LEIPZIGER PL.

Ⓑ Ⓤ
#200, 300,
M41 & N2 *Potsdamer Platz*

WC

Ⓑ
#200, 300,
M41 & N2

POTSDAMER STR.

PANORAMAPUNKT

CLOCK TOWER

Ⓢ
Potsdamer Platz Bahnhof

⑧

DDR WATCH-TOWER

To Kulturforum

POTSDAMER PLATZ 1

ALTE POTSDAMER STR.

FORUM TOWER

HAUS-HUTH

LIEBKNECHT MONUMENT BASE

INNER WALL FRAGMENT

ERNA-BERGER-STR.

MINISTRY OF ENVIRONMENT

Tilla-Durieux-Park

KÖTHENER STRASSE

GABRIELE-TERGIT-PROMENADE

STUDIO BY THE WALL

DESSAUER STRASSE

STRESEMANNSTRASSE

BERNBURGER

FORMER

① Checkpoint Charlie
② Museum of the Wall
③ Zimmerstrasse
④ Fragment of the Wall
⑤ Topography of Terror
⑥ Former Air Ministry
⑦ Building the Republic Mural
⑧ Potsdamer Platz
⑨ Sony Center

up here in 1961. Afterwards, this spot on Friedrichstrasse was one of the few places where people could legally pass between East and West—provided they had the proper documents, of course. That generally meant foreigners and officials from the Allies—not East Germans.

The East Germans fortified their side of the checkpoint heavily. There was the Wall, a watchtower, concrete barriers to prevent cars from speeding through, barbed-wire fences, and even a garage where vehicles could be checked for smuggled goods or people. (None of these structures stand today.)

On the US side, there was...Checkpoint Charlie. This was a humble shack for the document-checking GIs. It sat on a traffic island in the middle of Friedrichstrasse, fortified with a few piles of sandbags. While the actual checkpoint has long since been disman-

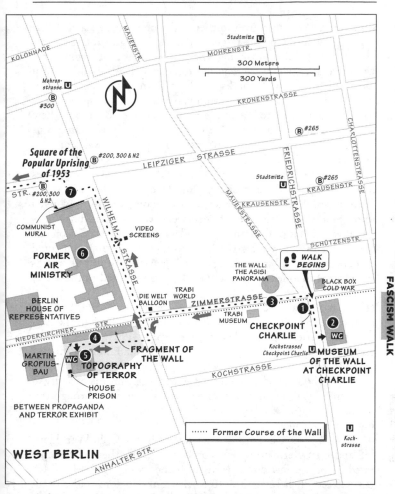

tled, you can see a **mock-up,** with a guard station, sandbags, and a US flag. There's a replica of the original sign, which warned omi-

nously in several languages: "You are leaving the American sector." Larger-than-life posters show an American soldier facing east and a young Soviet soldier facing west—look at these portraits and consider the decades of armed stand-offs here.

Imagine crossing this checkpoint as a Western visitor. Friends in West Berlin would load you up with care packages (and possibly contraband) to deliver to their loved ones in the East. While you knew you weren't the target of the machine gun-toting guards on watchtowers, approaching the border was still frightening. Upon crossing, you were required to change a certain amount of Deutschmarks into Ostmarks (the East German equivalent), leaving you with far more money than you could possibly spend (since there was very little to buy in the East). You entered a room where the guards might search you if they thought you were hiding contraband or foreign currency. At last, your passport was stamped, and you were allowed to go.

Stepping from West to East (as I did as a tourist many times in the 1980s) was the opposite of Dorothy opening the door to Oz: From a world of color, vibrancy, and freedom, you were plunged into a monochromatic, soot-stained scene, with beaten-down people always looking over their shoulders. You kept an eye on the clock, since there was a strict limit to how much time you could be here. Finally, after spending or giving away your last Ostmarks (you were forbidden to take any back), you retreated to the safety of the West.

Lots of dramatic history has happened on this spot. In 1961, a car came speeding up Friedrichstrasse, crashed through the East German barriers, and made it to freedom. In 1962, Peter Fechter tried running to the West through no-man's-land, but got tangled in barbed wire, was shot, and was left there, where he bled to death with the whole world watching—the first high-profile casualty of the Berlin Wall. Numerous escapees snuck their way through this checkpoint with forged documents, hidden inside cars, or via other ingenious schemes.

Checkpoint Charlie was a flashpoint in the Cold War. Here, US and East German soldiers could stare each other down, separated by only a few dozen yards of barbed wire. In 1961, 10 US tanks faced off here against 10 Soviet tanks...before cooler heads (and negotiations by Robert F. Kennedy) prevailed, thankfully averting a possible World War III. In 1963, President John F. Kennedy came to this spot to show solidarity with the embattled West Berliners.

Today, the area around Checkpoint Charlie has become a kind of Cold War freak show and kitschy tourist trap. A couple of actors posing as GIs will take a selfie with you for a fee. Sidewalk vendors nearby sell Cold War-era memorabilia—chunks of the Wall, Soviet and US medals, DDR-era soft-serve ice cream, and so on. Be warned: Hustlers charge an exorbitant €10 for a Cold War-era stamp in your passport. Technically, this invalidates your passport—which has caused some tourists big problems.

As if celebrating the final victory of crass capitalism, a KFC and a McDonald's now defiantly overlook the scene. Despite all the kitsch, the history here is real.

• *For a more sober look at the checkpoint's history, the Wall, and the many daring escape attempts, head a half-block past Checkpoint Charlie to find (on your left) the...*

❷ Museum of the Wall at Checkpoint Charlie

The museum traces the history of the famous border crossing, with a focus on the many brave and clever escape attempts over, under, and through the Wall.

More than that, the museum itself is a piece of Cold War history. Since 1962, this exhibit has stood here defiantly—within spitting distance of the border guards—showing the whole world the tragedy of the Wall. During the Cold War years, many famous people came here just to show their solidarity with West Berliners and lovers of freedom.

Today, the yellowed descriptions, which have scarcely changed since that time, tinge the museum with nostalgia. Chunks of the Wall stand like trophies at its door. The mazelike museum itself feels like an artifact: cluttered, cramped, dusty, disorganized, and overpriced, with lots of reading involved. While the museum is not for everyone (and serious historians will prefer the more thoughtful Berlin Wall Memorial), Checkpoint Charlie's Museum of the Wall has retro charm and tells its escape stories well. For more information on the museum, see page 64.

• *Outside the museum, at the giant* "You are leaving" *sign, you're at the cross street called Zimmerstrasse. We'll turn left and follow Zimmerstrasse a couple of blocks (with several Cold War sightseeing options).*

❸ Zimmerstrasse: A Cold War Carnival

Zimmerstrasse—connecting Checkpoint Charlie to the Topography of Terror area—is lined with tourist attractions. These range from thoughtful to tacky, and from free to overpriced. Note that this area continues to be developed, so most of these attractions are, to some degree, temporary. But the history here is fascinating, and it's well explained in the many **information posters** radiating out from the corner of Zimmerstrasse and Friedrichstrasse. The posters offer a helpful visualization of Checkpoint Charlie history—with illustrations, maps, and descriptions of events.

At the same corner, facing the Checkpoint Charlie action, are

The Trabi

Communist East Germany (a.k.a. the DDR) is forever linked to its trademark automobile— the Trabant, or, affectionately, the Trabi (TRAH-bee). Built in Zwickau, Saxony starting in 1957, the Trabi was the DDR's big play to compete with the popular West German Volkswagen Beetle. But its design and engineering (limited by a centrally planned economy) were nowhere near VW standards.

A ride in a Trabi was cramped, bumpy, and smelly. To gas up your Trabi, you'd open the hood and pour a gas-oil mix into a tank above the two-cylinder, two-stroke engine, which used gravity instead of a fuel pump. The body was made of a recycled, cloth-reinforced plastic resin called Duroplast. (So the body was as "green" as the engine was polluting.) On the upside, the construction was so simple that handy East Germans (who, out of necessity, were excellent do-it-yourselfers) could fix just about any problem with a hammer, a screwdriver, and a wrench. Production was limited, so the privilege of owning a Trabi required you to sign up on a waiting list and be prepared to wait many years.

In the summer of 1989, when Hungary suddenly opened its borders, whole fleets of Trabis were left behind by East Germans who went to vacation on Lake Balaton...and decided to flee West, never to come home. The Trabi remained in production until 1991, totaling more than three million rattletraps with lawnmower engines on Eastern Europe's roads.

The best thing about the Trabi were the jokes it generated:
• Why is the Trabi the world's quietest car? Because your knees cover your ears.
• How do you double a Trabi's value? Fill the tank.
• "I'd like two windshield wipers for my Trabi." "Sounds like a fair trade."
• How many workers does it take to build a Trabi? Three: One to cut, one to fold, and one to paste.
• Why is the Trabi's back window heated? To keep your hands warm while pushing.
• When does a Trabi reach top speed? When it's being towed.
• What's the longest car on the market? The Trabi, of course, at 60 feet long—6 feet of car and 54 feet of smoke.

Who says Germans don't have a sense of humor?

Like the *Ampelmann* (traffic-light man), the Trabi is enjoying a renaissance as a bit of "Ost-algic" communist kitsch. Old Trabis are being rehabilitated and souped up for tourist trips. Just be ready to get out and push.

two paid exhibits (neither worth the price): **Black Box Cold War** displays a few artifacts and documents on Checkpoint Charlie and the Wall, but essentially repeats information in better museums around town. Across the street, **The Wall: The**

Asisi Panorama is an oversized, 360-degree panorama illustration (by local artist Yadegar Asisi) that immerses you in a photorealistic painted re-creation of the Kreuzberg neighborhood in the shadow of the Wall. While strangely engrossing for Cold War buffs, it's outrageously overpriced for what it delivers (€10, daily 11:00-18:00).

From here, head west down Zimmerstrasse (past the panorama building). You're walking along the former "death strip," the no-man's-land between the inner and outer layers of the Wall. Along the left side of the street, you can see the **double row of cobbles** marking the exact route of the Berlin Wall. Throughout the city, cobbles like this trace 25 miles of the 96-mile-long wall that surrounded West Berlin (for background on the Berlin Wall, see page 213).

Follow Zimmerstrasse (and its cobbles) two blocks, passing more temptations: The **Trabi Museum** on the left at #14 (little more

than a shop featuring the oft-ridiculed East-German tin-can car); **Trabi World,** farther along on the right (where you can book a Berlin tour in a Trabi); and the "Die Welt" **balloon ride,** offering aerial views over Berlin.

Notice that many of these attractions fill vacant lots—undeveloped prime real estate in the heart of Berlin. Thanks to a complicated history, it can still be difficult to establish ownership. Under the Nazis, Jews were forced to sell their property. After the war, the Soviets occupied it. Then the DDR government seized private property. And after the fall of the Wall, many East Berliners flocked west, while adventurous young West Germans came here to squat in abandoned property and claim it as their own. So, who owns it today? For a few pieces of land, it's still not clear.

FASCISM WALK

• *Soon, where the road becomes Niederkirchnerstrasse, the sidewalk cobbles dead-end at an actual, surviving...*

❹ Fragment of the Berlin Wall

Intact segments of the Berlin Wall are rare in this high-rent downtown area. This block-long section survived because it abuts the

ruins of a Nazi building (the SS and Gestapo headquarters) that was intentionally left as a memorial, while the rest of the death strip was razed and rebuilt. This stretch of the Wall is especially evocative because, with its holes, you can see its rebar innards. This fit the DDR mantra of "cheap but efficient" for constructing the Wall. The tube-shaped top made it difficult for escapees to get a grip or attach a grappling hook. Ahead of you was the American sector on the left and the Soviet zone on the right.

• *This Berlin Wall section stands near the heart of Hitler's political and military administration. Eventually we'll turn right to see the Nazi former air ministry. But first let's explore the wall ahead of you and the Nazi history site along its left side. Cross the street and step into a big, gravel-filled lot with the wall along its right side.*

❺ Topography of Terror (Topographie des Terrors)

This free memorial and history exhibit (with an outdoor section on your right and the museum ahead) stands on what was once the

most feared address in Berlin: the Gestapo and SS headquarters. This is where Hitler's reign of terror was hatched, where prisoners were detained and tortured, and where Heinrich Himmler plotted the Final Solution. (Today, virtually nothing survives from that time. The stark, gray, boxy museum before you is completely new.)

The Topography of Terror is one of the few memorial sites that focuses on the perpetrators rather than the victims of the Nazis. It's chilling to see just how seamlessly and bureaucratically the Nazi institutions and state structures merged to become a well-oiled terror machine.

Visiting the Site: While there are few actual artifacts displayed, both the outdoor exhibit and the museum are excellent.

FASCISM WALK

Heinrich Himmler's SS State

Hitler's right-hand man was Heinrich Himmler (1900-1945). Among Hitler's inner circle, Hermann Göring was the military mastermind, Martin Bormann was the chief of staff concerned with domestic matters, and Joseph Goebbels was the propagandist. But the close-cropped, bespectacled Himmler—who looked more like a meek accountant than a war criminal—was responsible for the most despicable legacy of the Nazis: He controlled both the SS and the Gestapo and was the primary architect of the Holocaust. And his work was based right here, on the site of today's Topography of Terror.

This was the headquarters of the Reich Main Security Office, or *Reichssicherheitshauptamt* (RSHA), under Himmler's command. Their mission was to fight "enemies of the state" both inside and outside Germany—a terrifyingly broad authority that Himmler wielded unrelentingly.

Himmler oversaw three interrelated organizations: The Gestapo *(Geheime Staatspolizei)* was a secret state police force. The SS *(Schutzstaffel)* began as Hitler's personal bodyguards and evolved into a dreaded paramilitary force (the *Waffen-SS*). The lesser-known SD *(Sicherheitsdienst)* was the Nazi intelligence agency, which spied on foreign governments—but also on their own German people to root out spies and traitors. Together, they amounted to a state-within-a-state, with talons in every corner of German society. The Gestapo, the SS, and the SD were considered omnipotent, omnipresent, and omniscient. The threat of *Schutzhaft* ("protective custody") was enough to terrify civilians into compliance.

The Nazi worldview was rooted in the idealistic notion of a *Volksgemeinschaft* ("people's community") of a purely Germanic culture and race—which empowered Hitler to create a pervasive illusion that "we're all in this together." Anyone who was not an Aryan was *Untermensch*—subhuman—and must be treated as such.

It was from these headquarters that Himmler administered the concentration camps, where enemies of the state were rounded up, imprisoned, and worked to death. And later, it was from here that the Nazis firmed up plans for their genocide of Jews. Himmler and his SS were specifically tasked with the "racial purification" of German-held lands, especially Eastern Europe: the "Final Solution to the Jewish Question." Special concentration camps were set up specifically to murder Jews by the thousands—super-efficient factories for the mass production of death.

Himmler oversaw everything from his giant office building, where bureaucrats clocked in and dispassionately documented it all in triplicate. The cold-blooded paper-pushing at this site is what philosopher Hannah Arendt had in mind when she originated the phrase "the banality of evil."

Powerful photos and good English descriptions take you chronologically through the rise of Nazism, and the repression of all dissent through the organizations headquartered here. A free audioguide (available in the museum) covers the indoor exhibit and the grounds, but not the exhibit along the Wall.

Along the Wall: In the trench that runs along the surviving stretch of Wall is an exhibit called "Berlin 1933-1945: Between Propaganda and Terror." It covers the post-WWI Weimar Republic all the way through the ragged days just after World War II. The information lining the trench is similar to what's in the museum but not as in-depth.

Museum: In the lobby, study a model of the neighborhood showing the home of the German government at the outbreak of World War II. (We're standing at #20.) Back in the 1930s and '40s, this was just one of many governmental office buildings along Wilhelmstrasse. Seeing this sprawling bureaucratic quarter gives you a sense of how much mundane paperwork was involved in administering Hitler's reign of terror in an efficient, rational way. In the small theater nearby, the six-minute film provides context for the exhibit (and can be shown in English upon request).

The ground floor houses the permanent collection. Stepping in, you begin a chronological journey (with a timeline of events,

old photographs, documents, and newspaper clippings) through the evolution of Nazism, the reign of terror, the start of World War II, and the Holocaust.

Following the numbers, you'll trace: 1) the rise of Nazism and consolidation of power; 2) the institutionalization of terror; 3) the use of concentration camps and racism; 4) the spreading of Nazism with World War II; and 5) the end of the war and postwar life.

The displays illustrate how Hitler, Himmler, and their team expertly manipulated the German people to build a broadly supported

"dictatorship of consent." You'll learn about the web of intersecting organizations whose duties were run from here. And you'll learn about the Gestapo and SS *(Schutzstaffel)*, and their brutal methods—including their chillingly systematic implementation of the Holocaust.

FASCISM WALK

Some images here are indelible. Gleeful SS soldiers, stationed at Auschwitz, yuk it up on a retreat in the countryside (as their helpless prisoners were being gassed and burned a few miles away). A German woman, head shaved, is publicly humiliated for fraternizing with a Polish prisoner. On a street corner, jeering SS troops cut off the beard of an elderly Jewish man. A Roma woman's eye color is carefully analyzed by a doctor performing "racial evaluation." Graphic images show executions—by hanging, firing squad, and so on.

The exhibits end with the conclusion of the war in 1945. A photo shows this former building in total ruins. The finale is a wall of colored cards used in collecting data for the postwar trials of the people who worked here. While the Nazi leadership was captured and prosecuted at the Nürnberg trials, the majority of midlevel bureaucrats who worked in this building—and who routinely facilitated genocide with the flick of a pen—were never brought to justice. (They say there are two great miracles in modern Germany: After 1945 there were no Nazis, and after 1989 there were no communists.)

With more time, use the audioguide and posted signs to explore the grounds surrounding the blocky building.

Around the corner (to the right facing the museum entrance) are the scant remains of the **House Prison** outlined in cement. The building was equipped with dungeons, where the Gestapo detained and tortured thousands of prisoners. The  general public knew what went on here, and its very existence sent a message.

• *Leave the Topography of Terror by walking back between the wall and the long exhibit in the trench. At the corner where you entered, turn left and head down Wilhelmstrasse (with the massive building on your left, and the vacant lot filled with Trabi cars on your right). Pause when you reach the main courtyard of that building, set back behind a heavy fence.*

❻ Former Air Ministry (Reichsluftfahrtministerium)

The only major Hitler-era government building that survived the war's bombs, this once housed the headquarters of the Nazi Luftwaffe (Air Force). The building—completed in 1936—exemplifies Hitler's bigger-is-better, fascist aesthetic. It's designed to intimidate...to make the average person feel small and powerless. This

FASCISM WALK

is what much of Berlin looked like back when Germany occupied nearly all of Europe. (The courtyard is often used by modern film producers needing a Nazi backdrop.) While you're not allowed in the building, you may be able to discreetly step into the courtyard.

Large as it is, this building was constructed mostly in secret. Imagine: It's the mid-1930s in Berlin. Hitler has just come to power as chancellor, then grabs even more (with the Reichstag fire) to become führer. But Germany—just 15 years removed from its loss in World War I—is still subject to the Treaty of Versailles. One of the treaty's provisions is that Germany is not allowed to have an air force. But Hitler and his military leader, Hermann Göring, have a secret "Four Year Plan" to re-arm Germany, including the re-creation of the Luftwaffe. In the summer of 1936, the world comes to Berlin for the Olympics...and sees that Germany now has an Air Ministry. Hitler is probing, provoking, testing...will anyone put a stop to it? They do not. Later that same year, Hitler remilitarizes the Rhineland—another illegal act. And again, nobody has the will to push back. Historians cite 1936 as the pivotal year when Hitler realized how much he could get away with, emboldening him to build an empire and go on the offensive. And it all began with the Air Ministry.

After the war, this building became the headquarters for the Soviet occupation. And it was here, on October 7, 1949, that the German Democratic Republic (a.k.a. communist East Germany) was officially founded. The DDR used the building to house their—no joke—Ministry of Ministries. In this building, on June 15, 1961, East German Premier Walter Ulbricht reassured nervous East Berliners, "Nobody has any intention of building a wall." Less than two months later, the first bricks were laid. (Today, the building houses the German Finance Ministry.)

Across the street from the main courtyard, look for the information kiosk with a series of **video screens.** It can be hard to envision the weighty history at a monumental site like this, but these screens help—showing original footage of historic moments from 1914 (World War I) through 2014 (Angela Merkel).

• *Continue to the far end of the giant building. There, just around the corner with Leipziger Strasse, you'll find a small plaza cut into the structure.*

❼ Building the Republic Mural (1953)

Look under the Air Ministry's portico to find a vivid (and unusually well-preserved) example of communist art. The mural, Max Lingner's *Aufbau der Republik*, is classic Socialist Realism, showing the entire society—industrial laborers, farm workers, women, and children—all happily singing the same patriotic song. Its subtitle:

"The importance of peace for the cultural development of humanity and the necessity of struggle to achieve this goal."

On the far left, notice the highly educated young graduate with the briefcase. In the 1950s, the DDR experienced a serious brain drain with many  such potential leaders leaving for the West. The East needed a way to stop the emigration. Locals like to point out that the hands of the blue maidens are proof that Germans can't clap with the beat. The small children in blue kerchiefs represent the generation born in the rubble of World War II, who grew up knowing nothing but DDR values. They are the "lost generation," who, after German unification, had the toughest time dealing with freedom and change. These people are the demographic that is most "Ost-algic," often anti-immigrant, and likely to vote for extremist parties in Germany today.

This mural shows the communist ideal. But the reality was quite different. Step farther away from the mural beyond the large black-and-white photo embedded in the square. It shows an angry 1953 crowd with arms linked in solidarity—marching against a government that was as warm and accommodating as the architecture looming above.

When the DDR barricaded its borders with West Germany in 1952, the economy floundered—and it quickly became clear that the West was better off. After Josef Stalin died in March of 1953, people across the Eastern Bloc hoped for change. On June 16 of that year, workers who were busy constructing the ambitious Soviet-style boulevard "Stalinallee" (now Karl-Marx-Allee) laid down their tools, went on strike, and marched to this square to demand change. The next day, on June 17, a general strike went into effect across East Germany. But the uprising never had a chance to gain momentum—it was shut down by Soviet tanks. Today this square is officially named the "Square of the Popular Uprising of 1953."

• *Continue west down Leipziger Strasse to the towering skyscrapers in the distance. At the big intersection, make your way to the small, hexagonal clock tower near the big glass tubes, midway between the two cubical S-Bahn entrances marked* Bahnhof Potsdamer Platz.

❾ Potsdamer Platz

Before World War II, Potsdamer Platz was the "Times Square of Berlin," and possibly the busiest square in all of Europe. But it was pulverized in World War II, and stood at the intersection of the

American, British, and Soviet postwar sectors. When the Wall went up, the platz was cut in two and left a deserted no-man's-land for 40 years. As throughout Berlin, two subtle lines in the pavement indicate where the Wall once stood. With reunification, a redevelopment campaign was immediately started (christened by a 1990 concert of Pink Floyd's *The Wall*). Since then, Sony, Daimler, and other major corporations have turned the square once again into a city center. Like great Christian churches built upon pagan holy grounds, Potsdamer Platz—with its corporate logos flying high and shiny above what was the Wall—trumpets the triumph of capitalism.

The small green **clock tower** is a replica of the first electronic traffic light in Europe, which once stood at the six-street intersection of Potsdamer Platz.

Take in the skyscrapers around you—representing the rousing recovery of Berlin from its miserable 20th century. Start with the easy-to-spot **DB Tower**—a curved, green-glass, crescent-shaped building. This is the corporate headquarters for Deutsche Bahn, the national train system. Hiding behind the DB building is the (much lower) tent-like roofline of the Sony Center (where this walk ends).

To the right of the DB Tower is the **Beisheim Center.** Its twin, blocky-gray buildings are meant to recall the early skyscrapers of 1920s-era Chicago.

To the left of the DB Tower is the 25-story, red-brick **Potsdamer Platz 1** building. Though it looks like a retro Art Deco building from 1920s New York, it was built in 1999. This plays host to Daimler-Benz and big-name law firms. You can go up the tower to the Panoramapunkt for great views (see page 81).

The next skyscraper to the left is the glass-wedge, 18-story **Forum Tower.** It's by Renzo Piano, the renowned Italian architect who created the master plan for the entire Potsdamer Platz renovation.

Now turn your attention to the street level of Potsdamer Platz. The slanted glass cylinders sticking out of the ground help light the underground train station. Mirrors on the tops of the tubes move with the sun to collect light and send it underground.

DDR Watchtower Detour: If you just have to get another dose of the Berlin Wall, from here you can detour five minutes to a rare surviving DDR watchtower (turn left as Potsdamer Platz becomes Stresemannstrasse, then turn left again on Erna-Berger-Strasse and walk a long block). Built in 1966, the watchtower (on the left) was constantly manned by two guards. The guards were forbidden to get to know each other (no casual chatting), so they could effectively guard each other from escaping. You can pay to climb to the tower's tiny interior and peek out its windows (€3.50, open daily roughly 11:00-15:00, longer in summer).

• *Otherwise, let's continue to the grand (capitalist) finale of our walk: a shopping mall/entertainment complex that embodies the last generation's changes in Berlin. It's tucked behind the towering DB skyscraper. From the clock tower, cross the street to the second S-Bahn entrance. (Check out the slabs of Berlin Wall that stand like capitalist trophies of war.) Ride the escalator down. The first level below offers a peek at this massive underground transportation hub (there used to be a big train station above you). The vision is to promote public transit, so parking is almost non-existent around here.*

From here, follow signs to Sony Center. *At the top of the next escalator, you'll walk past a series of interesting historic photos that show and tell the story of what was "Europe's largest piece of urban wasteland" and the epic construction project that changed that. Finally, ride the escalator up and enter the...*

❾ Sony Center

The complex sits under a grand canopy, designed to evoke Mount Fuji. At night, multicolored floodlights play on the underside of this tent. There's a Lego-land and other touristy attractions. Office workers and tourists eat here by the fountain, enjoying the parade of people. The modern Bavarian Linden-bräu beer hall—the Sony boss wanted a *Brauhaus*—serves traditional food.

The Sony Center is a hub for Berlin's thriving cinema scene. It hosts red-carpet events, where major stars come to greet fans and promote their latest movie. Berlin has a major film festival ("Berlinale") each February. And there are several movie theaters here, along with the **Deutsche Kinemathek Film and TV Museum**

(described on page 80). A huge screen shows big sporting events on special occasions.

For all the attempts to make Potsdamer Platz a "city center" like it once was...it isn't. The corporate-sponsored buildings feel pretty soulless. But then, Berlin has never had a single "main square" the way, say, Munich has its Marienplatz. Berlin is more a collection of former towns that now compose dozens of distinct neighborhoods—Prenzlauer Berg, Charlottenburg, Kreuzberg, and so on.

Potsdamer Platz may not be Berlin's "center," but it is a major hub for transportation and shopping. The place remains lively after dark—a sure sign something must be happening here. Locals are unimpressed by the grandeur and the overpriced tourist restaurants, but they do admit, it's a good place to catch a movie.

• *You've survived this historical minefield of terrible topography and jarring architecture, representing the full span of Berlin's 20th century.*

*From here, art lovers are a short stroll away from the **Kulturforum**—boasting some of Berlin's best museum collections, from Old Masters (the Gemäldegalerie) to decorative arts to musical instruments. It's about a 10-minute walk from here, just past the far end of Sony Center; ▢ see the Gemäldegalerie & Kulturforum Tour chapter.*

FASCISM WALK

KREUZBERG WALK

The sprawling Kreuzberg (KROYTS-behrk) neighborhood, just south of the center, is most often described as Berlin's "Turkish neighborhood," or its "edgy multicultural district." It's those things, yes...and much more.

Kreuzberg is a huge area (four square miles, with 150,000 people), but it's really a collection of fascinating little *Kieze* (small neighborhoods), each with a unique personality. This walk focuses on the characteristic core around Kottbusser Tor, which gives you a general feel for the entire neighborhood. (For those who are intrigued, I've suggested other Kreuzberg *Kieze* to explore under "The Rest of Kreuzberg," at the end of this chapter.)

This walk offers a convenient, accessible, and representative introduction to Kreuzberg. Along the way—between tempting opportunities to sample the rich food scene—we'll get a crash course in the neighborhood's history, from its Industrial Age roots to its Turkish guest-worker boom of the postwar years to its current *Multikulti* (multiculturalism) and intense gentrification.

Orientation

Length of This Walk: About an hour.

When to Go: This walk can be done at any time, but to enjoy the Turkish street market in full swing, come on Tuesday or Friday (11:00-18:30). Given its thriving food scene, Kreuzberg is ideal for a stroll between sightseeing and dinner time—but if you're out late, don't stray too far from the main thoroughfares. (Berliners avoid sketchy Görlitzer Park at night.)

Getting There: Kreuzberg is well served by the north-south U8 line and the east-west U1 and U3 lines; these cross at the epicenter of Kreuzberg, Kottbusser Tor, which is also the starting and ending point for this walk.

Eateries: Kreuzberg is a foodie hotspot. Come hungry. I've pointed out several handy stops for a quick bite along this route. For a sit-down, "destination" restaurant, survey my recommendations in the Eating in Berlin chapter before you set out. For browsers and explorers, at the end of this chapter I've suggested some eateries in other parts of Kreuzberg, just beyond the central zone covered by this walk.

Starring: Berlin's thriving Turkish expat community, counterculture/squatter/punk heritage, and a trendy, up-and-coming vibe.

The Walk Begins

• *Ride the U1, U3, or U8 line to Kottbusser Tor, and head outside. To drop yourself right into the thick of Kreuzberg, make your way to the north side of the U-Bahn station and stand in the lively square in front of the Rossmann drugstore.*

❶ Kottbusser Tor

Nicknamed "Kotti" by locals, this area is a lesson in contrasts. The giant, semicircular apartment building—subsidized housing wrapping around the northern part of the square—defines a public space that corrals a lot of street life. With the U-Bahn station in the center, an elevated train line overhead, a busy arterial running through its heart, and a half-dozen smaller roads all converging on this circle, it's always full of activity.

As Berlin boomed with the Industrial Age in the late 19th century, Kreuzberg expanded like crazy to house workers (much like Prenzlauer Berg, to the north). During the Cold War, Kreuzberg was in the West but surrounded on three sides by the Wall. Its buildings, already damaged by WWII bombs, became further dilapidated as property owners—fishing for government support—refused to invest in repairs.

All of this made Kreuzberg the least desirable neighborhood in West Berlin. Much of the area around you dates from the 1970s, when the neighborhood's low rents attracted two groups: draft-dodging West German punks who squatted in Kreuzberg's ramshackle tenements, and immigrants—largely Turkish guest work-

Kreuzberg Walk

1 Kottbusser Tor
2 Admiralstrasse
3 Double Admiral Statue
4 Admiralsbrücke & Landwehr Canal
5 Graefekiez
6 Kottbusser Brücke & Turkish Street Market
7 Paul-Lincke-Ufer
8 Omar ibn Al Khattab Mosque & Community Center
9 Oranienstrasse
10 Adalbertstrasse
11 FHXB Museum

ers *(Gastarbeiter)* trying to scrape together a living in their adopted country.

Over the last decade or so, Kreuzberg has been in transition, as Berliners have been priced out of more expensive, central neighborhoods and moved south. While it still retains some of its squatter and Turkish roots (notice the many satellite dishes, which pick up Turkish stations), Kreuzberg has blossomed into one of the most diverse and exciting parts of town—and has rapidly gentrified. But it sticks to its fringe roots: Kreuzberg is Germany's only electoral district with a directly elected Green delegate in parliament.

Here on Kotti, you'll find a rainbow of people both busy and just hanging out, perhaps some sketchy-looking drug users and dealers, and usually a low-key police presence keeping an eye on things. Look up Adalbertstrasse (under the yellow arch that proclaims *Zentrum Kreuzberg*): This street used to dead-end at the Wall four blocks north of here. Our circular walk will eventually bring us down that street back to Kottbusser Tor.

• *Head under the train tracks, then go south down...*

❷ Admiralstrasse

On the immediate right is the recommended **Südblock,** an inviting beer terrace that prides itself in bringing this multidimensional community together. Across the street, a **community help center**—little more than a shack—helps locals with rent issues, drug problems, and so on.

Walk to the intersection with a ❸ statue called the **Double Admiral.** Erected in the 1980s (notice the feathered, punk hairdo of the figure at the base), it's clearly inspired by the name of the street: Two admirals stand at the top of the hourglass, peering in opposite directions. Maybe, as time passes, they're looking for their old Berlin...

Carrying on past the statue, you'll pass a graffiti-covered **primary school** on the left. With high unemployment here, there's lots of idle time and frustration. Just add a can of spray paint, and this is the result.

• *Soon you reach a waterway.*

❹ Admiralbrücke and the Landwehr Canal

This canal (the *Landwehrkanal*), was built in the 1840s before steam trains were established and runs roughly parallel to the Spree

River. It slices through the middle of Kreuzberg and adjoining districts, and through a corner of the huge Tiergarten Park. The canal was a critical link for shipping as Berlin entered its Industrial Age boom time. Today it's mostly recreational.

The bridge before you, called **Admiralbrücke,** functions as a delightful community gathering point on balmy evenings, a sign of prosperous times. A generation ago, the bridge and nearby embankments were the site of "The Battle of the Fraenkelufer," a 1980 rumble between squatters and the police, with riots, barricades, and beatings. The squatter movement had been growing in Kreuzberg for several years, and this standoff proved to be a turning point: Would the police succeed in evicting them, or would

Berlin's *Kiez* Culture

Berliners have a strong sense of community. They manage this in a big city by enjoying a strong neighborhood identity. Your neighborhood is called your *Kiez* ("keets"). This doesn't refer to a large swath of the city (like Prenzlauer Berg or Kreuzberg), but a microscopic sub-sub-sub-neighborhood. A *Kiez* can be just a few blocks, barely big enough to contain a smattering of key services (grocery store, school, park), and typically named for a major street or square. People tend to live lives very focused on their *Kiez,* and rarely stray. Some Berliners venture to other *Kieze* only when entertaining out-of-town visitors.

Each *Kiez* has its own personality—but things are definitely in flux. As a traditionally low-rent district, once surrounded on three sides by the Berlin Wall, Kreuzberg used to be thought of as being home to two types of people: draft-dodging, alternative-lifestyle German squatters and hard-working, lower-middle-class Turkish immigrants. And to an extent, you'll still see both groups in Kreuzberg. However, over the last decade or so, several Kreuzberg *Kieze* have gone through a predictable life cycle of gentrification: Artists and hipsters, lured by the *Kiez*'s low rents and ramshackle funkiness, move in. They open up gourmet ramen shops and fair-trade coffee houses, stoking a buzz. As these areas become hip and desirable, rents increase—often forcing out long-time residents and ultimately changing the face of the *Kiez.*

As you talk to Berliners, you'll learn that these issues of class, gentrification, and socioeconomic stratification are a huge preoccupation. Some make a hobby of chasing the latest trendy neighborhoods around town before they "go mainstream." Others grow disgruntled at having to move farther and farther from the center, priced out by über-rich yuppies. Throughout its history, Berlin has been a city in transition. I imagine that for just as long, the local pastime has been complaining about those changes...and today is no exception.

the squatters back down? While several were arrested, the fracas inspired even more squatters to come to Kreuzberg. Within several months, they occupied more than 160 area homes.

• *Those days are long gone, as will be clear when you cross the bridge and enter...*

❺ Graefekiez

This trendy, delightful-to-explore *Kiez* feels quite different from the area we just left. Berliners think of Kreuzberg in terms of its two postal codes, which have very different personalities: "Kreuzberg 36" (SO36), which we just left, is considered the grittier "other side of the tracks" (or canal); and "Kreuzberg 61" (SW61), which we just entered, which is thought of as sleepy and bourgeois.

Keep going into "The 61," enjoying the vibe on the square just past the bridge. Beloved neighborhood hangouts here include **Isabel,** an Italian-style ice-cream shop (Böckhstrasse 1), and the cheap-and-cheery **Il Casolare** pizzeria (Grimmstrasse 30).

Head down Böckhstrasse to see classic Graefekiez. Many of these buildings survived WWII bombings. Balcony culture is in vogue here. You may see lots of strollers, as Berlin is experiencing a baby boom—neighborhoods like this, with relatively affordable rents and a melting pot at your doorstep, are great for young families.

When you reach **Graefestrasse,** the main drag, pause to notice the gentrification. Kreuzberg's residents value a strong sense of community and support family businesses (you won't see big chain stores here). It's been a long struggle for this community and they know the value of working together.

Turn left up Graefestrasse back toward the canal. As you stroll, enjoy window-shopping through the characteristic shops and eateries. But be careful—at #7 (on the left) is **Eismanufaktur Berlin,** the local favorite for gourmet ice cream.

• *Busy Graefestrasse leads back to the Landwehr Canal and the...*

❻ Kottbusser Brücke and Turkish Street Market

To your right, along the south bank of the canal (Maybachufer Strasse), stretches Kreuzberg's vibrant Turkish street market. Ber-

lin is the largest Turkish city outside of Turkey itself, and that's most evident on a Tuesday or Friday when the market is in action. It's worth planning your visit to Kreuzberg around this lively scene, with a commotion of sights, sounds, and smells like you might experience at the bazaars in Istanbul: vibrant rugs, piles of olives, aromatic teas, and sizzling food carts, along with everyday items like clothes and kitchenware. (For more on this market, see the Shopping in Berlin chapter.)

• *If the market's on, give it a slow lap up and down Maybachufer, returning to the bridge where you started. When you're ready to move on, cross the canal and head right, along the northern embankment of the Landwehr Canal on...*

KREUZBERG WALK

❼ Paul-Lincke-Ufer

This mostly residential area is a pleasant place to stroll and enjoy some of Berlin's trendiest restaurants, including the recommended **Horváth** (which owns a Michelin star) and **Cocolo Ramen X-berg** (always crowded with happy people slurping noodles; for more recommendations on this street, see the Eating in Berlin chapter).

You could keep walking along this delightful embankment (for details, see "The Rest of Kreuzberg," later), but to continue our walk, turn left after a long block onto **Manteuffelstrasse** and walk a couple of blocks. Most of the apartment complexes here share the same story as those in Prenzlauer Berg and elsewhere in this neighborhood: built to house Industrial Age workers, survived WWII bombs, and neglected in communist times. After the Wall fell, they were largely abandoned and filled with squatters, poor immigrant workers, and counterculture types. When you see a vacant lot, it may have been bombed in WWII—or perhaps developers started demolishing houses only to be thwarted by local outcry. This was common in the 1980s, and similar debates rage today. There's long been an uneasy friction between longtime residents—who love their scruffy Kreuzberg just as it is—and developers who see dollar signs in the potential here.

By the way, we've crossed from posh "Kreuzberg 61" back into edgy "Kreuzberg 36"...can't you tell?

• *Carry on two blocks. Soon you'll reach the overhead train tracks marking the U-Bahn station at Görlitzer Bahnhof (to your right). Look right, through the small square, to see the big, glassy...*

❽ Omar ibn Al Khattab Mosque and Community Center

Built in 2008 and partly funded by Saudi Arabia, this glass-domed building on the corner is a mosque and community center for the large Muslim population in this neighborhood. Anyone is welcome to drop in and check it out—including you. Young, progressive Berlin embraces its *Multikulti* (a phrase made popular by the German Green Party in the 1980s), and celebrates the many different kinds of lifestyles, faiths, and backgrounds that come together here. The center also hosts an interesting eatery: The Maschari Cafeteria offers a cheap menu of items made in the mosque, including Turkish pizza.

• *From here, consider an optional detour to the...*

Markthalle Neun Food Hall: A short walk north is this wonderfully restored, 19th-century brick market hall, where hip food stalls rub shoulders with traditional vendors. Exploring this beautiful building, you'll find a wide variety of eating options. To get there now, head straight across Skalitzer Strasse and under the train tracks, and continue three blocks up Manteuffelstrasse.

When you reach Muskrauer Strasse, head right for one block and find the hall on your left (the approach is through a borderline-seedy area; just stay alert). If you don't make the trip now, keep this food hall in mind for a meal later (it's described in more detail in the Eating in Berlin chapter).

• *To continue our walk from Görlitzer Bahnhof, cross under the tracks and head left, down the main shopping street of "Kreuzberg 36" called...*

❾ Oranienstrasse

Oranienstrasse is Kreuzberg's "shopping mile." Like most of Kreuzberg, gentrification has brought more bars and restaurants, but this street retains its traditional character: No malls or chains, just small family-run shops, liberal bookstores, cultural centers, and so on. Venture into a courtyard or two. As throughout Berlin, so much hides behind the facades.

At Oranienstrasse #2 (on the right), **Coretex** record store was a mecca for the counterculture scene in the 1980s and provides a vivid reminder that Kreuzberg has long been about more than Turkish culture. It's fun for souvenirs, and they also sell concert tickets.

Farther along, you'll pass through a huge, octagonal intersection. Continue straight ahead, noticing (on the right, at #16) **Angry Chicken**—part of a recent trend of Korean fried chicken restaurants.

At the start of the next block (on the left at #190), **Club SO36** is a venerable punk concert hall made famous in the 1980s and still a thriving music venue. Gen-X Berliners think of this place fondly, and can still hear the ringing in their ears.

Carry on to the end of this long block. At #27, on the right, drop by the Smyrna Kuruyemis **nut shop.** Step up to the counter, choose from a huge selection of nuts and dried fruit, get a bowl and a drink, and sit down with the neighborhood gang outside and watch the scene while you munch.

• *At the intersection, turn left on Adalbertstrasse. From here, it's a straight shot back to Kotti and your starting point.*

❿ Adalbertstrasse

On the left is the recommended **Hasir,** a popular Turkish restaurant. After finding success here, Hasir opened a branch in the trendy, central Hackescher Markt area—bringing upmarket Turkish cooking from deep in the *Kieze* into downtown Berlin. They have a smaller branch just two doors farther down that's a bit less formal, with more kebabs.

Just beyond that (at #9) is **Kılıçoğlu,** the baklava shop of your honey-soaked dreams. Across the street (at #93), **Maroush** is an authentic hole-in-the-wall Lebanese joint, popular for its chicken shawarma.

Just beyond that, duck into the courtyard on the right to find the humble ❶ **FHXB Museum** (free, Tue-Fri 12:00-18:00, Sat-Sun 10:00-20:00, closed Mon, www.fhxb-museum.de). This museum celebrates the strong spirit and history of two communities, Kreuzberg and Friedrichshain—the neighborhood with a Kreuzberg-like vibe just across the river, to the northeast. It's really two museums that became one (the Kreuzberg Museum and the Heimatmuseum Friedrichshain), with the "X" in the name representing the crossover between the similar districts.

• *Finally, you'll pass under the* "Zentrum Kreuzberg" *sign—now in Turkish* ("Kreuzberg Merkezi") *on this side—and find yourself back where you started, right in the middle of Kotti.*

Our walk is finished. You could hop on the U1, U3, or U8 at Kottbusser Tor and head back to the city center. Or, if you're intrigued to see more of this area, consider these next options.

THE REST OF KREUZBERG

Now that you have your bearings, let yourself be drawn deeper into Kreuzberg. There are plenty of *Kieze* to explore, each with its own character, and each clustered around a U-Bahn station—making it easy to hopscotch between them. Use this rundown of some of Kreuzberg's most appealing *Kieze* to inspire you to explore further. The first two can easily be spliced into this walk; the last two are a U-Bahn ride away. For locations of many of the eateries and sights mentioned next, see the "Kreuzberg" section of the Eating in Berlin chapter on page 296, with a map and even more dining recommendations.

Extended Stroll on Paul-Lincke-Ufer (Between U8: Schönleinstrasse and U1/U3/U8: Görlitzer Bahnhof)

My self-guided walk offers a glimpse of this inviting embankment (along the Landwehr Canal, just east of Kottbusser Brücke). On a sunny day, you can venture farther—it's one of Berliners' favorite spots for a Sunday stroll. From Kottbusser Brücke, just head east. Just up Lausitzer Strasse at #22 (on the left) is a sign pointing to the funky, artsy squatters' courtyard called **Regenbogenfabrik** ("Rainbow Factory"), still run as a collective with its own cinema, kindergarten, and bike-repair shop. Back on Paul-Lincke-Ufer, between Forster Strasse and Liegnitzer Strasse you'll see popular public **lawn-bowling courts.** From this point on, you can peel off from Paul-Lincke-Ufer and head north to Görlitzer Park and beyond to Wrangelkiez (described later).

Mariannenplatz (U1/U3/U8: Kottbusser Tor)

Another appealing detour from the spine of my walk is this leafy square. Simply head a couple of blocks north of Oranienstrasse on Mariannenstrasse (from the big octagonal intersection) and pass the firefighters monument.

On the left side of the park, the huge turreted building is a hospital-turned-arts center called **Kunstquartier Bethanien.** Its courtyard hosts an atmospheric restaurant/beer garden and a summer outdoor movie series (www.kunstquartier-bethanien.de).

At the northeast edge of this long park, just beyond the Sankt-Thomas-Kirche, is the **Baumhaus an der Mauer**—a strange little nub of land where the Wall once ran. Locals love to tell the story of the Kreuzberg resident who realized this land belonged to the East, but somehow wound up just outside the Wall. He claimed it for his own and built a treehouse here, which stands to this day—like a ragged *Robinson Crusoe* shantytown in the middle of the street.

Wrangelkiez (U1: Schlesisches Tor)

Wrangelstrasse, running between Markthalle Neun and the river, is a trendy drag that defines the up-and-coming Wrangelkiez neighborhood. This tidy, grid-planned zone feels equal parts German and Turkish hipsters. You may see red paint or rude graffiti splashed on some of the trendier eateries: Locals tapping the brakes on the transformation of their *Kiez*. Görlitzer Park, at the southern edge of this area, is fine by day—but after dark, it's best avoided.

Note that Wrangelkiez is just across the river (on the picturesque Oberbaumbrücke—the Oberbaum Bridge) from the East Side Gallery—an easy add-on if you're exploring there (see page 74).

Eating in Wrangelkiez: This area is loaded with restaurants. Beer pilgrims appreciate **Hopfenreich,** with 22 good microbrews on tap, but no food (daily 16:00-24:00, on the corner of Wrangelstrasse and Sorauer Strasse at #31, +49 30 8806 1080). For a delicious and authentic Georgian meal, make your way to **$$ Schwiliko**—with owners (and ingredients) from the Republic of Georgia (daily 17:00-24:00, Schlesische Strasse 29, +49 30 6162 3588, www.schwiliko-berlin.de). And on the Landwehr Canal just to the east, **$$ Freischwimmer** serves a range of European dishes and is a great place to break on a sunny day thanks to its peaceful location (daily 12:00-22:00, Vor dem Schlesischen Tor 2a, +49 30 6107 4309).

Bergmannkiez (U7: Gneisenaustrasse)

The most upscale of the Kreuzberg *Kieze* (in the posh "Kreuzberg 61"), the Bergmannkiez gentrified long before gentrification was all the rage. This is where many Kreuzberg revolutionaries from the 1970s and 1980s moved once they grew up and settled down.

From the Gneisenaustrasse U-Bahn stop, go south down Mittenwalder Strasse. You'll soon reach the glass-walled **Marheineke Markthalle**—filled with appealing food counters serving Greek, Asian, Spanish tapas, French crêpes and galettes, grilled fish, pizza, Berliner specialties, and so on (Mon-Fri 8:00-20:00, Sat until 18:00, closed Sun, Marheinekeplatz 15). The square  out front (Marheinekeplatz) is a delight. A block to the east is a classic, parklike Prussian cemetery with a fine little **café.**

Or head west down the neighborhood's main artery, **Bergmannstrasse**—a fun place to browse (its pleasant side streets hold inviting little shops). Crossing Mehringdamm, continue up Kreuzbergstrasse to **Viktoriapark,** where a sturdy hike takes you up to "the" Kreuzberg—a frilly pillar with a cross *(Kreuz)* on top of a steep hill *(Berg),* designed by Karl Friedrich Schinkel to commemorate the Franco-Prussian War—which gave its name to this whole area.

After the hike, reward yourself with a tankard at the thriving **Golgatha Gaststätten** beer garden (near the stadium, behind the hill; daily 9:00-18:00, closed in bad weather, Dudenstrasse 40, +49 30 785 2453).

Eating near Marheineke Markthalle: The market hall itself is an easy place to find good food, but there are other options nearby, including a pair of restaurants that Berliners swear by for traditional Austrian cuisine: the aptly named **$$$ Austria Restaurant,**

in business since 1858 (Tue-Sun 12:00-23:00, Mon from 18:00, cash only, Bergmannstrasse 30, +49 30 4058 7763), and the smaller, trendier-feeling **$$ Felix Austria** (daily 10:00-24:00, a half-block away at Bergmannstrasse 26, +49 30 6167 5451). Nearby, the wine bar **Not Only Riesling** has an array of German vintages (Mon-Fri 13:00-22:00, Sat from 10:00, closed Sun, Schleiermacherstrasse 25, +49 30 200 039 557).

Street Food: Two beloved-by-Berliners joints stand a few steps apart on the west side of Mehringdamm street, near the U-Bahn stop (U6/U7). Both have long hours daily. **$ Mustafa's Gemüse Kebab** is famous for its top-quality kebabs...and its extremely long lines. Nearby, **$ Curry 36** is a local favorite for *Currywurst* and generally has a shorter/faster-moving line.

GEMÄLDEGALERIE & KULTURFORUM TOUR

The Kulturforum, with its collection of various museums, libraries, and concert halls, rivals Museum Island as Berlin's cultural heart. Established after many of the city's artistic treasures were lost behind the Wall, the Kulturforum's modernist buildings were mostly erected in the 1960s. Today, its collections pick up where those of Museum Island leave off, covering art from the late Middle Ages to the present.

The main sight here is the **Gemäldegalerie**—a world-class collection of European paintings that ranks alongside the greatest museums anywhere. Here you'll see works by Rembrandt, Dürer, Vermeer, Rubens, and others. There aren't a lot of "must-see" iconic paintings, but visitors with some background in art will find many that are instantly recognizable.

The Kulturforum's next-best sight is the **Decorative Arts Museum,** a breezy look at an assortment of beautiful objects through the ages. You'll see jeweled medieval reliquaries, elegant Louis XIV furniture, and a parade of ladies' dresses that even lowbrow tourists find interesting.

The complex is also home to the **Musical Instruments Museum,** the **Berlin Philharmonic's concert hall,** and the Mies van der Rohe-designed **New National Gallery** (closed for renovation).

Orientation

Combo-Ticket: Each Kulturforum museum has a separate ticket (listed later). If you're visiting at least two of the museums, get the €12 combo-ticket, which covers all the museums listed here (can cost more if a special exhibit is on, www. kulturforum-berlin.de). These museums are also covered by the Museum Pass Berlin.

Planning Your Visit to the Kulturforum

To hit the main highlights of the Kulturforum's collections, orient yourself to the various buildings of the sprawling campus. Start at the Gemäldegalerie with its collection of world-class paintings (allow an hour). When you're done there, head next door to the Museum of Decorative Arts or to the Musical Instruments Museum, just a block away (allow 30-45 minutes each).

Supplement my descriptions in this chapter with the maps and audioguides available at each museum.

When to Go: The museums are rarely crowded—anytime works well.

Getting There: The Kulturforum is a 10-minute walk from Potsdamer Platz: Ride the S-Bahn or U-Bahn to Potsdamer Platz, walk west along Potsdamer Strasse, then turn right on Scharounstrasse to enter the heart of the complex. (As you walk from Potsdamer Platz to the Kulturforum, consider stopping into the Sony Center—it's right on the way.) It's efficient to combine your Kulturforum visit with my 📖 Fascism & Cold War Walk.

You can also take bus #200 to the Philharmonie stop or bus #300 to the Philharmonie Sud stop.

Gemäldegalerie: €14; Tue-Fri 10:00-18:00, Thu until 20:00, Sat-Sun 11:00-18:00, closed Mon; Matthäikirchplatz 4, +49 30 266 424 242, www.smb.museum.

Museum of Decorative Arts: €8; Tue-Fri 10:00-18:00, Sat-Sun from 11:00, closed Mon; Matthäikirchplatz 5, +49 30 266 424 242, www.smb.museum/kgm.

Musical Instruments Museum: €6; Tue-Fri 9:00-17:00, Sat-Sun from 10:00, closed Mon; low-profile white building east of the big yellow Berlin Philharmonic concert hall (find the easy-to-miss entrance down Ben-Gurion-Strasse, facing the back of the Sony Center), +49 30 2548 1178, www.simpk.de.

New National Gallery: Closed for years-long renovation; for the latest, consult www.smb.museum.

Berlin Philharmonic: You can visit the concert hall with a guided one-hour **tour** in English (€5, daily at 13:30 except none July-Aug, same-day tickets sold at 12:00 at the artists' entrance—facing the busy road and the park). Also consider attending a **performance** or free **lunch concert,** held on most Tuesdays (for details, see page 311 of the Entertainment in Berlin chapter).

Getting Oriented: Locate the Kulturforum's various buildings

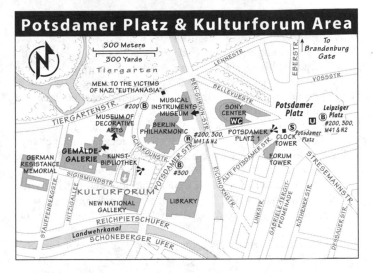

by first finding the green steeple of the St. Matthäus Church. Just to the left and beyond the church is the glass-walled New National Gallery. To the right of the church is the low-lying, sprawling Gemäldegalerie—this area's highlight. Farther right is the cubical Museum of Decorative Arts. Then comes the golden, angular Philharmonic concert hall and behind it, the Musical Instruments Museum (not really visible).

Tours: Each museum has a good, free audioguide; for insights beyond my tour, pick one up as you enter.

Services: You'll find WCs, free lockers, and a cloakroom at the Gemäldegalerie.

Cuisine Art: The Gemäldegalerie has a decent **$$** cafeteria/salad bar (upstairs, cash only); otherwise, you'll find touristy eateries a 10-minute walk away, around Potsdamer Platz and the Sony Center.

Starring: European masters, musical instruments, glittering treasury items, and women's fashion through the ages.

Gemäldegalerie

The Gemäldegalerie—literally the "Painting Gallery"—is Germany's top collection of 13th- to 18th-century European paintings (more than 1,400 canvases). They're beautifully displayed on one vast floor in a building that's a work of art in itself. Virtually every major European artist has at least one quality work, and connoisseurs could spend days here. The focus here is on Northern art, especially German (Holbein, Cranach, and Dürer) and Dutch (Rembrandt and Vermeer), with a few Italians and others thrown in.

❯ SELF-GUIDED TOUR

This "top dozen or so highlights tour" will get you started. I've selected artists and paintings that are famous, unique, and fairly easy to find in this sprawling museum. But you'll walk past many more fine paintings in the Gemäldegalerie's extensive collection. To go beyond my choices, make ample use of the excellent included audioguide.

When you buy your ticket, pick up the current museum map for help locating specific paintings (artwork locations may change from descriptions below). Northern Art is on one side (where we'll begin) and Italian art is on the other (where we'll end).

Note that inner rooms have Roman numerals (I, II, III), while adjacent outer rooms use Arabic numerals (1, 2, 3). We'll work counterclockwise (and roughly chronologically) through the collection.

• From the entrance, turn right through Rooms I and II, then turn right again into **Room 1** (not Room I—got it?).

Northern Art

The German paintings that fill Rooms 1-4 and I-III are a snapshot of Germany in the early 1500s. The many portraits of middle-class businessmen and town burghers are a testament to Germany's booming trade and craftsmanship. In those days, the austere Protestant Reformation was brewing, and there are few bubbly paintings of Madonnas and saints. Artistically, the style is realistic and down to earth. Colors are dark, and there's a meticulous attention to detail. Many depicted items are symbolic, with meanings passed down since medieval times.

❶ Hans Holbein the Younger, 1497-1543

Typical of German painting of the period is work by Hans Holbein. Holbein's sober, unvarnished portraits chronicle the movers and shakers of the early 1500s, from Martin Luther to Erasmus to Henry VIII.

Holbein's portrait *Merchant Georg Gisze* (*Der Kaufmann Georg Gisze*, 1532) depicts a wealthy 34-year-old German businessman. Gisze glances up from his work in his Hanseatic branch office in London. His black beret and immaculate clothes mark him as a successful dealer in cloth. Around him are the tools of his trade—logbooks, business letters with wax seals, signet rings, scales, and coins. The Turkish tablecloth and Venetian-glass vase remind us of Gisze's cosmopolitan tastes.

Holbein adds another layer of complexity to this seemingly

Gemäldegalerie Tour

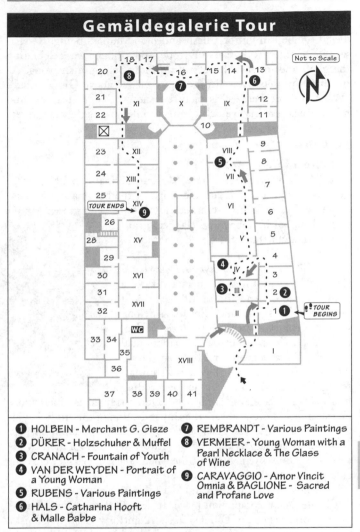

1 HOLBEIN - Merchant G. Gisze
2 DÜRER - Holzschuher & Muffel
3 CRANACH - Fountain of Youth
4 VAN DER WEYDEN - Portrait of a Young Woman
5 RUBENS - Various Paintings
6 HALS - Catharina Hooft & Malle Babbe
7 REMBRANDT - Various Paintings
8 VERMEER - Young Woman with a Pearl Necklace & The Glass of Wine
9 CARAVAGGIO - Amor Vincit Omnia & BAGLIONE - Sacred and Profane Love

straightforward portrait. Typical of detail-rich Northern European art, the canvas is bursting with highly symbolic tidbits. To the left, on the wall, is the motto *Nulla sine merore voluptas* ("No joy without sorrow"), a hint that Gisze's success has been hard-won. The clock (on the table, inside the small gold canister) reminds the viewer that time passes and worldly success fades. The unbalanced scales over his shoulder suggest that wealth is fleeting. Those negative symbols are counterbalanced by the hopeful image of the carnations and herbs in the vase, representing Gisze's upcoming marriage and his eternal devotion to his betrothed bride.

But the overwhelming impression Holbein leaves is not of medieval symbolism but of a flesh-and-blood human being. Renaissance humanism was alive in Europe, and Holbein was celebrating the glory and intrinsic beauty of an individual human being. As the artist himself wrote (in the white plaque above Gisze's head): "What you see here—this picture—shows Georg's features and figure. These are his eyes, this is his profile, just as they are in real life."

• *In **Room 2** are works by...*

❷ Albrecht Dürer, 1471-1528

In 1494, the young Dürer traveled from Germany to Italy, where he soaked up the technique and spirit of the burgeoning Renaissance movement. Dürer returned home and melded Italian harmony and classical grandeur with a Northern European attention to detail.

In his portrait *Hieronymus Holzschuher* (1526), Dürer captured the personality of a white-bearded friend from Nürnberg, right down to the sly twinkle in his sidelong glance. Technically the portrait is perfection: Look closely and see each individual hair of the man's beard and fur coat. Dürer does not gloss over the 57-year-old's unflattering features like the wrinkles or receding hairline (with the clever comb-over). Dürer, trained as a meticulous engraver, could even capture the tiny reflection of the studio's windows in the man's eyes. Also notice Dürer's little pyramid-shaped, D-inside-A signature. Signing one's work was a revolutionary assertion of Dürer's renown at a time when German artists were considered anonymous craftsmen.

Painted the same year and the same size, the portrait *Jakob Muffel* may be a companion piece. It depicts the mayor of Nürnberg (another friend of Dürer's) in a straightforward way, against a neutral background. We see the man's wrinkles, duck-billed nose, and prominent cranial bones. Muffel has a blank, calm expression, as though lost in thought. His high forehead reinforces the "highmindedness" of this incorruptible public servant.

• *To get to our next stop, head through Rooms 3 and 4, turn left into Room IV, then left again into Room III. (Confused yet?)* **Room III** *has some large-scale works by...*

❸ Lucas Cranach the Elder, 1472-1553

Cranach was a court painter for the prince electors of Saxony and a close friend of Martin Luther. He painted solemn portraits of

these men. But Cranach also painted religious and mythological subjects.

His *Fountain of Youth* (*Der Jungbrunnen*, 1546) depicts the perennial human pursuit of eternal youth. Ladies flock to bathe in the swimming pool of youth. They arrive (on the left) as old women—by wagon, on horseback, carried by men, even in a wheelbarrow. They strip and enter with sagging breasts, frolic awhile in the pool, rinse and repeat, then emerge (on the right) young again. Newly nubile, the women go into a tent to dress up, snog with noblemen in the bushes (right foreground), dance merrily beneath the trees, and dine grandly beneath a landscape of mountains and towers.

• *Head back into* **Room IV** *to see some masterworks by ...*

❹ Rogier van der Weyden, 1400-1464

Netherlandish painters—represented in the next several rooms—were early adopters of oil paint (as opposed to older egg tempera).

Its relative ease of handling allowed them to brush the super-fine details for which they became famous.

Rogier van der Weyden was a virtuoso of the new medium. In *Portrait of a Young Woman* (*Bildnis einer jungen Frau*, 1440-1445), the subject wears a typical winged bonnet, addressing the viewer directly with her fetching blue eyes. The subjects (especially women) of most portraits of the time look off to one side; some art historians guess that the confident woman shown here is Van der Weyden's wife.

In the same room is a remarkable, rare trio of three-panel altarpieces by Van der Weyden: The *Marienaltar* shows the life of the Virgin Mary; the *Johannesaltar* narrates the life of John the Baptist—his birth, baptizing of Christ (with God and the Holy Spirit hovering overhead), and gruesome death by decapitation; and the *Middelburger* altar tells the story of the Nativity. Savor the fine details in each panel of these altarpieces.

• *Browse through the next several rooms (V-VII, and the adjoining 5-8), with early Flemish artists. Ignore several undeniable masterworks—by the likes of Van Eyck, Bruegel, and Bosch—as you keep going to our next stop,* **Room VIII.**

❺ Peter Paul Rubens, 1577-1640

Here in Room VIII (and adjoining rooms) are works by Rubens. We've fast-forwarded a hundred years, and it's apparent how much the Protestant Reformation changed the tenor of Northern European art. Rubens' paintings represent the Catholic response, the Counter-Reformation.

You'll see huge, brightly-colored canvases of Mary, alongside angels, bishops, and venerated saints (like the arrow-pierced martyr, St. Sebastian). This exuberant Baroque style trumpeted the greatness of the Catholic Church. The Church had serious competition for the hearts and minds of its congregants. Exciting art like this became a way to keep people in the pews. Notice the quivering brushstrokes and almost too-bright colors.

You'll also see fleshy nudes and mythological scenes in the Italian tradition, such as *Perseus Freeing Andromeda* (*Perseus befreit Andromeda,* c. 1622, next to St. Sebastian). Rubens painted for wealthy Catholic nobles who were schooled in the classical imagery and sensual nudes of Renaissance art.

Finally, find a portrait of Rubens' first wife, the noble-looking Isabella Brandt. You may also see glimpses of Rubens' second wife, Helene Fourment, in mythological scenes such as *Andromeda* (1638). Helene, the amply-figured nymph with a sweetly smiling face, came to define the phrase "Ruben-esque."

• *Continue through a few more rooms to the museum's far-right corner,* **Room 13.** *You'll have to refocus your eyes from Rubens' huge colorful canvases to the tiny, dark slices-of-life of Dutch art.*

❻ Frans Hals, c. 1582-1666

Dutch painters captured convivial portraits of everyday folk during Holland's Golden Age of sea-trading prosperity.

Hals' *Portrait of Catharina Hooft with Her Nurse* (*Bildnis der Catharina Hooft mit ihrer Amme,* 1619-1620) presents a startlingly self-possessed baby (the newest member of a wealthy merchant family), dressed in the lacy, jeweled finery of a queen and clutching a golden rattle. The smiling nurse supporting the tyke offers her a piece of fruit, whose blush of red perfectly matches the nanny's apple-fresh cheeks. By the way, baby Catharina would grow up to marry the mayor of Amsterdam.

At the other end of the social spectrum is Hals' *Malle Babbe* (1633-1635). The subject, a notorious barfly nicknamed "Crazy" Babbe, was well known in Hals' hometown. Hals captures her in a snapshot from the local pub, hefting her pewter beer stein and turning to laugh at a joke. The messy brushstrokes that define her collar and cap are as wild and lively as her over-the-top personality. The bird perched on Babbe's shoulder was a sign to everyone that she was (as they used to say) "drunk as an owl."

• *Continue counterclockwise to Room 16 and the large, adjoining Room X.*

❼ Rembrandt van Rijn, 1606-1669

The ultimate Dutch master, Rembrandt was propelled to fame in his lifetime by his powers of perception and invention. His style—

dark brown canvases highlighted by a few brightly-lit details—is moody and dramatic.

Browse these rooms to get a taste of the range of Rembrandt's work. There are storytelling scenes, taut with pulse-racing emotion. In *The Rape of Persephone* (1631, Room 16), Pluto grabs Persephone from his chariot and races toward the underworld, while other goddesses cling to her robe, trying to save her. Cast against a nearly-black background, the almost overexposed, action-packed scene is shockingly expressive.

There are Bible scenes: In *Samson and Delilah* (1628-1629, Room 16), Delilah cradles Samson's head in her lap while silently signaling to a goon to shear Samson's hair, the secret to his strength. The larger-scale *Samson Threatens His Father-in-Law* (*Samson bedroht seinen Schwiegervater*, 1635, Room X) captures the moment just after the mighty Samson (with his flowing hair, elegant robes, and shaking fist) has been told by his wife's father to take a hike. I wouldn't want to cross this guy.

You may see the famous *Man with the Golden Helmet* (*Der Mann mit dem Goldhelm,* 1650-1655, Room 16). This is probably *not* by Rembrandt, but it shows how his style was so mimicked by followers that it's sprouted a cottage industry of art scholars trying to authenticate Rembrandt paintings.

In Room X, a *Self-Portrait* (1634) shows Rembrandt wearing

a beret. The 28-year-old genius was already famous. He soon married the beautiful Saskia (*Portrait of Saskia,* 1643, Room 16), and seemed to have it all. But then Saskia died, Rembrandt declared bankruptcy, his painting style went out of fashion, and he moved in with his young housekeeper, Hendrickje Stoffels (depicted in *Young Girl in an Open Door/Junge Frau am geöffneter Tür,* 1656-1657)...all of which contributed to his brooding, dark canvases.

• *Continue counterclockwise a couple of rooms, to* **Room 18.**

❽ Johannes Vermeer, 1632-1675

Today, Vermeer is just as admired as Rembrandt, though he was little known in his day, probably because he painted relatively few works for a small circle of Delft collectors. Vermeer was a master at conveying a complicated story through a deceptively simple scene with a few significant details—whether a woman reading a letter at a window, a milkmaid pouring milk from a pitcher into a bowl, or a woman with a pearl necklace.

Though not as famous as *Girl with the Pearl Earring* (which inspired a novel), *Young Woman with a Pearl Necklace* (*Junge Dame mit Perlenhalsband,* 1664) is classic Vermeer. He lets us glimpse an intimate, unguarded moment in the life of an everyday woman. She wears a beautiful yellow coat with an ermine fur lining, ribbons in her hair, and pearl earrings. As she completes her *toilette,* adjusting her necklace with the ribbon ties, she pauses for a moment. What catches her attention? It's as though a thought bubble hangs in the empty space between her and the mirror—the center of the composition.

This painting has many signature elements of Vermeer's style. Two colors dominate: the yellow of her jacket and the ultramarine blue of the bunched-up tablecloth (Vermeer liberally used this blue pigment, despite its being made from incredibly expensive powdered lapis lazuli). The scene is lit from a window at left, creating a soft, diffuse atmosphere. Vermeer tells us a bit about the woman with objects on the table: her comb, make-up brush, and water bowl.

Who is this young woman? Vermeer painted her on other occasions, and she may be the woman who became his wife.

Vermeer's *The Glass of Wine* (*Das Glas Wein,* 1661) lets us glimpse a racier subject. A young man offers a drink to a young lady. Her elegantly-dressed seducer has been playing his lute (which now sits, discarded, on a chair) and is hoping to seal the deal with some alcohol. The woman is finishing one glass of wine, and her suitor stands ready—almost *too* ready—to pour her another.

His sly smirk hints at his hopes for what will come next. Vermeer has perfectly captured the exact moment of "Will she or won't she?" The painter offers some clues—the coat of arms in the window depicts a woman holding onto the reins of a horse, staying in control—but ultimately, only he (and the couple) know how this scene will end.

• *Continuing counterclockwise, turn the corner into the South Wing, and skip ahead to* **Room XIV,** *where our tour concludes.*

Italian Art

The South Wing is dedicated primarily to art from Italy (with a smattering from France and Spain). We'll focus on just one artist, whose sensational originality turned the Italian art world on its head.

❾ Caravaggio, 1573–1610

In the year 1600, living in Rome, Caravaggio burst onto the scene with a new and shocking art style. He populated his canvases with everyday people drawn directly from life, set in a dark background and lit by a harsh, dramatic, unflattering light. (Remember Rembrandt? Well, Rembrandt sure remembered Caravaggio.) Even religious and allegorical subjects got his uncompromising, gritty, ultrarealistic treatment.

In Caravaggio's *Amor Vincit Omnia* (*Amor als Sieger,* 1601-1602), "Love Conquers All." Cupid stands victorious over all the

vain accomplishments of ambitious men: Military triumphs (symbolized by the fallen armor), Art (the discarded musical instruments), Literature (paper and pen), Science (a globe), Grand Architecture (compass and square), and Power (the crown). Cupid—a young, naked boy—mocks those grown-up ambitions. He laughs derisively and splays his genitals over the fallen symbols. This Cupid was Caravaggio's favorite male model, fitted with obviously fake stage-prop wings. The photorealistic style broke the fourth wall of illusion in what should be a high-falutin' allegorical painting. A secular-minded noble bought the painting and made it the showpiece of his collection.

For the next phase of Caravaggio's story, turn your attention to a painting in Room XIV by a different artist—**Giovanni**

Baglione's *Sacred and Profane Love (Der himmlische Amor besiegt den irdischen Amor,* 1602-1603).

Baglione was hired by the secular noble's brother—a conservative cardinal—to paint a moralizing response. Here, the main figure is a more upright incarnation of love—Sacred Love—embodied by a radiant angel. He corners his rascally counterpart, the cowering and "Profane" little Cupid (lower right). This breaks up the illicit tryst between Profane Love and the Devil (lower left). Baglione was satirizing Caravaggio's rude painting and also satirizing Caravaggio's groundbreaking style of dark/light contrasts.

The plot thickens. When Caravaggio saw Baglione's satire, he was furious. Baglione began spreading rumors that Caravaggio was sodomizing young boys. Baglione even painted a second version of this painting, with Caravaggio himself as the Devil. Caravaggio responded with dirty limericks about Baglione's own sex life, charged that he'd plagiarized his unique style (true), and harshly critiqued Baglione's "clumsy" work. Baglione successfully sued Caravaggio for libel, sending the young genius to jail for a few weeks.

Caravaggio's star began to fall. He became increasingly quick-tempered, killed a man in a street fight, spent years as an outlaw, and eventually died of a knife wound. After Caravaggio's death, his bad-boy reputation was cemented by his first biographer—none other than Baglione.

• *The rest of the South Wing features lesser-known works by great Italian Renaissance painters. Check out several Raphael Madonnas (Room 29), Titian's* Venus and the Organ Player *(Room XVI), and much, much more.*

Museum of Decorative Arts

With displays covering a thousand years of applied arts—porcelain, fine *Jugendstil* furniture, Art Deco, and reliquaries—the huge space of the Museum of Decorative Arts (Kunstgewerbemuseum) will delight some and bore others. But everyone will love one display: an impressive collection of clothing (mostly women's) through the ages.

COLLECTION HIGHLIGHTS

Entering the museum, pick up the free map and get oriented—you're on the "Mode/Foyer/Entrance" level. Go downstairs to the "Alte Kunst/Ground Floor" level, do a U-turn, and head for the door marked Mittelalter. You'll step into Room I.

The Guelph Treasure through History

The precious ecclesiastical objects of the Guelph Treasure were made in medieval times and for centuries belonged to the Braunschweig Cathedral. In 1671, the town's ruling noble family, the Guelphs, acquired the Treasure from the cathedral. Some 350 years later, in 1928, the cash-strapped descendants of the Guelphs sold the entire collection to a consortium of Jewish art dealers. They in turn took the Treasure on tour through America, offering it for sale (they sold off about half of the 82 pieces, many to museums). In 1935, with the Nazis now in power, the German state (under the art-loving Hermann Göring) "bought" the remaining bits of the Treasure from the art dealers. The timing of the sale begged the question—was it a fair bargain, or were the dealers pressured by the Nazis because of their Jewish heritage? After the war, the dealers' heirs sued the German government, asserting that the sale had been made under duress for less than true market value. In 2015, after years of legal wrangling, a German court declared the Guelph Treasure to be the property of the German state and a national treasure. But the legal maneuvering is not over, though, as the heirs are pursuing their claim in a still-pending civil suit.

Guelph Treasure

The more than 40 gleaming gold, silver, and bejeweled objects in Room I are known as the Guelph Treasure. Ranging in date from the 8th to 15th centuries, most are reliquaries, which once held reminders of long-dead saints—a piece of bone, a bicuspid, a shred of clothing, or a sliver of their walking stick. By standing in the presence of such remains, housed in gloriously decorated reliquaries, medieval Christians experienced awe and a closer connection to their saints. For centuries, they were venerated by medieval pilgrims in the Cathedral of Braunschweig, a town 150 miles west of Berlin, ruled by the Guelph family.

Start (in the center of the room) with the most treasured of the Treasure, the **Dome Reliquary** (Kuppelreliquar). It's shaped like a tiny jeweled church (18 inches tall), topped with a dome. This magnificent container, created c. 1175 by artists in Cologne, once housed the skull of brainy St. Gregory the Theologian (c. 329-390), whose writings helped define the mystery of the Trinity. The saint's remains were brought from his resting spot in Constantinople to Germany by a Guelph Crusader. The domed reliquary may have been modeled after Jerusalem's famed Dome of the Rock Church, which the Crusaders were bent on liberating from Muslim control.

Admire the beauty and workmanship of the Dome Reliquary. Its wood core is covered with gilded copper, and the dome is plated with colorful enamels of blue, green, and red, traced with intertwining vines. The church rests on four crouching griffins of gilt bronze, and is topped with a globe of gold filigree. Ringing the base of the dome are 13 majestic figures on thrones carved from walrus-tusk ivory—the 12 apostles plus Christ. Each has a different hairstyle, beard, and robe, and each holds an identifying attribute: Peter, for example (at Christ's right hand), holds his keys to the kingdom of heaven. The lower part of the reliquary has more carved ivory saints and four intricately carved scenes of the Crucifixion, the women at Christ's tomb, the Holy Family, and the Three Magi. Though small and stiff, these scenes are the infancy of what would grow into Renaissance realism.

Browse **other reliquaries of the Guelph Treasure** in this room. Some are shaped like arms (to hold the arm bone of a saint);

others are busts, crosses, or boxes. Some have a transparent rock-crystal receptacle where you can actually see the relic inside. All are magnificently gilded, silvered, enameled, jeweled, and pearled. Is the security guard eyeing you a little too closely? Well, the total value of the Guelph collection in this room has been estimated at €250 million.

• *To see more treasure, face the Dome Reliquary, turn right, and follow* Rundgang *signs on a counterclockwise loop.*

First up, in Room II, are Renaissance **tapestries and porcelain** from southern Europe. Then comes Room III, to the right, with

still more finely-crafted Renaissance wonders from northern Europe, including a cache of **silver** from the civic treasury in Lüneburg. Look for two charming hand-washing pots—one in the shape of a lion, the other an elephant. They're both marvels of beauty and function. Lift either by the tail, and water pours out its mouth. These were prized pieces of tableware in the messy days before silverware was introduced.

• *Exit past the elephant into the foyer and head upstairs to the "Mode/ Entrance" level. Enter the series of rooms devoted to...*

Fashion

These rooms trace ladies' fashions from 1845 to 2000. (Earlier fashions, from 1700-1845, are found on the upper floor.) Altogeth-

er about 130 costumes (and nearly as many accessories) are presented in chrono-logical order and accom-panied by bits of historical context that make fashion seem more fascinating than fickle, even to the style-challenged (we know who we are). In a long, dark hallway, you'll walk past Victorian-era dresses with narrow waists and floor-length hemlines, including elegant ballgowns. There's a peek at ladies' undergarments—hoop skirts, corsets, pad-ded bras, and bustles (for the bootylicious Victorian)—that accen-tuated the shape of the dress in order to reflect the era's ideal body type. Continuing through history, you'll see slinky and shapeless 1920s-era flapper dresses, 1940s business suits, 1960s miniskirts and hot pants, 1970s women's-libber pantsuits and short skirts, and late-century designer labels such as Yves Saint Laurent, Chanel, and Versace.

• *Continue upstairs to the Neue Kunst/Upper Floor level and turn left through the door marked* Renaissance bis Barock *for a look at...*

Renaissance to Baroque, 1500-1800

Heaven's garage sale might look like this: room after room of exqui-sitely beautiful, handmade objects. Browse through elegant Delft-ware porcelain, Versailles-era furniture, "Kunstkammer" curiosity chests, ceremonial beer steins, and Tiffany lamps and carved-wood furniture from the Art Nouveau *(Jugendstil)* era.

Rest of the Kulturforum

Musical Instruments Museum: The Musikinstrumenten Mu-seum fills a striking hall with 600 exhibits, spanning the 16th century to modern times. This place is fascinating if you're into pianos. Highlights include a pre-piano keyboard (the Bach Cem-balo), Stradivarius violins, venerable church organs, Frederick the Great's flute, a silent-movie-era Wurlitzer organ, electric guitars, and 20th-century synthesizers—once cutting-edge, now museum pieces. Wander among old keyboard instruments and funny-looking tubas. Pick up the included audioguide and free English brochure at the entry. In addition to the English commentary, the audioguide lets you listen to various instruments being played; while the musical snippets are beautiful, there are too few of them.

New National Gallery: The Neue Nationalgalerie—currently closed for a lengthy renovation—features 20th-century art, with ever-changing special exhibits. The building, which opened in 1968, was the last commission completed by esteemed architect Ludwig Mies van der Rohe.

Berlin Philharmonic: Poke into the lobby of the yellow, pentagonal-shaped Berlin Philharmonic concert hall and see if there are tickets available for performances during your stay (for more on ticketing, see page 311). The hall is famous for its extraordinary acoustics. Even from the outside, this is a remarkable building, designed by a nautical engineer to look like a ship—notice how different it appears from each angle.

Memorial to the Victims of Nazi "Euthanasia": Immediately north of the Philharmonic, facing the park, was the building where the Nazis administered a campaign of what they called "euthanasia" against mentally and physically disabled people. The memorial fills the long blue wall between the Philharmonic and Tiergartenstrasse.

GEMÄLDEGALERIE & KULTURFORUM

SLEEPING IN BERLIN

Choosing the right neighborhood in Berlin is as important as choosing the right hotel. I've focused my recommendations in safe, colorful areas convenient to sightseeing. In northern Berlin, Prenzlauer Berg—my favorite area to sleep—offers a local neighborhood vibe, easy transit connections, and an excellent selection of eateries; the old Jewish quarter, also with good restaurants, is closer to the sights but more impersonal than Prenzlauer Berg. Farther out, City West—the heart of the former West Berlin—is an upscale, residential neighborhood. I recommend the best accommodations values for each, from €20 bunks to deluxe €300 doubles. Most of my listings cluster around the €100-160 range.

Berlin for the most part lacks the characteristic, traditional, family-run hotels that I typically favor. Outside of a few small hotels in Prenzlauer Berg and near Savignyplatz in City West, most of my listings are larger, business-oriented hotels—often part of a chain. Pricing at these big hotels fluctuates with demand; since the hotels themselves are fairly standard, I recommend picking a few places and comparing prices for your travel dates. For some travelers, short-term, Airbnb-type rentals can be a good alternative; search for places in my recommended hotel neighborhoods.

A few notes about hotels in Berlin:

- Berlin charges a daily tourist tax (5 percent of the room rate). This may be included in the room price or may appear as an extra charge on your bill.
- Most hotels offer an optional breakfast buffet for about €15-

20 per person, though it's often not included in their quoted rates (you can choose whether to add breakfast when booking). Light eaters and budget travelers can opt out of the hotel breakfast and get coffee and a pastry at a neighborhood café for less.

- Air-conditioning is relatively rare (I've noted hotels that have it in all rooms). If it's important to you, ask about it when you book.
- Many hotels offer bike rentals to guests (usually €10-12/day).

I rank accommodations from $ budget to $$$$ splurge. For the best deal, contact family-run hotels directly by phone or email. When you book direct, the owner avoids a commission and may be able to offer a discount. Book well in advance for peak season or if your trip coincides with a major holiday or festival (see the appendix). Rooms can be in especially short supply when big trade shows are in town (including Green Week in mid-January and the ITB travel show in mid-March).

For details on reservations, short-term rentals, and more, see the "Sleeping" section in the Practicalities chapter.

PRENZLAUER BERG

My favorite Berlin neighborhood to call home, Prenzlauer Berg offers easy transit connections to sightseeing; diverse eateries, coffeehouses, and nightspots; and a welcoming personality. A onetime hipster mecca, this area is now gentrified and more sedate—yet it still retains a bit of its alternative edge (think of all that graffiti as just some people's way of saying they care). If staying here, orient yourself with my 🕮 Prenzlauer Berg Walk. For eating, shopping, and nightlife options, see my recommendations in those chapters.

Most of my recommended hotels are between Kastanienallee and Prenzlauer Allee. The area's transit hub is the Eberswalder Strasse U-Bahn station (U2 line). Trams also serve this neighborhood: The #M1 and #12 run up and down Kastanienallee, connecting to the Rosenthaler Platz U-Bahn (#M1 continues all the way to the Hackescher Markt S-Bahn station), while the #M10 heads west from Eberswalder Strasse along Bernauer Strasse to the Berlin Wall Memorial and eventually to the Hauptbahnhof.

$$$ Hotel Jurine (zhoo-REEN—the family name) is a pleasant and well-run 53-room business-style hotel on a peaceful street. Its good-value rooms are priced at the low end of this range. If you want calm atmosphere in a comfortable and quality building, with more German guests than tourists, your own peaceful back garden, and a very friendly staff, this is my choice (mention Rick Steves when you book for a free upgraded room, breakfast extra, elevator, pay parking—reserve ahead, Schwedter Strasse 15, 5-minute walk to #M1: Zionskirchplatz or U2: Senefelderplatz, +49 30 443 2990, www.hotel-jurine.de, mail@hotel-jurine.de).

$$$ Hotel Oderberger has 70 modern rooms filling part of a Neo-Renaissance bathhouse complex (originally opened in 1902, renovated and reopened in 2016). From the reception, you can peek into the elegant old swimming pool area. It's a fine choice, with its understated elegance, historic aura, and good location, tucked away on a quiet side street near the most happening stretch of Kastanienallee (elevator, guest discount for swimming pool, Oderberger Strasse 57, +49 30 780 089 760, www.hotel-oderberger.de, info@hotel-oderberger.berlin).

$$$ Linnen rents five rooms above a cozy and characteristic café, along a busy street between the Eberswalder Strasse U-Bahn station and Mauerpark. Linnen stays true to its motto, "more home, less hotel"—the vibe is casual, and the spacious, stylishly decorated rooms feel homey. This place pleases well-heeled hipsters (breakfast extra at downstairs café, Eberswalder Strasse 35, +49 30 4737 2440, www.linnenberlin.com, booking@linnenberlin.com).

$$ Myer's Hotel rents 50 comfortable rooms decorated with lots of bold colors and gold accents. Located on a tranquil, tree-lined street, and overlooking a sleepy courtyard, Myer's is closer to charming Kollwitzplatz than to the Kastanienallee action. Staying at this peaceful hub, you'll find it hard to believe you're in the heart of a capital city. The gorgeous public spaces, including an art-filled patio and garden, host frequent cultural events (air-con, elevator, sauna, Metzer Strasse 26—midway between U2: Senefelderplatz and #M2 tram: Prenzlauer Allee/Metzer Strasse, #M2 goes to/from Alexanderplatz, +49 30 440 140, www.myershotel.de, info@myershotel.de).

$$ Hotel Kastanienhof feels less urban-classy and more like a traditional small-town German hotel. It's wonderfully located on the Kastanienallee #M1 tram line, with easy access to the Prenzlauer Berg bustle (but since trams run all night, ask for a room in the back). Its 44 rooms come with helpful service (breakfast extra, deluxe top-floor rooms offer air-con and/

or balcony, elevator, wheelchair-accessible room, pay parking, 20 yards from #M1: Zionskirchplatz at Kastanienallee 65, +49 30 443 050, www.kastanienhof.berlin, info@kastanienhof.berlin). The hotel's recommended Ausspanne restaurant serves excellent German dishes with a modern twist.

Prenzlauer Berg Hotels & Restaurants

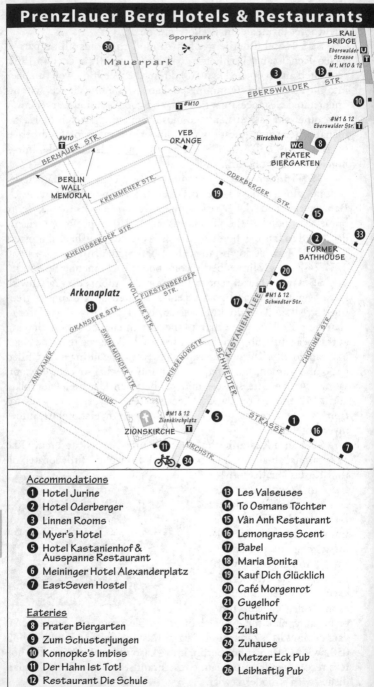

SLEEPING

Accommodations

1 Hotel Jurine
2 Hotel Oderberger
3 Linnen Rooms
4 Myer's Hotel
5 Hotel Kastanienhof & Ausspanne Restaurant
6 Meininger Hotel Alexanderplatz
7 EastSeven Hostel

Eateries

8 Prater Biergarten
9 Zum Schusterjungen
10 Konnopke's Imbiss
11 Der Hahn Ist Tot!
12 Restaurant Die Schule
13 Les Valseuses
14 To Osmans Töchter
15 Vân Anh Restaurant
16 Lemongrass Scent
17 Babel
18 Maria Bonita
19 Kauf Dich Glücklich
20 Café Morgenrot
21 Gugelhof
22 Chutnify
23 Zula
24 Zuhause
25 Metzer Eck Pub
26 Leibhaftig Pub

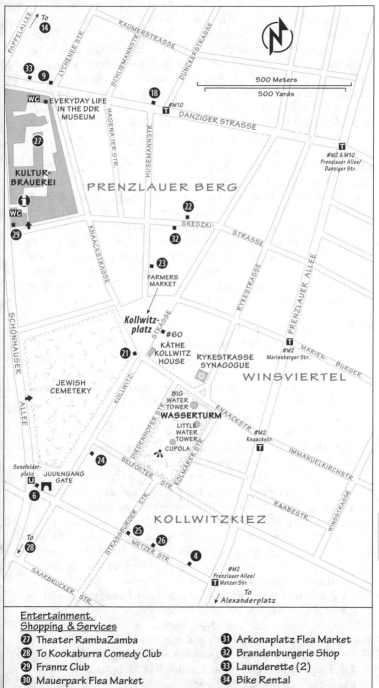

Entertainment, Shopping & Services

27 Theater RambaZamba
28 To Kookaburra Comedy Club
29 Frannz Club
30 Mauerpark Flea Market

31 Arkonaplatz Flea Market
32 Brandenburgerie Shop
33 Launderette (2)
34 Bike Rental

¢ **Hostels:** A convenient branch of the hostel/budget hotel **Meininger** is at Senefelderplatz; for details, see page 283. **East-Seven Hostel** rents 100 of the best cheap beds in Prenzlauer Berg. Modern and conscientiously run, it offers all the hostel services plus an inviting lounge, guest kitchen, backyard terrace, and bike rental. Children are welcome. Easygoing people of any age are comfortable here (private rooms available, no curfew, 100 yards from U2: Senefelderplatz at Schwedter Strasse 7, +49 30 9362 2240, www.eastseven.de, info@eastseven.de).

OLD JEWISH QUARTER

The old Jewish quarter, south of Prenzlauer Berg, makes for a fine home base thanks to its good location (close to public transportation and easy walking distance to the center) and traveler-friendly offerings, including cozy restaurants, independent shops, the delightful Monbijoupark, and a few interesting sights. It's closer to the historic core than Prenzlauer Berg but feels less residential, and the hotels here are bigger and less personable. To get your bearings, take my 🕮 Old Jewish Quarter Walk. You can find recommendations for eateries, shopping, and entertainment in those chapters.

Near Rosenthaler Platz

Rosenthaler Platz is halfway between Hackescher Markt and the heart of the Prenzlauer Berg scene (on Kastanienallee). Though bustling and congested, it makes a good base for getting around the city thanks to its U-Bahn stop (U8: Rosenthaler Platz) and tram service (#M1 heads north to Kastanienallee/Eberswalder Strasse and south to the Hackescher Markt S-Bahn hub; #M8 connects to the Hauptbahnhof).

$$ The Circus Hotel is fun, entirely comfortable, and a great value. The achingly hip lobby has a café serving delicious (optional) breakfasts, and the 60 rooms are straightforward and colorful. Run by the same folks who manage the popular Circus Hostel (listed later), it's service oriented, with a very "green" attitude and special events for guests. As the hotel overlooks a busy intersection, ask for a quieter back room (breakfast extra, elevator, Rosenthaler Strasse 1, +49 30 2000 3939, www.circus-berlin.de, info@circus-berlin.de). The Circus also offers spacious, modern **$$$ apartments** within the hotel and two blocks away at Choriner Strasse 84.

$$ Amano Hotel, while big (163 rooms) and impersonal, is well-priced for what you get: chic contemporary design and all the little amenities you don't need but appreciate nonetheless (breakfast extra, air-con, elevator, pay parking, Auguststrasse 43, +49 30 809 4150, www.amanogroup.de, amano@amanogroup.de).

$ EasyHotel Berlin Hackescher Markt is part of an unapologetically cheap, Europe-wide chain where you pay for exactly what you use—nothing more, nothing less. You're charged a low base rate, then pay à la carte for each service you add (Wi-Fi, housekeeping, etc.). The 125 orange-and-gray rooms are very small, basic, and feel popped out of a plastic mold (no breakfast, elevator, call to request a quieter back room after booking online, Rosenthaler Strasse 69, +49 30 4000 6550, www.easyhotel-berlin. de, enquiries@berlinhm.easyhotel.com).

¢ **The Circus Hostel** is a brightly colored, well-run place with 250 beds, plenty of social networking, and a trendy lounge and microbrewery. It has typical hostel dorms as well as some hotel-like private rooms; for a few big steps up in comfort,  consider the Circus Hotel, listed earlier (no curfew, elevator, Weinbergsweg 1A, +49 30 2000 3939, www.circus-berlin.de, info@circus-berlin.de).

By Hackescher Markt

Lively Hackescher Markt, just north of the river, is brimming with people, eateries, and on some days, an open-air market. It's also home to an S-Bahn station and is connected to Prenzlauer Berg by tram #M1.

Of the following listings, the first two (Adina and Hotel Alexander Plaza) are in a characterless glass-and-concrete zone just south of Hackescher Markt. The others face each other across the tracks of a tram depot (ask for a quieter room). These hotels are all bigger than they are charming.

$$$ Adina Apartment Hotel Berlin Hackescher Markt has 134 studio and one-bedroom apartments with kitchenettes, though breakfast is available for an extra fee (air-con, elevator, pay parking, An der Spandauer Brücke 11, +49 30 209 6980, www.adinahotels. com, berlinhm@adina.eu).

$$$ Hotel Alexander Plaza offers 94 brightly appointed, business-style rooms (breakfast extra, elevator, pay parking, Rosenstrasse 1, +49 30 240 010, www.hotel-alexander-plaza.de, frontoffice@hotel-alexander-plaza.de).

$$$ Monbijou Hotel's 101 rooms are small, but they make up for it with pleasing public spaces, a postcard-worthy rooftop terrace (with views of the cathedral and TV Tower), and a flair for design—from reclaimed wood and antique furnishings to plenty of natural light (breakfast extra, family rooms, air-con, elevator, pay

Old Jewish Quarter Hotels & Restaurants

Accommodations

1 The Circus Hotel
2 Amano Hotel
3 EasyHotel Berlin Hackescher Markt
4 The Circus Hostel
5 Adina Apartment Hotel Berlin Hackescher Markt
6 Hotel Alexander Plaza
7 Monbijou Hotel
8 Hotel Hackescher Markt
9 Hotel Zoe by Amano
10 Hotel Augustinenhof
11 Calma Berlin Mitte
12 NH Collection Berlin Mitte Friedrichstrasse
13 Hotel Eurostars Berlin
14 Leonardo Hotel Berlin Mitte
15 To Hotel Albrechtshof
16 To Motel One Hackescher Markt
17 Meininger Hotel

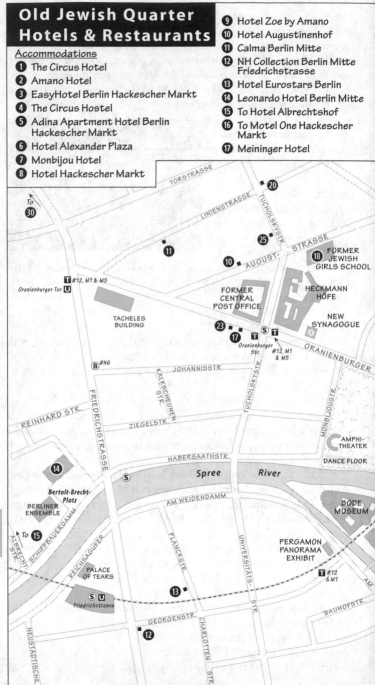

SLEEPING

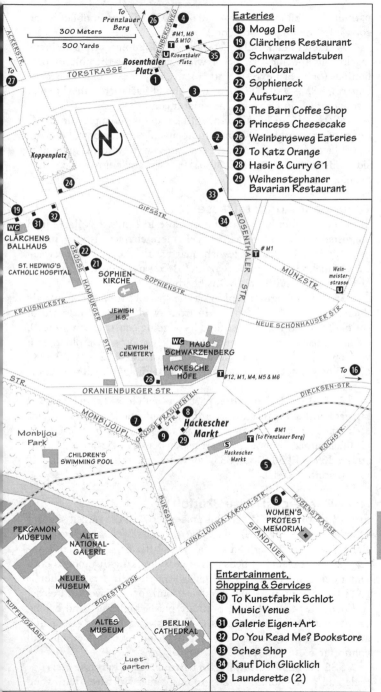

Eateries
- 18 Mogg Deli
- 19 Clärchens Restaurant
- 20 Schwarzwaldstuben
- 21 Cordobar
- 22 Sophieneck
- 23 Aufsturz
- 24 The Barn Coffee Shop
- 25 Princess Cheesecake
- 26 Weinbergsweg Eateries
- 27 To Katz Orange
- 28 Hasir & Curry 61
- 29 Weihenstephaner Bavarian Restaurant

Entertainment, Shopping & Services
- 30 To Kunstfabrik Schlot Music Venue
- 31 Galerie Eigen+Art
- 32 Do You Read Me? Bookstore
- 33 Schee Shop
- 34 Kauf Dich Glücklich
- 35 Launderette (2)

SLEEPING

parking, Monbijouplatz 1, +49 30 6162 0300, www.monbijouhotel.com, info@monbijouhotel.com).

$$ Hotel Hackescher Markt, with 32 rooms, offers an inviting lounge and modern decor without being predictable or pretentious (breakfast extra, family rooms, elevator, Grosse Präsidentenstrasse 8, +49 30 280 030, www.hotel-hackescher-markt.com, reservierung@hotel-hackescher-markt.com).

$$ Hotel Zoe by Amano, with 88 rooms and a pleasant rooftop bar, is a trendy and slightly more upscale branch of the Amano Hotel listed earlier (breakfast extra, air-con, elevator, Grosse Präsidentenstrasse 6, +49 30 2130 0150, www.amanogroup.de, zoe@amanogroup.de).

On or near Auguststrasse

These good-value hotels are on or close to fun, art gallery-lined Auguststrasse, in an area that feels more characteristic than my other listings in the old Jewish quarter. They're located between the Oranienburger Strasse S-Bahn (S1/S2) and Oranienburger Tor U-Bahn (U6), and tram #M1 is nearby.

$$ Hotel Augustinenhof has 66 spacious rooms, nice woody floors, and firm beds. Rooms in front overlook the courtyard of the old Imperial Post Office (and its ongoing construction project), rooms in back are a bit quieter, and some rooms have older, thin windows (breakfast extra, elevator, Auguststrasse 82, +49 30 3088 6710, www.hotel-augustinenhof.de, augustinenhof@albrechtshof-hotels.de).

$$ Calma Berlin Mitte, part of a small local chain, is a good budget bet. Its 46 straightforward but comfortable, modern rooms are tucked away on a tranquil courtyard, just steps from the lively Oranienburger Strasse scene (breakfast extra, elevator, Linienstrasse 139, +49 30 9153 9333, www.lindemannhotels.de, calma@lindemannhotels.de).

Near Friedrichstrasse Station

Straddling the Spree River, this area—between the transit stations Oranienburger Tor (U6) and Friedrichstrasse (U6 and several S-Bahn lines)—feels big and sterile, with little personality. But hotels here have plenty of beds and are easy walking distance to both Unter den Linden and the old Jewish quarter. The first two hotels (NH Collection and Eurostars) are south of the river and closer to Friedrichstrasse Station; both are plush, high-end, and belong to international Spanish chains. The last two listings (Leonardo and Albrechtshof) are north of the river and a bit simpler, but still comfortable.

$$$ NH Collection Berlin Mitte Friedrichstrasse feels upscale and professional. Its 268 rooms come with sleek hardwood floors, high ceilings, and red accents (breakfast extra, air-con, elevator, gym, sauna, Friedrichstrasse 96, +49 30 206 2660, www.nh-collection.com, nhcollectionberlinfriedrich@nh-hotels.com).

$$$ Hotel Eurostars Berlin is a classy hotel with 221 spacious, rich wood rooms towering over the everyday hustle and bustle. As it faces train tracks, ask for a quieter room—several face into the lobby atrium (breakfast extra, air-con, elevator, gym, spa, Friedrichstrasse 99, +49 30 701 736 284, www.eurostarsberlin.com, info@eurostarsberlin.com).

$$ Leonardo Hotel Berlin Mitte occupies a modern building set back on a little park overlooking the river. It features retro public spaces and a mazelike floor plan leading to 309 tight, tidy, stylish rooms (breakfast extra, air-con, elevator, gym, spa, limited pay parking, Bertolt-Brecht-Platz 4, +49 30 374 405 000, www.leonardo-hotels.com, info.berlinmitte@leonardo-hotels.com).

$$ Hotel Albrechtshof is a bit scruffier than its sister hotel, the Augustinenhof (described earlier), but still a good choice. It has the most personality of the hotels in this area. The 98 rooms come with a similar design, friendly staff, peaceful courtyard, and weekly chapel services. Martin Luther King Jr. once stayed here and attended one (breakfast extra, elevator, Albrechtstrasse 8, +49 30 308 860, www.hotel-albrechtshof.de, albrechtshof@albrechtshof-hotel.de).

CITY WEST

City West—the heart of the former West Berlin—is a pleasant, upscale, low-impact residential neighborhood. While most travelers prefer to sleep closer to the center, City West can be an ideal home base if you don't mind a longer commute to sightseeing. The area retains an artsy aura, going back to the cabaret days of the 1920s, when it was the center of Berlin's gay scene. Today, City West feels sedate and posh (if quite touristy along Ku'damm). Travelers sleeping in City West have several transit options: Bus #100 is slow but scenic (see my "Do-It-Yourself Bus #100 Tour" on page 36), while the S-Bahn zips much faster from Savignyplatz or Zoologischer Garten to the center.

Near Europa Center

$$$$ 25hours Hotel Bikini Berlin is your trendy hotel option overlooking Europa Center in the busiest and buzziest part of City West. Filling a high rise adjacent to the Berlin Zoo and the Bikini Berlin shopping mall, it has 149 plywood-and-concrete rooms and public spaces with an industrial-zoo ambience. This is where trendsetters sleep in City West (breakfast extra, air-con, elevator, Budapester Strasse 40, +49 30 120 2210, www.25hours-hotels.com, bikini@25hours-hotels.com).

City West Hotels & Restaurants

Accommodations
1. 25hours Hotel Bikini Berlin
2. Hecker's Hotel
3. Hommage à Magritte B&B
4. Hotel-Pension Funk
5. Hotel Augusta
6. Pension Peters
7. Motel One Ku'damm

Eateries & Nightlife
8. Restaurant Marjellchen
9. Dicke Wirtin
10. Café im Literaturhaus
11. Heno Heno
12. Diener Tattersall
13. To Weyers
14. Bleibtreustrasse Eateries
15. Curry 36
16. Schleusenkrug Beer Garden
17. KaDeWe Winter Garden Buffet
18. A Trane Jazz Club
19. Bar Jeder Vernunft

Around Savignyplatz

These listings huddle around the delightful, tree-lined Savigny-platz, which has a neighborhood charm and an abundance of simple, small, friendly, good-value places to sleep and eat. The first two hotels, located between Savignyplatz and Ku'damm, are close to the Uhlandstrasse U-Bahn station (U1). For the others, ride the S-Bahn directly to Savignyplatz—or get off at Zoologischer Garten (with more connections) and walk about 10 minutes.

$$ Hecker's Hotel is an excellent value, with 69 big, fresh, well-maintained rooms and all the Euro-comforts. Herr Kiesel's "superior" rooms have air-conditioning and more-modern furnishings—and cost a bit more—than his "comfort" rooms (a few rooms with kitchenettes, free breakfast for Rick Steves readers, elevator, pay parking, Grolmanstrasse 35, +49 30 88900, www.heckers-hotel.de, info@heckers-hotel.de).

$$ Hommage à Magritte is a spiffy, tidy B&B in a classic old

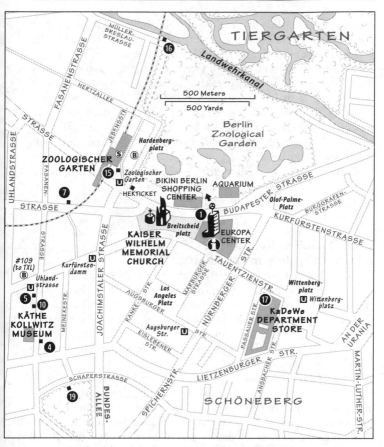

apartment building on a quiet street. Its 17 rooms come with an artistic touch, inspired by its namesake, the Belgian Surrealist painter René Magritte (Grolmanstrasse 32, +49 30 8956 7087, www.hommage-a-magritte.com, info@hommage-a-magritte.com).

$$ Hotel-Pension Funk, the former home of a 1920s silent-movie star, is a delightfully quirky, only-in-Berlin time warp. Kind manager Herr Michael Pfundt and his right-hand man, Ding, offer 15 elegant old rooms with rich Art Nouveau furnishings and hardly any modern trappings. Most guests adore it; some are put off by its old-fashioned feel. Figure out which you'll be before you book (cheaper rooms with shared bath, cash preferred, no TVs, a long block south of Ku'damm at Fasanenstrasse 69, +49 30 882 7193, www.hotel-pensionfunk.de, berlin@hotel-pensionfunk.de).

$$ Hotel Augusta, run by mother-and-daughter team Julia and Danuta—and their friendly staff—fills an early-20th-century building with 45 smartly decorated rooms, most with hints of the building's *Jugendstil* origins. Superior rooms come with coffee makers and air-con, while others have balconies overlooking Ku'damm (breakfast extra, elevator, Fasanenstrasse 22, +49 30 883 5028, www.hotel-augusta.de, info@hotel-augusta.de).

$ Pension Peters, run by a German-Swedish couple, is sunny and central, with a cheery breakfast room and super-friendly staff who go out of their way to help guests. With sleek Scandinavian decor and 33 rooms, it's a good choice. Some ground-floor rooms facing the back courtyard are a bit dark—and cheaper. If street noise bothers you, request a quiet room. Annika and Christoph (with help from his sister, Daisy, as well as Uwe and others) have been welcoming my readers for decades (breakfast extra, RS%, family rooms, 10 yards off Savignyplatz at Kantstrasse 146, +49 30 312 2278, www.pension-peters-berlin.de, info@pension-peters-berlin.de).

OTHER SLEEPING OPTIONS
Business Hotels in the Historic Core
Berlin's historic core is handy to sightseeing, but—frankly—pretty dull. Locals who don't work in this area rarely venture here, making it sleepy at night. But these large, business-oriented hotels are worth considering if you're looking to sleep in the very center of town and can score a deal. Breakfasts here are expensive add-ons. For locations see the "Historic Core Hotels & Restaurants" map in the Eating in Berlin chapter.

$$$$ Hotel de Rome, holding court on Frederick the Great's showpiece Bebelplatz and facing Unter den Linden, is *the* Berlin splurge, with 108 rooms and all the luxurious little extras. If money is no object, this is a tempting choice for your Berlin address (air-con, elevator, Behrenstrasse 37, +49 30 460 6090, www.roccofortehotels.com, info.derome@roccofortehotels.com).

$$$ NH Collection Berlin Mitte am Checkpoint Charlie is an elegant chain hotel on a busy street a short walk from Gendarmenmarkt, with nearly 400 fresh, interchangeable rooms at reasonable rates (air-con, elevator, Leipziger Strasse 106, U2: Stadtmitte, +49 30 203 760, www.nh-hotels.com, nhcollectionberlinmitte@nh-hotels.com).

In Eastern Berlin's Friedrichshain
$$ Michelberger Hotel, right across from the Warschauer Strasse S-Bahn station (the gateway to gritty, quickly gentrifying Friedrichshain), is so artsy and self-consciously hip that it'd all be just too much...if it weren't for its helpful staff. Its 133 bright rooms are reasonably priced, and its common spaces—a bar/lounge and a breezy all-organic courtyard restaurant—are welcoming (breakfast extra, family rooms, elevator; from atop Warschauer Strasse S-Bahn station, turn left to cross the bridge—it's across from the

U-Bahn station and #M10 tram stop at Warschauer Strasse 39; +49 30 2977 8590, www.michelbergerhotel.com, reservations@ michelbergerhotel.com).

Good-Value Chain Hotels

$ Motel One has multiple locations across Berlin; all have the same aqua-and-brown decor and posh-feeling but small rooms. The four most convenient locations are between Hackescher Markt and Alexanderplatz (Dircksenstrasse 36—see the "Old Jewish Quarter Hotels & Restaurants" map, +49 30 2005 4080, berlin-hackeschermarkt@motel-one.com); near the Zoologischer Garten station (Kantstrasse 10—see the "City West Hotels & Restaurants" map, +49 30 3151 7360, berlin-kudamm@motel-one.com); just behind the Hauptbahnhof (Invalidenstrasse 54, +49 30 3641 0050, berlin-hauptbahnhof@motel-one.com); and a few blocks east of Gendarmenmarkt (Leipziger Strasse 50, U2: Spittelmarkt, +49 30 2014 3630, berlin-spittelmarkt@motel-one.com). For the last two locations, see the "Historic Core Hotels & Restaurants" map in the Eating in Berlin chapter.

Meininger is a Europe-wide budget-hotel chain with several locations in Berlin. With both ¢ cheap dorm beds and $$ comfortable, hotelesque private rooms, Meininger is basic but lively, modern, and generally a solid budget option, even for nonhostelers. They have three well-located branches: in Prenzlauer Berg ("Alexanderplatz" branch, actually at Schönhauser Allee 19 on Senefelderplatz—see the "Prenzlauer Berg Hotels & Restaurants" map); in the old Jewish quarter (Mitte "Humboldthaus" branch, next to the recommended Aufsturz pub at Oranienburger Strasse 67—see the "Old Jewish Quarter Hotels & Restaurants" map); and near the Hauptbahnhof at Ella-Trebe-Strasse 9—see the "Historic Core Hotels & Restaurants" map in the Eating in Berlin chapter (all locations have elevator and 24-hour reception, pay parking at some, +49 30 666 36100, www.meininger-hostels.com, welcome@ meininger-hostels.com).

Apartment Rentals

Consider this option if you're traveling as a family, in a group, or staying four nights or longer. Websites such as Airbnb and VRBO let you correspond directly with European property owners or managers. For more information on renting apartments, see the "Sleeping" section of the Practicalities chapter.

SLEEPING

EATING IN BERLIN

Berlin hosts a world of ever-changing restaurants. While the city abounds with traditional German eateries, Berliners consider this cuisine old-school; when they eat out, they're usually not looking for traditional local fare. Nouveau German is California cuisine with scant memories of wurst, kraut, and pumpernickel.

Berlin is also a place to venture beyond German cuisine. As one of Europe's primary melting pots, you'll find sushi, Turkish, Italian, Peruvian, Cuban, Thai, Georgian, Indian, Argentinian, and lots of Vietnamese—usually done quite well. In recent years, Michelin-star restaurants and fancy steak houses have attracted attention from celebrities and travelers who appreciate finer dining. The result: From simple to sophisticated, Berlin's cuisine scene has something for every taste bud—and budget.

I rank eateries from **$** budget to **$$$$** splurge. For more advice on eating in Germany, including ordering, tipping, and typical cuisine and beverages, see the "Eating" section of the Practicalities chapter.

EATING TIPS

Berlin has far more quality restaurants than could fit in any guidebook—and the scene changes so fast, anything in print is already dated. It's hard to go wrong by just browsing a neighborhood until you find something that strikes your fancy. Lunches are especially easy, as the city is crammed with places selling fresh, affordable sandwiches and salads, and finer restaurants with wonderful €10 lunch plates. Consider picking up the annual *Zitty Essen Gehen*, with reviews and photographs of the city's hottest eateries, produced by a local culture magazine (German only, sold at newsstands, www.zitty.de/gastro).

Berlin Specialties: Don't be too determined to eat "Berlin-style." The city is best known for its street food—*Currywurst* and kebabs (see the "Berliner Street Food" sidebar).

But if you do eat German food in Berlin, popular dishes include *Buletten* and *Königsberger Klopse* (both meatball dishes), plus other meaty plates, such as *Schnitzel Holstein* (veal cutlet with egg), *Eisbein* (boiled ham hock), *Leber Berliner Art* (veal liver), *Kassler* (or *Kasseler;* smoked pork), and *Mett* (or *Hackepeter;* minced pork). Also popular are *Aal grün* (boiled eel), *Rollmops* (pickled herring), and *Senfeier* (hard-boiled eggs with potatoes). As for sweets, *Berliner Pfannkuchen* is the local jelly doughnut, and *Berliner Luft* is a popular dessert. These dishes are described in more detail in the Practicalities chapter (under "Traditional German Fare," starting on page 414).

HISTORIC CORE

While this government/commercial area is hardly a hotspot for eateries, I've listed a few places handy for your sightseeing, all a short walk from Unter den Linden.

On and near Museum Island

The Altes, Neues, and Bode museums all have simple cafés. My favorite Berlin museum restaurant is in the neighboring German History Museum. And the streets around Hackescher Markt, a 10-minute walk away in the old Jewish quarter, hold plenty of options (see that neighborhood description, later in this chapter).

$$ Deponie No. 3 is a rustic if touristy Berlin *Kneipe* (pub). Garden seating in the back is nice but comes with the noise of the S-Bahn passing directly above. The bar interior is cozy and woody with several inviting spaces. They serve basic salads, traditional Berlin dishes, and hearty daily specials (daily 10:00-24:00, S-Bahn arch #187 at Georgenstrasse 5, +49 30 2016 5740).

Near the TV Tower: $$ Brauhaus Lemke is a big, lively beer hall (modern but still in its 1970s DDR shell) that makes its own brews and offers a menu of Berliner specialties and Bavarian dishes. They have decent salads and serve a six-beer sampler board. You can venture upstairs any time to see the actual brewery (daily 12:00-24:00, across from the TV Tower and tucked a bit back from the street at Karl-Liebknecht-Strasse 13, +49 30 3087 8989).

Nikolai Quarter: A short walk from Museum Island and Karl-Liebknecht-Strasse, Berlin's rebuilt "old town" (the Nikolai

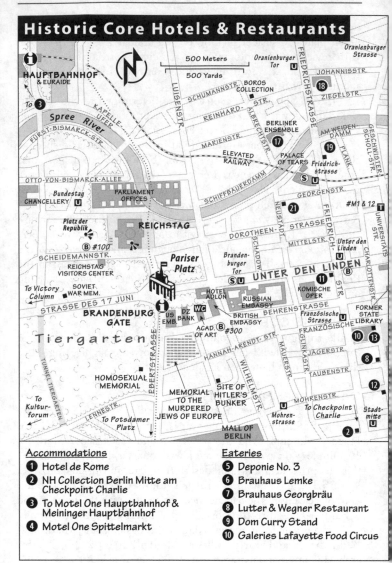

Historic Core Hotels & Restaurants

500 Meters
500 Yards

Accommodations

1 Hotel de Rome
2 NH Collection Berlin Mitte am Checkpoint Charlie
3 To Motel One Hauptbahnhof & Meininger Hauptbahnhof
4 Motel One Spittelmarkt

Eateries

5 Deponie No. 3
6 Brauhaus Lemke
7 Brauhaus Georgbräu
8 Lutter & Wegner Restaurant
9 Dom Curry Stand
10 Galeries Lafayette Food Circus

Quarter) feels pretty soulless by day but is a popular restaurant zone at night. **$$ Brauhaus Georgbräu,** a thriving beer hall teeming with German tourists, serves homemade suds on a picturesque courtyard overlooking the Spree River. Eat in the lively and woody but mod-feeling, hops-infused interior, or outdoors with fun riverside seating. It's a good place to try *Eisbein* (boiled ham hock) with sauerkraut and mashed peas with bacon, a typical Berlin dish. Their statue of St. George once stood in the courtyard of Berlin's old castle—until the Nazis deemed it not "German" enough (daily

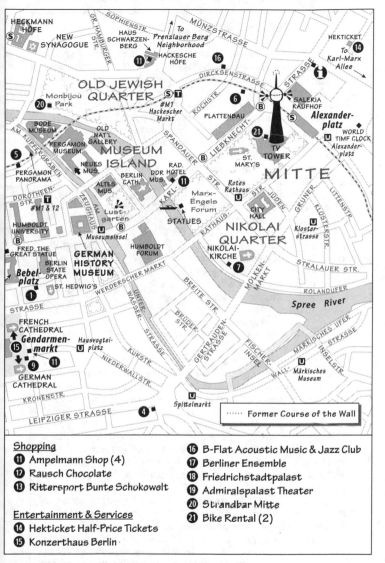

12:00-24:00, 2 blocks south of Berlin Cathedral and across the river at Spreeufer 4, +49 30 242 4244).

Near Gendarmenmarkt

South of Unter den Linden, Gendarmenmarkt, with its twin churches, is a delightful place for an al fresco meal. Here you'll find business lunch-type places that offer midday specials, though they're pricey at night. For more options, browse the eateries along Charlottenstrasse.

Berliner Street Food

In Berlin, it's easy to eat cheap, with a glut of *Imbiss* snack stands, bakeries (for sandwiches), and falafel/kebab counters. Train stations have grocery stores, as well as bright and modern fruit-and-sandwich bars.

Sausage stands are everywhere—including the reigning local favorites, Konnopke's Imbiss (see page 290) and Curry 36 (see pages 252 and 301). You may even see portable human hot-dog stands—cooks in clever harnesses that let them grill and sell hot dogs from under an umbrella.

Most sausage stands specialize in **Currywurst,** created in Berlin after World War II, when a fast-food cook got her hands on some curry and Worcestershire sauce from British troops stationed here. It's basically a grilled pork sausage smothered with curry sauce. *Currywurst* comes either *mit Darm* (with casing) or *ohne Darm* (without casing). If the casing is left on to grill, it gives the sausage a smokier flavor. (*Berliner Art*— "Berlin-style"—means that the sausage is boiled *ohne Darm,* then grilled.)

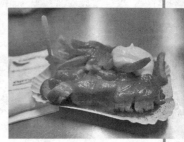

Either way, the grilled sausage is then chopped into small pieces or cut in half (East Berlin style) and topped with sauce. While some places simply use ketchup and sprinkle on some curry powder, real *Currywurst* joints use a proper *Currysauce:* tomato paste, Worcestershire sauce, and curry. With your wurst comes either a toothpick or small wooden fork; you'll usually get a plate of fries as well, but rarely a roll. You'll see *Currywurst* on the menu at some sit-down restaurants, but purists say that misses the point: You'll get a more authentic dish (and pay a third less) at a street stand under elevated S-Bahn tracks.

The other big Berlin street food is fast Turkish and Middle Eastern food. Shawarma and falafel joints are cheap and tasty. And the kebab—either **döner kebab** (Turkish-style skewered meat slow-roasted and served in pita bread) or the recently trendy, healthier, vegetarian alternative, **Gemüse kebab** (with lots of veggies, and sometimes falafel)—is a quick way to fill up for a couple euros. Other variations include the *döner teller* (on a plate instead of in bread) and *döner dürüm* (in a thin flatbread wrap, also called *dürüm kebab* or *yufka*). Just as Americans drop by a taco truck for a quick bite, Germans find a kebab stand.

$$$$ Lutter & Wegner Restaurant is a Berlin institution respected for its Austrian cuisine (*Schnitzel* and *Sauerbraten*). Popular with businesspeople, it's dressy, with fun sidewalk seating or a dark and elegant interior. Weekday €9 lunch specials are an affordable way to sample their cooking (daily 12:00-24:00, Charlottenstrasse 56, +49 30 202 9515, www.l-w-berlin.de). Another location is inside the Sony Center.

$ Dom Curry, behind the German Cathedral, is a *Currywurst* stand that works for a quick bite out on the square (daily 12:00-20:00).

$$ Galeries Lafayette Food Circus is a French festival of fun eateries surrounding the glass atrium in the basement of the landmark department store—ideal for a quality lunch. You'll find sandwiches, savory crêpes, quiches, sushi bar, oyster bar, *les macarons,* and so on. Eat in or take advantage of their handy to-go items (Mon-Sat 10:00-20:00, closed Sun, Friedrichstrasse 76, U6: Französische Strasse, +49 30 209 480).

PRENZLAUER BERG

Prenzlauer Berg is bursting with excellent restaurants, serving up every cuisine imaginable. Even if you're not staying in this area, it's worth venturing here for dinner (consider combining it with my ☐ Prenzlauer Berg Walk). Before choosing a restaurant, I'd spend at least a half-hour strolling and browsing through this bohemian wonderland of creative eateries. Or consider one of my recommendations (for locations, see the "Prenzlauer Berg Hotels & Restaurants" map in the Sleeping in Berlin chapter).

The epicenter of this neighborhood is Kastanienallee (between the Eberswalder Strasse U-Bahn station and Zionskirche), and surrounding streets. It's a youthful and trendy place to eat and drink. I've organized my recommendations in four categories: German cuisine, international options, places for a drink or snack, and options in the gentrified Kollwitzkiez area, near a pleasant park.

German Food

$ Prater Biergarten has been in business since 1837—back when Prenzlauer Berg was a forested hill—and is Berlin's oldest beer garden. It's a classic *Gemütlichkeit* (cozy and convivial) scene—mellow, shaded, and super-cheap—with a family-friendly outdoor area, including a playground (no table service, order food at one counter, beer at the other). They serve just basic pub grub, but the price is right and there's a wide range of beers. Prater's rustic indoor restaurant (more expensive, with table service) serves well-executed German classics with proper veal schnitzel and good salads. Both sections proudly pour Prater's own microbrew (restaurant open Mon-Sat 18:00-24:00, Sun from 12:00; beer garden open daily in

EATING

Berlin's Brew and Beverage Scene

Although Berliners leave it to Bavarian brewers to be the masters of traditional brews, Berlin is the epicenter of Germany's growing small-batch craft beer scene. Specialty craft-beer bars and microbreweries are popping up all around the city, such as the recommended Hopfenreich, in Kreuzberg.

The city does have its own mass-produced beers, too. Most famous are the fizzy Berliner Weisse and the basic Berliner Kindl pilsner. Berliner Weisse is commonly served *mit Schuss*—with a shot of fruity syrup in your suds. Choose either *rot* (red) or *grün* (green) syrup. These beers are—locals readily admit—uninspired at best. (Maybe that's why they need to add syrup.)

A good place to sample the local brew is at a beer hall, beer garden, or one of the city's *Kneipen*. These traditional, colorful pubs, offering a fine old-Berlin ambience, not only serve drinks, but also light, quick, and easy meals. Classic Berlin *Kneipen* listed in this chapter include Metzer Eck and Zum Schusterjungen (Prenzlauer Berg), Aufsturz and Sophieneck (old Jewish quarter), and Dicke Wirtin (City West, near Savignyplatz).

For all its other hallmarks of a great foodie city, Berlin does not have a particularly good craft cocktail scene, though all of the standards are available. Nonalcoholic specialties to look for include Fritz-Cola, a high-end soft-drink brand, and Club-Mate (MAH-tay), a carbonated iced-tea drink made of yerba mate leaves, with as much caffeine as a cup of coffee. It comes in several varieties, and is sometimes mixed into a cocktail (which helps keep the party going).

good weather 12:00-24:00, closed in winter; Kastanienallee 7, +49 30 448 5688).

$$ Zum Schusterjungen ("The Cobbler's Apprentice") is a classic, old-school, German-with-attitude eatery that retains its circa-1986 DDR decor. Famous for its filling meals (including various types of schnitzel and Berlin specialties such as pork knuckle), it's a no-frills place with quality ingredients and a strong local following. It serves the needs of those Berliners lamenting the disappearance of solid, traditional German cooking amid the flood of ethnic eateries (small 40-seat dining hall plus outdoor tables, daily 12:00-24:00, corner of Lychener Strasse and Danziger Strasse 9, +49 30 442 7654).

$ Konnopke's Imbiss, a super-cheap German-style sausage stand with a small section of covered picnic tables underneath the ever-rumbling U2 train tracks, has been a Berlin institution since 1930. It was family-owned even during DDR times. Loyal Berliners say Konnopke's cooks up some of the city's best *Currywurst;* they also serve a wide variety of other wurst specialties  (Tue-Sat 10:00-20:00, Sun 12:00-18:00, closed Mon; Schönhauser Allee 44A—underneath elevated train tracks where Kastanienallee dead-ends, +49 30 442 7765). If you'd rather have very cheap, finger-licking-good, halal fried chicken, head across the street and join all the kids at Risa's.

$$$ Ausspanne looks like a traditional, uninspired hotel restaurant. But the small, always fresh menu boldly elevates German classics with surprising flourishes—such as a puff of habanero foam with duck breast and red cabbage. It offers an interesting and reasonably priced take on modern German cooking (daily 17:00-22:00, in recommended Hotel Kastanienhof at Kastanienallee 65, +49 30 4430 5199).

$$$ Der Hahn Ist Tot! ("The Rooster Is Dead!") has whimsical style and cozy outdoor tables facing the Zionskirche, on a pleasant Prenzlauer Berg square. They serve only four-course, €24 dinners. The small menu is a thoughtful combination of rustic German and French dishes (always a fish, meat, and vegetarian option), and prices are decent. It's as tiny as it is popular—book ahead (Tue-Sun 18:30-23:00, closed Mon, Zionskirchstrasse 40, +49 30 6570 6756, www.der-hahn-ist-tot.de).

$$$ Restaurant Die Schule is a dressy, spacious, modern eatery where you can sample €3 tapas-style plates of old-fashioned German food. They have several varieties of *Flammkuchen* (German pizza—a flatbread dish from the French borderlands) and seasonal main dishes. The vibe is sober and nondescript inside and out (daily 11:00-22:00, Kastanienallee 82, +49 30 780 089 550).

International Eateries

$$$ Les Valseuses is a hole-in-the-wall French bistro with an open kitchen. Everything is simple and unpretentious, from the subway tile-clad exterior to the cozy, stripped-down interior, to the short menu (fish, meat or vegetarian). Reserve ahead (daily 18:30-23:00, Eberswalder Strasse 28, +49 30 7552 2032).

$$$ Osmans Töchter ("Ottoman Daughters"), run by sisters from Istanbul, is a fun mash-up of industrial-mod interior and modern Turkish cuisine. Although the service can be a bit full of

---

Food Tours

Most Berlin culinary tours either focus on traditional German fare or the trendier foodie scene, some do a combination of both, and virtually all include a *Currywurst*. Some well-established tour operators—including **Original Berlin Walks** and **Fat Tire Bike Tours**—have added food and craft beer tours to their lineup (see "Tours in Berlin" in the Orientation chapter). Meanwhile, an array of specialty companies focus on doing only food tours. As this is a quickly evolving scene, it's difficult to recommend a specific company. But for starters, consider the following: **Fork and Walk Tours** (higher-end, combines sightseeing with food stops, www.forkandwalktoursberlin.com), **Bite Berlin** (a smaller operation with thoughtful tours, www.biteberlin.com), and **The German Food Tour** (brief and affordable, www.thegermanfoodtour.de). Check their websites (and online reviews) to find a tour that suits your interests and travel philosophy.

---

itself, this popular restaurant is the most appealing place in Prenzlauer Berg to sample well-executed Turkish dishes. Reservations are smart (daily 17:30-24:00, Pappelallee 15, +49 30 3266 3388, www.osmanstoechter.de).

$$ Vân Anh Restaurant serves finer Vietnamese dishes than you might expect. Harried waiters barely take time to talk, but the creative menu—with dishes from stir fries to salads and steaks—makes ordering fun. It has a successful and youthful energy with stripped-down woody decor. You can enjoy the Oderberger Strasse and Kastanienallee action from sidewalk tables wrapping around a central corner of Prenzlauer Berg, or join the high-energy yet mellow tighter seating inside (daily 12:00-23:00, cash only, Oderberger Strasse 7, +49 30 4171 7294).

$ Lemongrass Scent is a hardworking little spot on a quiet street serving fresh and tasty Asian dishes for a great price. It's fast, friendly, and has a comfy interior and tables with benches on the street (daily 12:00-23:00, Schwedter Strasse 12, +49 30 4057 6985).

$$ Babel is a Lebanese restaurant popular with locals for its generous portions of shawarma, falafel, and kafta served at flower-bedecked sidewalk tables. Their mix-and-match lunch plates and two-person platters are an especially good value (daily 11:00-24:00, Kastanienallee 33, +49 30 4403 1318).

$ Maria Bonita is an American-run Mexican bistro on a busy street offering some of the most authentic tacos in Berlin (daily 12:00-23:00, equidistant from Kollwitzplatz and Eberswalder Strasse U-Bahn stations at Danziger Strasse 33, +49 30 2025 5338).

Browsing Kastanienallee: For other ethnic options, simply wander down Kastanienallee from the Eberswalder Strasse trestle. In just a few blocks, you'll see Italian, Vietnamese, falafel, and *Gemüse kebab,* along with burgers, funky cafés, colorful *Kneipen,* and much more.

Waffles or a Hippy Bar in the Center of Prenzlauer Berg

The following places are good for lingering over a drink and/or snack, ideally at an outdoor table where you can soak up the essence of Prenzlauer Berg.

Kauf Dich Glücklich makes a great capper to a Prenzlauer Berg dinner. It serves an enticing array of sweet Belgian waffles and homemade ice cream in an inviting candy-sprinkled, bohemian lounge and a garden-like front terrace on a great street (or get your dessert to go, daily 10:00-23:00, Oderberger Strasse 44, +49 30 4862 3292).

Café Morgenrot ("Red Dawn") is actually a bar. This Prenzlauer Berg classic, a holdover from the neighborhood's squatter days, brings together the community—gay, straight, local, foreign—and is still run by an artists' collective (Tue-Sun 11:00-24:00, closed Mon, vegan options, Kastanienallee 85, +49 30 4431 7844).

Kollwitzkiez Area

This small neighborhood, a few blocks east of Kastanienallee, is Prenzlauer Berg's gentrified heart—quieter and more residential. Hip parents bring their hip kids to the hip leafy playground park at its center, Kollwitzplatz. The first listing (Gugelhof) is a pricier sit-down option right on the park; the others allow you to enjoy great food and this area on the cheap. Some of these (and many others in the neighborhood) offer takeaway; grab something to go, and find a bench on this prime square.

$$$$ Gugelhof is famous for its Alsatian German cuisine—French quality with German proportions. It has a kids' menu, a selection of *Flammkuchen* (Alsatian pizzas), fun fixed-price meals, and professional service. A smart local clientele fills its minimalist yet classy interior; in good weather, outdoor seating sprawls along its sidewalk (Mon-Fri 17:00-23:00, Sat-Sun from 10:00, reservations smart, where Knaackstrasse meets Kollwitzplatz, +49 30 442 9229, www.gugelhof.de).

$ Chutnify offers a modern take on Indian street food. You can get a *dosa* (southern India's version of a burrito, with various fillings), a *thali* (mixed platter), or a curry, either to eat in the cozy interior or dine with the neighborhood street-side (daily 12:00-23:00, Sredzkistrasse 43, +49 30 4401 0795).

$ Zula is handy for cheap hummus wraps to enjoy at an outside table on one of Prenzlauer Berg's finest streets, or take to Kollwitzplatz, just down the way (daily 11:00-23:00, Husemannstrasse 10, +49 30 4171 5100).

$$ Zuhause specializes in picnic-perfect deli-style dishes. Choose from a fresh selection of salads, veggie dishes, or traditional Berlin comfort food—*Sauerbraten, Buletten,* and *goulash.* Save room for a meal-capping slice of *kuchen* (Mon-Fri 11:00-21:00, Sat from 12:00, closed Sun, Kollwitzstrasse 26, +49 30 6431 2315).

Pubs near Senefelderplatz: Two options—a few blocks south of Kollwitzplatz, handy to the Senefelderplatz U-Bahn—are good choices for beer with grub. **$ Metzer Eck** is a time-warp *Kneipe* with cozy charm and a family tradition dating to 1913. It serves cheap, basic, old-fashioned Berlin grub with five beers on tap (Mon-Fri 16:00-24:00, Sat from 18:00, closed Sun, Metzer Strasse 33, on the corner with Strassburger Strasse, +49 30 442 7656). **$$ Leibhaftig** is the modern yin to Metzer's yang, serving their own brews and Bavarian tapas—small plates of nouveau German cuisine, with plenty of vegetarian options (Mon-Sat 18:00-24:00, closed Sun, Metzer Strasse 30, +49 30 5481 5039).

OLD JEWISH QUARTER

Of Berlin's trendy dining zones, this is the closest to the main sightseeing core. Most of these places are a reasonable walk from Unter den Linden and within 10 minutes of the Hackescher Markt S-Bahn station. For locations, see the "Old Jewish Quarter" map in the Sleeping in Berlin chapter.

On and near Auguststrasse

The best place to find good eateries in the old Jewish quarter is along or near Auguststrasse, Berlin's "art gallery row" (close to the New Synagogue and my ▯ Old Jewish Quarter Walk). Though the Hackescher Markt places are easier to reach, Auguststrasse has attracted a fun cross-section of creative chefs and is worth the short detour.

The nearby and much bigger Oranienburger Strasse is jammed with dime-a-dozen Indian, Cuban, and Singapore-themed restaurants serving tropical cocktails. While this street is trendy, the places I recommend here are more interesting and more respected by locals.

$$ Mogg Deli is a foodie favorite, serving a short but thoughtful menu of soups, salads, and sandwiches. While dishing up international cuisine, it's inspired by a New York deli. They're known for their home-cured pastrami, especially their monster, designed-to-be-shared Reuben (Mon-Sat 11:00-22:00, Sun until 20:00; inside the huge red-brick former Jewish girls' school at Auguststrasse 11, +49 30 330 060 770).

$$ Clärchens Restaurant fills the courtyard in front of

Clärchens Ballhaus (a classic old Berlin ballroom) with twinkle lights, ramshackle furniture, and a bohemian-chic atmosphere—especially nice on a balmy evening. They serve German and Italian dishes, including brats, pizza, and homemade

cakes. You can also eat in the dance hall or in a garden out back. After 21:00, the DJ cranks up the music in the ground floor dance hall, creating a fun, high-energy yet neighborly scene (daily 12:00-22:00, Auguststrasse 24, +49 30 282 9295).

$$$ Schwarzwaldstuben is a Black Forest-themed pub—which explains the antlers, cuckoo clocks, and painting of a thick forest on the wall. It's friendly, with good service, food, and prices. The staff chooses the music (often rock or jazz), and the ambience is warm and welcoming. If they're full, you can eat at the long bar (daily 12:00-23:00, Tucholskystrasse 48, +49 30 2809 8084).

$$$ Cordobar is a cozy wine bar with a clean, trendy vibe and an appealing range of both German and international wines by the glass, paired with upscale small plates. Come here not for a filling meal, but to enjoy a posh local scene and try some interesting wines. It's popular, so reserve ahead (Tue-Sat 19:00-24:00, closed Sun-Mon, Grosse Hamburger Strasse 32, +49 30 2758 1215).

$$ Sophieneck upholds its *Kneipe* roots as the neighborhood's ersatz living room, serving hearty Berliner specialties like *Buletten* and *Eisbein* on a breezy corner to a happy mix of locals and tourists (daily 12:00-22:30, Grosse Hamburger Strasse 37, +49 30 283 4065).

$$ Aufsturz is a lively pub that's more for serious drinkers than serious eaters. It has a huge selection of beer and whisky and dishes up traditional Berliner pub grub to a young crowd (daily 12:00-24:00, Oranienburger Strasse 67, +49 30 2804 7407).

Coffee: At **The Barn,** curt baristas serve up some of Berlin's best gourmet coffee with an extra shot of pretense. Hipster coffee snobs will be satisfied (Mon-Fri 8:00-18:00, Sat-Sun from 10:00, Auguststrasse 58).

Dessert: For your afternoon *Kaffee und Küchen,* stop at **Princess Cheesecake,** beloved by locals and selling several varieties of cheesecake (daily 10:00-20:00, Tucholskystrasse 37, +49 30 2809 2760).

Rosenthaler Platz Area

This busy neighborhood thrives with millennials and the youth hostel crowd and has some enticing options. It's roughly between the old Jewish quarter and Prenzlauer Berg, near the U8: Rosenthaler Platz station, and on the tram #M1 line that runs between Kastanienallee and the Hackescher Markt S-Bahn station.

Eclectic Eats on Weinbergsweg: Don't miss the first block of Weinbergsweg, the narrower, tram track-lined lane that heads north to Prenzlauer Berg. In just one block, you'll find cafés, bakeries, superfoods and organic juice, *Gemüse kebab, döner kebab,* an Italian deli, Mexican street food, Russian, Korean barbecue, a French bistro, Chinese dumplings, and gelato.

$$$$ Katz Orange is a mecca for foodies, and feels regal from the moment you enter its intimate courtyard. It's surprisingly affordable and delightfully cozy-chic. The menu is small and sharp, known for its "candy on the bone" slow-cooked meat, and changes with the season (daily 18:00-23:00, reservations recommended, Bergstrasse 22, +49 30 983 208 430, www.katzorange.com).

Hackescher Markt Area

$$$ Hasir is a popular, upscale, somewhat stuffy opportunity to splurge on Turkish and Anatolian specialties amid candles and hardwood floors. While a bit past its prime and with hit-or-miss service, Hasir remains respected, and enjoys a handy location (large and splittable portions, daily 16:00-24:00, a block from the Hackescher Markt S-Bahn station at Oranienburger Strasse 4, +49 30 2804 1616).

$$ Weihenstephaner Bavarian Restaurant serves traditional Bavarian food in an air-conditioned traditional-yet-sleek interior, down in an atmospheric cellar, on an inner courtyard, or on a busy people-watching terrace facing the delightful Hackescher Markt square; and, of course, it has excellent beer. If you want to eat right on Hackescher Markt, this is your best bet (daily 11:00-24:00, Neue Promenade 5 at Hackescher Markt, +49 30 8471 0760).

$ Curry 61 serves up, for many, the best *Currywurst* in Berlin; vegetarians and vegans appreciate good options too. Eat in or grab a €5 meal to eat on a bench at the fine Monbijoupark across the street (daily, long hours, Oranienburger Strasse 6).

KREUZBERG

To dig into Berlin's up-and-coming food scene, head to Kreuzberg. This southern Berlin neighborhood—historically known for its large immigrant community and counterculture squatters—has taken off as *the* place for upwardly mobile young Berliners to eat out. As this is a very trendy destination, it's smart to reserve ahead at most of my listings—especially on weekends—or avoid prime meal times.

Most of the places I've listed here are in the neighborhood known as "Kreuzberg 36." Consider combining a visit here with my

□ Kreuzberg Walk, which includes even more eating options, such as lots of handy street food places and restaurants in other parts of Kreuzberg, including Wrangelkiez and Bergmannkiez.

Markthalle Neun

Kreuzberg's best foodie destination is this refurbished 19th-century market hall, filled with local producers and fun food stalls.

You'll find gourmet butchers, wine shops, tapas, Berlin meatballs *(Buletten)*, tofu sandwiches, fair trade spices, Turkish dishes, and a supermarket. It's most worthwhile on "Street Food Thursdays," when extra eateries open from 17:00 to 22:00 (most vendors open Mon-Sat 10:00-18:00, closed Sun, Eisenbahnstrasse 42, U1: Görlitzer Bahnhof, www.markthalleneun.de). Attached to the market is **$$$$ Weltrestaurant Markthalle,** with classic *Kneipe* decor and big portions of traditional German dishes (daily 12:00-24:00, Pücklerstrasse 34). Note: The Görlitzer Bahnhof area can feel seedy, especially at night.

Near Kottbusser Tor U-Bahn Station and Oranienstrasse

$$$ Hasir is a big, clean, and unstressful place tourists appreciate for high-quality Turkish cuisine at high prices. It's well-run, dressy, and spacious, with great energy and a big open kitchen (daily 12:00-24:00, Adalbertstrasse 10 at corner of Oranienstrasse, +49 30 6165 9222, http://hasir.de).

$ Südblock, Kreuzberg's take on a beer garden, brings together all walks of local life: Turk, Berliner, gay, straight, and tourist. It's a convivial vibe, best when balmy, with shared tables filling a corner plaza under trees and umbrellas or inside with cramped seating under disco balls (the DJ turns up the music nightly at 21:00). The menu includes German standards, stuffed baked potatoes, Tex-Mex, *Flammkuchen,* vegan, and lots of booze (daily from 11:00, where Admiralstrasse hits Kottbusser Tor, +49 30 6094 1853).

$$ Max und Moritz is an old-time *Wirtshaus* half a block from Oranienplatz. They pride themselves on doing traditional Berlin food the right way—with equal amounts respect for the origins, and disregard for anyone who might not like it that way (daily 17:00-23:00, cash only, reservations smart, Oranienstrasse 162, +49 30 6951 5911, www.maxundmoritzberlin.de).

Cheap Turkish-Style Eats: Two doors down from Hasir,

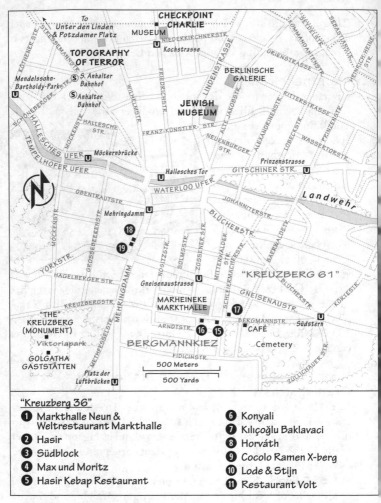

"Kreuzberg 36"

1 Markthalle Neun & Weltrestaurant Markthalle
2 Hasir
3 Südblock
4 Max und Moritz
5 Hasir Kebap Restaurant
6 Konyali
7 Kılıçoğlu Baklavaci
8 Horváth
9 Cocolo Ramen X-berg
10 Lode & Stijn
11 Restaurant Volt

$ Hasir Kebap Restaurant, at Adalbertstrasse 12, is a bit more casual and has more kebab options (daily until late). **$ Konyali,** a cheap kebab joint just off Kottbusser Tor, offers the closest thing to an Istanbul vibe and crowd, with great prices and solid Turkish cuisine and fun seating outside (Reichenberger Strasse 10, +49 30 6900 4567). For dessert, head down to the friendly **Kılıçoğlu Baklavaci** bakery for enticing honey-soaked sweets sold by weight (daily until late, Adalbertstrasse 9).

High-End Foodie Splurges on and near Paul-Lincke-Ufer

The Paul-Lincke-Ufer strip along the north bank of the Landwehr Canal (across from the Turkish market) is home to several top-tier

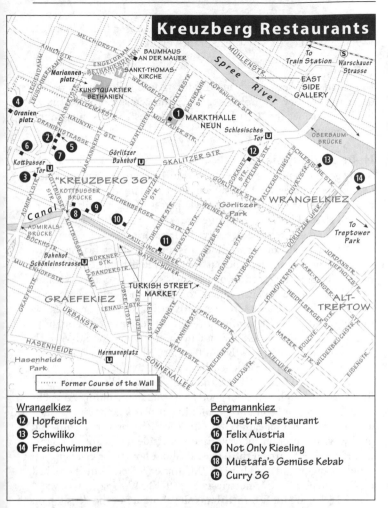

Kreuzberg Restaurants

Wrangelkiez
- ⑫ Hopfenreich
- ⑬ Schwiliko
- ⑭ Freischwimmer

Bergmannkiez
- ⑮ Austria Restaurant
- ⑯ Felix Austria
- ⑰ Not Only Riesling
- ⑱ Mustafa's Gemüse Kebab
- ⑲ Curry 36

Berlin eateries (U8: Schönleinstrasse). I've listed these in the order you reach them, heading east from Kottbusser Brücke.

$$$$ Horváth, a Michelin-star restaurant, serves elevated Austrian/international-fusion fare (Wed-Sun 18:30-22:00, closed Mon-Tue, #44a, +49 30 6128 9992, www.restaurant-horvath.de).

$$ Cocolo Ramen X-berg, a wildly popular outpost of a high-end Japanese restaurant, dishes up slurpy noodle bowls (Mon-Sat 12:00-24:00, closed Sun, #39, +49 30 9833 9073, www.kuchi.de).

$$$$ Lode & Stijn features the eclectic high-end cooking (without pretense) of two talented Dutch-transplant chefs (Tue-Sat 18:00-22:00, closed Sun-Mon, Lausitzer Strasse 25, +49 30 6521 4507, www.lode-stijn.de)

$$$ Restaurant Volt serves upscale international dishes in a

EATING

former power station (Tue-Sat 18:00-24:00, closed Sun-Mon, #21, +49 30 338 402 320, www.restaurant-volt.de).

CITY WEST

I've listed these eateries primarily for travelers sleeping here. (In other words, they are not worth traveling across Berlin to enjoy.) For locations, see the "City West Hotels & Restaurants" map in the Sleeping in Berlin chapter.

Near Savignyplatz

Many good restaurants are on or within 100 yards of Savignyplatz, near my recommended hotels. Savignyplatz is lined with attractive, relaxed, mostly Mediterranean-style places. Take a walk and survey the places I list here; continue your stroll along Bleibtreustrasse to discover many trendier, creative little eateries.

$$$ Restaurant Marjellchen is a trip to East Prussia, with big portions of hearty, delicious German/Polish cuisine. Dine in cozily cluttered elegance in one of two six-table rooms. While it doesn't have to be expensive, plan to go the whole nine yards here, as this can be a great experience, with caring service. The menu is inviting, and the place family-run—all the recipes were brought to Berlin by the owner's East Prussian mother after World War II. Reservations are smart (daily 17:00-22:30, Mommsenstrasse 9, +49 30 883 2676, www.marjellchen-berlin.de).

$$ Dicke Wirtin ("Fat Landlady") has a traditional old-Berlin *Kneipe* atmosphere, seven good beers on tap (including Andechs from Bavaria), and solid home cooking at reasonable prices—such as their famously cheap *Gulaschsuppe*. Their interior is fun and pubby, with soccer on the TV; their streetside tables are also inviting. Pickled eggs are on the bar—ask about how these can help you avoid a hangover (daily 11:00-23:00, dinner served from 18:00, just off Savignyplatz at Carmerstrasse 9, +49 30 312 4952).

$$$$ Café im Literaturhaus sits above a rare-books shop on a delightfully tranquil garden courtyard, facing the Käthe Kollwitz Museum. It has the ambience of an Old World villa, with classy gold Art Deco accents—perfect for their evening poetry and other literary readings. While the full menu is quite pricey, you can enjoy the place far more affordably with a sandwich or coffee and cake (daily 9:00-24:00, reservations smart, Fasanenstrasse 23, +49 30 882 5414).

$ Heno Heno is a very popular Japanese hole-in-the-wall, serving a variety of rice bowls, noodle dishes, and soups (but no sushi) in a long, sleek, minimalist space (Mon-Sat 12:00-22:00, closed Sun, Wielandstrasse 37, +49 30 6630 7370).

$ Diener Tattersall is a neighborhood favorite *Kneipe* with a complicated history. The building started as a horse riding school, later became a casino, and was eventually bought by the German heavyweight champion Franz Diener, who attracted an eclectic clientele of boxers and artists to his *Kneipe*. Today it's known for the affordable menu, specializing in homemade liver sausage (daily from 18:00, Grolmanstrasse 47, +49 30 881 5329).

$$ Weyers offers modern German cuisine in a simple, elegant setting, with dining tables spilling out into the idyllic neighborhood park in the summer (daily 8:00-24:00, Pariser Strasse 16—facing Ludwigkirchplatz at intersection with Pfalzburger Strasse, +49 30 881 9378).

On Bleibtreustrasse: On the stretch just south of the Savignyplatz S-Bahn tracks, Bleibtreustrasse is lined with an eclectic array of dining options—wander and take your pick: **$$ Zillemarkt,** an old-time beer hall with nice atmosphere and uninspired service (#48A); **$ Ali Baba,** with pizzas and outdoor seating (#45); **$ Repke Spätzlerei** (*Flamkuchen*, spaetzle, and buttery dumplings, #46); and **Nibs Cacao** (churros and chocolate, also at #46).

Near Zoologischer Garten Station

In addition to a beer garden and department-store cafeteria, there's plenty of fast food near the Zoologischer Garten station and on Ku'damm.

$ Curry 36—the locally beloved *Currywurst* vendor from Kreuzberg—has a handy outpost just outside of the station.

$$ Schleusenkrug beer garden is hidden in the park overlooking a canal between the Zoologischer Garten and Tiergarten stations. Choose from an ever-changing self-service menu of huge salads, pasta, and some German dishes (daily 11:00-24:00, food served 11:30-21:30, shorter hours and more basic menu off-season, cash only; from Zoologischer Garten station it's  a 5-minute walk following the path into the park between the zoo and train tracks; +49 30 313 9909).

KaDeWe: The top floor of this famous department store holds the **$$ Winter Garden Buffet** cafeteria, while its sixth-floor deli/food department is a picnicker's nirvana. Its arterials are clogged with more than 1,000 kinds of sausage and 1,500 types of cheese (Mon-Sat 10:00-20:00, closed Sun, U1/U2/U3: Wittenbergplatz, +49 30 2121 2623).

EATING

SHOPPING IN BERLIN

Berlin is a good shopping city—if not quite a great one. While Berlin isn't known for any single must-buy item, those who enjoy browsing design boutiques with clever hipster housewares are on cloud nine here, and you can find fun areas to window-shop anywhere you go. This chapter focuses mainly on markets, neighborhoods, and streets where browsing is its own reward...even if you don't buy anything.

Most Berlin shops keep similar hours: Monday through Friday from about 9:00 or 10:00 to somewhere between 18:00 and 20:00, often somewhat shorter hours on Saturday, and typically closed on Sunday.

For information on VAT refunds and customs regulations, see page 399.

WHAT TO BUY

Shops all over town stock the typical array of **souvenirs** (T-shirts, posters, bottle openers, etc.) emblazoned with icons of Berlin: Brandenburg Gate, TV Tower, Berlin Wall, bears (the namesake and official mascot of "Bear-lin"), and so on.

One big draw is **communist kitsch.** Gift shops at museums (such as the DDR Museum or the Museum of the Wall at Checkpoint Charlie) sell a variety of "East Berlin" paraphernalia: circa-1968 city maps that mysteriously leave out West Berlin, postcards and posters of DDR propaganda or famous Wall escapes, miniature Trabis, old DDR military armbands and medals, defunct communist

currency, and little plastic chicken-shaped egg holders that every East German family had on their breakfast table. While you can get modern replicas all over town, for authentic communist artifacts, head to VEB Orange (in Prenzlauer Berg, described on page 207) or the flea market by the Ostbahnhof (Sun mornings, described later).

Maybe *the* top communist-kitsch souvenir is something— anything—with the image of the *Ampelmann* (traffic-light man), the DDR-era crossing-guard symbol that's become Berlin's unofficial mascot. The best selection is at the local chain of Ampelmann shops, with locations all over the city. The flagship store—with a hunk of Berlin Wall autographed by David

Hasselhoff (no joke)—is along Unter den Linden at #35 (at the corner with Friedrichstrasse). Others are near Gendarmenmarkt (Markgrafenstrasse 37), between Museum Island and the TV Tower (Karl-Liebknecht-Strasse 5), in the Hackesche Höfe (described later), at Potsdamer Platz, in the Hauptbahnhof, and on City West's Kurfürstendamm (at #20).

One communist-era souvenir to avoid is an **"authentic" chunk of the Berlin Wall**—enough of which have been sold since 1989 to encircle all of Germany. Don't trust any vendor who swears they chipped it off the Wall themselves. (And, because the few remaining stretches of Wall are now protected monuments, it's bad form to chisel off your own souvenir.)

Berlin's true forte is **design.** In this city of stylish young urbanites, the streets are lined with hipster gift shops that sell ironic T-shirts, clever kitchen or desk gadgets, snarky books and postcards, and so on. Stroll through home decor, housewares, and furniture shops: Even if what they sell is too big to pack home, you'll get an eye-opening look at how locals furnish their lives.

Other shopping options to consider include Berlin's many appealing **bookstores** (consider Do You Read Me? at Auguststrasse 28 in the old Jewish quarter; or Ocelot, near Rosenthaler Platz at Brunnenstrasse 181); CDs of quality **music,** perhaps performed by the renowned Berlin Philharmonic (shop at the Philharmonic building itself Saturdays 11:00-14:00, also check out the big Dussmann book-and-record store at Friedrichstrasse 90; for something more recent, Hard Wax in Kreuzberg at Paul-Lincke-Ufer 44A is *the* seminal record shop in town); or **museum gift shops,** which stock books and prints of artwork that you enjoyed seeing in person.

FLEA MARKETS AND FARMERS MARKETS

In such an outdoorsy city, some of the most enjoyable "shopping" experiences aren't in shopping malls or hole-in-the-wall boutiques, but at sprawling outdoor markets.

Flea Markets *(Flohmarkt)*

Virtually every Berlin neighborhood hosts a regular flea market.

Prenzlauer Berg: The Sunday rummage market in the **Mauerpark** isn't just about buying and selling—it's an excuse for a big, weekly, community-wide party. If it's nice out, people come here simply to chill, drink, barbecue, and socialize. You'll find lots of inventive snack stalls and, in the afternoon, karaoke in the park's amphitheater (Sun 10:00-18:00, U2: Eberswalder Strasse, www.flohmarktimmauerpark.de). On Sundays there's also a lively "junk market" *(Trödelmarkt)* several blocks south on **Arkonaplatz** (10:00-16:00, U8: Bernauer Strasse or a 10-minute walk from Mauerpark).

Old Jewish Quarter: Just across the Spree from Monbijoupark, the riverbank facing the **Bode Museum** hosts a weekend antique-and-book market (Sat-Sun 11:00-17:00, tram #M1 or #12 to Am Kupfergraben or a 10-minute walk from Hackescher Markt or Friedrichstrasse S-Bahn stations, www.antik-buchmarkt.de). Nearby, **Hackescher Markt** hosts a twice-weekly market with an odd variety of produce, clothes, trinkets, jewelry, hats, and food stalls; while smaller, more touristy, and less funky than the best Berlin markets, it's conveniently located (Thu 9:00-18:00, Sat from 10:00).

Kreuzberg: Along the south bank of Landwehr Canal, the twice-weekly **Turkish street market** is a very local place to shop for everything from clothes and fabrics to basic housewares to produce and meat. The clientele is a mix of Turkish and Middle Eastern immigrants, Kreuzberg punks, and a smattering of tourists. While you can pick up some tasty Turkish-style snacks (such as mint tea and dried fruits and nuts), I'd come  here more for the people-watching than for souvenirs (Tue and Fri 11:00-18:30, U8: Schönleinstrasse). Also in Kreuzberg—in the ritzier Bergmannkiez—the leafy and delightful **Marheinekeplatz** hosts a weekend flea market (Sat-Sun 11:00-16:00, U7: Gneisenaustrasse). For more on this area see the Kreuzberg Walk chapter.

Friedrichshain: The swiftly gentrifying square **Boxhagen-**

er Platz (affectionately called "Boxi" by locals) hosts a lively flea market on Sundays (10:00-18:00, U5: Samariterstrasse or U- and S-Bahn hub Warschauer Strasse; also a Sat farmers market—see later). On Sunday mornings, the **Antikmarkt Ostbahnhof** (9:00-17:00, on the north side of the Ostbahnhof S-Bahn station) is the place to pick through the Cold War knickknacks that keep turning up in the basements of former East Berliners.

Near Tiergarten Park: One of Berlin's largest flea markets is right next to Tiergarten Park on **Strasse des 17 Juni,** with great antiques, more than 200 stalls, collector-savvy merchants, and fun German fast-food stands (Sat-Sun 10:00-17:00, S-Bahn: Tiergarten, www.berlinertroedelmarkt.com).

City West: Consider the big flea market on **Fehrbelinner Platz** in Charlottenburg (Sat-Sun 10:00-16:00, U3/U7: Fehrbelinner Platz), or the smaller one in front of the **Schöneberg City Hall** (Sat-Sun 8:00-16:00, U4: Rathaus Schöneberg; for more on this area see page 87).

Food and Farmers Markets

Weekly farmers markets are huge in this city of foodies, and the biggest include stalls proffering fresh snacks of all kinds.

The city's best food market is Kreuzberg's **Markthalle Neun,** with a variety of vendors and even more activity during the thrice-weekly farmers market and on "Street Food Thursdays."

Another local favorite is on **Boxhagener Platz** in Friedrichshain (farmers market Sat 9:00-15:30, see also Sunday flea market, listed earlier). Prenzlauer Berg also has options: **Kollwitzplatz** (Thu 12:00-19:00 and Sat 9:00-16:00) and in the courtyard of the **Kulturbrauerei** (Sun 12:00-18:00). In City West, head for **Wittenbergplatz** (near KaDeWe, Thu 10:00-18:00).

BROWSING AREAS
Prenzlauer Berg

My favorite hotel and dining neighborhood is also an enjoyable place to window-shop. It's a delight to simply wander colorful Kastanienallee between Eberswalder Strasse (with a U-Bahn station) and Weinbergspark.

On Kastanienallee: Perhaps the most satisfying place to browse in Berlin—with so many shops in such a small area—Kastanienallee is made-to-order for a shopping stroll. Here's just some of what you'll see as you work your way downhill from Eberswalder

SHOPPING

Strasse: **Stoffbruch** (#99, set back on a modern plaza on the left) is a concept store with stylish clothes "designed in Berlin, fair-produced in Europe." **Da Capo** (#96) is a funky, classic Prenzlauer Berg vintage record-and-book shop.

After crossing Oderberger Strasse, you're near two fashion outposts: **Fein und Ripp** (#91) has hip, made-in-Germany clothes, while **Thatchers Fashion Berlin** (across the street at #21) is a bit more upscale. Farther down, **Uhranus** (#31) is perhaps the most enjoyably eclectic Kastanienallee design shop, with tea towels, bags, and prints that celebrate Berlin. In the next block, **Heimat Berlin** (#40) is part of a small chain of fun-to-explore hipster gift shops; **Musik Department** (#41) is an appealingly grungy base-ment record store; **Kleine Fabriek** (#63, on the left) has high-end artisanal stuff for kids; and **Grünbein** (#47) sells fashionable, Swiss-made shoes and boots. Near the bottom of Kastanienallee, facing Weinbergspark, is **Glücklich am Park**—a branch of the popular Oderberger Strasse waffle café, Kauf Dich Glücklich, with its own little fashion boutique upstairs.

Elsewhere in Prenzlauer Berg: The **Kulturbrauerei** brewery-turned-cultural center (described on page 60) has a smattering of little shops, including Green Living (with environmentally friendly housewares and home decor). The Kollwitzkiez (a few blocks east) is mostly residential, but you'll also find some pleasant shops here. For locally produced goods, stop by **Brandenburgerie,** with a va-riety of mostly edible products (meat, cheese, chocolate, juices, schnapps) made in the Brandenburg region that surrounds Berlin (closed Sun-Mon, Sredzkistrasse 36).

Rosenthaler Strasse

The otherwise nondescript street that connects the Hackescher Markt and Rosenthaler Platz areas (along the handy tram #M1 route) attracts those interested in Berlin's fashion and design scene. Most shops along here are **pop-up** spaces, giving you a glimpse at what local designers are up to right now. A couple of permanent fixtures are worth checking out: **Kauf Dich Glücklich,** a ram-shackle Berlin café famous for its waffles (see page 293), but which has since moved into fashion (at #17, www.kaufdichgluecklich-shop.de); and **Schee,** with appealing handmade items, including prints and textiles (at #15, www.schee.net).

Hackesche Höfe

This delightfully restored old series of eight interlocking shopping courtyards sits in the heart of the old Jewish quarter (and is de-scribed on page 186 in the Old Jewish Quarter Walk). While not cheap, it's a convenient and tempting place to window-shop. Your options include Auerbach (top-end leather goods and men's fashion), Königliche Porzellan-Manufaktur (locally made porcelain), Sawade (gourmet chocolates), Hoffnung Berlin (handmade belts),

Home on Earth (products made of natural materials—felt, cork, wicker, and so on), Eat Berlin (artisanal local foods), Golem (decorative *Jugendstil* tiles), Ampelmann (goods featuring the kitschy DDR-era traffic-light man), and more (shops typically open Mon-Sat from 10:00 or 11:00 until 19:00, closed Sun, Rosenthaler Strasse 40, www.hackesche-hoefe.com).

The Hackesche Höfe connects directly from courtyard #6 into another series of shopping courtyards called the **Rosenhöfe.** Though this space has a nice, slinky *Jugendstil* flair, its shops are less characteristic (with more international chains, like H&M and MAC).

Kreuzberg's Bergmannkiez

While a bit less colorful than the areas described above, Kreuzberg's classy Bergmannkiez can be fun to browse for designer boutiques and plenty of antiques. Most are concentrated along Bergmannstrasse, but you'll find more options on the side streets. For more on exploring this area, see the Kreuzberg Walk chapter.

Chocolate Shops on Gendarmenmarkt

The delightful square called Gendarmenmarkt—a short detour south of Unter den Linden—has two very different chocolate shops that are fun to browse: one bourgeois, and the other proletarian. For locations see the map on page 286.

Rausch claims to be Europe's biggest chocolate store. After 150 years of chocolatemaking, this family-owned business proudly displays its sweet delights—250 different kinds—on a 55-foot-long buffet. Truffles are picked at your direction by white-gloved maidens (it's fun to compose the fancy little eight-piece box of your dreams). Upstairs is an el-

egant café with fine views. The displays feature giant chocolate models of Berlin landmarks—Reichstag, Brandenburg Gate, Kaiser Wilhelm Memorial Church, TV Tower, a chunk of the Wall, and so on (Mon-Sat 10:00-

20:00, Sun from 11:00, corner of Mohrenstrasse at Charlotten-strasse 60—look for green awnings directly behind German Cathedral, +49 30 757 882 440).

If you're a choco-populist, head to the opposite end of Gendarmenmarkt, near the French Cathedral, for the Volkswagen of candy. **Ritter Sport Bunte Schokowelt** is home to the flagship store of Ritter Sport, the famous chocolate company—*"quadratisch, praktisch, gut"* ("square, practical, good"). This is basically Germany's answer to the M&M's store. While you can find Ritter Sport in any grocery store, it's fun to see floor-to-ceiling walls of chocolate, stop at their café, and create a make-your-own chocolate-bar souvenir: Select milk, dark, or white chocolate; add three "mix-ins"; wait 30 minutes (browsing the attached retail shop) while it cools, and *voilà* (daily 10:00-19:00, Französische Strasse 24, +49 30 200 950 810).

BIG, GLITZY DEPARTMENT STORES

Consumerism—the Cold War victor—has taken root with a vengeance in Berlin, where super-modern malls and department stores abound.

Central Berlin

Unter den Linden is lined with some high-end shops, but for a wider selection, head a few blocks south.

The stretch of **Friedrichstrasse** near Gendarmenmarkt was slated to become Berlin's "Fifth Avenue" shopping district after the fall of the Wall. While it hasn't quite taken off the way developers had hoped, the French department store **Galeries Lafayette** has a large outpost here with several floors of high-end goods under a glass dome (top-quality basement food court; Mon-Sat 10:00-20:00, closed Sun, Französische Strasse 23).

Several blocks west is the massive, recently opened, state-of-the-art **Mall of Berlin,** with 270 shops surrounding a cavernous glass-covered passageway (Mon-Sat 10:00-21:00, closed Sun, Vossstrasse 35, www.mallofberlin.de). Nearby, **Potsdamer Platz** and **Sony Center** have additional shops.

City West

Several swanky shops line **Kurfürstendamm,** the area's main boulevard (and the place to go if you're in the market for another Rolex).

The trendy **Bikini Berlin** shopping center faces the Europa Center on one side and the Berlin Zoo on the other. This "concept mall" has a mix of international chains, artisan boutiques, temporary art exhibits, food stalls, a small Edeka supermarket, and "pop-up boxes" highlighting Berlin vendors (plus a free glimpse of the zoo's monkeys; Mon-Sat 10:00-20:00, closed Sun, Budapester Strasse 38, www.bikiniberlin.de).

City West's most venerable shopping is a couple blocks east (near the Wittenbergplatz U-Bahn), at **KaDeWe**— one of Europe's fanciest department stores, in business since 1907 and a worthwhile sight in itself (for more, see page 87).

Farther west, the Charlottenburg neighborhood's **"Antique Mile"** stretches along Suarezstrasse (between Kantstrasse and the Sophie-Charlotte-Platz U-Bahn stop).

ENTERTAINMENT IN BERLIN

In the 18th century, Frederick the Great transformed Berlin into a cultural capital. In the early 20th century, the city emerged as Europe's counterculture capital—with a flourishing of edgy performing arts, from Marlene Dietrich's cabaret-singer origins to Bertolt Brecht's intentionally alienating theatrical staging. And today, Berlin remains a hub of both mainstream and alternative arts. This city has three opera companies, multiple symphonies and chamber orchestras, and organ concerts in churches nearly every day of the week. But you'll also find wild dance clubs, hipster ballrooms, dilapidated techno beach bars, and smoky jazz cellars.

This chapter focuses on two big facets of Berlin's entertainment scene: live music and how to spend your time after hours. In this sprawling city, options are many; I've focused on an (admittedly narrow) selection of ideas, with an emphasis on my favorite neighborhoods. Use these resources as a starting point to find entertainment and nightlife to meet your interests.

Entertainment Info: The TI can provide basic information about what's on; for classical music, look for the free, monthly *Concerti* magazine. For good live music listings, see www.askhelmut.com or shell out a few euros for a Berlin magazine (sold at kiosks): *Zitty* (www.zitty.de) and *Tip* (www.tip-berlin.de) are the top guides to alternative culture (mostly in German); *Exberliner Magazine* is colorfully written in English (www.exberliner.com). Also pick up the free *030* schedule in bars and clubs (www.berlin030.de).

Half-Price Tickets: Berlin's ticket clearinghouse, **Hekticket,** offers advance tickets to concerts, cabaret, theater, etc. Every day after 14:00, they sell deeply discounted last-minute tickets (up to half off, tickets usually €10-40). You can either call or go online (+49 30 230 9930, www.hekticket.de, pay by credit card), or visit one of their locations (cash only) to see what's on the push list for that evening. Booths are near Alexanderplatz (Mon-Fri 10:30-19:00, closed Sat-Sun, Alexanderstrasse 1 across from Hotel Park Inn) and in City West (Mon-Sat 12:00-20:00, Sun 14:00-18:00, across from Zoologischer Garten train station at Hardenbergstrasse 29).

Smoking: Berlin bars that don't sell food may allow smoking (unlike in much of Europe). Travelers who are sensitive to smoke should check in advance that their chosen bar is nonsmoking.

Late-Hours Sightseeing: Berlin's museums typically close at 18:00, but many stay open later at least one day a week. Three of the biggies are open late every day: the Reichstag (until midnight, last entry at 22:00), the Museum of the Wall at Checkpoint Charlie (until 22:00), and the Topography of Terror (until 20:00). All the Museum Island museums are open until 20:00 on Thursdays. Outdoor monuments such as the Berlin Wall Memorial and the Memorial to the Murdered Jews of Europe are accessible, safe, and well lit late into the night, though their visitor centers close earlier.

CLASSICAL MUSIC
Berlin Philharmonic

Housed in a striking, modern building at the Kulturforum cultural complex, the Berlin Philharmonic is among the world's top ten orchestras. Inexpensive and  legitimate tickets are often sold on the street an hour before performances. You can also buy tickets at the box office, by phone, or online (ticket office open Mon-Fri 15:00-18:00, Sat-Sun 11:00-14:00 except closed July-Aug, +49 30 2548 8999, www.berliner philharmoniker.de). The philharmonic also presents a popular series of free lunch concerts (most Tue at 13:00 except in July-Aug, tickets handed out in person the same day—try to arrive by 12:00). For more on the building, see the end of the Gemäldegalerie & Kulturforum Tour chapter.

Other Classical Music Venues

In the historic core, these include the gorgeous, Schinkel-designed **Konzerthaus Berlin** on Gendarmenmarkt (home of the Konzerthausorchester symphony orchestra, popular 45-minute "espresso concert" series Wed at 14:00, +49 30 203 092 101, www. konzerthaus.de) and the cutting-edge, Frank Gehry-designed **Pierre Boulez Saal** (theater-in-the-round chamber music, not far from Bebelplatz at Französische Strasse 33D, +49 30 4799 7411, www.boulezsaal.de). To enjoy an affordable (sometimes free) recital by talented students, consider the **Hochschule für Musik Hanns Eisler,** with two venues in the historical center (facing Gendarmenmarkt at Charlottenstrasse 55, and on Museum Island at Schlossplatz 7, +49 30 203 092 101, www.hfm-berlin.de).

Opera

The most historic opera venue is the stately **Staatsoper,** on Bebelplatz overlooking Unter den Linden (box office located at Unter den Linden 7, +49 30 2035 4555, www.staatsoper-berlin.de). Quite different is Berlin's famous **Komische Oper,** with a long tradition for avant-garde, adventurous performances (near Unter den Linden and Friedrichstrasse at Behrenstrasse 55, +49 30 4799 7400, www.komische-oper-berlin.de). The modern **Deutsche Oper** building (in Charlottenburg, near City West) houses both its own opera company and the Berlin State Ballet (Bismarckstrasse 35, U2: Deutsche Oper, +49 30 3438 4343, www.deutscheoperberlin.de).

Concerts in Churches

Several Berlin churches and other venues offer frequent daytime and early-evening concerts. Note that each of these is a historic building described in the Sights in Berlin chapter (and often in one of my walks or tour chapters). Even "free" concerts request a donation. Any of these can cancel unexpectedly, so confirm before making a special trip.

St. Mary's Church: Along Karl-Liebknecht-Strasse near the TV Tower, free organ concerts twice weekly (Thu and Fri at 13:30, www.marienkirche-berlin.de), as well as a variety of other concerts

Nikolaikirche: In the Nikolai Quarter, 30-minute organ concerts on Fridays at 17:00 (€4, www.en.stadtmuseum.de/nikolaikirche)

French Cathedral: On Gendarmenmarkt, 30-minute organ concerts on Tuesdays at 15:00 (€3, www.franzoesische-friedrichstadtkirche.de), plus a variety of other organ and choral worship services

St. Hedwig's Catholic Cathedral: On Bebelplatz, free 30-minute organ concerts on Wednesdays at 15:00 (www.hedwigs-kathedrale.de)

Berlin Cathedral: On Museum Island, evening weekend concerts ranging from organ to choral (tickets at door—prices vary, starts between 18:00 and 20:00, www.berlinerdom.de)

Kaiser Wilhelm Memorial Church: In City West, quality concerts (some free, sporadic schedule, often choral, www.gedaechtniskirche-berlin.de)

Clärchens Ballhaus: Not a church but the old Jewish quarter's beloved classic ballroom, concerts most Sunday evenings in its twinkling upstairs Mirror Room, the Spiegelsaal (€12, often piano or small ensembles, usually begins at 19:00 or 19:30, www.sonntagskonzerte.de)

MODERN MUSIC AND THEATER
Jazz

Berlin has a lively jazz scene (for schedules, see www.jazzclubinberlin.com). The following are close to my recommended accommodations; each has live music nightly from 21:00 (doors open at 20:00).

In City West (near Savignyplatz), consider **A Trane Jazz Club** (great stage and intimate seating, €10-25 cover depending on act, Bleibtreustrasse 1—see map on page 280, +49 30 313 2550, www.a-trane.de).

Near the TV Tower, **B-Flat Acoustic Music and Jazz Club** has live shows and jam sessions (from free to €15, in Alexanderplatz at Dircksenstrasse 40—see map on page 286, +49 30 283 3123, www.b-flat-berlin.de).

Kunstfabrik Schlot, northwest of the old Jewish quarter, is another respected venue (from free to €15, tucked in a cellar, in a courtyard at Invalidenstrasse 117, see map on page 276, U6: Naturkundemuseum, +49 30 448 2160, www.kunstfabrik-schlot.de).

Theater and Variety Shows

Since the cabaret days, Berlin has had a flair for the dramatic. Most of these offerings are in German only. If you're adventurous or speak some German, this can be a plus; if not, confirm the language carefully before you book. For the big spectacles, the language matters less.

Bar Jeder Vernunft, in City West, offers modern-day cabaret a short walk from my recommended Savignyplatz hotels. This variety show—under a classic old tent perched atop the modern parking lot of the Berliner Festspiele theater—is a hit with German speakers and can be worthwhile even for those who don't speak the language (as some of the shows are in a sort of *Deutsch*-English hybrid). Some Americans even perform here periodically (€25-30, performances generally Mon-Sat at 20:00, Sun at 19:00, seating can be cramped, south of Ku'damm at Schaperstrasse 24—see map on page 280, U3 or U9: Spichernstrasse, +49 30 883 1582, www.bar-jeder-vernunft.de).

Berliner Ensemble—a venerable company made famous

under the direction of Bertolt Brecht—stages a dozen or so different productions each month ranging from classic to contemporary. The performances are housed in the majestic Theater am Schiffbauerdamm, across from the Friedrichstrasse Bahnhof, just off the river (€12-50, performances generally daily at 19:30 or 20:00, box office open Mon-Sat 10:00-18:30, Bertolt-Brecht-Platz 1, +49 30 2840 8155, www.berliner-ensemble.de).

The **Friedrichstadtpalast** just north of Unter den Linden stages glitzy spectacles—going for Las Vegas-style bombast (Friedrichstrasse 107, www.palast.berlin).

Nearby, a bit closer to Unter den Linden, the historic **Admiralspalast Theater** features lower-key concerts, plays, and musicals (including the Distel Cabaret Theater company—an East Berlin cabaret troupe, Friedrichstrasse 101, www.admiralspalast.theater).

Other venues to consider: **Theater RambaZamba,** in Prenzlauer Berg's Kulturbrauerei, highlights performers who are disabled and creatively transforms those "disabilities" into assets (www.rambazamba-theater.de). **Chamäleon,** inside Hackesche Höfe and handy to many recommended accommodations, channels the creative spirit of 1920s Berlin and bills itself as a contemporary circus, mixing acrobatics, theater, music, and dance (www.chamaeleonberlin.com). **Kookaburra,** between my old Jewish quarter and Prenzlauer Berg hotels, is a comedy club that regularly presents acts in English (usually Tue at 20:00, Schönhauser Allee 184, www.comedyclub.de). And the **Berliner Festspiele** often hosts a variety of Off-Broadway-type fringe theater (www.berlinerfestspiele.de).

Live Music

Berlin has a staggering array of smaller music venues. Here's a sampling: **Frannz Club,** in Prenzlauer Berg's Kulturbrauerei, was a DDR-era hotspot; today it attracts talented rock and alternative bands (www.frannz.com). Though it's a dance hall, **Clärchens Ballhaus** also has live music Friday and Saturday nights; **Ballhaus Berlin** is another good option (see descriptions for both later, under "Dancing"). **Aufsturz** pub, the

recommended pub in the old Jewish quarter, hosts jazz and other music (www.aufsturz.de). And **SO36,** on Oranienstrasse in Kreuzberg, is Berlin's most venerable punk venue (www.so36.de).

Big concerts are often held at **Olympic Stadium, Mercedes-Benz Arena** in Friedrichshain, the **Spandau Citadel,** and the outdoor **Waldbühne** ("Forest Stage").

NIGHTLIFE
Al Fresco Summer Fun
Berliners have a knack for enjoying life without spending a lot of money. On a warm summer evening, it seems everyone's out, simply enjoying their city.

Great places to **stroll** while people-watching Berliners include the Spree riverbank (especially around Monbijoupark and Museum Island); Prenzlauer Berg's Kastanienallee, Oderberger Strasse, and Helmholtzplatz; and Kreuzberg's Paul-Lincke-Ufer, a leafy embankment on the Landwehr Canal with upscale homes and a lively *boules* court. The old Jewish quarter's Oranienburger Strasse (near the New Synagogue) and City West's Europa Center/Kurfürstendamm boulevard are packed, but are more tourist-oriented.

To nurse a drink, stop by a ***Biergarten.*** Big, beloved, and lively choices include Prater Biergarten, in Prenzlauer Berg; Schleusenkrug in City West, tucked back in the park near the Zoologischer Garten train station; and Golgatha Gaststätten in Kreuzberg's Viktoriapark.

You can also start or end your evenings on a **rooftop bar.** Favorites include the posh **Hotel de Rome** (overlooking Gendarmenmarkt); **25hours Hotel's Monkey Bar** (with views into the zoo residents' enclosure); and **Hugos Restaurant** (inside the Intercontinental on the edge of Tiergarten).

An even more summery variation is Berlin's emerging **beach bar** scene—where people grab a drink along the riverfront and watch the excursion boats go by. The classic spot is the **Strandbar Mitte** in Monbijoupark, with a breezy and scenic setting overlooking the Bode Museum on Museum Island. Others are farther afield, in the Friedrichshain and Kreuzberg neighborhoods: **Yaam** is funky, with playgrounds, real sand, an African theme, and often live music (near the Ostbahnhof and Radialsystem—described later, www.yaam.de). Two more are farther east (close to U1:

Schlesisches Tor): **Badeschiff,** a floating swimming pool with a bar (May-Sept daily, www.arena.berlin/en/location/badeschiff); and **Club der Visionaere,** a very cramped wooden pier with DJs spinning throbbing electronic music (Mon-Fri 15:00-late, Sat-Sun 12:00-later, www.clubdervisionaere.com).

Gallery Hopping

Berlin, a magnet for new artists, is a great city for gallery browsing. Many galleries stay open late and welcome visitors who are "just looking." The most famous gallery district is in the old Jewish quarter, along **Auguststrasse** (branches off from Oranienburger Strasse). Check out the Berlin outpost of the edgy-yet-accessible art of the New Leipzig movement at Galerie Eigen+Art (Tue-Sat 11:00-18:00, closed Sun-Mon, Auguststrasse 26, +49 30 280 6605, www.eigen-art.com).

Dancing

The old ballroom **Clärchens Ballhaus** has been a Berlin institution since 1913 (described in the Old Jewish Quarter Walk chapter). At some point, everyone in Berlin comes through here, as the dance hall attracts an eclectic Berlin-in-a-nutshell crowd of grannies, elegant women in evening dresses, yuppies, scenesters, and hippies. Every night from 21:00 on the DJ cranks it up and people dance like no one's watching. The music changes every day—swing, waltz, tango, or cha-cha. There's live music on Friday and Saturday (from 23:00, €5 cover, Auguststrasse 24—see map on page 276, S-Bahn: Oranienburger Strasse, +49 30 282 9295, www.ballhaus.de). Dancing lessons are also available (€6-9, beginner lessons generally Mon-Fri at 19:00, Sun at 12:00, 1.5 hours).

The **$$** Gipsy Restaurant, which fills a huge courtyard out front, serves reasonably priced German and Italian food. If you enjoy the *Ballhaus* scene, consider the campy (and less venerable) **Ballhaus Berlin,** just west of Prenzlauer Berg (Chausseestrasse 102, U6: Naturkundemuseum, www.ballhaus-berlin.de).

Berlin boasts the largest **tango** scene outside Buenos Aires (well-described at www.tango-argentino-online.com). In summer, it's easy to get a taste of tango on any balmy night in the riverside **Monbijoupark,** between Museum Island and Hackescher Markt. Most nights also include sessions with one or two other dance styles (€5-10, beginner classes often available; www.monbijou-theater.de). Also check out **Tangoloft** in Wed-

ENTERTAINMENT

ding, northwest of Prenzlauer Berg (Gerichtstrasse 2, take S-Bahn to Wedding station, www.tangoloft-berlin.de).

Pub Crawls

The "free" tour companies that cater to students offer wildly popular pub crawls, promising "four cool bars and one hot club" for about €12. Just imagine what kind of bar lets in a tour of 70 college kids. It can be fun...if you want to get drunk with a bunch of American students in a foreign country.

Friedrichshain Nightlife

Prenzlauer Berg and Kreuzberg both have pockets of excitement. But these days, the most happening scene is a few tram stops or U-Bahn stops farther from the center, in the neighborhood of Friedrichshain (just east of Prenzlauer Berg). While this area is famous for its rowdy and exclusive dance clubs, here are some more accessible options.

One striking venue is **Radialsystem,** a red-brick industrial building right by the water and near the East Side Gallery. Priding itself on being a "space for arts and ideas," they host everything from classical music to electronica (and good €5 meals to boot, Holzmarktstrasse 33, take S-Bahn to Ostbahnhof station, www.radialsystem.de).

The edgier **RAW-Tempel,** just north of the Warschauerstrasse S-Bahn station, is a huge complex of industrial buildings that have been renovated by a community group dedicated to hosting low-cost arts events, including club nights, concerts, a bar, and even a circus. It's a ramshackle wonderland of twinkle lights and graffiti.

Across from the Warschauerstrasse S-Bahn station is the iconic **Monster Ronson's Ichiban Karaoke** bar, with private cabins and live music (daily 24 hours, Warschauerstrasse 34, www.karaokemonster.de).

BERLIN CONNECTIONS

This chapter covers Berlin's airports (which, by the time you visit, will likely include just the new Brandenburg airport); its main train station (Berlin Hauptbahnhof), including train connections to other German destinations and beyond; its bus depot; and the cruise port at Warnemünde.

By Plane

Berlin's airport situation has been in flux, but the much-delayed Berlin Brandenburg Airport should be open by the time you visit. For years, two older airports—Tegel and Schönefeld—did their best to handle Berlin's heavy air traffic; Brandenburg will replace Schönefeld while Tegel will likely have closed by the time you visit. For current airport information, see www.berlin-airport.de.

Berlin Brandenburg / Schönefeld Airport
The state-of-the-art **Brandenberg Airport** (airport code: BER), 11 miles south of central Berlin, should finally be open by the time you visit, absorbing the Cold-War era Schönefeld Airport.

Brandenburg will have three terminals: T1 and T2 are the main terminals located in the new building; T5 will take over Schönefeld's terminal. The two terminal buildings will be connected by frequent S-Bahn trains and buses.

The airport's train station (Flughafen BER) sits directly under the new terminal and will connect the airport with downtown Berlin plus regional and international destinations. Airport Express trains (FEX) will run to Berlin's Hauptbahnhof, where buses, trains, and trams fan out across the city. S-Bahn and regional trains will also connect the airport station with the city center.

When you arrive, the S9 S-Bahn line may be your best bet

into town. It's especially handy for Prenzlauer Berg and old Jewish quarter hotels: From the Schönhauser Allee stop, tram #M1

runs south along Kastanienallee, then all the way to Hackescher Markt. You can also take Airport Express RE and RB trains directly to Ostbahnhof, Alexanderplatz, Friedrichsstrasse (near some old Jewish quarter hotels), Hauptbahnhof, and Zoologischer Garten (handy for City West hotels; train runs 2/hour, direction: Nauen or Dessau). Either train is covered by an ABC transit ticket (€3.60, buy at machine and validate before boarding). Check all connections when you arrive to get the most current information. A taxi to the city center costs about €45.

Tegel Airport

Tegel (airport code: TXL) will likely have closed by the time you visit. Just four miles northwest of the center, it served as Berlin's main airport while the new Brandenburg airport underwent years of renovation. If further delays to Brandenburg occur, and you arrive at Tegel, the easiest way to get downtown is to hop on bus #TXL (follow the little bus icons to exit D), which runs every six minutes to the Hauptbahnhof, where you can connect to the U-Bahn or a bus to your hotel. A taxi from Tegel Airport costs about €30 to Alexanderplatz or €20 to City West.

By Train

Virtually all long-distance trains pass through the **Berlin Hauptbahnhof** ("Berlin Hbf" on schedules)—a massive, state-of-the-art

temple of railroad travel in the heart of the city. This mostly underground train station is where the national train system meets Berlin's S-Bahn—unique for the way its major lines come in at right angles. Note that many arriving trains (especially regional ones) stop at multiple Berlin stations, one of which may be more convenient to your hotel than the Hauptbahnhof. Before you arrive, figure out which station is best for you.

Orientation: The gigantic station has five floors, but its open

layout makes it easy to navigate...once you understand the
signage. The main floor, at
street level, is labeled "EG" (for
Erdgeschoss), or level 0. Below
that are UG1 (level -1) and UG2
(level -2), while above it are
OG1 (level +1) and OG2 (level
+2). Tracks 1-8 are on UG2,
while tracks 11-16 and the S-

Bahn are on OG2. Shops and services are on the three middle levels. Enter and exit the station on level EG: The Washingtonplatz
entrance faces south (toward the Reichstag and downtown, with a
taxi stand). The north entrance is marked *Europaplatz.*

CONNECTIONS

Services: On the main floor (EG), you'll find the **TI** (just inside the north/Europaplatz entrance) and the **"Rail & Fresh WC"**
facility (public pay toilets, near the food court, follow gold signs).
Up one level (OG1) are a 24-hour **pharmacy** and **lockers** (directly
under track 14 on the east side). **Car rental** offices are down one
level (UG1), near platforms 7-8.

Train Information and Tickets: The Deutsche Bahn *Reisezentrum* information center is up one level (OG1), between
tracks 12 and 13 (on the west side; open long hours daily).

EurAide is an English-speaking information desk with answers to your questions about train travel around Europe. It's located at counter 12 inside the *Reisezentrum* on the first upper level
(OG1). It's American-run, so communication is simple. This is an
especially good place to make fast-train and *couchette* reservations
(generally open Mon-Fri 11:10-18:50, until 20:00 May-Aug, check
website for specific hours, closed Jan-Feb and Sat-Sun year-round;
www.euraide.com).

Shopping: The Hauptbahnhof is home to 80 shops with long
hours—some locals call the station a "shopping mall with trains"
(many stores open Sun). The REWE City supermarket (UG1, follow signs for tracks 1-2) is handy for assembling a picnic for your
train ride.

Getting into Town: Taxis and buses wait outside the station
on the Washingtonplatz side, but the S-Bahn is probably your best
bet for connecting to most hotels. It's simple: S-Bahn trains are on
tracks 15 and 16 at the top of the station (level OG2). Trains on
track 15 go east, stopping at Friedrichstrasse, Hackescher Markt,
Alexanderplatz, and Ostbahnhof; trains on track 16 go west, toward Zoologischer Garten and Savignyplatz (best for City West
hotels). Your train ticket to Berlin covers any connecting S-Bahn
ride (but for the U-Bahn, trams, or buses, you'll need an additional
ticket).

To reach most hotels in northern Berlin's **Prenzlauer Berg** neighborhood, it's fastest to take any train on track 15 two stops to Hackescher Markt. Once there, follow signs to *Hackescher Markt* down the stairs, then exit to Spandauer Strasse and cross the tracks to the tram stop. Here you'll catch tram #M1 north (direction: Schillerstrasse), which trundles north through Rosenthaler Platz and up Kastanienallee to Eberswalder Strasse. (For Rosenthaler Platz hotels, it's even more direct to hop on tram #M8, which leaves from in front of the Hauptbahnhof's Europaplatz entrance.)

For **old Jewish quarter** hotels, you'll also take the S-Bahn from track 15. Some of these hotels are closer to the Friedrichstrasse station (first stop), while others are closer to Hackescher Markt (second stop).

To reach **City West** hotels, catch any train on track 16 to Savignyplatz, where you're within a five-minute walk of most recommended hotels.

The **U5 U-Bahn line** connects the Hauptbahnhof, Reichstag, and strategic stops along the city's main sightseeing spine: Brandenburger Tor, Unter den Linden (near Bebelplatz), Museumsinsel (Museum Island, due to open sometime in 2021), Rotes Rathaus (City Hall, near the Nikolai Quarter), and Alexanderplatz.

Airport Express trains (FEX) will connect the Hauptbahnhof with the new Brandenburg airport (Flughafen BER; 4/hour, 30 minutes), and are covered by an ABC transit ticket (€3.60, buy at machine and validate before boarding).

Destinations

For help buying tickets, stop by the EurAide office in the Hauptbahnhof (described earlier). Before buying a ticket for any long train ride from Berlin (over 7 hours), consider taking a cheap flight instead (buy well in advance for the best fare). Train info: www.bahn.com.

From Berlin by Train to: Potsdam (2/hour, 30 minutes on RE1 train; or take S-Bahn from other points in Berlin, S7 direct, S1 with a change at Wannsee, 6/hour, 30-50 minutes—see page 326 for details), **Oranienburg** and Sachsenhausen Memorial and Museum (hourly, 25 minutes on the RE5; or take the S1 line from Friedrichstrasse or other stops in town, 2/hour, 50 minutes), **Wittenberg** (a.k.a. *Lutherstadt Wittenberg*, hourly on ICE, 40 minutes), **Dresden** (hourly direct, 2 hours; more with a transfer in Leipzig, 3 hours), **Leipzig** (hourly, 1.5 hours), **Erfurt** (1-2/hour, 2 hours), **Eisenach** and Wartburg Castle (every 2 hours direct, 2.5 hours; more with transfer in Erfurt), **Hamburg** (1-2/hour, 2 hours), **Frankfurt** (at least hourly, 4 hours), **Bacharach** (every 2 hours with transfer in Frankfurt, 5.5 hours; more with 2-3 changes), **Würzburg** (hourly, 4 hours, transfer points vary),

CONNECTIONS

Rothenburg (hourly, 5.5 hours, 3 changes), **Nürnberg** (1-2/hour, 3.5 hours), **Munich** (1-2/hour, 4.5 hours, longer night train possible), **Cologne** (hourly, 4.5 hours), **Amsterdam** (every 2 hours direct, 6.5 hours; more with change in Hannover; wise to reserve in advance), **Brussels** (8/day, 7 hours with transfer in Cologne, some require reservations), **Budapest** (1/day direct, more with transfer in Prague, 11 hours, via Czech Republic and Slovakia; if your rail pass doesn't cover these countries, consider a longer route via Nürnberg), **Copenhagen** (2/day, 8 hours, reservation required in summer, change in Hamburg; 1 direct bus 4/week at 11:30, daily in summer, accepts rail pass), **London** (4-6/day, 10 hours, 2 changes, reservations required), **Paris** (9/day, 8 hours with 1 transfer, reservations required in France), **Zürich** (hourly, 8-9 hours, transfer in Hannover or Basel or 1 direct 12-hour night train), **Prague** (6/day direct, 4 hours, wise to reserve in advance), **Warsaw** (4-6/day, 6.5 hours, reservations required), **Kraków** (transfer in Warsaw, 9 hours; 1 bus/day direct, accepts rail pass, 8 hours), **Vienna** (7/day, 8 hours via Nürnberg or 9 hours via Prague, night train possible; others with 2 changes; trains with a change in Nürnberg or Munich avoid Czech Republic—useful if it's not covered by your rail pass).

Night trains run from Berlin to Munich, Basel, Zürich, and Vienna. A *Liegeplatz,* a.k.a. *couchette* berth (€15-36), is a great deal; inquire at EurAide at the Hauptbahnhof for details. Beds generally cost the same whether you have a first- or second-class ticket or rail pass. Trains are often full, so reserve your *couchette* a few days in advance from any travel agency or major train station in Europe.

By Bus

The city's bus station, **ZOB** (Zentraler Omnibusbahnhof), is west of Zoologischer Garten (Berlin Zoo), in Charlottenburg (Masurenallee 4, U2: Kaiserdamm or S41/S42: Messe Nord, www.zob. berlin). **FlixBus, MeinFern,** and **Eurolines** all operate from here to locations around Germany and Europe.

By Cruise Ship at the Port of Warnemünde

Many cruise lines advertise a stop in "Berlin," but ships actually put in at the Baltic seaside town of Warnemünde—a whopping 150 miles north of downtown Berlin. By train, by tour bus, or by Porsche on the autobahn, plan on at least six hours of travel time round-trip between Warnemünde and Berlin. The easiest option is to book a package excursion from your cruise line. You can also book a tour with a local Berlin-based operator such as Original Berlin Walks; see contact information on page 35). Otherwise, several train connections run each day from Warnemünde's train station to Berlin (roughly every 2 hours, 3 hours, transfer in Rostock).

For more details on visiting Berlin while on a cruise, pick up the *Rick Steves Scandinavian & Northern European Cruise Ports* guidebook.

DAY TRIPS

*Potsdam • Sachsenhausen
Memorial and Museum •
Wittenberg*

While you could spend days in Berlin and not run out of things to do, a few worthwhile side trips are within an hour of downtown. Frederick the Great's opulent playground at Potsdam is a hit for its mix of Prussian history and ornate palaces surrounded by pretty parks; the town also has a fun-to-explore center and some interesting Cold War sights. On the opposite side of Berlin—and the sightseeing spectrum—the Sachsenhausen Memorial and Museum commemorates the tens of thousands of prisoners who died at this concentration camp during the Holocaust. And for a small-town experience that packs a huge historical wallop—head 45 minutes to Wittenberg, where, 500 years ago, Martin Luther famously nailed his 95 Theses to the church door, kicking off the Protestant Reformation.

Potsdam

Squeezed between the Wannsee and a lush park strewn with the escapist whimsies of Frederick the Great, the once-important, now-sleepy town of Potsdam has long been Berlin's holiday retreat. Potsdam's palaces are your best opportunity to get a taste of Prussia's Hohenzollern royalty.

Beyond these royal retreats, Potsdam is simply enjoyable—a swanky bedroom community, where, thanks to its aristocratic heritage, everything seems bigger and better than it needs to be. Cold War buffs might focus on Cecilienhof (site of the famous post-WWII Potsdam Conference) and nearby KGB Prison Memorial. And anyone can enjoy Potsdam's well-manicured town center as a kind of sightseeing eye-candy. Don't come here just for the

palaces—come here to escape the bustle of Berlin, and to spend a sunny day exploring a stately burg and its picnic-friendly park.

GETTING TO POTSDAM

Potsdam is 15 miles southwest of Berlin, easy to reach by train. You have two train options for zipping from the city to Potsdam's Hauptbahnhof, both covered by a Berlin transit day pass (€9.60, with zones ABC; if you have a pass for just zones AB, buy a €1.70 *Anschlussfahrausweis*—extension ticket—to get here, valid 2 hours).

Regional Express/RE1 trains go direct to Potsdam and depart twice hourly from three different Berlin stations: Zoologischer Garten (20 minutes to Potsdam), Hauptbahnhof (30 minutes), and Friedrichstrasse (35 minutes; any train to Brandenburg or Magdeburg stops in Potsdam). Note: Some RE1 trains continue past the Potsdam Hauptbahnhof to a stop called Park Sanssouci, which is closer to the New Palace.

The **S-Bahn** is slightly slower (30-50 minutes depending on starting point), but more frequent (6/hour) and handier from some areas of Berlin. The S7 line goes directly to Potsdam from downtown Berlin. Another option is to ride the S1 to the end of the line at Wannsee, cross the platform, and ride the S7 train three more stops to Potsdam.

Avid cyclists can rent a bike in Berlin, take it on the train (€1.90 extra), and combine a visit to Potsdam with an enjoyable ride along skinny lakes and through green parklands back into the city.

PLANNING YOUR TIME

There are three dimensions to a visit to Potsdam: the garrison town itself (centered near the main train station); Sanssouci Park with

its many palaces and imperial delights; and a handful of Cold War sights a mile north of town. To see it all is a very long day with long walks, lots of biking, or plenty of bus rides.

The town's delightful main square, Alter Markt, is a couple blocks from the main train station. The Potsdam Museum (on the square) is worth an hour for history buffs who want context for the rest of the sights.

Potsdam's main draw is its vast park dotted with frilly palaces. The two main palaces are the New Palace (no lines, smart to buy a combo-ticket with a Sanssouci timed-entry here) and the more famous and popular Sanssouci (long lines, required timed entry). Each comes with an audioguide and takes about an hour to tour. The two palaces are connected by the park—it's a pleasant 30-minute walk or a 10-minute bus ride between them.

While Sanssouci is an exquisite little palace with eight unforgettably lavish rooms, the New Palace is much bigger, more historic, and its state rooms are pleasantly plush. If one palace is plenty, you could happily tour the interior of the New Palace and enjoy the views and gardens around Sanssouci without bothering to go into the other palace. Keep in mind that Sanssouci is closed on Monday and the New Palace is closed on Tuesday.

Potsdam also has three fascinating 20th-century sights for Cold War enthusiasts: Cecilienhof, the KGB Prison Memorial, and the Bridge of Spies. On your way back to Berlin, you could hop off the train at the Wannsee station for a boat ride on the lake or dinner in a wonderful beer garden.

Orientation to Potsdam

Potsdam (pop. 170,000) borders Berlin, on the lake called Wannsee. (During the Cold War, Potsdam was barely in East Germany, just outside West Berlin—the Wall ran right along the lakeshore.)

DAY TRIPS

DAY TRIPS

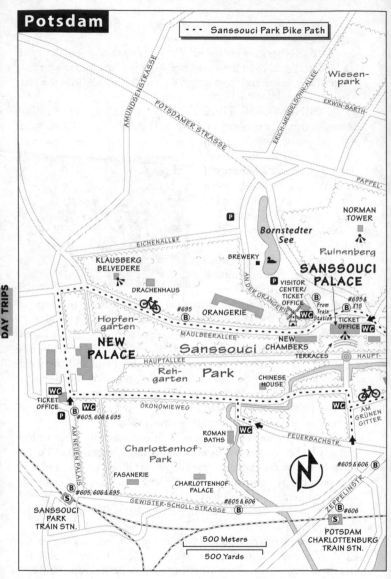

Potsdam

- - - Sanssouci Park Bike Path

Wiesen-park

ERWIN-BARTH-

PAPPEL-

AMUNDSENSTRASSE

POTSDAMER STRASSE

ERICH-MENDELSOHN-ALLEE

NORMAN TOWER

Ruinenberg

P

Bornstedter See

EICHENALLEE

KLAUSBERG BELVEDERE

BREWERY

AN DER ORANGERIE

P VISITOR CENTER/ TICKET OFFICE

SANSSOUCI PALACE

DRACHENHAUS

#695

Hopfen-garten

ORANGERIE

B

WC

B From Train Station

#695 & X15

B

TICKET OFFICE

WC

NEW PALACE

MAULBEERALLEE

Sanssouci

NEW CHAMBERS

HAUPTALLEE

TERRACES

HAUPT-

Reh-garten

Park

CHINESE HOUSE

WC

AM GRÜNEN GITTER

WC TICKET OFFICE

P

B #605, 606 & 695

WC

ÖKONOMIEWEG

FEUERBACHSTR.

ROMAN BATHS

WC

AM NEUEN PALAIS

Charlottenhof Park

FASANERIE

CHARLOTTENHOF PALACE

#605 & 606 **B**

#605 & 606 **B**

B #605, 606 & 695

S

GEWISTER-SCHOLL-STRASSE

ZEPPELINSTR.

B #606

SANSSOUCI PARK TRAIN STN.

S

POTSDAM CHARLOTTENBURG TRAIN STN.

500 Meters

500 Yards

Sights cluster in three areas, each a long walk or a short bus ride apart: the city center, just across the bridge from the train station; Sanssouci Park, a vast royal park at the western edge of town, peppered with grand Hohenzollern palaces (Sanssouci and New Palace are best); and, to the north, the park called Neuer Garten, where Cecilienhof Palace looks out over Wannsee and a former KGB prison lurks nearby.

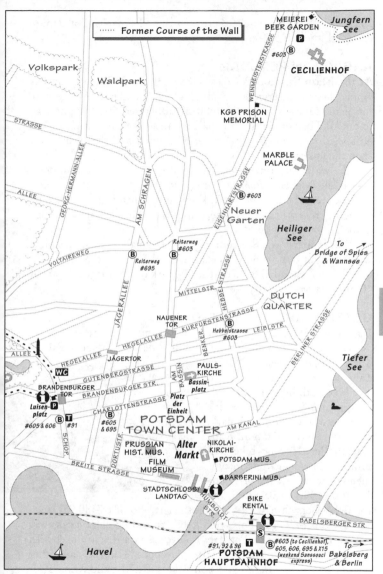

MEIEREI
BEER GARDEN

Jungfern See

#603

CECILIENHOF

Volkspark

Waldpark

STRASSE

GEORG-HERMANN-ALLEE

ALLEE

VOLTAIREWEG

AM SCHRAGEN

JÄGERALLEE

WEINMEISTERSTRASSE

KGB PRISON
MEMORIAL

MARBLE
PALACE

EISENHARTSTRASSE

Neuer
Garten

Heiliger See

To
Bridge of Spies
& Wannsee

Reiterweg
#603

Reiterweg
#695

MITTELSTR

HEBBELSTRASSE

DUTCH
QUARTER

BERLINER STRASSE

Tiefer See

NAUENER
TOR

HEGELALLEE

KURFÜRSTENSTRASSE

BENKERT

LEIBLSTR.

Hebbelstrasse
#603

HEGELALLEE

ALLEE

JÄGERTOR

WC

GUTENBERGSTRASSE

BRANDENBURGER
TOR

BRANDENBURGER STR.

AM BASSIN

PAULS-
KIRCHE

Bassin-
platz

*Luisen-
platz*

#605 & 606

#91

CHARLOTTENSTRASSE

*Platz
der
Einheit*

POTSDAM
TOWN CENTER

AM KANAL

SCHOP

#605
& 695

DORTUSTR.

PRUSSIAN
HIST. MUS.

*Alter
Markt*

NIKOLAI-
KIRCHE

POTSDAM MUS.

BREITE STRASSE

FILM
MUSEUM

BARBERINI MUS.

STADTSCHLOSS/
LANDTAG

HUMBOLDT STR.

BIKE
RENTAL

BABELSBERGER STR.

Havel

#91, 92 & 96

**POTSDAM
HAUPTBAHNHOF**

#603 (to Cecilienhof),
605, 606, 695 & X15
(weekend Sanssouci
express)

To
Babelsberg
& Berlin

····· Former Course of the Wall

DAY TRIPS

TOURIST INFORMATION

Potsdam has three handy TIs: inside Potsdam's **main train station** (near track 7, Mon-Sat 9:30-18:30, Sun until 15:00, +49 331
2755 8899, www.potsdamtourismus.de); on the old main square,
Alter Markt, across the bridge from the station (Mon-Sat 9:30-
19:00, Sun 10:00-16:00, Humboldtstrasse 1); and at **Luisenplatz,**
on the eastern end of Sanssouci Park (Mon-Sat 9:30-18:00, Sun

10:00-16:00). While you're there, buy the TI's map of Potsdam—it's worth the minor fee.

ARRIVAL IN POTSDAM

At the Main Station (Potsdam Hauptbahnhof): This station has ample shops and services including a large Kaufland grocery store for picnic supplies (Mon-Sat 6:00-22:00, closed Sun). On arrival, to take the **bus or tram** to the palaces, head out the exit past track 4, labeled *Friedrich-Engels-Strasse;* here you'll find the tram stops, then the bus stops.

To **walk** into town—or rent a **bike**—use the opposite door, past track 7, labeled *Babelsberger Strasse.* Exiting, turn left to find the bike-rental office. To walk, keep going, turn right at the traffic light, cross a bridge, and head for Alter Markt (with the huge dome).

Sanssouci Park Station: From this smaller station, simply walk straight out (or hop a local bus) and head up the boulevard called Am Neuen Palais, with the big park on your right. In about 10 minutes, you'll reach the New Palace.

GETTING AROUND POTSDAM

By Bike: Flat Potsdam is ideal by bike, and from the station it's a pleasant and well-signed 20-minute ride to Sanssouci Palace.

There's one caveat: Within Sanssouci Park you're restricted to a bike path between the palaces; you can't even walk with a bike anywhere else in the park. At the main train station, **Radstation/Pedales** rents bikes and provides a map showing recommended routes (Mon-Fri 7:00-19:00, Sat-Sun 9:30-18:00, out the Babelsberg Strasse exit and on the left, +49 331 7480 057).

By Bus or Tram: Potsdam's public transit efficiently connects most points of interest. Potsdam is covered by a Berlin ticket with zones ABC, but not by one with just zones AB. You can either buy *Anschlussfahrausweis*/extension tickets (€1.70, valid 2 hours), or individual tickets covering Potsdam transit: €2.10/ride, €4.20 all day (buy tickets from machine on board). These are the buses you're most likely to take and the lane from which they depart at the main train station:

Bus **#695**—most handy for tourists—goes through the town center to Sanssouci Palace and then to the New Palace (3/hour, from lane 4).

Bus **#X15** runs only on summer weekends and makes a beeline to Sanssouci Palace (3/hour, from lane 4).

Buses **#606** and **#605** go directly to the New Palace (3/hour, lane 4).

Bus **#603** runs on summer weekends from the main train station up to Cecilienhof Palace, then loops back down past the KGB Prison Memorial (Persiusstrasse stop) and the Dutch Quarter (Hebbelstrasse) before returning to the station (3/hour, lane 6). If you visit during the week or off-season, catch bus #603 at Platz der Einheit, a 15-minute walk past the Alter Markt (reachable by multiple bus or tram lines from the station).

Tram **#91** is good for a scenic walk through the terraced palace gardens: Get off at Luisenplatz, then walk 20 minutes through the park, which lets you enjoy a classic view of Sanssouci Palace (3/hour from lane 1, direction: Bahnhof Pirscheide).

By Foot: It's a long (but scenic) 45-minute walk from the station to Sanssouci Palace (get a map at the TI). Tram #91, described above, shaves off the least interesting part of this hike.

By Taxi or Uber: A taxi can help link up otherwise difficult-to-connect sights (for example, €15 between the New Palace and Cecilienhof—avoiding a time-consuming bus connection).

Tours in Potsdam

Local Tours
Various bus tours (including hop-on, hop-off options) conveniently connect this town's spread-out sights. Most start at the main train station. Pick up brochures at the TI or check their website (www.potsdamtourismus.de).

Tours from Berlin
Original Berlin Walks and Insider Tour offer inexpensive all-day tours from Berlin to Potsdam. They rely on public transit, focus on the park and the palace exteriors, and don't actually go inside the palaces as a group (€17, admissions and public transportation not included; for contact info see "Tours in Berlin" in the Orientation chapter).

Sights in Potsdam

Potsdam's sights cluster in three areas: the city center; Sanssouci Park; and the Cold War sights near Neuer Garten.

POTSDAM'S TOWN CENTER
The easy-to-stroll town center has pedestrianized shopping streets lined with boutiques and eateries. For a small town, this was once

a cosmopolitan place: Frederick the Great imported some very talented people.

▲Alter Markt

Potsdam's "Old Market Square" is marked by the massive dome of the Nikolaikirche—visible from all over town. This square, always pleasant, has been further rejuvenated by the opening of the Museum Barberini. It's worth a quick stroll through here to ogle the striking Hohenzollern architecture.

Stand in the middle of the square, facing the giant church. The obelisk dates from 1753 and is decorated with medallions celebrating Prussian kings. Remember, Potsdam was essentially a garrison town for the Hohenzollern dynasty. Do a clockwise spin-tour starting at the church to get oriented.

The **Nikolaikirche,** designed by architect Karl Friedrich Schinkel, is an icon of Potsdam. Step inside to see its austere, very Protestant, Neoclassical interior—a well-ordered world of perfectly formed domes and Corinthian columns. The flier explains how this was built following Schinkel's plans in 1850, destroyed in 1945, and rebuilt in 1981 (€2 donation, daily 10:00-21:00).

To the right sits the **Altes Rathaus** (Old Town Hall), with its frilly cupola topped by a "Goldfinger" Atlas supporting the world.

Next is the **Potsdam Museum** (rated ▲▲). This surprisingly interesting museum fills two floors with lots of well-described artifacts that give context to the town, its palaces, and its history. It shows life as a Hollenzollern, and everyday life under the dynasty. It also covers the tragic drama of Potsdam's bombing in 1945, postwar reconstruction, the Soviet era, and the spy-exchange drama on Glienicke Bridge (€5, Tue-Fri 10:00-17:00, Sat-Sun until 16:00, closed Mon, audioguide-€2, +49 331 289 6868, www.potsdam-museum.de).

The **Museum Barberini,** a state-of-the-art museum filling a beautifully restored old building, shows off temporary exhibits of world-class artists to the delight of Berlin art snobs. Check what's on (€14, Wed-Mon 10:00-19:00, closed Tue, audioguide-€2, www.museum-barberini.com).

Humboldtstrasse, further to the right, leads to the TI (and is the quickest route to the train station).

Next is the stately, salmon-colored **Stadtschloss** (Brandenburg State Capitol). Germany is made up of 16 states *(Länder).* The city of Berlin is itself a state. And you're standing just outside the "state" of Berlin in the state of Brandenburg. Potsdam is the capital of Brandenburg, the *Land* that completely surrounds Berlin. Step inside the sterile courtyard, rebuilt after 1945, to see Brandenburg's state capitol and three flags: the EU, Germany, and Brandenburg.

Finally, spinning back toward the church, you see a construction site (or new building) where an ugly, concrete, functionalist building from the DDR once stood. It's now being replaced by a modern building designed to fit the historic tone of the city center. Bit by bit, the ugly communist-era architecture is being replaced.

Other Town Center Sights

Potsdam seems to have a museum for every interest, including a good film museum and a museum of Prussian history (both near Breite Strasse). I'd skip Potsdam's much-promoted Wannsee boat rides, which are pretty dull. (If you're in a mood to relax on a lake, consider stopping off at Wannsee for some beach time on your way home to Berlin—see "Near Potsdam," later).

For a quick visit to the Low Countries, walk about 10 minutes north of the Alter Markt until you see pretty brick gables of the

Dutch Quarter (Holländisches Viertel). Frederick the Great imported Dutch engineers and workers to build his city's canals and drain the swamps here in the 18th century. They also built a little bit of home. Radiating out from the intersection of Mittel-  strasse and Benkertstrasse (just behind Bassinplatz) you'll find a cute zone with gables, red bricks, and shutters—just like a town in the Netherlands...minus the Dutch people. It's very touristy today, with lots of boutiques, restaurants, and cafés (some selling Dutch pancakes and *poffertjes*).

FREDERICK THE GREAT'S PALACES AT SANSSOUCI PARK

The dynamic Frederick the Great put Prussia on the map in the 18th century with his merciless military prowess. Yet he also had tender affection for the finer things in life: art, architecture, gardens, literature, and other distinguished pursuits. During his reign, Frederick built an impressive ensemble of palaces and other grand buildings around Sanssouci Park, with the two  top palaces located at either end. Frederick's small, super-Rococo Sanssouci Palace is dazzling, and his massive New Palace was built to wow guests and disprove rumors that Prussia was running out of money after the costly Seven Years' War.

Background: For a little historic context, read the "Prussian King Frederick the Great" sidebar (page 114) before your visit.

Getting Between the Palaces: It's about a 30-minute walk between Sanssouci and the New Palace, and about 10 minutes by bike. Otherwise hop on bus #695, which takes you between the palaces in either direction (€1.50 *Kurzstrecke* ticket). If you do walk, you'll find the park wilder, more forested, and less carefully manicured than those in other big-league European palace complexes (such as Versailles or Vienna's Schönbrunn). The park's €2 suggested donation gets you a helpful map.

Combo-Ticket: A €19 combo-ticket covers nearly all the royal buildings in the park. It's worthwhile only if you're visiting both Sanssouci and the New Palace (for most visitors, those two are more than enough). The combo-ticket is sold online and at the ticket offices at Sanssouci Palace and the New Palace. The combo-ticket comes with an appointed entry time for Sanssouci Palace (which you select according to what's available).

Audio Tours: All tickets include an audioguide.

Information: +49 331 969 4200, www.spsg.de.

▲▲Sanssouci Palace

Sans souci means "without a care," and this was the carefree summer home of Frederick the Great (built 1745-1747). Of all the palatial buildings scattered around Potsdam, this was his actual residence. While the palace is small and the audioguide does little to capture the personality of its former resident, the palace is worth seeing for its opulence.

Cost and Hours: €14, covered by combo-ticket, Tue-Sun 10:00-17:30, Nov-March until 16:30, closed Mon year-round.

Crowd-Beating Tips: If you arrive right at 10:00, you can generally go right in. Arrive later and you'll be given an entry time a couple hours later in the day. If you buy a combo-ticket (described earlier), you'll also book a timed entry for Sanssouci. You can do this online in advance or the same day. A good plan is to go first to the New Palace, buy the combo-ticket with an entry time for Sanssouci later that day, tour the New Palace, and explore the garden until your Sanssouci appointment. If you need to kill time, the palace kitchen and the nearby windmill are both interesting.

Visiting the Palace: This cute little palace was where Frederick the Great spent his summers. You'll stroll through the classic Rococo interior, where golden grapevines climb the walls and frame the windows. First explore the Royal Apartments, containing one of Frederick's three libraries (he found it easier to buy extra copies of books rather than move them around), the "study bedroom" where he lived and worked, and the chair where he died. The domed, central Marble Hall resembles the Pantheon in Rome (on a smaller scale), with an oblong oculus, inlaid marble floors, and Corinthian columns made of Carrara marble.

Finally, you'll visit the guest rooms, most of which empty straight out onto the delightful terrace. Each room is decorated differently: Chinese, Italian, and so on; the niche at the back was for a bed. The happiest is the yellow Voltaire Room, where realistic animals and flowers dangle from the walls and ceiling. As you exit (through the servants' quarters), keep an eye out for the giant portrait of Frederick by Andy Warhol.

Nearby: The **palace kitchen** (Schlossküche) gives a peek at a well-preserved and fully-equipped mid-19th-century royal kitchen. Hike down the tight spiral staircase to the wine cellar, with an exhibit about the grapes that were grown on the terraced vineyards out front (€4, covered by combo-ticket, Tue-Sun 10:00-17:30, closed Mon and Nov-March). The **historic windmill** was busy from 1787 grinding grain for the royals. Today it's filled with a very vertical six-floor exhibit (in German only). When the wind turns the sails, you can see the miller at work and feel the entire mill tremble (€4, covered by combo-ticket, daily 10:00-18:00, shorter hours off-season).

▲▲New Palace (Neues Palais)

This gigantic showpiece palace (with more than 200 rooms) is grander than the intimate Sanssouci. Frederick the Great built the New Palace (1763-1769), but he rarely stayed here—it was mostly used to host guests and dazzle visiting dignitaries. But other Prussian kings—and later German emperors—called it home. The highlights are the lavishly decorated Grotto Hall

and Marble Hall, and several other fine apartments, each a stunning example of the exuberant Rococo style. Together, they're an artistic ensemble with the same theme. And unlike at Sanssouci, there's no concern about a long line.

Cost and Hours: €6, covered by combo-ticket, Wed-Mon

DAY TRIPS

10:00-17:30, Nov-March until 16:30, closed Tue year-round, last entry one hour before closing.

Getting In: Buy your ticket (which comes with an entry time—generally within 10 or 20 minutes) at the visitors center near the bus stop. I'd skip the eight-minute introductory film—but not the WC here, as there's none in the palace. Then head to the palace at the appointed time to pick up your audioguide.

Visiting the Palace: The audioguide takes you through the palace's ornate halls and state rooms. On the main floor, the highlight is the Grotto Hall, whose marble walls are encrusted with a quarter of a million seashells, semiprecious stones, and fossils. From there, continue on through the eight suites of the Lower Princes' Apartments, which accommodated guests and royal family members. In the 19th and early 20th centuries, German emperors Frederick III and Wilhelm II (the last kaiser) resided here. The Gentlemen's Bedchamber holds the red-canopy bed where Kaiser Frederick III died in 1888. The Ladies' Bedchamber is a reminder that noblemen and their wives slept separately.

Upstairs, the Upper Princes' Quarters include a small blue-tiled bathroom that was installed for Kaiser Wilhelm II (he lived here until 1918), and a bedchamber shared by a married couple—my, how times have changed. You'll also find Wilhelm's bedroom, as well as a small painting gallery with portraits of Frederick the Great and Russia's Catherine the Great (who was born a German princess). The grand finale is the sumptuous, 52-foot-high Marble Hall, with its dramatic ceiling painting and floors inlaid with Silesian marble. Through the windows, enjoy views of the gardens.

Other Palaces

The two main palaces (Sanssouci and the New Palace) are just the beginning. Sprawling Sanssouci Park contains a variety of other palaces and royal buildings, many of which you can enter: the sprawling Italian-style **Orangery**; the **New Chambers** (a royal guesthouse); the **Chinese Tea House**; and other viewpoints, such as the **Klausberg Belvedere** and the **Norman Tower.**

Cost and Hours: Each has its own entry fee (€2-6; all but the Belvedere covered by the €19 combo-ticket). Some are open weekends and/or April-October only (get complete details at Potsdam TI, palace ticket office, or www.spsg.de).

COLD WAR SIGHTS

At the north end of town, another (much more modest) park, called Neuer Garten, is delightfully set on the idyllic Wannsee. This is where you'll find several stirring sights for those interested in Cold War history, and a fine lakeside brewery.

Getting There: While getting to these sights by public transit is possible, you'll do better with a bike or taxi. The Neuer Garten area is connected to the center by bus #603 (see "Getting Around Potsdam," earlier). Tram #93 takes you from the main train station to the Bridge of Spies. It's about a 20-minute walk between the Neuer Garten sights and the bridge.

▲Cecilienhof

This early-20th-century villa was the site of the historic Potsdam Conference for two weeks in the summer of 1945. For Cold War buffs, it's worth ▲▲. Touring the rooms with an audioguide, you'll hear how, during those meetings, Harry Truman, Winston Churchill, and Joseph Stalin negotiated how best to punish Germany for dragging Europe through another devastating war. It was here that the postwar map of Europe was officially drawn, setting the stage for a protracted Cold War that would drag on for more than four decades. There's no wait, and a stop here pairs well with a drink or meal at the fine Meierei brewery and a visit to the KGB Prison Memorial—each less than a 10-minute walk away.

Cost and Hours: €10, includes audioguide, Tue-Sun 10:00-17:30, Nov-March until 16:30, closed Mon year-round, +49 331 969 4200, www.spsg.de. Note: A separate ticket is required to visit the upper floor of elegant state rooms (open only with an hourly German-language tour).

Visiting the Palace: This Tudor-style villa—designed to appear smaller and more modest than it actually is—was built in 1912 to house Crown Prince Wilhelm and his wife Cecilie, who would have ruled Germany, had Kaiser Wilhelm II not lost World War I. It's certainly less striking than Potsdam's other palaces. The draw here is the 1945 history. You'll tour the palace using an excellent, 45-minute audioguide, which does a marvelous job of re-animating history. You'll hear all about those tense days in July 1945, including sound bites from meeting participants. You'll see the private offices of Stalin, Churchill, and Truman, as well as the grand meeting hall with the round table where they faced off to negotiate. It's both chilling and fitting to think that, just 20 years later, the Berlin Wall would run through the park right in front of the palace—cutting off idyllic views of the Wannsee. This was also where Truman told Stalin about the atomic bomb and issued the "Potsdam Declaration"—demanding that Japan unconditionally surrender to end the war once and for all. Japan refused—and the US dropped atomic bombs on Hiroshima and Nagasaki.

Eating: The **$ Meierei Biergarten,** named for a 19th-century creamery, now functions as a brewery, producing beer rather than milk. Delightfully set on the lake under an evocative industrial age chimney, it has two zones: a cheery, self-service beer garden (basic beerhall food and drink, open only in summer and good weather) and a more serious, pricier restaurant (with seating under vaults where cows were once milked and outside overlooking the lake). The setting here is tranquil and romantic. It's a short, thought-provoking walk from Cecilienhof as you pass through what was once the death strip of the Berlin Wall (Wed-Sun 12:00-22:00, closed Mon-Tue, a 10-minute stroll north of Cecilienhof—follow *Meierei* signs to Im Neuen Garten 10, +49 331 704 3211).

▲KGB Prison Memorial at Leistikowstrasse (Gedenkstätte Leistikowstrasse Potsdam)

Standing in stark contrast to all of Potsdam's pretty palaces and Hohenzollern bombast, this crumbling concrete prison has been turned into a memorial and documentation center to the Cold War victims of USSR "counterintelligence."

Cost and Hours: Free, Tue-Sun 14:00-18:00, Nov-March 13:00-17:00, closed Mon year-round, Leistikowstrasse 1, +49 331 201 1540, www.leistikowstrasse-sbg.de.

Visiting the Memorial: On the nondescript Leistikowstrasse, a few steps from the lakeside park, the KGB established a base in August 1945 (mere days after the Potsdam Conference), which remained active until the fall of the USSR in 1991. The centerpiece of their "secret city" was this transit prison in which enemies of the Soviet regime were held and punished in horrible conditions before entering the USSR "justice" system—to  be tried, executed, or shipped off to notorious gulag labor camps. While most prisoners were Russian citizens, until 1955 the prison also held Germans who were essentially kidnapped by the USSR in retribution for their wartime activities.

From the blocky modern reception building at the corner, you'll enter the complex. In the yard find a model illustrating how this was just the inner core of a walled secret city that (until 1991) was technically Soviet territory run by the KGB. Then head inside the prison, where the hallways and cells are an eerie world of peeling paint, faded linoleum, and rusted hinges. The two floors host a well-presented exhibit explaining the history of the building (which was a vicarage before being seized by the Soviets) and profiling several individuals who were held here.

Bridge of Spies

Until the building of the Berlin Wall, the Glienicke Bridge was a nondescript bridge across the Havel River, connecting the state of Berlin with the state of Brandenburg. But during the Cold War, the river became the border between the US and Soviet sectors. Because this was a handy place to swap prisoners and spies, it became known as the "Bridge of Spies."

The bridge had long been part of a key transportation route between the royal residence in Potsdam and Berlin. A fine brick-and-wood bridge was built here in 1834, then replaced with a modern iron one in 1904. After serious bomb damage, it was rebuilt in 1949. After construction of the Berlin Wall in 1961, the bridge was closed to the public, and guarded as a border crossing.

Spies and dissidents—most famously Gary Powers (who piloted the U-2 spy plane shot down over the USSR in 1960) and Soviet activist Natan Sharansky—were traded on this bridge. The 1962 exchange of KGB agent Rudolf Abel for Powers inspired the Steven Spielberg film *Bridge of Spies,* starring Tom Hanks (2015). The Villa Schöningen at the west end of the bridge has an exhibit covering the historic border crossing (€9, Fri-Sun 12:00-18:00, closed Mon-Thu, Berliner Strasse 86, +49 331 200 1739, www.villa-schoeningen.de).

NEAR POTSDAM
Babelsberg

Movie buffs might already know that the nearby suburb of Babelsberg (just east of Potsdam) hosts the biggest film studio in Germany, where classics such as *The Blue Angel* and *Metropolis,* as well as more recent films *The Reader* and *Inglourious Basterds,* were filmed (for visitor info, see www.filmpark-babelsberg.de).

Wannsee

To see Berliners at play on a hot summer day, consider hopping off the train at Wannsee. (The name may be familiar as the site of the 1942 Wannsee Conference, when Nazis came up with their "Final Solution" to the "Jewish Question.")

Today this big lake is a popular near-the-city getaway for urbanites who appreciate strolling, sunbathing, splashing, and *See-*faring on lazy cruises. The action at Wannsee is down on the lake, where you'll find a park and promenade, lazy lake cruises (two-hour, seven-lake trip is best, hourly departures). For a quicker and cheaper cruise option, for the cost of a transit ticket, the BVG ferry to Kladow departs on the hour.

A popular activity for locals is to rent a rustic floating "lounge" with a small motor for a day of swimming, sunning, drinking, and lazing on the waters. You don't need a license, and some boats come with a BBQ and WC—and even a minikeg to keep your beer fresh and flowing.

Above the train tracks is **$$ Loretta am Wannsee Biergarten.** This idyllic beer garden fills a forested bluff with Bavarian *gemütlichkeit*—look for lots of rustic tables, a self-serve food-and-drink counter, and a kids' area. It's popular as the sun sets on the lake. Berliners young and old travel here to spend a convivial evening eating beer-garden classics and drinking good local beer.

As you go by Wannsee on the train, you'll pass pea-patch gardens dotted with simple country homes. These little pleasure shantytowns, while extremely basic, come with warm memories for many Berliners. Further out, in the DDR, these were called *Datsche*—a Russian tradition (allowing even humble workers to escape periodically to the countryside) that caught on here in Cold War times.

Sachsenhausen Memorial and Museum

About 20 miles north of downtown Berlin, the small town of Oranienburg was the site of one of the most notorious Nazi concentration camps. Sachsenhausen's proximity to the capital gave it special status as the place to train camp guards and test new procedures.

It was also the site of the Third Reich's massive counterfeiting operation to destabilize Great Britain by flooding the monetary system with forged pound notes. Today the Sachsenhausen Memorial and Museum *(Gedenkstätte und Museum Sachsenhausen)*, worth ▲▲, honors the camp's victims and

survivors, and teaches visitors about the atrocities that took place here.

GETTING TO SACHSENHAUSEN

Take a train to the town of Oranienburg (20-50 minutes, covered by zone ABC ticket; if you have a pass for just zones AB, buy a €1.70 *Anschlussfahrausweis* (extension ticket) to get here—valid for 2 hours; from there, it's a quick trip by bus or taxi to the camp, or a 20-minute walk. The whole journey takes just over an hour each way.

From Berlin Hauptbahnhof, the **Regional Express/RE5** train speeds to Oranienburg (hourly, 25 minutes). Or you can take the S-Bahn (S1) line from various stops in downtown Berlin, including Potsdamer Platz, Brandenburger Tor, Friedrichstrasse, and Oranienburger Strasse (2/hour, 50 minutes).

At Oranienburg, the **bus** to the memorial departs from lane 4, right in front of the train station (on weekdays, hourly bus #804 is timed to meet most regional trains; on weekends it runs only every 2 hours, and doesn't sync with S-Bahn arrivals; direction: Malz; bus #821 also possible, runs 5/day, no buses Sat-Sun, direction: Tiergarten; €1.70, covered by Berlin transit day pass for zones ABC or *Anschlussfahrausweis,* get off at Gedenkstätte stop). You can also take a **taxi** (€8, ask for the *Gedenkstätte*—geh-DENK-shteh-teh).

To **walk** 20 minutes to the memorial, turn right from the train station and head up Stralsunder Strasse for about two blocks. Turn right under the railroad trestle onto Bernauer Strasse, following signs for *Gedenkstätte Sachsenhausen.* At the traffic light, turn left onto André-Pican-Strasse, which becomes Strasse der Einheit. After two blocks, turn right on Strasse der Nationen, which leads right to the camp.

PLANNING YOUR TIME

Make your pilgrimage to Sachsenhausen any day in summer. The museums are closed on Monday from mid-October to mid-March (the grounds are open daily year-round). You'll need at least three hours to appreciate the many worthwhile exhibits here. Factoring in transit time, give yourself at least five hours round-trip from central Berlin.

ORIENTATION TO SACHSENHAUSEN

Cost and Hours: Free, daily 8:30-18:00, mid-Oct-mid-March until 16:30, on Mon off-season only the grounds and visitors center are open, Strasse der Nationen 22.

Information: +49 3301 200 200, www.gedenkstaette-sachsenhausen.de

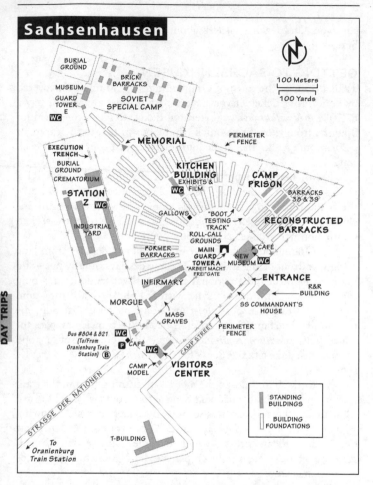

Sachsenhausen

BURIAL GROUND

MUSEUM

GUARD TOWER E

WC

BRICK BARRACKS

SOVIET SPECIAL CAMP

100 Meters

100 Yards

MEMORIAL

PERIMETER FENCE

EXECUTION TRENCH

BURIAL GROUND

CREMATORIUM

STATION Z

WC

INDUSTRIAL YARD

KITCHEN BUILDING

EXHIBITS & FILM

WC

CAMP PRISON

BARRACKS 38 & 39

RECONSTRUCTED BARRACKS

GALLOWS

"BOOT TESTING TRACK"

ROLL-CALL GROUNDS

FORMER BARRACKS

MAIN GUARD TOWER A

"ARBEIT MACHT FREI" GATE

NEW MUSEUM

CAFÉ

WC

INFIRMARY

ENTRANCE

R&R BUILDING

MORGUE

SS COMMANDANT'S HOUSE

MASS GRAVES

PERIMETER FENCE

Bus #804 & 821 (To/From Oranienburg Train Station) B

WC

P CAFÉ

WC

CAMP STREET

CAMP MODEL

VISITORS CENTER

STANDING BUILDINGS

BUILDING FOUNDATIONS

STRASSE DER NATIONEN

To Oranienburg Train Station

T-BUILDING

DAY TRIPS

Visitor Information: The map in this book is sufficient, but the map sold at the visitors center is worthwhile for its extra background information. Skip the overlong audioguide and instead make use of this chapter's self-guided tour and ample information posted within the camp.

Services: The visitors center has WCs, a bookshop, and a helpful information desk.

Tours: A tour helps you understand the camp's complicated and important story. The Sachsenhausen **visitors center** offers €14 guided tours Tue, Thu, and Sun at 10:20 from the entrance of the Oranienburg train station, and at 10:50 and 14:00 from the visitors center (just show up—no reservation necessary).

Virtually all **walking-tour companies** in Berlin offer side trips to Sachsenhausen (meet in the city, then ride together by train to Oranienburg). The round-trip takes about six hours, much of which is spent in transit—but your time at the camp is made very meaningful by your guide's commentary.

Check walking-tour companies' websites or compare brochures to find an itinerary that fits your schedule (typically €19, April-Oct daily at 10:00, less frequent off-season). Options include **Original Berlin Walks** (www.berlinwalks.de) and **Insider Tour** (www.insidertour.com). Don't book a tour on an off-season Monday, when the grounds are open, but not the museum exhibits.

Eating: Pack a lunch or buy one en route, as dining choices at the camp are minimal. The little "Info Café" inside the camp offers small snacks, and Bistro To Go, just outside the visitors center, serves basic fare (wurst, soup).

BACKGROUND

Completed in July 1936, Sachsenhausen was the first concentration camp built under SS chief Heinrich Himmler. The triangle-shaped grounds, contained by three walls, enabled observation of the entire camp from a single point, the main guard tower. The design was intended to be a model for other camps, but it had a critical flaw that prevented its widespread adoption: It was very difficult to expand without interfering with sight lines.

Sachsenhausen was not, strictly speaking, a "death camp" for mass murder (like Auschwitz); it was a labor camp, intended to wring hard work out of the prisoners. Many toiled in a brickworks, producing materials to be used in architect Albert Speer's grandiose plans for erecting new buildings all over Berlin.

Between 1936 and 1945, about 200,000 prisoners did time at Sachsenhausen; about 50,000 died here, while numerous others were transported elsewhere to be killed (in 1942, many of Sachsenhausen's Jews were taken to Auschwitz). Though it was designed to hold 10,000 prisoners, by the end of its functional life the camp had up to 38,000 people. In the spring of 1945, knowing that the Red Army was approaching, guards took 35,000 able-bodied prisoners on a death march, leading them into the forest for seven days and nights with no rations. Rather than "wasting" bullets to kill them, SS troops hoped that the prisoners would expire from exhaustion. On the eighth day, after 6,000 had died, the guards abandoned the group in the wilderness. When Soviet troops liberated Sachsenhausen on April 22, 1945, they discovered an additional 3,000 prisoners who had been too weak to walk and were left there to die (all but 300 survived).

Just three months after the war, Sachsenhausen was converted into Soviet Special Camp No. 7 for the USSR's own prisoners. It was a notorious "silent camp," where prisoners would disappear—

DAY TRIPS

allowed no contact with the outside world and their imprisonment officially unacknowledged. The prisoners were Nazis as well as anti-Stalin Russians. By the time the camp closed in 1950, 12,000 more people had died here.

In 1961, Sachsenhausen became the first former concentration camp to be turned into a memorial. The East German government created the memorial mostly for propaganda purposes, to deflect attention from the controversial construction of the Berlin Wall and to exalt the USSR as the valiant antifascist liberators of the camp and all of Germany.

Since the end of the DDR, Sachsenhausen has been redeveloped into a true memorial, with updated museum exhibits and an emphasis on preservation—documenting and sharing the story of what happened here. While difficult to take in, as with all concentration camp memorials, the intention of Sachsenhausen is to share its story and lessons—and prevent this type of brutality from ever happening again.

◉ SELF-GUIDED TOUR

The camp's various exhibits are scattered throughout the grounds in various buildings, and offer more information than you probably have time to absorb. This outline covers the key parts of your visit.

Entrance

In the courtyard next to the visitors center, a **model** of the camp illustrates its unique triangular layout. Guards stationed in tower A (at the main gate) could see everything going on inside those three walls. Along the left (west) side of the triangle is the crematorium, called Station Z. Outside the main triangle are the workshops, factories, and extra barracks that were added when the camp ran out of room.

Walk up the dusty lane called Camp Street. On the right is the SS officers' R&R building, nicknamed the **"Green Monster,"** where prisoners dressed in nice clothes were forced to wait on their keepers. Officials mostly chose Jehovah's Witnesses for this duty, because they had a strong pacifist code and could be trusted not to attempt to harm their captors.

A left turn through the fence takes you into the courtyard in front of **guard tower A.** The clock on the tower is frozen at 11:07—the exact time that the Red Army liberated the camp. The building on the right—the **New Museum**—has an interesting DDR-era stained-glass window inside, as well as thoughtful temporary exhibits and a small café.

Go through the gate cruelly marked *Arbeit Macht Frei*—"Work will set you free."

Main Grounds

Entering the triangular field, you can see that almost none of the original buildings still stand. Following the war, locals salvaged the barracks here for much-needed building materials. Tracing the perimeter, notice the electric fence and barbed wire. A few feet in front of the wall is a gravel track called the **neutral zone**—any prisoner setting foot here would be shot. This became a common way for prisoners to attempt suicide. Guards quickly caught on: If they sensed a suicide attempt, they'd shoot to maim instead of kill. It was typical upside-down Nazi logic: Those who wanted to live would die, and those who wanted to die would live.

Every morning, after a 4:15 wake-up call, prisoners would scramble to eat, bathe, and dress in time to assemble in the **roll-call**

grounds in front of the guard tower by 5:00. Dressed in their thin, striped pajama-like uniforms and wooden clogs, prisoners would line up while guards, in long coats and accompanied by angry dogs, barked orders and accounted for each person, including those who had died in the barracks overnight. It could take hours, in any weather. A single misbehaving prisoner would bring about punishment for all others. One day, after a prisoner escaped, SS officer Rudolf Höss (who later went on to run Auschwitz-Birkenau) forced the entire population of the camp to stand here for 15 hours in a foot of snow and subzero temperatures. A thousand people died.

To the far right from the entrance, the wooden **barracks** (with good museum displays) are reconstructed from original timbers. Barrack 38 focuses on the Jewish experience at Sachsenhausen, as well as the general mistreatment of German Jews under the Nazis (including anti-Semitic propaganda). Barrack 39 explains everyday life, with stories following 20 individual internees. You'll see how prisoners lived: long rows of bunks, benches for taking paltry meals, latrines crammed wall-to-wall with toilets, and communal fountains for washing. Inmates would jockey for access to these facilities. The strongest, meanest, most aggressive prisoners—often here because they had been convicted of a violent crime—would be named *Kapo,* the head of the barrack (to discourage camaraderie, the worst prisoners, rather than the best, were "promoted"). Like at many other camps, the camp leaders at Sachsenhausen ran a system of organized rape, whereby they brought in inmates from the women's-only Ravensbrück concentration camp and forced them to "reward good prisoners" at Sachsenhausen.

Next to the barracks is the **camp prison,** where political prisoners or out-of-line inmates were sent. It was run not by the SS, but by the Gestapo (secret police), who would torture captives to extract information. Other prisoners didn't know exactly what went on here, but they could hear screams from inside and knew it was no place they wanted to be. This was also where the Nazis held special hostages, including three Allied airmen who had participated in a bold escape from a Nazi prisoner-of-war camp (the basis for *The Great Escape;* they later managed to escape from Sachsenhausen as well, before being recaptured) and Joseph Stalin's son, Yakov Dzhugashvili, who had been captured during the fighting at Stalingrad. (The Nazis offered to exchange the young man for five German officers. Stalin refused, and soon after, Yakov died here under mysterious circumstances.) The cells contain exhibits about the prisoners and the methods used by their captors.

Just outside the back of the building stand three **posts** (out of an originwal 15) with iron pegs near the top. Guards cruelly executed people by tying their hands behind their backs, then hanging them on these pegs by their wrists until they died—a medieval method called *strappado.*

Walk around the inner semicircle toward the buildings in the middle of the camp. On this **"boot-testing track,"** prisoners were forced to put on boots two sizes too small and walk in a circle on uneven ground all day, supposedly to "test" the shoes for fighting at Stalingrad.

The rectangles of stones show where each of the original barrack buildings once stood. At the center, a marker represents the location of the gallows, where prisoners would be publicly executed as a deterrent to others.

In the middle of the triangle, on the right, is the kitchen building, with exhibits that trace the chronological history of the camp. You'll learn how Sachswenhausen was built by prisoners and see original artifacts, including the gallows, a bunk from the barracks, uniforms, and so on. There are also photos, quotes, and a 22-minute film.

Memorial and Crematorium

Head back to the far end of the camp, which is dominated by the towering, 130-foot-tall, 1961 communist **DDR memorial** to the victims of Sachsenhausen. The 18 triangles at the top are red, the color designated for political prisoners (to the communists, they were more worthy of honor than the other victims who died here). At the base of the monument, two prisoners are being liberated by a noble Soviet soldier. The prisoners are unrealistically robust, healthy, and optimistic (they will survive and become part of the proud Soviet proletariat!). The **podium** in front was used by the East German army for speeches and rallies—exploiting Sachsenhausen as a backdrop for their propaganda.

From here, head left and go through the gap in the fence to find the execution trench, used for mass shootings. When this system proved too inefficient, the Nazis built "Station Z," the nearby

crematorium, where they could execute and dispose of prisoners more systematically. Its ruins are inside the white building (prior to the camp's liberation by Soviet troops, Nazi guards destroyed the crematorium to remove evidence of their crimes).

The crematorium's ramp

took prisoners down into the "infirmary," while the three steps led up to the dressing room. This is where, on five occasions, the Nazis tested Zyklon-B (the chemical later responsible for killing hundreds of thousands at Auschwitz). Most of the building's victims died in the room with the dou-

ble row of bricks (for soundproofing; the Nazis also blasted classical music to mask noise). Victims would report here for a "dental check," to find out if they had gold or silver teeth that could be taken. They would then stand against the wall to have their height measured—and a guard would shoot them through a small hole in the wall with a single bullet to the back of the skull. (The Nazis found it was easier for guards to carry out their duties if they didn't have to see their victims face-to-face.)

Bodies were taken to be incinerated in the ovens (which still stand). Notice the statue of the emaciated prisoner—a much more accurate depiction than the one at the DDR monument. Outside, a burial ground is filled with ashes from the crematorium.

The Rest of the Camp

Back inside the main part of the camp you can head left, up to the tip of the triangle (behind the big monument) to find a museum about the postwar era, when Sachsenhausen served as a **Soviet Special Camp.** Nearby is a burial ground for victims of that camp. At this corner of the triangle, the gate in the fence—called **tower E**—holds a small exhibit about the relationship between the camp and the town of Oranienburg.

Heading back toward the main guard tower, along the wall toward the front corner, are the long, green barracks of the **infirmary,** used for medical experiments on inmates (as explained by the exhibits inside). This was also where Soviet soldiers found the 3,000 remaining survivors when they liberated the camp. The small building in back was the morgue—Nazis used the long ramp to bring in the day's bodies via wheelbarrows. Behind that is a field with six stones, each marking 50 bodies for the 300 prisoners who died after the camp was freed.

Wittenberg

You need only look at its official name—Lutherstadt Wittenberg—to know this small city's claim to fame. The adopted hometown of Martin Luther, and the birthplace of his Protestant Reformation, little Wittenberg has a gigantic history that belies its straightforward townscape. With a pair of historic churches—the Town Church of St. Mary, where Luther preached, and the Church of All Saints (Castle Church), where he famously hammered his 95 Theses to the door—and an excellent museum about Luther's life (Luther House), Wittenberg can be a worthwhile stop even for those unfamiliar with the Great Reformer. And for Lutherans, it's a pilgrimage. The notable painter Lucas Cranach the Elder, a contemporary and friend of Luther who also lived and worked in Wittenberg, left behind a slew of masterful paintings and woodcuts, and you can see where he lived as well.

Centuries of Germans have celebrated Wittenberg for its ties to Luther. In 1983, which marked Martin Luther's 500th birthday, Wittenberg was part of communist East Germany, whose atheistic regime was tearing down proud old churches elsewhere. But ignoring the Luther anniversary would have made the East German government, already unpopular, seem woefully out of touch. (The government also sensed an opportunity to attract Luther tourists and much-needed hard Western currency.) So the communists swallowed hard and rehabilitated the memory of Luther, tidying up the sights devoted to him. This may be why Wittenberg emerged from communism in better shape than many other East German towns.

The city received another round of upgrades in 2017, when it celebrated the 500th anniversary of Luther's famous 95 Theses—it's newly spiffed up and sparkling. Most tourists here are Germans (and American Lutherans), and the town is also a stop for riverboat cruise groups heading from Hamburg to Dresden and Prague. And yet, Wittenberg isn't unpleasantly touristy. Its pedestrianized main street feels quiet—sometimes almost deserted—and its sights are satisfying and quickly seen. Wittenberg works perfectly as a side trip from Berlin (offering a refreshing small-town break from the intense city), and also works well on the way between Berlin and Leipzig, Erfurt, or even Dresden (handy lockers at Wittenberg train station).

GETTING TO WITTENBERG

It's a speedy 40 minutes from Berlin on ICE trains, or 1.5 hours on cheaper regional (RE) trains. All trains depart from the Berlin Hauptbahnhof; some regional trains also stop at Potsdamer

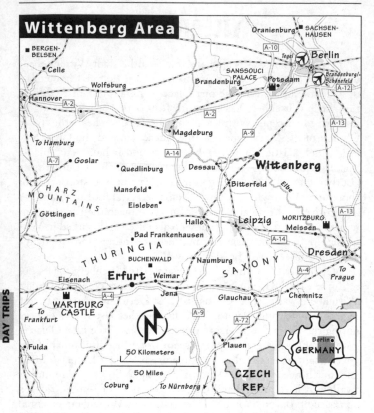

Wittenberg Area

BERGEN-BELSEN
Celle
Wolfsburg
Oranienburg
SACHSEN-HAUSEN
A-10
Tegel
Berlin
Brandenburg-Schönefeld
SANSSOUCI PALACE
Brandenburg
Potsdam
A-12
Hannover
A-2
A-2
A-13
To Hamburg
Magdeburg
A-9
A-7
Goslar
A-14
Dessau
Wittenberg
Quedlinburg
HARZ MOUNTAINS
Mansfeld
Bitterfeld
Elbe
Göttingen
Eisleben
Halle
Leipzig
MORITZBURG
Meissen
A-13
Bad Frankenhausen
A-14
THURINGIA
BUCHENWALD
Naumburg
SAXONY
Dresden
Eisenach
Erfurt
Weimar
A-4
To Prague
WARTBURG CASTLE
A-4
Jena
Glauchau
Chemnitz
To Frankfurt
A-9
A-72
Fulda
Plauen
50 Kilometers
50 Miles
Coburg
To Nürnberg
CZECH REP.
Berlin
GERMANY

DAY TRIPS

Platz. If you're a small group day-tripping from Berlin, and are willing to take the slower regional trains, you can save a bundle with the **Brandenburg-Berlin-Ticket** (not valid on ICE). Available through Deutsche Bahn, this covers unlimited regional train travel throughout the Brandenburg region during one day, for up to five people, all for €29.

PLANNING YOUR TIME

Wittenberg's sights can be seen in just a few hours. For an efficient visit, from the train station ride the public bus to Marktplatz, start at the TI and Castle Church, then work your way downhill through town—sightseeing and possibly having lunch as you go. From the last couple of sights—Luther House and Asisi's Wittenberg 360 Panorama—it's about a 15-minute, downhill walk back to the train station.

Background on Martin Luther

Luther lived a turbulent life. In early adulthood, the newly ordained Catholic priest suffered a crisis of faith before finally emerging as "born again." In 1517, he openly protested against Church corruption and was later excommunicated. Defying both the pope and the emperor, he was declared a heretic and hid out in a friendly prince's castle, watching as his ideas sparked peasant riots. In his castle refuge he translated the New Testament from Greek to German. He later composed hymns such as "A Mighty Fortress is Our God," sparred with fellow Reformers, and tried to harness and guide the religious, social, and political firestorm he helped ignite.

DAY TRIPS

Early Life

Luther was born on November 10, 1483, in Eisleben, south of Berlin. His dad owned a copper smelter, affording Luther a middle-class upbringing—a rarity in the medieval hierarchy of nobles, clergy, and peasants.

Luther enrolled at the University of Erfurt in 1501. There he earned a liberal-arts degree, entered law school, and earned himself

two nicknames—"the philosopher" for his wide-ranging mind, and "the king of hops" for his lifelong love affair with beer.

Then came July 2, 1505. While riding through the countryside, Luther was caught up in an intense thunderstorm, and a bolt of lightning knocked him to the ground. Luther cried out, "St. Anne, save me, and I will become a monk!" Surviving the storm, Luther was determined to make good on his promise. He returned to Erfurt, sold his possessions, and told his friends, "After this day, you will see me no more." The next morning, he knocked on the door of Erfurt's Augustinian Monastery and dedicated his life to Christianity.

But Luther soon realized that pious monastic life did not suit his inquisitive nature. He returned to academia, was ordained a priest in 1507 in Erfurt's cathedral, and by 1508 was teaching theology part-time at the university in nearby Wittenberg.

In 1509, Luther set out for Rome on foot, a pilgrimage that

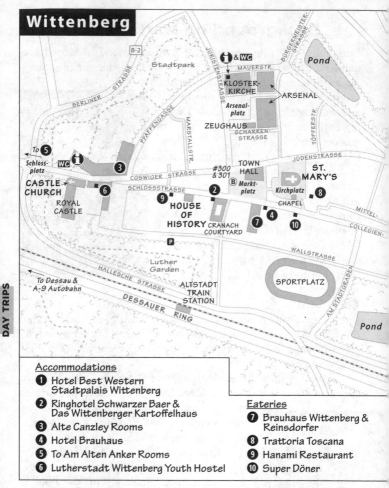

Wittenberg

Accommodations
1. Hotel Best Western Stadtpalais Wittenberg
2. Ringhotel Schwarzer Baer & Das Wittenberger Kartoffelhaus
3. Alte Canzley Rooms
4. Hotel Brauhaus
5. To Am Alten Anker Rooms
6. Lutherstadt Wittenberg Youth Hostel

Eateries
7. Brauhaus Wittenberg & Reinsdorfer
8. Trattoria Toscana
9. Hanami Restaurant
10. Super Döner

would change him forever. Upon arriving in the Eternal City, he was dismayed to find rich, corrupt priests and bishops selling "indulgences," which supposedly guaranteed entry to heaven to those able to pay the price. This was the Rome of Pope Julius II, who was in the midst of an expensive, over-the-top remodel of Vatican City—and the lucrative sale of indulgences helped refill the papal treasury. At the time of Luther's visit, Michelangelo was lying aloft on his back in the Sistine Chapel, executing detailed frescoes on the ceiling, while Raphael was slathering nearby hallways with his own Renaissance masterpieces.

This traffic in indulgences and luxury clashed violently with Luther's deeply held belief that people's faith, not their pocketbooks, would determine the final destination of their souls. Indul-

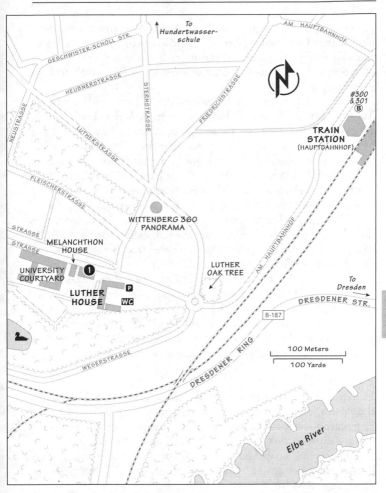

gences were an insult to his worldview—and, to Luther, a betrayal of the Christian faith.

Professor and Preacher

After returning to Germany in 1512, Luther received his doctorate and got a job teaching theology at the university in Wittenberg. The prince elector of Saxony, Frederick the Wise, had decided to make this backwater town his royal seat, so he invited the region's best and brightest to populate his dynamic new burg. Here, Luther mingled with other great thinkers (including fellow professor Philipp Melanchthon) and artists (most notably Lucas Cranach the Elder).

During these early years, Luther was consumed with the notion that he was a sinner. He devoured the Bible, looking for an answer and finding it in Paul's letter to the Romans. Luther concluded that God makes sinners righteous through their faith in Jesus Christ, not by earning it through good deeds. As this concept of "unearned grace" took hold, Luther said, "I felt myself to have been born again."

Energized, he began a series of Bible lectures at Wittenberg's Town Church of St. Mary. The pews were packed as Luther quoted passages directly from the Bible. Speaker and audience alike began to see discrepancies between what the Bible said and what the Church was doing. Coincidentally, a friar happened to arrive in Wittenberg around this time, selling letters of indulgence that promised "forgiveness for all thy sins, transgressions, and excesses, howsoever enormous they may be"...a bargain at twice the price.

Outraged at the idea that God's grace could be bought, Luther thought the subject should be debated openly. On October 31, 1517, he nailed his now-famous 95 Theses (topics for discussion) to the door of Wittenberg's Castle Church. The theses questioned indulgences and other Church practices and beliefs. Thesis #82 boldly asked: "If the pope redeems a number of souls for the sake of miserable money with which to buy a church, why doesn't he empty purgatory for the sake of holy love?" With the newfangled printing presses belonging to Lucas Cranach, Luther's propositions were turned into pamphlets that became the talk of Germany.

Excommunication

Luther didn't set out to start a new church; he wanted to reform the existing one. He preached throughout the region, spreading his provocative ideas and publicly debating his positions in such venues as Leipzig's town hall. In 1520, a furious Pope Leo X sent the rebellious monk a papal bull threatening excommunication. Luther burned the edict on the spot, and soon after, Leo X formally excommunicated him.

Luther was branded a heretic and ordered to Rome to face charges, but he refused to go. Finally, the most powerful man in Europe, Emperor Charles V, stepped in to arbitrate, calling an Imperial Diet (congress) at Worms in 1521. Luther made a triumphal entry into Worms, greeted by cheering crowds. The Diet convened, and Luther took his place in the center of the large hall, standing next to a stack of his writings. Inquisitors grilled him while the ultra-conservative Charles looked on. Luther refused to disavow his beliefs.

The infuriated emperor declared Luther an outlaw and a heretic. Being "outside the law" meant that he could be killed at will. After leaving Worms, Luther disappeared. He was kidnapped—by supporters—and given refuge in Frederick the Wise's Wartburg Castle. There Luther wore a beard to disguise himself as Junker

Jörg ("Squire George"). He spent 10 months fighting depression and translating the Bible's New Testament from the original Greek into German. This "September Testament" was revolutionary, bringing the Bible to the masses and shaping the modern German language.

Meanwhile, Luther's ideas caught on back home in Wittenberg, where his followers had continued to pursue reform. By the time Luther returned to the city in 1522, popular uprisings led by more radically-minded reformers were undermining law and order.

Later Life

In 1525, Luther's friend and follower Thomas Müntzer used Luther's writings to justify an uprising known as the Peasants' Revolt. Poor farmers attacked their feudal masters with hoes and pitchforks, fighting for more food, political say-so, and respect. Thousands of peasants died, and Müntzer was executed. Luther decried the uprising, preaching that Church corruption did not justify outright societal rebellion. In fact, he supported the violent suppression of the Peasants' Revolt.

In 1525, the 41-year-old ex-priest married a 26-year-old ex-nun, Katharina von Bora, "to please my father and annoy the pope."

(Their wedding set the precedent of allowing Protestant clergy to marry.) They moved into the former Wittenberg monastery where Luther had once lived (today's Luther House, the best museum anywhere on the Reformation and Luther), where they rented rooms to students. Luther turned his checkbook over to "my lord Katie," who ran the family farm and raised their six children and 11 adopted orphans.

Luther traveled, spreading the Protestant message. In 1529, at Marburg Castle (just north of Frankfurt), he attended a summit of leading Protestants to try and forge an alliance against Catholicism. They agreed on everything except a single theological point: whether Christ was present in the wine and bread of Communion in a physical sense (according to Luther) or symbolic sense (per the Swiss reformer Ulrich Zwingli). The disagreement doomed the Protestant movement to splinter into dozens of sects.

In 1534, Luther finished translating the Bible. Lucas Cranach illustrated it with woodcuts and published it on his printing presses. The Martin Luther Bible was to German-speaking Christians what the King James Bible would be to English-speaking Christians—essentially codifying an entire language. Luther also wrote a German Mass, catechisms, and several hymns, including the still-beloved "A Mighty Fortress is Our God."

In his fifties, Luther's health declined and he grew bitter, a fact made clear in such writings as "Against the Papacy at Rome Founded by the Devil" and "Of the Jews and Their Lies." A general tone of anti-Judaism pollutes his later work. Luther was less concerned with the ethnicity of Jews—as the Nazis later were—than he was by their refusal to accept Christianity. Luther's words were later invoked to justify anti-Semitic speech and actions during the early days of Nazism.

Martin Luther died on February 18, 1546, and was buried in Wittenberg. To read more about the Protestant Reformation, see the "Luther's Legacy" sidebar, later. And watch my one-hour public television special, Rick Steves' *Luther and the Reformation* (RickSteves.com/luther).

Orientation to Wittenberg

Literally "White Hill," Wittenberg (Germans say VIT-tehn-behrk, pop. 50,000) sits atop a gentle rise above the Elbe River. The tourists' Wittenberg is essentially a one-street town: Its main drag runs about three-quarters of a mile from the Luther House (where the street is called Collegienstrasse) to the Castle Church (where it's called Schlossstrasse). The rest of the Old Town consists only of a few side streets. The modern part of town sprawls mostly to the north and east.

Don't confuse Wittenberg with Wittenberge, a town north of Berlin. (The correct Wittenberg sometimes shows up as "Kleinwittenberg" on GPS maps or "Lutherstadt Wittenberg" on some websites.)

TOURIST INFORMATION

Wittenberg's TI is at the far end of town from the train station, across the street from Castle Church (daily 9:00-18:00; Nov-March 10:00-17:00; Schlossplatz 2, +49 3491 498 610, www.lutherstadt-wittenberg.de). The TI rents a town audioguide (€7, 2 hours of commentary—must return before closing time), and there's a pay WC next door. A second, less comprehensive branch of the TI is at the northern edge of the Old Town, in the Stadthaus (shorter hours than main TI).

Wittenberg in the Early 1500s

As you explore Wittenberg, mentally time-travel to the days of Luther—the first few decades of the 16th century. The Renaissance was percolating to the south in Italy (where Michelangelo and Raphael were hard at work redecorating the Vatican), and a spirit of new ideas was also beginning to take hold in Germany.

The influential prince elector Frederick III "the Wise" (1463-1525), who had inherited half of Saxony from his father, chose sleepy Wittenberg as his royal seat. He built a stout castle here in 1492 (not open to visitors, but viewable from the park just beyond the town gate), and began remaking this humble fishing village into a proper Renaissance town. (That explains Wittenberg's grid of streets, compared with the twisty medieval muddle of many other German towns.) Frederick the Wise hired Lucas Cranach the Elder to be his official court painter. Cranach—along with his wife, Barbara, and son Lucas Cranach the Younger—lived in a big mansion on Market Square (today a museum; his statue—pictured above—is in the courtyard). Frederick also founded a university here (in 1502) and stocked it with some of the brightest minds of his time, including the promising young theologian Martin Luther and the brilliant classical-languages specialist Philipp Melanchthon. Cranach, Luther, Melanchthon, and others were good friends who regularly socialized and swapped ideas.

Although he remained a devout Catholic until the end of his life, Frederick the Wise supported Luther and the reformers in their darkest hour, likely saving them from obscurity or worse. Wittenberg would not be famous if not for Luther—but, most likely, if not for Frederick the Wise, Luther would not be famous, either.

ARRIVAL IN WITTENBERG

Wittenberg's **main train station** (listed on schedules as Lutherstadt Wittenberg) is a dull 15-minute walk from the Luther House and a 25-minute walk from the TI and Castle Church. (The smaller Lutherstadt Wittenberg Altstadt station, while closer to the Old Town, only serves trains on a small branch line.) The station building has handy lockers, a café, and a ticket office. Nearby (on the other side of the big, white tent) are **bus** stops for the ride into town. Look for bus #300 (toward Coswig) or bus #301 (toward Straach); these leave from bus stop #1 (every 30 minutes, 10-minute ride, €1.30/ride, €2.50/day pass, buy tickets from driver). Stops aren't announced;

you want the Marktplatz stop, right at the Old Town's main square (ask the driver to confirm). A **taxi** from the station to Schlossplatz (near the TI) should cost about €10 (if no taxis are waiting, call +49 3491 666 666). To **walk,** head left from the station, walk beneath the overpass, and look for signs directing you to the city center.

Drivers will find plenty of free on-street **parking** just outside the mostly pedestrianized town center.

HELPFUL HINTS

Festivals: Various festivals dot Wittenberg's calendar, including a three-day celebration of the wedding of Luther and Katharina (second weekend in June) and special events for **Reformation Day** (Oct 31, when Luther nailed his 95 Theses to the church door).

Tours: Most walking-tour options (you'll likely see costumed Martin Luthers and Katharina von Boras leading groups through town) are in German only. For an English tour, hire your own local guide—gracious **Katja Köhler** does a great job telling Wittenberg's story (€80/2-hour tour, €130/4-hour tour, mobile +49 177 688 8218, katjakoehler@gmx.net).

English Worship Services: Local Lutherans offer English-language services in historic Wittenberg churches during the summer (April-Oct Wed-Fri at 16:00 in small Corpus Christi chapel next to Town Church of St. Mary; Sat at 17:00 in either Castle Church or Town Church of St. Mary; confirm times at www.wittenbergenglishministry.com).

Classical Concerts: It seems like there's always a concert on in one of the town's churches. If you're spending the night, check at the TI to find out when and where you can enjoy some classical music. (Luther—who said "to sing is to pray double"—loved music.)

Sights in Wittenberg

MARTIN LUTHER SIGHTS

I've organized these sights roughly in order from the TI end of town (with the Castle Church) to the Luther House end of town.

▲▲Castle Church (Schlosskirche)

This Church of All Saints was the site of one of the most important moments in European history: Martin Luther nailing his 95 Theses to the church door. That door—and most of the church as it existed in Luther's time—are long gone (destroyed in 1760, during the Seven Years' War). But in the late 19th century, as Germany was uniting as a nation for the first time, the church and the door were rebuilt in the Romantic style as a temple to Luther and his fellow reformers. You'll find Luther's humble tombstone inside.

Cost and Hours: Free; Mon-Sat 10:00-18:00, Sun from 11:30; Nov-March Tue-Sat 10:00-16:00, Sun from 11:30, closed Mon; Schlossplatz, +49 3491 506 9160, www.schlosskirche-wittenberg.de.

Visiting the Church: Before entering, take a close look at that famous **side door** (in the middle of the church, to the left of the present-day entrance). According to most accounts, on October 31, 1517, a frustrated Martin Luther nailed a handwritten copy of 95 Theses—topics for discussion—to the wooden door that was here then. (What you see is a 19th-century bronze door engraved with the Latin theses.) The act wasn't quite as defiant as it sounds—the door served as a sort of community bulletin board. But the strong arguments Luther made about ending the practice of indulgences and other forms of Church corruption were revolutionary...as was his timing. Normally, Wittenbergers worshipped at the Town Church of St. Mary, but the day after Luther's act—All Saints' Day—was the one day each year that the Castle Church's interior was open to the public, who were invited to come inside, view Frederick the Wise's vast collection of relics, and purchase indulgences. Historians quibble over the exact day Luther made his theses public and whether he actually nailed them to the door, but there's no doubt that his work spurred a nascent sentiment of reform and cemented his role as that movement's leader.

Above the door is a glittering image of the crucified Christ flanked by Luther (on the left) and his fellow Reformer Philipp Melanchthon (on the right), with the skyline of Wittenberg behind them.

Go inside, walk down the **nave,** and look up. Notice the colorful coats of arms on the upper stained-glass windows, which represent German cities that became Protestant when they joined Luther's Reformation. The carved coats of arms on the railing honor larger principalities that also adopted Protestantism. The lower stained-glass windows, with images of Reformers, were grudgingly added for Luther's 500th birthday, in 1983, by the aggressively atheistic East German government...and it shows.

In the middle of the church, to the right (in front of the pulpit, with a raised

plaque), you'll see the flower-bedecked **tomb of Martin Luther.** On the wall behind it is a replica of the large bronze tomb marker that originally covered Luther's remains. While this wasn't his home church (that would be the Town Church of St. Mary, just up the street and described later), this university church was traditionally where professors like Luther were entombed. On the left side of the nave is a similar raised plaque marking the grave of Luther's right-hand man and fellow professor, **Philipp Melanchthon.**

Proceed to the front of the church. In front of the high altar are large tomb markers for the **prince electors** who called Witten-

berg home and provided safe harbor for Luther's provocative ideas. On the left is Frederick the Wise, and on his right is his younger brother, John the Stead-fast. While Frederick remained de-voutly Catholic throughout his life, his support for Luther, Melanchthon, and the early Protestant Reformers never wavered. Frederick's successor, John, converted to Protestantism and, in a fit of iconoclasm, destroyed his brother's impressive collection of relics. Flank-ing these markers are larger plaques and statues (from the original church) that depict these important brothers.

▲Market Square (Marktplatz)

This wide square is much the same today as it was in Luther's time. An all-purpose space back then, it was used for everything from tournaments to executions. The square is dominated by the Renaissance-style **Town Hall** (Rathaus). Notice the seven small, filled-in doors at the right side of the building, which led to a shopping gallery back when the building's cellar hosted a little mar-ketplace (today the Town Hall houses a 20th-century Christian art collection). In one cor-ner of the square you'll find a metal model of Wittenberg's Old Town. In the middle of the square are 19th-century **statues** of Martin Luther (pictured here) and Philipp Melanch-thon (pictured on next page).

The main street through town is lined by delightful gurgling **canals,** as in a few other German cities, like Freiburg and Augsburg. When Luther first moved to Wittenberg, he was disgusted by these, which carried drinking water (on the

Philipp Melanchthon (1497-1560)

While everyone who comes to Wittenberg has heard of Martin Luther, many are surprised to find another important figure celebrated here with almost equal reverence: Philipp Melanchthon. The Garfunkel to Luther's Simon, Melanchthon was a brainy university professor who also played a critical role in the Protestant Reformation.

Born Philipp Schwartzerdt in southern Germany, he later changed his name to its Greek translation, Melanchthon ("black soil"). Although he was short, young, sickly, and notoriously unattractive, Melanchthon impressed everybody in Wittenberg with his keen intellect. In fact, when Melanchthon became disillusioned with Wittenberg and threatened to move away, Frederick the Wise persuaded him to stay by arranging a marriage for him (to the mayor's daughter, no less). While Luther was no intellectual slouch, Melanchthon was even more brilliant—he taught several topics (specializing in ancient languages, pedagogy, and theology) and encouraged women to pursue university study. Particularly gifted with languages, he provided Luther with invaluable assistance when translating the Bible into German from the original Greek and Hebrew texts.

DAY TRIPS

way into town) and smelly sewage (on the way out). Years later, they were covered over by the modern street. But recently they were opened up to the air to evoke the ambience of Luther's time.

Cranach Courtyard (Cranachhof)

Find the big beige Renaissance building at Schlossstrasse 1, in one corner of the square, with a pharmacy (the Lucas-Cranach-Apotheke) on the ground floor. This building, circling a surprisingly large courtyard, was the residence of the artist Lucas Cranach the Elder. Enter the courtyard to see a statue of Cranach sketching at the far end.

As the official court painter for Frederick the Wise, Cranach was one of the most esteemed men in town, but he was also an entrepreneur who dabbled in endeavors like printing and running a pharmacy. Cranach and Luther were fast friends. The artist was the only painter who had permission to do portraits of Luther and his family (Cranach and his school produced and re-produced some 2,000 Luther portraits), and he was one of the first printers of Luther's writings. Cranach's house is also where Luther's future bride, Katharina von Bora, lived when she first came to Wittenberg (fresh out of the convent).

For decades, this space sat in ruins (see the pre-1989 photo in the entry arch.) But it's been converted into a kind of cultural center, hosting artists' studios, a small bar, a gift shop, comfortable hotel rooms, and—at the far end of the courtyard—an old-fashioned print shop *(Druckerstube)*. Operated by a quirky printer who speaks some English and enjoys explaining the importance of Luther's statement, "This is a German nation—the people speak German," the shop uses traditional methods to create postcards and replicas of works by Luther and Cranach (closed Sun). There's a small Cranach museum a few doors away (at #4 on Market Square).

▲▲Town Church of St. Mary (Stadtkirche St. Marien)

Towering over a row of buildings at the end of Market Square, this is the oldest building in town and an impressively historic place to be surrounded by Luther lore.

Before stepping inside, notice that the tops of the twin towers don't quite match the rest of the building. Formerly pointy Gothic steeples, these were knocked down during a 1546 battle. They were later rebuilt in the round Renaissance style you see today.

Cost and Hours: Free to enter, Mon-Sat 10:00-18:00, Sun from 11:30, Nov-Easter daily until 16:00, free organ concerts May-Oct Fri at 18:00, +49 3491 62830, www.stadtkirchengemeinde-wittenberg.de.

Visiting the Church: The interior of the Town Church of St. Mary is striking for its pure, uncluttered feel. Once ornately painted and slathered with chapels, statues, and ornamentation, it was cleaned out when it became Lutheran. Sit in a pew and enjoy the Doublemint freshness of the space.

For most of his life, this was Luther's home church—where he was married, where his children were baptized, and where he preached over 2,000 times. This is where what many consider to be the first-ever Protestant service took place, on Christmas Day in 1521 (although Martin Luther wasn't in attendance—he was hiding out at Wartburg Castle). The readings were in German (not Latin), communion was taken by everyone (not just priests), and

hymns were sung by the congregation—actually quite radical at the time.

At the front of the church, the **baptismal font** is where Luther's own children were baptized. Notice the tube extending from the basin directly down toward the ground. This allowed water, after having washed away sin, to be drained directly into what was a sandy floor, so it could be transmitted, unimpeded, to hell. Around the lower legs of the font, notice the many demons attempting to reach the baby being baptized up top—but their progress is blocked by the righteous saints.

The focal point of the church is the colorful, engaging, almost whimsical **altar painting** by Lucas Cranach the Elder, the Younger, and their school (completed in 1547, the year after Luther died).

The gang's all here: All the big-name early Protestants and their buddies have showed up to reenact classic ecclesiastical scenes. In the spirit of the Reformation, these aren't saints or royals—they're just people.

The bottom panel shows Martin Luther preaching from a pulpit, one hand on the Bible and the other pointing to Christ, as he engages an enthralled group of worshippers. The fluttering loincloth of Jesus helps to convey the message from preacher to parishioner. But notice that, true to life, some of those people aren't paying attention—they're chatting and looking around. The woman watching Luther most intently is his wife, Katharina. She's surrounded by their many children. Cranach (with the big white beard) is in the back.

The panel on the left shows Philipp Melanchthon (who was not a priest) baptizing a baby. The early reformers believed that lay people—not exclusively priests—could perform baptisms. In the foreground, the extravagantly dressed woman with her back to us is Cranach's wife, Barbara. Supposedly, she grew frustrated that her husband was always painting Luther, Katharina, and others, but never her. "Fine," he said. "I'll include you in the altarpiece."

On the right panel, Johannes Bugenhagen (among reformers, he ranks third after Luther and Melanchthon) is hearing confession from two very different people. Over the head of the obviously distraught and repentant man on the left, Bugenhagen holds the key of heaven—the sinner has done right by confessing and will reap eternal rewards. The man on the right, however, is trying to buy his way into heaven—but his hands are tied and the key of heaven is behind him, indicating he can't purchase paradise.

The central panel features the Last Supper, with the reformers standing in for the apostles. Notice the round table, which symbolizes how, in Protestantism, all are equal. People from all walks of life are actively engaging each other. It's easy to pick out Judas in the foreground (he wears yellow, as evildoers often do in Cranach paintings). On the opposite side of the table, Martin Luther (clad in black, wearing the bearded disguise of Junker Jörg) is being handed a chalice by Lucas Cranach the Younger. In contrast to Catholic worship at the time, Protestant services invited everybody to participate in communion.

Circle behind the painting and look at the lower panel, which appears as though it's been defaced by some no-good teenagers. It was...centuries ago. Around Luther's time, students of theology came here at the end of their studies and scratched their names or initials into the painting: on the left, in the river of knowledge, if they'd done well—or on the right, in hell, if they'd flunked. Looking carefully among the damned (higher up, on a skull), you can find the name "Johannes Luther"—Martin's son. (Thankfully, he had more success after he switched to law.)

The zone behind the altar has several interesting paintings. Most important is a painting labeled *Epitaph for Paul Eber and his Family* (better known as *The Vineyard of the Lord*), by Lucas Cranach the Younger. This work's propaganda-for-the-Reformation motives are obvious: On the right, the reformers tend to the garden of the Lord (that's Martin Luther raking and Philipp Melanchthon pulling water from the well—just as the reformers went back to the original source to translate their Bible). On the left, the pope and his cronies (in their excessively opulent robes) trash all their hard work. In the lower-left corner, everyone lines up to receive their reward from Jesus. The pope (wearing yellow, again symbolizing evil) has already received

his, but keeps his hand outstretched, expecting more than his share. In the lower right, the reformers (in their simple black robes) pray reverently.

As you head back up the nave to exit, look up: The grand **organ** dates from the communist period (1983), and booms out short organ concerts in summer. Luther's greatest musical hit, "A Mighty Fortress is Our God," was first sung here.

Exiting the way you came in, turn left and go to the back

corner of the church. Look up at the bottom of the roofline to find the relief of a pig, called the **Judensau** ("Jewish sow"). This bit

of medieval anti-Semitic propaganda was designed to intimidate Wittenberg's Jews, who lived in the area just behind the church. Look carefully at the pig, which is considered unclean in the Jewish faith: Jewish children are suckling from it, and a rabbi seems to be peering inquisitively into its rear end. When restoring the church, church authorities asked the Jewish community in Berlin what they should do with this painful remnant of a less-enlightened time. Rather than cover it, they suggested leaving it here as a part of the town's heritage, and adding a modern monument: Look for the plaque in the cobbles directly below the pig, where four paving stones look as if they're being pried apart by something bubbling up from beneath. The message: You can't hide uncomfortable facts; they will find a way to see the light of day. The adjacent cedar tree was donated by students in Tel Aviv.

Behind you, go through the gap between the buildings near the pig to see one of Wittenberg's 16th-century **fountains.** Part of Frederick the Wise's improvements, this network of fountains (with wooden pipes) still works—but nobody knows quite how.

▲▲Luther House (Lutherhaus)

Luther's former home has been converted into an excellent mu-

seum displaying original paintings, manuscripts, and other Luther-era items—including the pulpit from which Luther preached, famous portraits of Luther and the other reformers by Lucas Cranach, and Luther's original New Testament and Bible translations into High German. Everything is fully described, and touch-screen stations provide more depth.

Cost and Hours: €8, €10 combo-ticket with Melanchthon House; daily 10:00-18:00; Nov-March Tue-Sun 10:00-17:00, closed Mon; Collegienstrasse 54, +49 3491 420 3171, www.martinluther.de.

Visiting the House: From the street, step through the passage (at #59) into the inner courtyard to see the giant, turreted

building. Not really a "house," this was originally a monastery. Luther lived here first as a monk and again later, after he had married Katharina von Bora (the building was a wedding gift from a prince elector who took Luther under his wing). Katharina rented out rooms to students, and kept the family fed and watered by cultivating a garden, brewing beer, and even breeding cattle. In the middle of the courtyard is a **statue of Katharina.** Erected on her 500th birthday in 1999, the sculpture symbolizes her leaving her former life at a nunnery and beginning a new one with Martin Luther.

Head inside through the gateway on your right. From the ticket desk, go straight into the first room to see a simplified model of Wittenberg during Luther's time; paintings by Lucas Cranach (including a portrait of Frederick the Wise, the prince elector who supported Luther); and a woodcut print of a knights' tournament at Market Square.

The next room juxtaposes several **historic items.** Flanking the door are an indulgence chest and an original letter of indulgence *(Ablassurkunde),* from 1492. Those who bought indulgences would supposedly be rescued from their sins...while generating substantial income for the Catholic Church. Money raised was applied directly to an ambitious building project at the Vatican: On the right, see the engraving of St. Peter's Basilica, with its spectacular dome still under construction. Albrecht of Brandenburg (as the archbishop of Mainz, he was Luther's direct superior) and Pope Leo X (both pictured at right), stunningly influential and wealthy, were part of a finely tuned business of selling forgiveness to

mostly illiterate Christians frightened they'd spend eons in purgatory...or worse.

In contrast to the opulence in Roman Catholic churches, see Martin Luther's original lindenwood **pulpit** from the Town Church of St. Mary. Notice how relatively humble it is—imagine him climbing up to the top and bringing the Reformation message

Luther's Legacy

It'd be difficult to overstate the impact Luther and the Protestant Reformation he led had on European history.

Even during Luther's lifetime, the Reformation raged across northern Europe. In Holland, Protestant extremists marched into Catholic churches, lopped off the heads of holy statues, stripped gold-leaf angels from the walls, and shattered stained-glass windows in a fit of anti-Catholic iconoclasm. Switzerland—with its deep roots in democracy and self-rule—was a haven for free thinkers, led by Ulrich Zwingli (1484-1531) and the exiled Frenchman John Calvin (1509-1564), who established a theocratic government and inspired French followers called Huguenots. When England's charismatic King Henry VIII (r. 1509-1547) was excommunicated for divorcing Catherine of Aragon so he could marry Anne Boleyn, Henry "divorced" England from the Catholic Church, established the Church of England (or "Anglican Church") and "dissolved" (destroyed) England's many countryside abbeys.

The Vatican responded to these Protestant revolutions with the Counter-Reformation, which was an attempt to put the universal Catholic Church back together using a carrot-and-stick approach. On the one hand, the Church worked diligently to eliminate corruption from within, reach out to alienated members, do missionary work, and inspire the faithful with exalted Church art. This "Counter-Reformation" art, Baroque and bubbly, gave worshippers a glimpse of the heaven that awaited those who remained faithful. On the other hand, when need be, the Church resorted to propaganda, intimidation, and outright force—as doled out by the dreaded Inquisition.

The Reformation spawned a century of Catholic-versus-Protestant wars, with each side convinced that God favored them. When these wars finally ended, Western civilization realized what it should have known from the start: Catholics and Protestants would have to live together. The Peace of Westphalia (1648) decreed that the leader of each country would decide the religion of his nation. Ultimately this divided Europe in half: the generally Protestant north (Scandinavia, the Low Countries, northern Germany, and England), and the predominantly Catholic south (Spain, Portugal, Italy, and southern Germany).

It's clear that Luther's legacy lives on. If you are a Lutheran, Presbyterian, Methodist, Baptist, Episcopalian—or any one of a number of other Protestant faiths—you're the spiritual descendant of this German monk.

to a packed church. Nearby is the first printed version of Luther's troublemaking 95 Theses.

Continue into the **refectory,** where students would sit around a long table to dine. At the far end of this great hall is Cranach's wonderful painting *The Ten Commandments* (1516). This was originally designed for the Town Hall so that anybody could see it; and today, as then, it's handy for a review of Sunday school lessons. See if you can identify each of the 10 commandments being broken (and followed)— and note that the same noble-man (in yellow and black) is responsible for half the sins. In each panel, an eerie-eyed demon prods the sinners.

In a side passage near the refectory, you can peruse a small but endearing exhibit with wood-carved figures acting out daily life in Luther's time.

Up on the **first floor** is a rare painting of a relatively young Martin Luther by Cranach (1520). In the little dimly lit alcove, find the Cranach-printed first edition (1522) of Luther's German translation of the New Testament, illustrated with Cranach woodcuts. Nearby is the "community chest," the first systematized charity for poor people—Protestants began steering donations to the needy rather than into Church coffers. (Compare this to the Church's indulgence chest we saw earlier.)

Pass through a lecture hall dominated by a fancy gilded lectern into the actual private **residence** of the Luther family (which still smells like the 16th century). Look for his-and-hers Cranach paintings of Martin and Katharina, three years after their wedding. Imagine the lifestyle of these newlyweds—he a former monk and priest, she a former nun. While the idealistic Luther took little or no payment for preaching and writing, and depended on the charity of wealthy local supporters, Katharina was a businesswoman who balanced the books and kept this huge household going. Look for the lockbox they used to protect their valuables. Katharina kept the key so Luther wouldn't give everything they owned to the poor.

The centerpiece is the "Lutherstube"—the room with benches, a stove, and the table where Luther engaged in spirited conversations with his colleagues. Notice the names scratched into the ceiling, left behind by visiting VIPs (on the door, protected by glass, is the John Hancock of Russian Czar Peter the Great). Luther's adjoining study contains a collection of his beer mugs (Luther loved his suds).

DAY TRIPS

In the final room, see Luther's translation of the complete Bible from 1534, printed and illustrated by Cranach with 266 woodcuts, and a tiny hymnal from 1533. Luther, who believed that music should be an important part of worship, composed hymns that are still sung today.

An adjacent room features an old printing press and cases filled with booklets that Luther authored and Cranach illustrated. In this room you can find (on the wall) an etching of "the pope as Satan," a case full of anti-Jewish-themed books Luther wrote late in his life, and covers with more of Cranach's political cartoon etchings—designed so even the illiterate could get the gist of Luther's message. Perhaps the first PR genius to "go viral," Luther sold more than a quarter million books and was the best-selling German author of the 16th century.

Now climb the stairs to the **top floor,** which features a small treasury filled with 16th-century documents (including a small printed indulgence from 1515 with empty blanks for the purchaser to fill in, and a big indulgence from 1492 worth 100 fewer days in purgatory). This exhibit finishes with an intriguing exhibit of images showing how Luther has been represented in the centuries after his death. At the very end, check out Luther posters from Hitler's time and from communist days (including the 1982 East German illustration showing Luther conversing at a table with Che Guevara and other revolutionaries). The East German government decided that it was OK to tell Luther's story—as long as it was linked to the ideals of socialist revolution.

Luther Sights near Luther House

Several other Reformation sights cluster along Collegienstrasse, at the Luther House end of town:

Leaving the Luther House, turn right down Collegienstrasse with your back toward the town center (toward the ring road). At the big roundabout (see map), at the edge of the park on the left, is the famous **"Luther Oak" tree** marking the spot where Luther burned the papal bull that threatened him with excommunication.

About a block toward Market Square from the Luther House are two other buildings of interest to Lutherans. At #60 (with the rounded gables) is the **Melanchthon House** (Melanchthonhaus)— given to Philipp Melanchthon to persuade him to stay in Wittenberg when he threatened to move elsewhere, and now a museum about his life. Nothing survives from Melanchthon's household, but the museum tries hard to bring him to life, and everything is described in English (€5, €10 combo-ticket with Luther House; daily 10:00-18:00; Nov-March Tue-Sun until 17:00, closed Mon; +49 3491 420 3110).

At #62a, duck through the doorway into the **university court-**

DAY TRIPS

yard. These are some of the original buildings where Luther, Melanchthon, and their colleagues worked. Wall plaques ringing the courtyard celebrate famous professors and alumni.

▲Wittenberg 360 Panorama: Luther 1517

Berlin artist Yadegar Asisi—who has created these immersive, 360-degree panorama paintings around eastern Germany—has arrived in Wittenberg. A giant bunker-like structure in a park near the Luther House is home to this nearly 12,000-square-foot work that wraps entirely around the viewer. Using a combination of photographed models and digitally reconstructed historic buildings, Asisi recreates a day in the life of the grubby, crowded, and colorful town on the cusp of the Reformation—standing right in front of the Castle Church. Light and sound effects highlight different parts of the giant illustration, inviting you to tune into various details (pick up the leaflet, which explains some of the tableaus you'll see). You can climb up the metal tower in the middle of the room for a higher vantage point. Panorama paintings like this one were all the rage in the 19th century, and Asisi does a good job of updating the magic for the modern era. While certainly overpriced, this could be worth the splurge to round out your Luther experience.

Cost and Hours: €11, daily 9:00-18:00, Lutherstrasse 42, www.wittenberg360.de.

Luther Garden

This orchard of ecumenism, a short walk just south of Market Square, is a leafy statement that Christian communities—Protestant, Catholic, and Orthodox—can cooperate. Hundreds of trees from many Christian communities from all over the world have been planted, and each has a sister tree planted in its community of origin.

OTHER WITTENBERG SIGHTS
▲House of History (Haus der Geschichte)

Those intrigued by the communist chapter of Wittenberg's history will enjoy this museum's three floors of everyday items from East German times (1949-1989). For Cold War buffs, it's worth ▲▲. The *Wende* (German reunification) in 1989 erased an entire culture, and in the space of a few years East German toys, food brands, cars, schoolbooks, and much more were replaced by Western ones—awakening nostalgia even in those who otherwise welcomed the end of communism. Over the past two decades, a dedicated staff has collected thousands of items that memorialize the world of their youth. The museum also includes a few rooms showing furnishings and fashions from the 1920s and 1930s. On the ground floor, you'll find a fully stocked communist-era grocery store, a cozy DDR pub, and an exhibit (German only) on the life of Soviet troops posted to East Germany. The museum is directed at nostalgic German visitors, but the €1 audioguide makes it more meaningful to tourists.

Cost and Hours: €6, daily 10:00-18:00; Nov-Feb Tue-Sun until 17:00, closed Mon; Schlossstrasse 6, +49 3491 409 004, www.pflug-ev.de.

Historical Town Information Center (Historisches Stadtinformation)

This slick new facility—in two buildings facing Arsenalplatz, a couple of blocks north of Marktplatz—illustrates the history of Wittenberg beyond the life of its most famous resident. The Zeughaus (former armory) displays a large model of Wittenberg in 1873, offering a good look at its earthen ramparts and moat. Across the square—displayed in the enclosed ruins of the Klosterkirche (former Franciscan monastery)—are exhibits on the Ascanian dukes of Saxony, who ruled this area before Luther. (This building adjoins the Stadthaus, with a branch TI, a concert hall, and a free WC.) While presented with modern flair, there's only so much to say—making this, mostly, a "so what?" experience.

Cost and Hours: €2; daily 9:00-18:00; Nov-March Tue-Sun 10:00-17:00, closed Mon; Zeughaus at Juristenstrasse 16a, Klosterkirche at Mauerstrasse 18.

Hundertwasserschule

This formerly drab communist-era public school, on the northeast outskirts of town, was redecorated in 1993 with wildly colorful and imaginative flair by Austrian architect Friedensreich Hundertwasser. Most intriguing to architecture buffs, it's a long 30-minute walk from the city center (interior closed to the public but exterior viewable anytime, officially called "Luther-Melanchthon-Gymnasium," Schillerstrasse 22a, www.hundertwasserschule.de).

Cruises and Biking the Elbe River Valley

While you can pay to take a brief cruise on the Elbe River, there's not much to see other than a panoramic view of town (details at TI). The Elbe Valley also attracts many bicycle tourists, following the bike path called the Elberadweg (cycling route info at www.elberadweg.de).

DAY TRIPS

Sleeping in Wittenberg

Wittenberg has a wide range of charming hotels at fine prices. My listings (except Am Alten Anker) are right in the heart of the Old Town. Air-conditioning is rare.

$$$ Hotel Best Western Stadtpalais Wittenberg is a professional-feeling place with 78 rooms offering predictable business-class comfort right on the main drag, near the Luther House (some rooms have air-con, elevator, pay parking, Collegienstrasse 56, +49 3491 4250, www.stadtpalais.bestwestern.de, info@stadtpalais. bestwestern.de).

$$ Ringhotel Schwarzer Baer ("Black Bear") has 32 modern, comfortable rooms—each a bit different, but all of them stylish—in a period building with hardwood floors right off Market Square (elevator, free parking, Schlossstrasse 2, +49 3491 420 4344, http://schwarzer-baer-wittenberg.de, info@schwarzer-baer-wittenberg.de).

$$ Alte Canzley, right next to the TI and across from the Castle Church, has nine enormous, well-equipped (if somewhat dated) rooms above a restaurant in a historic building from 1391. You'll pay extra for a small kitchenette or a view of the Castle Church (elevator, free parking, Schlossplatz 3, +49 3491 429 110, www.alte-canzley.com, info@alte-canzley.de).

$$ Hotel Brauhaus, a lesser value, rents 34 straightforward rooms over a restaurant and antique shop fronting Market Square (lots of stairs, no elevator, free parking, Markt 7, +49 3491 443 3130, www.brauhaus-wittenberg.de, info@brauhaus-wittenberg. de).

$ Am Alten Anker, above a restaurant in a drab area at the far end of town (about a 15-minute walk beyond the TI, or a 30-minute walk or quick taxi ride from the train station), has 20 basic but comfortable rooms at a reasonable price (Dessauer Strasse 286, +49 3491 768 760, www.amaltenanker.de, info@amaltenanker.de).

¢ Lutherstadt Wittenberg Youth Hostel, an official HI hostel, has 160 beds in 3- to 6-bed dorms, each with its own bath. This modern hostel is perfectly located, filling a sleek building by the Castle Church (private rooms available, elevator, pay Wi-Fi, lots of school groups, doors close at 22:00, lunch or dinner available, tucked behind Castle Church at Schlossstrasse 14, +49 3491 505 205, www.jugendherberge-wittenberg.de, wittenberg@ jugendherberge.de).

Eating in Wittenberg

You'll find a fun variety of good, affordable restaurants within a couple blocks of Market Square.

$$ Brauhaus Wittenberg serves up traditional meals and great local beer in a fun-loving beer garden that feels closer to Bavaria than to Saxony. From Mar-

ket Square, you'll enter the classic old courtyard filled with jovial tables; at the end, go inside to find comfortable seating on two levels, surrounding big copper vats where they brew their own "Wittenberger Original" pilsner. The menu includes big portions of tasty German standards (daily 11:00-22:30, Markt 6, +49 3491 433 130).

$$ Das Wittenberger Kartof-felhaus serves up hearty, heavy skillets piled high with potatoes, potatoes, potatoes, prepared in fun and creative ways. The interior is cozy and brimming with kitschy decor, and the outdoor seating is on the relaxing pedestrian drag, just off Market Square (Schlossstrasse 2, daily 11:00-22:00, +49 3491 411 200).

$$ Trattoria Toscana is a popular choice for Italian meals. Tucked in a "Little Italy" corner of town behind the Town Church of St. Mary, it has a fancy interior, romantic piazza seating, and down-to-earth prices (kid-friendly, daily 11:00-24:00, Mittelstrasse 1, +49 3491 433 188).

$ Hanami, a family-run spot with a classy dining room, specializes in Vietnamese cooking and sushi. Like many Asian restaurants in eastern Germany, the Vietnam connection dates back to the communist days (cash only, usually daily 11:00-15:00 & 17:00-21:00, Schlossstrasse 8, +49 3491 459 7068).

$ Reinsdorfer is good for a quick lunch on the go—there's a bakery on one side of the shop (sandwiches made to order) and a butcher's counter on the other (grilled sausages and prepared side dishes sold from the counter's back end, take out or eat at simple tables, Mon-Fri 8:00-18:00, Sat until 12:00, closed Sun, Markt 6).

$ Super Döner serves up super *döner kebabs* to go from a hardworking little hole-in-the-wall just off Market Square at Collegienstrasse 86 (Mon-Sat 10:30-19:00, closed Sun).

DAY TRIPS

Wittenberg Connections

From Wittenberg by Train to: Berlin (hourly on ICE, 40 minutes; also every 2 hours on slower regional train, 1.5 hours), **Leipzig** (6/day on ICE, 40 minutes; also hourly on regional trains, 1 hour, some with transfer in Bitterfeld), **Erfurt** (every 2 hours, 1.5 hours direct, more with transfer in Leipzig), **Eisenach** and Wartburg Castle (at least hourly, 2.5 hours, transfer in Erfurt or Leipzig), **Dresden** (1-2/hour, 2-3 hours, transfer in Leipzig and sometimes also Bitterfeld), **Frankfurt** (every 2 hours, 4 hours, transfer in Naumburg), **Hamburg** (nearly hourly direct on ICE, 3 hours; also possible about hourly with transfer in Berlin, 3.5 hours), and **Nürnberg** (every 2 hours direct on ICE, 4.5 hours). Train info: www.bahn.com.

DAY TRIPS

GERMANY: PAST & PRESENT

A united Germany has only existed since 1871, but the cultural heritage of the German-speaking people stretches back 2,000 years.

ROMANS (AD 1-500)

German history begins in AD 9, when Roman troops were ambushed and driven back by the German chief Arminius. For the

next 250 years, the Rhine and Danube rivers marked the border between civilized Roman Europe (to the southwest) and "barbarian" German lands (to the northeast). While the rest of Western Europe's future would be Roman, Christian, and Latin, most of Germany followed a separate, pagan path.

In AD 476, Rome fell to the Germanic chief Theodoric the Great (a.k.a. Dietrich of Bern). After that, Germanic Franks controlled northern Europe, ruling a mixed population of Romanized Christians and tree-worshipping pagans. Rome's imprint on Germany remains in place names like Cologne ("Colonia" was an important Roman city) and great monuments like Trier's Porta Nigra.

CHARLEMAGNE AND THE FRANKS (AD 500-1000)

For Christmas in AD 800, the pope gave Charlemagne the title of Holy Roman Emperor. Charlemagne, the king of the Franks, was the first of many German kings to be called *Kaiser* ("emperor," from "Caesar") over the next thousand years. Allied with the pope, Charlemagne ruled an empire that included Germany, Austria,

France, the Low Countries, and northern Italy.

Charlemagne (Karl der Grosse, or Charles the Great, r. 768-814) stood a head taller than his subjects, and his foot became a standard unit of measurement. The stuff of legend, Charlemagne had five wives and four concubines, producing descendants with names like Charles the Bald, Louis the Pious, and Henry the Quarrelsome. His eldest son, Pippin the Hunchback, led a failed coup against Charlemagne and was exiled to a monastery. When Charlemagne died of pneumonia (814), he lacked a clear heir. His united empire was divided into (what would become) Germany, France, and the lands in between (Treaty of Verdun, 843). As this treaty was signed not in Latin, but in the local languages, many mark 843 as the year Europe was born.

THE HOLY ROMAN EMPIRE (1000-1500)

Chaotic medieval Germany (about the size of Montana) was made up of more than 300 small, quarreling dukedoms ruled by the Holy Roman Emperor. The title was pretty bogus, implying that the German king ruled the same huge European empire as the ancient Romans. In fact, he was "Holy" because he was blessed by the pope, "Roman" to recall ancient grandeur, and the figurehead "Emperor" of what was an empire in name only.

Holy Roman Emperors had less hands-on power than other kings around Europe. Because of the custom of electing emperors by nobles and archbishops, rather than by bestowing the title through inheritance, they couldn't pass the crown from father to son. In addition, there were no empire-wide taxes and no national capital. This system gave nobles great power: Peasants had to huddle close to their local noble's castle for protection from attack by the noble next door.

When Emperor Henry IV (r. 1056-1106) tried to assert his power by appointing bishops, he was slapped down by the nobles, and forced to repent to the pope by standing barefoot in the alpine snow for three days at Canossa (in northern Italy, 1077). Ever since, the phrase "going to Canossa" has meant "to humble oneself."

Emperor Frederick I Barbarossa (1152-1190), blue-eyed and red-bearded (hence *barba rossa*), gained an international reputation as a valiant knight, gentleman, bon vivant, and lover of poetry and women. Still, his great victories were away in Italy and Asia (on the Third Crusade, where he drowned in a river), while back home nobles wielded the real power.

GERMAN HISTORY

Why We Call Deutschland "Germany"

Our English name "Germany" comes from the Latin *Germania,* the Roman name for the lands north of the Alps where "barbarian" tribes lived. The French and Spanish call it *Allemagne* and *Alemania,* respectively, after the Alemanni tribe. Italians call the country *Germania,* but in Italy the German language is known as *tedesco.* The Slavic peoples of Eastern Europe have a perhaps simpler approach, calling Germany *Německo* (Czech), *Niemcy* (Polish), and other variations of a word that basically means "people who can't speak right." The Hungarians borrowed this word from the Slavs and call anything German *német.*

To Germans, their country is *Deutschland,* their language is *Deutsch,* and they themselves are *Deutsche.* A few hundred years ago, this word was spelled *Teutsch* (later, the "t" changed to a "d"). The English word Teutonic, the Italian *tedesco,* and the Scandinavian *tysk* all come from this earlier form. *Alles klar?*

This was the era of Germany's troubadours *(Meistersinger),* who traveled from castle to castle singing love songs *(Minnesang)* and telling the epic tales of chivalrous knights (Tristan and Isolde, Parsifal, and the Nibelungen) that would later inspire German nationalism and Wagnerian operas.

While France, England, and Spain were centralizing power around a single ruling family to create nation-states, Germany lagged behind as a decentralized, backward, feudal battleground. It would remain so until the 19th century (and neighboring European powers preferred it that way).

MEDIEVAL GROWTH

Nevertheless, Germany was strategically located at the center of Europe, and trading towns prospered. Berlin was born when inhabitants of the region of Brandenburg settled on a marshy island in the Spree River. Several northern towns (especially Hamburg and Lübeck) banded together into the Hanseatic League, promoting open trade around the Baltic Sea. To curry favor at election time, emperors granted powers and privileges to certain towns, which were designated "free imperial cities." Some towns, such as Cologne, Mainz, Dresden, and Trier, held higher status than many nobles, as hosts of one of the seven "electors" of the emperor. To this day, every German town keeps careful track of whether it was "free" during the Middle Ages—or answered to a duke, king, archbishop, or elector in another place.

Textiles, mining, and the colonization of lands to the

The History of Berlin

Berlin was a humble, marshy burg until prince electors from the Hohenzollern dynasty made it their capital in the mid-15th century. Gradually their territory spread and strengthened, becoming the powerful Kingdom of Prussia in 1701. As the leading city of Prussia, Berlin dominated the northern Germanic world—both militarily and culturally—long before there was a united "Germany."

Thanks largely to Frederick the Great (1712-1786), the enlightened despot who was both a ruthless military tactician and a cultured lover of the arts, Prussia was well positioned to lead the German unification movement in the 19th century. And when Germany became a unified modern nation in 1871, Berlin was its natural capital. The city boomed with Germany's industrialization, quadrupling its population over the next 40 years. After Germany's humiliating defeat in World War I, Berlin thrived as an anything-goes cultural capital of the Roaring Twenties. During World War II, the city was Hitler's headquarters—and the place where the Führer drew his final breath.

When the Soviet Army reached Berlin in 1945, the protracted fighting left the city in ruins. Berlin was divided by the victorious Allied powers—the American, British, and French sectors became West Berlin, and the Soviet sector, East Berlin. The city became the main battlefield of the nascent Cold War. In 1948, the Soviets tried to starve the 2.2 million residents of the western half in an almost medieval-style siege, which was broken by the Allies' Berlin Airlift. Later, with the overnight construction of the Berlin Wall in 1961, an Iron (or, at least, concrete) Curtain completely encircled West Berlin—cutting Berlin in half. While East Berliners lived through difficult times, West Berlin became a magnet for artists, punks, squatters, and free spirits.

Finally, on November 9, 1989, the Wall came down. After wild celebrations, Berlin faced a fitful transition to reunification. Two cities—and countries—became one at a staggering pace. Some "Ossies" (impolite slang for Easterners) missed their security. Some "Wessies" missed military deferrals, subsidized rent, and tax breaks for living in an isolated city surrounded by the communist world.

Today, going on 30 years later, the old East-West divisions are a distant memory. Berlin's local government has been eager to charge forward, with little nostalgia for the past. Big corporations and the national government have moved in, and the dreary swath of land that was the Wall has been transformed. Berlin is a new city—ready to welcome visitors.

east made German states relatively wealthy and enabled the growth of a thriving middle class. In towns, middle-class folks (burghers), not aristocrats, began running things. In about 1450, Johann Gutenberg of Mainz figured out how to use moveable type for printing, an innovation that would allow the export of a new commodity: ideas. Around this time, Berlin came under the rule of the powerful Hohenzollern family, who began a palace complex on what is now that city's "Museum Island." The Hohen-

zollern's influence soon spread throughout northern Germany (Prussia).

RELIGIOUS STRUGGLES AND THE THIRTY YEARS' WAR (1500-1700)

Martin Luther—German monk, fiery orator, and religious whistle-blower—sparked a century of European wars by speaking out

against the Catholic Church. Luther's protests ("Protestantism") threw Germany into a century of turmoil, as each local prince took sides between Catholics and Protestants. In the 1525 Peasant Revolt, peasants attacked their feudal masters with hoes and pitchforks, fighting for more food, political say-so, and respect. The revolt was brutally put down.

The Holy Roman Emperor, Charles V (r. 1519-1556), sided with the pope. Charles was the most powerful man in Europe, having inherited an empire that included Germany and Austria, plus the Low Countries, much of Italy, Spain, and Spain's New World possessions. But many local German nobles took the opportunity to go Protestant—some for religious reasons, but also as an excuse to seize Church assets and powers.

The 1555 Peace of Augsburg allowed each local noble to decide the religion of his realm. In general, the northern and eastern lands became Protestant, while the south (today's Bavaria, along with Austria) and west remained Catholic.

Unresolved religious and political differences eventually expanded into the Thirty Years' War (1618-1648). This Europe-wide war, fought mainly on German soil, involved Denmark, Sweden,

GERMAN HISTORY

1000 Years — Each dashed line = 500 years — Each dashed line = 100 years — Each dashed

| 1000 | 0 | 500 | 1000 | 1100 | 1200 | 1300 | 1400 | 1500 | 1600 |

Jesus

Charlemagne

BLACK DEATH

CELTS

Constantine

Barbarossa

Luther

ROMAN

TREATY OF VERDUN

HRE ruled by Habsburgs from 1438 until it ends in 1806

Julius Caesar

FRANKS

30 YEARS WAR

DIET OF WORMS

HOLY ROMAN EMPIRE

ROMANS COLONIZE, BUILD BATHS, PLANT VINES

HENRY IV IN CANOSSA

RELIGIOUS

LUTHER'S 95 THESES

PEACE OF AUGSBURG

HISTORY

GUTENBERG BIBLE

PEASANTS REVOLT

COUNCIL OF TRENT

SACK OF ROME

CRUSADES

BARBARIANS

Attila

WITTELSBACH DYNASTY BEGINS

BAVARIA UNITED

BEER PURITY LAW

←To Neanderthal Era

DUCHY ESTABLISHED

BAVARIA

Nefertiti (Berlin)

MUNICH FOUNDED

HOHENZOLLERN RULE BEGINS

UNIFIED

EGYPT

PRINCIPALITY

BRANDENBURG-

GREECE

BERLIN FOUNDED

HABSBURG

Pergamon Altar (Berlin)

OTHER EMPIRES & EVENTS

Max. I Charles V

HANSEATIC LEAGUE

CELTIC

Cologne Founded

Palatine Chapel Aachen

Altdorfer

ROMAN

Grünewald

Porta Nigra

DARK

Riemenschneider

Trier Basilica

ROMANESQUE

Freiburg Cathedral

Holy Blood Altar Rothenburg

GOTHIC

Cologne Cathedral

RENAISSANCE

ARTS & ARCHITECTURE

Dürer

Cranach

Holbein

St. Michael's Munich

Wartburg

CASTLES

Marksburg

Rheinfels

Burg Eltz finished

MANY CASTLES BUILT ALONG RHINE & MOSEL

| 1000 | 0 | 500 | 1000 | 1100 | 1200 | 1300 | 1400 | 1500 | 1600 |

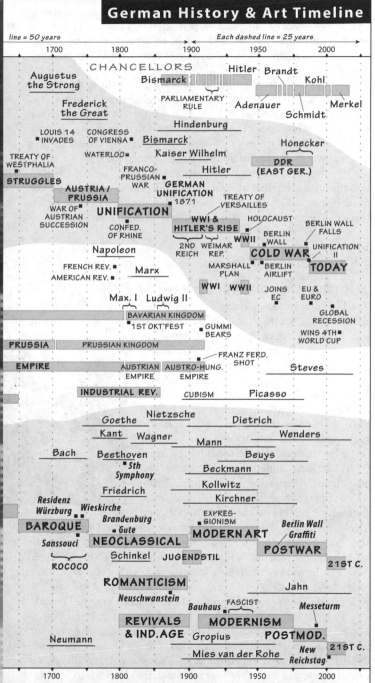

German History & Art Timeline

line = 50 years · Each dashed line = 25 years

1700 · 1800 · 1900 · 1950 · 2000

CHANCELLORS

Augustus the Strong · Bismarck · Hitler · Brandt · Kohl

Frederick the Great · PARLIAMENTARY RULE · Adenauer · Schmidt · Merkel

Hindenburg

LOUIS 14 INVADES · CONGRESS OF VIENNA · Bismarck

TREATY OF WESTPHALIA · WATERLOO · Kaiser Wilhelm · Honecker

STRUGGLES · FRANCO-PRUSSIAN WAR · Hitler · DDR (EAST GER.)

AUSTRIA / PRUSSIA · GERMAN UNIFICATION 1871 · TREATY OF VERSAILLES

WAR OF AUSTRIAN SUCCESSION · UNIFICATION · CONFED. OF RHINE · WWI & HITLER'S RISE · HOLOCAUST · BERLIN WALL FALLS

2ND REICH · WEIMAR REP. · WWII · BERLIN WALL · UNIFICATION II

Napoleon · COLD WAR

FRENCH REV. · Marx · MARSHALL PLAN · BERLIN AIRLIFT · TODAY

AMERICAN REV. · WWI · WWII · JOINS EC · EU & EURO

Max. I · Ludwig II · GLOBAL RECESSION

BAVARIAN KINGDOM · 1ST OKT'FEST · GUMMI BEARS · WINS 4TH WORLD CUP

PRUSSIA · PRUSSIAN KINGDOM · FRANZ FERD. SHOT

EMPIRE · AUSTRIAN EMPIRE · AUSTRO-HUNG. EMPIRE · Steves

INDUSTRIAL REV. · CUBISM · Picasso

Goethe · Nietzsche · Dietrich

Kant · Wagner · Mann · Wenders

Bach · Beethoven · Beuys

5th Symphony · Beckmann

Kollwitz

Friedrich · Kirchner

Residenz Würzburg · Wieskirche · EXPRES-SIONISM

BAROQUE · Brandenburg · Gute · MODERN ART · Berlin Wall Graffiti

Sanssouci · NEOCLASSICAL · POSTWAR

Schinkel · JUGENDSTIL · 21ST C.

ROCOCO

ROMANTICISM · Jahn

Neuschwanstein · Bauhaus · FASCIST · Messeturm

REVIVALS & IND. AGE · MODERNISM · POSTMOD.

Neumann · Gropius · New Reichstag · 21ST C.

Mies van der Rohe

1700 · 1800 · 1900 · 1950 · 2000

GERMAN HISTORY

France, and Bohemia (in today's Czech Republic), among others. It was one of history's bloodiest wars, fueled by religious extremism and political opportunism, and fought by armies of brutal mercenaries who worked on commission and were paid in loot and pillage.

By the war's end (Treaty of Westphalia, 1648), a third of all Germans had died, France was the rising European power, and the Holy Roman Empire was a medieval mess of scattered feudal states. In 1689, France's Louis XIV swept down the Rhine, gutting and leveling its once-great castles, and Germany ceased to be a major player in European politics until the modern era.

(For an entertaining one-hour education on Luther, the Reformation, and the wars of religion, see my public-television special produced in 2017 to celebrate the 500th anniversary of the Reformation. You can stream it on YouTube or at RickSteves.com.)

Sights
• Luther sights in Wittenberg

AUSTRIA AND PRUSSIA (1700s)
The German-speaking lands now consisted of three "Germanys": Austria in the south, Prussia in the north, and the rest in between.

Prussia—originally a largely Slavic region colonized by celibate ex-Crusaders called Teutonic Knights—was forged into a unified state by two strong kings. Frederick I (the "King Sergeant," r. 1701-1713) built a modern state around a highly disciplined army, a centralized government (with Berlin as its capital), and national pride.

His grandson, Frederick II "The Great" (r. 1740-1786), added French culture and worldliness, preparing militaristic Prussia to enter the world stage. A well-read, flute-playing lover of the arts and liberal ideals, Frederick also ruled with an iron fist—the very model of the "enlightened despot." Meanwhile, Austria thrived under the more laid-back rule of the Habsburg family. The Habsburgs gained power in Europe by marrying into it. They acquired the Netherlands, Spain, and Bohemia that way (a strategy that didn't work so well for Marie-Antoinette, who wed the doomed king of France).

In the 1700s, the Germanic lands became a cultural powerhouse, producing musicians (Bach, Haydn, Mozart, Beethoven), writers (Goethe, Schiller), and thinkers (Kant, Leibniz). Sophisticated Berlin became the epicenter of Prussian culture. But politically, fragmented Germany was no match for the modern powers.

After the French Revolution (1789), Napoleon swept through Germany with his armies, deposing feudal lords, emancipating Jews, confiscating church lands, and forcing the Holy Roman Emperor to hand over his crown (1806). After a thousand years, the Holy Roman Empire was dead.

Sights

- Frederick the Great's Bebelplatz (Berlin State Opera, St. Hedwig's Cathedral)
- Humboldt Forum on Museum Island
- Charlottenburg Palace
- Sanssouci and New Palace in Potsdam

GERMAN UNIFICATION (1800s)

Napoleon's invasion helped unify the German-speaking peoples by rallying them against a common foreign enemy. After Napoleon's defeat, the Congress of Vienna (1815), presided over by the Austrian Prince Metternich, realigned Europe's borders. The idea of unifying the three Germanic nations—Prussia, Austria, and the German Confederation, a loose collection of small states in between—began to grow. By mid-century, most German-speaking people favored forming a modern nation-state; the only question was whether the confederation would be under Prussian or Austrian dominance.

Economically, Germany was becoming increasingly efficient and modern, with a unified trade organization (1834), railroads (1835), mechanical-engineering prowess, and booming factories benefiting from a surplus of labor. Berlin was changing into a world-class city graced by Neoclassical buildings designed by architect Karl Friedrich Schinkel (including many of today's museums). By 1850, with its Unter den Linden boulevard and the Brandenburg Gate, Berlin rivaled Paris as Europe's most elegant promenade.

Energetic Prussia took the lead in unifying the country. Otto von Bismarck (served 1862-1890), the strong minister of Prussia's weak king, used cunning politics to engineer a unified Germany under Prussian dominance. First, he started a war with Austria, ensuring that any united Germany would be under Prussian control. (Austria remains a separate country to this day.) Next, Bismarck provoked a war with France (the Franco-Prussian War, 1870-1871), which united Prussia and the German Confederation against their common enemy, France.

Fueled by hysterical patriotism, German armies swept through France and, in the Hall of Mirrors at Versailles, crowned Prussia's Wilhelm I as Emperor (*Kaiser*) of a new German Empire, uniting Prussia and the German Confederation (but excluding Austria). Berlin was the obvious choice as the new imperial capital. This Sec-

Germany in the Early 1800s

ond Reich (1871-1918) featured elements of democracy (an elected *Reichstag*—parliament), offset by a strong military and an emperor with veto powers.

A united and resurgent Germany was suddenly flexing its muscles in European politics. Berlin's population boomed, prompting the construction of Prenzlauer Berg, Kreuzberg, and other outlying districts. With strong industry, war spoils, overseas colonies, and a large and disciplined military, Germany sought its rightful place at the global table.

Fueled by nationalistic fervor, patriotic *Volk* art flourished (Wagner's operas, Nietzsche's essays), reviving medieval German myths and Nordic gods. The rest of Europe saw Germany's rapid rise—and began arming themselves to the teeth. The old order was scrambled and peace was reliant upon a tenuous and confused web of bilateral treaties. In Berlin, the imposing Berlin Cathedral was built, announcing the über-nationalism of Kaiser Wilhelm II that would lead Europe into World War I.

Nazi Terminology

Many Nazi military terms are familiar to English speakers. "Nazi" is an abbreviation for *Nationalsozialismus* (National Socialism), Hitler's political party. Other terms you'll probably recognize are SS (short for *Schutzstaffel,* or "protective unit"), *Luftwaffe* (air force), and *Blitzkrieg* ("lightning war"). Nazis also devised the *Endlösung* ("final solution") for doing away with Jewish and other "undesirable" people, by interning and killing them in *Konzentrationslager* (KZ, concentration camps). The *Widerstand* (resistance) stood up against the Nazis. *Vergangenheitsbewaltigung* (coming to terms with the past) continues to be a major issue in Germany. Many concentration camps and other wartime symbols have been turned into *Gedenkstätte* (memorials). At a *Dokumentationzentrum* (documentation center), locals and visitors can learn about Nazi atrocities. The message of these sites is *Vergesst es nie—* "Never forget."

Sights
- Concert Hall on Gendarmenmarkt
- Neue Wache
- Museum Island
- Berlin Cathedral
- Prenzlauer Berg Walk

WORLD WAR I AND HITLER'S RISE (1914-1939)

When Archduke Franz Ferdinand, the heir to the Austro-Hungarian Empire, was assassinated in 1914, all of Europe took sides as the political squabble quickly escalated into World War I. Germany and Austria-Hungary attacked British and French troops in France, but were stalled at the Battle of the Marne. Both sides dug defensive trenches, then settled in for four brutal years of bloodshed, boredom, mud, machine-gun fire, disease, and mustard gas.

More than four years later, at 11:00 in the morning of November 11, 1918, the fighting finally ceased. Germany surrendered, signing the Treaty of Versailles in the Hall of Mirrors at Versailles. The war cost the defeated German nation 1.7 million men, precious territory, military rights, reparations money, and national pride.

A new democratic government called the Weimar Republic (1919) dutifully abided by the Treaty of Versailles, and tried to maintain order among Germany's many divided political parties. But after the humiliating defeat, the country was in ruins, its economy a shambles, and the war's victors demanded heavy reparations. Berlin attracted the disillusioned as the center of decadent cabaret nightlife—especially near today's Ku'damm and along Friedrich-

Germany During World War II
(1939-1945)

1939: Soldiers singing *"Muss i denn, Muss i denn zum Städtele hinaus"* ("Must I, must I leave my city") march off to war. On September 1, Germany invades Poland to seize the free city of Danzig (Gdańsk), sparking World War II. Germany, Italy, and Japan (the Axis) would eventually square off against the Allies—which included Britain, France, the United States, and the USSR.

1940: The Nazi Blitzkrieg (lightning war) quickly sweeps through Denmark, Norway, the Low Countries, and France; later it also conquers Yugoslavia and Greece. With fellow fascists ruling Italy (Mussolini), Spain (Franco), and Portugal (Salazar), the Continent is now dominated by fascists, creating a "fortress Europe."

1941: Hitler invades his former ally, the USSR. Bombastic victory parades in Berlin celebrate the triumph of the Aryan race over the lesser peoples of the world.

1942: Allied bombs begin falling on German cities. That autumn and winter, German families receive death notices from the horrific Battle of Stalingrad. The German army suffers around 850,000 casualties (by comparison, the US had roughly 214,000 casualties for the entire Vietnam War). Back home, Nazi officials begin their plan for the "final solution to the Jewish problem"—systematic execution of Europe's Jews in specially built death camps.

1943: Germany fights a two-front war: against tenacious Soviets on the bitter Eastern Front, and against Brits and Yanks advancing north through Italy on the Western Front. Germany's industrial output tries desperately to keep up with that of the Allies.

strasse. Elsewhere, communists rioted in the streets, fascists plotted coups, and inflation drove the price of a loaf of bread to a billion marks. War vets grumbled in their beer about how their leaders had sold them out. All Germans, regardless of their political affiliations, were fervently united in their apathy toward the new democracy. When the worldwide depression of 1929 hit Germany with brutal force, the nation was desperate for a strong leader with answers.

Adolf Hitler (1889-1945) was a disgruntled vet who had spent the post-World War I years homeless, wandering the streets of Vienna with sketchpad in hand, hoping to become an artist. In Munich, he joined other disaffected Germans to form the National Socialist

The average German suffers through shortages, rationing, and frequent trips to the bomb shelter.

1944: Hitler's no-surrender policy is increasingly unpopular, and he narrowly survives an assassination attempt by members of his own military. After the Allies reach France on D-Day, Germany counterattacks with a last-gasp offensive (the Battle of the Bulge) that slows but doesn't stop the Allies.

1945: Soviet soldiers approach Berlin from the east, and Americans and Brits advance from the west. Adolf Hitler commits suicide, and families lock up their daughters to protect them from rapacious Soviet soldiers. When Germany finally surrenders on May 8, the country is in ruins, occupied by several foreign powers, divided into occupation zones, and viewed by the world as an immoral monster.

War's Aftermath: German citizens are faced with the scope of the mass killings and atrocities committed by their leaders and accomplices. Over 11 million people have been systemically murdered—6 million Jews, as well as people with disabilities, homosexuals, prisoners of war, political dissidents, and ethnic minorities.

GERMAN HISTORY

German Workers' Party—the Nazis. In stirring speeches, Hitler promised to restore Germany to its rightful glory, blaming the country's current problems on communists, foreigners, and Jews. After an unsuccessful coup attempt (the Beer Hall Putsch in Munich, 1923), Hitler was sent to jail, where he wrote an influential book of his political ideas, titled *Mein Kampf (My Struggle)*.

By 1930, the Nazis—now wearing power suits and working within the system—had become a formidable political party in Germany's democracy. They won 38 percent of the seats in the Reichstag in 1932, and Hitler was appointed chancellor (1933). Two months later, the Reichstag building was mysteriously set on fire—an apparent act of terrorism with a September 11-sized impact—and a terrified Germany gave Chancellor Hitler sweeping powers to preserve national security.

Hitler wasted no time in using this Enabling Act to jail opponents, terrorize the citizenry, and organize every aspect of German life under the watchful eye of the Nazi Party. Plumbers' unions, choral societies, schoolteachers, church pastors, filmmakers, and artists all had to account to a Nazi Party official about how their work furthered the Third Reich.

For the next decade, an all-powerful Hitler revived Germany's economy, building the autobahns and rebuilding the military. Defying the Treaty of Versailles and world opinion, Hitler proceeded with his Four-Year Plan to re-arm Germany: He occupied the Saar region (1935) and the Rhineland (1936), annexed Austria and the Sudetenland (1938), and invaded Czechoslovakia (March 1939). The rest of Europe finally reached its appeasement limit—and World War II began—when Germany invaded Poland in September 1939. When the war was over (1945), countless millions were dead and most German cities had been bombed beyond recognition. The Third Reich was over.

(For a one-hour program on this topic, see my public television special "The Story of Fascism in Europe," produced in 2018. You can stream it on YouTube and at RickSteves.com.)

Sights

- Former Air Ministry
- Topography of Terror
- Site of Hitler's Bunker
- German Resistance Memorial
- Kaiser Wilhelm Memorial Church
- Sachsenhausen Memorial and Museum

TWO GERMANYS...AND REUNIFICATION (1945-2000)

After World War II, the Allies divided occupied Germany into two halves, split down the middle by an 855-mile border that Winston Churchill called an "Iron Curtain." By 1949, Germany was officially two separate countries. West Germany (the Federal Republic of Germany) was democratic and capitalist, allied with the powerful United States. East Germany (the German Democratic Republic, or DDR) was a communist state under Soviet control. The former capital, Berlin, sitting in East German

territory, was itself split into two parts, allowing a tiny pocket of Western life in the Soviet-controlled East. In 1961, the East German government erected a 12-foot-high concrete wall through the heart of Berlin—physically dividing the city in two, isolating West Berlin, and preventing East German citizens from fleeing to the West. Over the next decades, more than a hundred East Germans

would die or be arrested trying to cross that Wall. The Berlin Wall came to symbolize a divided Germany.

In West Germany, Chancellor Konrad Adenauer (who had suffered imprisonment under the Nazis) tried to restore Germany's good name, paying war reparations and joining international organizations of nations. Thanks to US aid from the Marshall Plan, West Germany was rebuilt, democracy was established, and its "economic miracle" quickly exceeded pre-WWII levels. Adenauer was eventually succeeded in 1969 by the US-friendly Willy Brandt.

Meanwhile, East Germany was a repressive communist state ruled with an iron fist by Walter Ulbricht (who had been exiled by the Nazis). In 1953, demonstrations and anti-government protests were brutally put down by Soviet—not German—troops. Erich Honecker (a kinder, gentler tyrant who had endured a decade of Nazi imprisonment) succeeded Ulbricht as ruler of the East in 1971.

Throughout the 1970s and 1980s, both the US and the Soviet Union used divided Germany as a military base. West Germans debated whether US missiles aimed at the Soviets should be placed in their country. Economically, West Germany just got stronger while East Germany stagnated.

As the Soviet Union collapsed, so did its client nation, East Germany. On November 9, 1989, East Germany unexpectedly opened the Berlin Wall. Astonished Germans from both sides climbed the Wall, hugged each other, shared bottles of beer, sang songs, and chiseled off souvenirs. At first, most Germans— West and East—simply looked forward to free travel and better relations between two distinct nations. But before the month was out, negotiations and elections to reunite the two Germanys had begun. October 3, 1990, was proclaimed German Unity Day, and Berlin reassumed its status as the German capital in 1991.

In the decade that followed, in reunified Berlin, Potsdamer Platz, formerly part of the Berlin Wall's "death strip," was redeveloped into a forest of skyscrapers. The glittering new dome atop the Reichstag—which had been damaged in World War II and sat unused for decades—formally opened, giving the German people a birds-eye view of their government at work. Formerly dilapidated neighborhoods (first Prenzlauer Berg, then Kreuzberg, now Friedrichshain) rapidly gentrified, and the city erected several monuments to the victims of both the Nazis and the Cold War divide. Germany was ready to set its painful past behind.

Sights
- Berlin Wall Memorial
- Museum of the Wall at Checkpoint Charlie
- East Side Gallery
- Tempelhof Field
- Alexanderplatz (TV Tower and World Clock)
- Karl-Marx-Allee
- DDR Museum
- Everyday Life in the DDR Museum
- Stasi Museum
- Palace of Tears
- Potsdamer Platz
- Reichstag Dome
- Memorials near the Reichstag
- KGB Prison Memorial and Bridge of Spies in Potsdam

GERMANY TODAY (2000-present)

Today Germany is a major economic and political force in Europe. It's a powerful member of the European Union—an organization whose original chief aim was to avoid future wars by embracing Germany in the economic web of Europe. Recently, however, Germany has outgrown its role as a mere member state to become, thanks to its economic might, the EU's de facto leader. (While many other European countries were hard-hit by the economic crisis of the last decade, Ger-

many—with the largest economy in the EU—emerged relatively unscathed.)

German elections in 2005 resulted in no clear victory, and both major parties formed a "Grand Coalition," sharing power equally under Germany's first female chancellor, Angela Merkel, who the media like to call "Mutti" (Mommy). While representing the center-right Christian Democratic Union, Merkel's cautious, centrist, pro-business policies earned her reelection in 2009, 2013, and 2017. Though she governs with coalition partners, she is considered one of the world's most powerful people. Returning for her fourth term in September 2017, Merkel is Europe's longest-serving elected female leader—breaking Margaret Thatcher's 11-year record.

Painfully aware of tensions that still linger even decades after World War II, many Germans have been reluctant to embrace their country's dominant role in Europe. But this hesitancy is slipping away. The 2006 World Cup is often cited as a turning point—not because Germany successfully hosted the huge event, but because that's when a new generation of Germans embraced their country's flag en masse. For the first time since World War II, Germans exhibited a national pride that they no longer feared would be confused with Nazi sentiment.

In 2014, the country's spirit got a huge boost when its soccer team won the World Cup, its first as a united nation. And while Chancellor Merkel's EU austerity measures are unpopular in many corners of Europe, her firm stance has been largely applauded by a German population that's increasingly comfortable calling the shots.

Merkel's popularity weakened somewhat in 2015 after she welcomed Syrian refugees fleeing that nation's civil war. About a million people were given asylum, and the flood of refugees taxed Germany's social services. Her decision was praised by some (she was named *Time* magazine's Person of the Year) but sparked a backlash among others, concerned about Germany's ability to absorb so many newcomers and the economic strain placed on the country's social services.

Like the US and other European nations, Germany has been the target of isolated terrorist incidents. During New Year's Eve celebrations in 2015, an orchestrated series of sexual assaults and thefts rippled through German cities; many of the perpetrators were determined to have been North African migrants. And in 2016, a 24-year-old Tunisian man plowed a tractor-trailer into Berlin's Christmas market, killing 12. These events increased pressure on Germany's leaders to take a tougher stance on immigration, though the country's population remains generally welcoming.

The long-term viability of the EU is another challenge facing Germany. As the biggest and staunchest EU booster, Germany must grapple with the implications of Brexit (Britain's decision to withdraw from the EU) and the rise of other European anti-EU movements.

For more on German history, consider *Europe 101: History and Art for the Traveler,* written by Rick Steves and Gene Openshaw (available at RickSteves.com). And for all the latest, travel to Berlin, buy someone a beer, and ask, "So, what's going on here in Germany?"

PRACTICALITIES

This chapter covers the practical skills of European travel: how to get tourist information, pay for things, sightsee efficiently, find good-value accommodations, eat affordably but well, use technology wisely, and get between destinations smoothly. For more information on these topics, see RickSteves.com/travel-tips.

Tourist Information

Germany's national tourist office **in the US** is a wealth of information. Before your trip, scan their website (www.germany.travel) for information on festivals and biking, as well as regional and thematic itineraries..

In Berlin, you'll find tourist information offices (abbreviated **TI** in this book) at a few major landmarks across the city.

While these are for-profit agencies in business to help you enjoy spending money in their town, they're mostly well organized and have English-speaking staff. Swing by to pick up free walking tour company brochures that include a decent city map (skip the TI's €1 map) and get information on public transit and special events.

Travel Tips

Travel Advisories: For updated health and safety conditions, including any restrictions for your destination, consult the US State Department's international travel website (www.travel.state.gov).

Emergency and Medical Help: For any emergency service—ambulance, police, or fire—call **112** from a mobile phone or landline (operators typically speak English). If you get sick, do as the locals do and go to a pharmacist for advice. Or ask at your hotel for help—they'll know the nearest medical and emergency services. The US Embassy & Consulates website for Germany has a list of English-speaking doctors (+49 30 83050, https://de.usembassy.gov, search for "Medical Assistance").

ETIAS Registration: The European Union may soon require US and Canadian citizens to register online with the European Travel Information and Authorization System (ETIAS) before entering Germany and other Schengen Zone countries (quick and easy process). For the latest, check www.etiasvisa.com.

Theft or Loss: To replace a passport, you'll need to go in person to an embassy (see next). If your credit and debit cards disappear, cancel and replace them (see "Damage Control for Lost Cards," later). File a police report, either on the spot or within a day or two; you'll need it to submit an insurance claim for lost or stolen rail passes or electronics, and it can help with replacing your passport or credit and debit cards. For more information, see RickSteves.com/help.

Embassies: US Embassy in Berlin—passport replacement by appointment only Wed-Thu, sign up online (Clayallee 170, +49 30 83050, http://de.usembassy.gov). **Canadian Embassy** in Berlin—consular services open Mon-Fri 9:00-12:00, closed Sat-Sun (Leipziger Platz 17, +49 30 2031 2470, www.germany.gc.ca).

Time Zones: Germany, like most of continental Europe, is generally six/nine hours ahead of the East/West Coasts of the US. The exceptions are the beginning and end of Daylight Saving Time: Europe "springs forward" the last Sunday in March (two weeks after most of North America) and "falls back" the last Sunday in October (one week before North America). For a handy time converter, use the world clock app on your phone or download one (see www.timeanddate.com).

PRACTICALITIES

Business Hours: In Germany, most shops are open from about 9:00 until 18:00-20:00 on weekdays; smaller stores generally close earlier on Saturdays, and most stores are closed all day Sunday (shops and grocery stores in train stations often have longer hours). Banks are generally open Monday to Friday from 9:00 to 15:00 (or later, up to 19:00). Many museums and sights are closed on Monday.

Watt's Up? Europe's electrical system is 220 volts, instead of North America's 110 volts. Most electronics (laptops, phones, cameras) and appliances (newer hair dryers, CPAP machines) convert automatically, so you won't need a converter, but you will need an adapter plug with two round prongs, sold inexpensively at travel stores in the US. Avoid bringing older appliances that don't automatically convert voltage; instead, buy a cheap replacement in Europe.

Rip up this book! Turn chapters into mini guidebooks: Break the book's spine and use a utility knife to slice apart chapters, keeping gummy edges intact. Reinforce the chapter spines with clear wide tape; use a heavy-duty stapler; or make or buy a cheap cover (see the Travel Store at RickSteves.com), swapping out chapters as you go.

Discounts: Discounts for sights are generally not listed in this book. However, seniors (age 65 and over), youths under 18, and students and teachers with proper identification cards (obtain from www.isic.org) can get discounts at many sights—always ask. Some discounts are available only to European citizens.

Online Translation Tips: Google's Chrome browser instantly translates websites; Translate.google.com and DeepL.com are also handy. The Google Translate app converts spoken or typed English into most European languages (and vice versa) and can also translate text it "reads" with your phone's camera.

Going Green: There's plenty you can do to reduce your environmental footprint when traveling. When practical, take a train instead of a flight within Europe, and use public transportation within cities. In hotels, use the "Do Not Disturb" sign to avoid daily linen and towel changes (or hang up your towels to signal you'll reuse them). Bring a reusable shopping tote and refillable water bottle (Europe's tap water is safe to drink). To find out how Rick Steves' Europe is offsetting carbon emissions with an innovative self-imposed carbon tax, go to RickSteves.com/about-us/climate-smart.

Money

Here's my basic strategy for using money in Europe:
- Upon arrival, head for an ATM at the airport and withdraw

Exchange Rate

1 euro (€) = about $1.20

To convert prices in euros to dollars, add about 20 percent: €20 = about $24, €50 = about $60. Like the dollar, one euro is broken into 100 cents. Coins range from €0.01 to €2, and bills from €5 to €200 (bills over €50 are rarely used).

Check www.oanda.com for the latest exchange rates.

some local currency, using a debit card with low international transaction fees.

- In general, pay for bigger expenses with a credit card and use cash for smaller purchases. Use a debit card for cash withdrawals.
- Keep your cards and cash safe in a money belt.

PLASTIC VERSUS CASH

Although credit cards are widely accepted in Europe, cash is sometimes the only way to pay for street food, taxis, tips, and local guides. Some businesses (especially smaller ones, such as B&Bs and mom-and-pop cafés and shops) may charge you extra for using a credit card—or might not accept credit cards at all. Having cash on hand helps you out of a jam if your card randomly doesn't work.

I use my credit card to book and pay for hotel reservations, to buy advance tickets for events or sights, and to cover most other expenses. But keep in mind that some shops and restaurants in Germany accept only the local "EC" debit cards—not American credit cards. Larger hotels, restaurants, and shops that do take US cards more commonly accept Visa and MasterCard than American Express.

WHAT TO BRING

I pack the following and keep it all safe in my money belt.

Debit Card: Use this at ATMs to withdraw local cash.

Credit Card: Handy for bigger transactions (at hotels, shops, restaurants, travel agencies, car-rental agencies, and so on), payment machines, and online purchases.

Backup Card: Some travelers carry a third card (debit or credit; ideally from a different bank), in case one gets lost or simply doesn't work.

A Stash of Cash: I carry $100-200 in US dollars as a cash backup, which comes in handy in an emergency (for example, if your ATM card gets eaten by the machine).

What NOT to Bring: Resist the urge to buy euros before your trip or you'll pay the price in bad stateside exchange rates. Wait until you arrive to withdraw money. European airports have plenty of ATMs.

BEFORE YOU GO

Use this pre-trip checklist.

Know your cards. US debit cards with a Visa or MasterCard logo will work in any European ATM. As for credit cards, Visa and MasterCard are universal, American Express is less common, and Discover is unknown in Europe.

Know your PIN. Make sure you know the numeric, four-digit PIN for all of your cards, both debit and credit. Request it if you don't have one, as it may be required for some purchases in Europe (see "Using Credit Cards," later). Allow time to receive the information by mail—it's not always possible to obtain your PIN online.

Report your travel dates. Let your bank know that you'll be using your debit and credit cards in Europe, and when and where you're headed.

Adjust your ATM withdrawal limit. Find out how much you can take out daily and ask for a higher daily withdrawal limit if you want to get more cash at once. Note that European ATMs will withdraw funds only from checking accounts, not savings accounts.

Ask about fees. For any purchase or withdrawal made with a card, you may be charged a currency conversion fee (1-3 percent) and/or a Visa or MasterCard international transaction fee (less than 1 percent). If you're getting a bad deal, consider getting a new debit or credit card. Reputable no-fee cards include those from Capital One, as well as Charles Schwab debit cards. Most credit unions and some airline loyalty cards have low or no international transaction fees.

IN EUROPE
Using Cash Machines

European cash machines have English-language instructions and work just like they do at home—except they spit out local currency instead of dollars, calculated at the day's standard bank-to-bank rate.

In most places, ATMs are easy to locate—in Germany ask for a *Geldautomat*. When possible, withdraw cash from a bank-run ATM located just outside that bank.

If your debit card doesn't work, try a lower amount—your request may have exceeded your withdrawal limit or the ATM's limit. If you still have a problem, try a different ATM or come back later.

Avoid "independent" ATMs, such as Travelex, Euronet, Moneybox, Your Cash, Cardpoint, and Cashzone. These have high fees, can be less secure, and may try to trick users with "dynamic currency conversion" (see next).

PRACTICALITIES

Dynamic Currency Conversion

When paying with a credit card, you'll often be asked whether you want to pay in dollars or in the local currency. Always refuse the conversion and choose the local currency. While DCC seems convenient, it comes with a poor exchange rate, and you'll wind up losing money. Many ATMs also offer DCC—again, always select "continue without conversion."

Exchanging Cash

Minimize exchanging money in Europe; it's expensive (you'll generally lose 5 to 10 percent). In a pinch you can find exchange desks at major train stations or airports. Banks generally do not exchange money unless you have an account with them.

Using Credit Cards

US credit cards generally work fine in Europe—with a few exceptions.

European cards use chip-and-PIN technology; most chip cards issued in the US instead require a signature. When presented with a US card, European card readers may generate a receipt for you to sign—or prompt you to enter your PIN. At self-service payment machines (such as transit-ticket kiosks), US cards may not work. In this case, look for a cashier who can process your card manually—or pay in cash.

"Tap to pay" cards and smartphone payment apps work in Europe just as they do in the US, and sidestep chip-and-PIN compatibility issues.

Drivers Beware: Drivers may encounter automated pay points (tollbooths, parking meters, gas pumps, etc.) where US cards are not accepted. Carry cash as a back-up and be prepared to move on to the next gas station if necessary (in some countries, gas stations sell prepaid gas cards, which you should be able to purchase with any US card). When approaching a toll plaza, use the "cash" lane.

Security Tips

Pickpockets target tourists. Keep your cash, credit cards, and passport secure in your money belt, and carry only a day's spending money in your front pocket or wallet.

Before inserting your card into an ATM, inspect the front. If anything looks crooked, loose, or damaged, it could be a sign of a card-skimming device. When entering your PIN, carefully block other people's view of the keypad.

Don't use a debit card for purchases. Because a debit card pulls funds directly from your bank account, potential charges incurred by a thief will stay on your account while the fraudulent use is investigated by your bank.

To access your accounts online while traveling, be sure to use a secure connection (see the "Tips on Internet Security" sidebar, later).

Damage Control for Lost Cards

If you lose your credit or debit card, report the loss immediately to the respective global customer-assistance centers. With a mobile phone, call these 24-hour US numbers: Visa (+1 303 967 1096), MasterCard (+1 636 722 7111), and American Express (+1 336 393 1111). From a landline, you can call these US numbers collect by going through a local operator.

You'll need to provide the primary cardholder's identification-verification details (such as birth date, mother's maiden name, or Social Security number). You can generally receive a temporary card within two or three business days in Europe (see RickSteves.com/help for more).

If you report your loss within two days, you typically won't be responsible for unauthorized transactions on your account, although many banks charge a liability fee.

TIPPING

Tipping in Germany isn't as automatic and generous as it is in the US. However, tips are appreciated and expected. As in the US, the proper amount depends on your resources, tipping philosophy, and the circumstances, but some general guidelines apply.

Restaurants: You don't need to tip if you order your food at a counter. At German restaurants that have a wait staff, it's common to tip by rounding up (about 10 percent) after a good meal. For details on tipping in restaurants, see page 413.

Taxis: For a typical ride, round up your fare a bit (for instance, if your fare is €4.70, pay €5). If the cabbie hauls your bags and zips you to the airport to help you catch your flight, you might want to toss in a little more.

Services: In general, if someone in the service industry does a super job for you, a small tip of a euro or two is appropriate. If you're not sure whether (or how much) to tip, ask a local for advice.

GETTING A VAT REFUND

Wrapped into the purchase price of your German souvenirs is a value-added tax (VAT) of 19 percent. You're entitled to get most of that tax back if you purchase more than €25 (about $30) worth of goods at a store that participates in the VAT-refund scheme. Typically, you must ring up the minimum at a single retailer—you can't add up your purchases from various shops to reach the required amount. (If the store ships the goods to your US home, VAT is not assessed on your purchase.)

Getting your refund is usually straightforward...and worthwhile if you spend a significant amount on souvenirs.

At the Merchant: Have the merchant completely fill out the refund document (they'll ask for your passport; a photo of your passport usually works). Keep track of the paperwork and your original sales receipt. Note that you're not supposed to use your purchased goods before you leave Europe.

At the Border or Airport: Process your VAT document at your last stop in the European Union (such as at the airport) with the customs agent who deals with VAT refunds. At some airports, you'll have to go to a customs office to get your documents stamped and then to a separate VAT refund service (such as Global Blue or Planet) to process the refund. At other airports, a single VAT desk handles the whole thing. Note that refund services typically extract a 4 percent fee and can refund your money in cash immediately or credit your card. Otherwise, you'll need to mail the stamped refund documents to the address given by the merchant. Allow plenty of extra time at the airport to deal with the VAT refund process.

CUSTOMS FOR AMERICAN SHOPPERS

You can take home $800 worth of items per person duty-free, once every 31 days. Many processed and packaged foods are allowed, including cheeses, dried herbs, jams, baked goods, candy, chocolate, oil, vinegar, condiments, and honey. Fresh fruits and vegetables and most meats are not allowed, with exceptions for some canned items. As for alcohol, you can bring in one liter duty-free (it can be packed securely in your checked luggage, along with any other liquid-containing items).

To bring alcohol (or liquid-packed foods) in your carry-on bag on your flight home, buy it at a duty-free shop at the airport. You'll increase your odds of getting it onto a connecting flight if it's packaged in a "STEB"—a secure, tamper-evident bag. But stay away from liquids in opaque, ceramic, or metallic containers, which usually cannot be successfully screened (STEB or no STEB).

For details on allowable goods, customs rules, and duty rates, visit http://help.cbp.gov.

Sightseeing

Sightseeing can be hard work. Use these tips to make your visits to Berlin's finest sights meaningful, fun, efficient, and painless.

MAPS AND NAVIGATION TOOLS

A good map is essential for efficient navigation while sightseeing. The maps in this book are concise and simple, designed to help you locate recommended destinations, sights, hotels, and restaurants. Simple maps are generally free at TIs and hotels.

You can also use a mapping app on your mobile device, which provides turn-by-turn directions for walking, driving, and taking public transit. Google Maps, Apple Maps, and CityMaps2Go allow you to download maps for offline use; ideally, download the areas you'll need before your trip. For certain features, you'll need to be online—either using Wi-Fi or an international data plan.

PLAN AHEAD

Set up an itinerary that allows you to fit in all your must-see sights. For a one-stop look at opening hours, see "Berlin at a Glance" in the Sights in Berlin chapter. Most sights keep stable hours, but you can easily confirm the latest by checking with the TI or visiting museum websites.

Don't put off visiting a must-see sight—you never know when a place will close unexpectedly for a holiday, strike, or restoration. Many museums are closed or have reduced hours at least a few days a year, especially on holidays such as Christmas, New Year's, and Labor Day (May 1). A list of holidays is in the appendix; check for possible closures during your trip. In summer, some sights may stay open late. Off-season hours may be shorter.

Going at the right time helps avoid crowds. This book offers tips on the best times to see specific sights. Try visiting popular sights very early or very late. Evening visits (when possible) are usually peaceful, with fewer crowds. Late morning is usually the worst time to visit a popular sight.

If you plan to hire a local guide, reserve ahead by email. Popular guides can get booked up.

Study up. To get the most out of the self-guided tours and sight descriptions in this book, read them before you visit.

RESERVATIONS, ADVANCE TICKETS, AND PASSES

Given how precious your vacation time is, I recommend getting reservations for any must-see sight that offers them (see page 40).

To deal with lines, many popular sights sell advance tickets that guarantee admission at a certain time of day and allow you to skip entry lines. It's worth giving up some spontaneity to book in advance. While hundreds of tourists sweat in long ticket-buying lines—or arrive to find the sight sold out—those who've booked ahead are assured of getting in. In some cases, getting a ticket in advance simply means buying your ticket earlier on the same day. But for other sights, you may need to book weeks or even months in advance. As soon as you're ready to commit to a certain date, book it.

AT SIGHTS

Here's what you can typically expect:

Entering: You may not be allowed to enter if you arrive too close to closing time. And guards start ushering people out well before the actual closing time, so don't save the best for last.

Many sights have a security check. Allow extra time for these lines. Most museums in Germany require you to check any bag bigger than a purse, and sometimes even purses. Museum lockers are free, but be prepared to pay a €1-2 deposit.

Photography: If the museum's photo policy isn't clearly posted, ask a guard. Generally, taking photos without a flash or tripod is allowed. Some sights ban selfie sticks; others ban photos altogether.

Audioguides and Apps: I've produced a free, downloadable audio tour for my Best of Berlin City Walk; look for the 🎧 in this book. For more on my audio tours, see page 22.

Many sights rent audioguides with useful recorded descriptions in English. Most of Berlin's top museums are run by the government and include excellent audioguides with admission (you'll need to leave an ID as a deposit). If you bring your own earbuds, you can often enjoy better sound. And if you don't mind being tethered to your travel partner, you'll save money by bringing a Y-jack and sharing one audioguide. Museums and sights often offer free apps that you can download to your mobile device (check their websites).

Temporary Exhibits: Museums may show special exhibits in addition to their permanent collection. Some exhibits are included in the entry price, while others come at an extra cost (which you may have to pay even if you don't want to see the exhibit).

Expect Changes: Artwork can be on tour, on loan, out sick, or shifted at the whim of the curator. Pick up a floor plan as you enter, and ask museum staff if you can't find a particular item.

Services: Important sights usually have a reasonably priced on-site café or cafeteria (handy and air-conditioned places to rejuvenate during a long visit). In Berlin, state-run museums offer free loaner stools, inviting you to camp out and really ponder your favorite work of art. The WCs at sights are free and generally clean.

Before Leaving: At the gift shop, scan the postcard rack or thumb through a guidebook to be sure you haven't overlooked something that you'd like to see. Every sight or museum offers

Sleep Code

Hotels in this book are categorized according to the average price of a standard double room with breakfast in high season.

$$$$	**Splurge:** Most rooms over €170
$$$	**Pricier:** €130-170
$$	**Moderate:** €90-130
$	**Budget:** €50-90
¢	**Backpacker:** Under €50
RS%	**Rick Steves discount**

Unless otherwise noted, credit cards are accepted, hotel staff speak basic English, and free Wi-Fi is available. Comparison-shop by checking prices at several hotels (on each hotel's own website, on a booking site, or by email). For the best deal, *book directly with the hotel.* Ask for a discount if paying in cash; if the listing includes **RS%**, request a Rick Steves discount.

more than what is covered in this book. Use the information I provide as an introduction—not the final word.

Sleeping

Extensive and opinionated listings of good-value rooms are a major feature of this book's Sleeping in Berlin chapter. Rather than list accommodations scattered throughout a town, I choose hotels in my favorite neighborhoods that are convenient to your sightseeing.

My recommendations run the gamut, from dorm beds to fancy rooms with all the comforts. I like places that are clean, central, relatively quiet at night, reasonably priced, friendly, small enough to have a hands-on owner or manager, and run with a respect for German traditions. I'm more impressed by a handy location and fun-loving philosophy than flat-screen TVs and a fancy gym. Most of my recommendations fall short of perfection. But if I can find a place with most of these features, it's a keeper.

Book your accommodations as soon as your itinerary is set, especially if you want to stay at one of my top listings or if you'll be traveling during busy times, such as Green Week in mid-January, the ITB travel show in mid-March, Easter weekend, the first weekend and Ascension weekend in May, or Germany Unity Day on October 3. See the appendix for a list of major holidays and festivals in Germany.

RATES AND DEALS

I've categorized my recommended accommodations based on price, indicated with a dollar-sign rating (see sidebar). Room prices can fluctuate significantly with demand and amenities (size, views,

PRACTICALITIES

Using Online Services to Your Advantage

From booking services to user reviews, online businesses play a greater role in travelers' planning than ever before. Take advantage of their pluses—and be wise to their downsides.

Booking Sites

Booking websites such as Booking.com and Hotels.com offer one-stop shopping for hotels. While convenient for travelers, they're both a blessing and a curse for independent, family-run hotels. Without a presence on these sites, small hotels become almost invisible. But to be listed, a hotel must pay a sizable commission...and promise that its own website won't undercut the price on the booking-service site.

Here's the work-around: Use the big sites to research what's out there, then book direct with the hotel by email or phone, in which case hotel owners are free to give you whatever price they like. Ask for a room without the commission mark-up (or ask for a free breakfast if not included, or a free upgrade). If you do book online, be sure to use the hotel's own website. The price will likely be the same as via a booking site, but your money goes to the hotel, not agency commissions.

As a savvy consumer, remember: When you book with an online booking service, you're adding a middleman who takes roughly 20 percent. To support small, family-run hotels whose world is more difficult than ever, book direct.

Short-Term Rental Sites

Rental juggernaut Airbnb (along with other short-term rental sites) allows travelers to rent rooms and apartments, often providing more value, space, and amenities than a cookie-cutter hotel. Airbnb fans appreciate feeling part of a real neighborhood and getting into a daily routine as "temporary Europeans." Depending on the host, Airbnb can provide an opportunity to get to know a local person, while keeping the money spent on your

room class, and so on), but these relative price categories remain constant. Taxes, which can vary from place to place, are generally insignificant (a dollar or two per person, per night).

Room rates are especially volatile at hotels that use "dynamic pricing" to set rates. Prices can skyrocket during festivals and conventions, while business hotels can have deep discounts on weekends when demand plummets. Of the many hotels I recommend, it's difficult to say which will be the best value on a given day—until you do your homework.

Booking Direct: Once your dates are set, compare prices at several hotels. You can do this by checking hotel websites and booking sites such as Hotels.com or Booking.com. After you've zeroed accommodations in the community.

Critics of Airbnb see it as a threat to "traditional Europe." Landlords can make more money renting to short-stay travelers, driving rents up—and local residents out to more affordable but less charming districts. When those long-term renters go, traditional businesses are replaced by ones that cater to tourists. And the character that made those neighborhoods desirable to the tourists in the first place goes too. Some cities have cracked down, requiring owners to obtain a license and to occupy rental properties part of the year (and staging disruptive "inspections" that inconvenience guests).

As a lover of Europe, I share the worry of those who see residents nudged aside by tourists. But as an advocate for travelers, I appreciate the value and cultural intimacy Airbnb provides.

User Reviews

User-generated review sites and apps such as Yelp and TripAdvisor can give you a consensus of opinions about everything from hotels and restaurants to sights and nightlife. If you scan reviews of a restaurant or hotel and see several complaints about noise or a rotten location, you've gained insight that can help in your decision-making.

But as a guidebook writer, my sense is that there is a big difference between the uncurated information on a review site and the vetted listings in a guidebook. A user-generated review is based on the limited experience of one person, who stayed at just one hotel in a given city and ate at a few restaurants there. A guidebook is the work of a trained researcher who forms a well-developed basis for comparison by visiting many restaurants and hotels year after year.

Both types of information have their place, and in many ways, they're complementary. If something is well reviewed in a guidebook and it also gets good online reviews, it's likely a winner.

in on your choice, book directly with the hotel itself. This increases the chances that the hotelier will be able to accommodate special needs or requests (such as shifting your reservation). And when you book by phone or email, the owner avoids the commission paid to booking sites, giving them wiggle room to offer you a discount, a nicer room, or a free breakfast (if it's not already included).

Getting a Discount: Some hotels extend a discount to those who pay cash or stay longer than three nights. And some accommodations offer a special discount for Rick Steves readers, indicated in this guidebook by the abbreviation **"RS%."** Discounts vary: Ask for details when you reserve. Generally, to qualify for this discount, you must book direct (not through a booking site), mention this book when you reserve, show this book upon arrival, and sometimes pay cash or stay a certain number of nights. In some cases, you may need to enter a discount code (which I've provided in the listing) in the booking form on the hotel's website. Rick Steves discounts apply to readers with either print or digital books. Understandably, discounts do not apply to promotional rates.

Berlin hoteliers charge a daily tourist tax (5 percent of the room rate). This may be included in the room price or may appear as an extra charge on your bill.

TYPES OF ACCOMMODATIONS
Hotels

In this book, the price for a double room in a hotel ranges from €50 (very simple, toilet and shower down the hall) to €400-plus (maximum plumbing and the works). Breakfast is generally not included in the quoted rate, but you can usually add or remove a breakfast option when booking (sometimes continental, but often buffet; see "Eating," later in this chapter).

Some hotels can add an extra bed (for a small charge) to turn a double into a triple; some offer larger rooms for four or more people (I call these "family rooms" in the listings). If there's space for an extra cot, they'll cram it in for you. In general, a triple room is cheaper than the cost of a double and a single. Three or four people can economize by requesting one big room.

Chain hotels can be a good value, especially in Berlin; along with those listed in the Sleeping in Berlin chapter, the Europe-wide Ibis/Mercure chain has many options (www.accorhotels.com). I'm also impressed with the homegrown, Hamburg-based German chain called Motel One, which specializes in affordable style and has several branches in Berlin (www.motel-one.com). Because hotel chains tend to have multiple branches scattered across a city, be sure you're booking the one you want.

Arrival and Check-In: Hotels and B&Bs are sometimes located on the higher floors of a multipurpose building with a secured door. In that case, look for your hotel's name on the buttons by the main entrance. When you ring the bell, you'll be buzzed in.

Hotel elevators are common, though small, and some older buildings still lack them. You may have to climb a flight of stairs to reach the elevator (if so, you can ask the front desk for help carrying your bags up).

The EU requires that hotels collect your name, nationality,

and ID number. When you check in, the receptionist will normally ask for your passport and may keep it for up to a couple of hours. If you're not comfortable leaving your passport at the desk for a long time, bring a photocopy to give them instead.

If you're arriving in the morning, your room probably won't be ready. Check your bag safely at the hotel and dive right into sightseeing.

In Your Room: Most hotel rooms have a TV, telephone, and free Wi-Fi (although in old buildings with thick walls, the Wi-Fi signal might be available only in the lobby). Simpler places rarely have a room phone.

In Germany, beds usually come with a top sheet and blankets or a comforter. A double bed comes with two comforters—rather than one bigger one. It also frequently has two separate mattresses and sometimes two separate (but adjacent) frames—even if the bed is intended for couples. (A "real" double bed with a single mattress is called a *Französisches Bett*—a French bed.) Rooms with truly separate twin beds are less common in German hotels. When Americans request separate beds, German hotels sometimes give them normal doubles with complete sincerity—reasoning that the mattresses, though adjacent, are separate.

Checking Out: While it's customary to pay for your room upon departure, it can be a good idea to settle your bill the day before, when you're not in a hurry and while the manager's in.

Hotelier Help: Hoteliers can be a good source of advice. Most know their city well, and can assist you with everything from public transit and airport connections to finding a good restaurant, the nearest launderette, or a late-night pharmacy.

Hotel Hassles: Even at the best places, mechanical breakdowns occur: Sinks leak, hot water turns cold, toilets may gurgle or smell, the Wi-Fi goes out, or the air-conditioning dies when you need it most. Report your concerns clearly and calmly at the front desk.

If you find that night noise is a problem (if, for instance, your room is over a nightclub or facing a busy street), ask for a quieter room in the back or on an upper floor. To guard against theft in your room, keep valuables out of sight. Some rooms come with a safe, and other hotels have safes at the front desk. I've never bothered using one and in a lifetime of travel, I've never had anything stolen from my room.

For more complicated problems, don't expect instant results. Above all, keep a positive attitude. Remember, you're on vacation. If your hotel is a disappointment, spend more time out enjoying the place you came to see.

Making Hotel Reservations

Reserve your rooms as soon as you've pinned down your travel dates. For busy national holidays, it's wise to reserve far in advance (see the appendix).

Requesting a Reservation: For family-run hotels, it's generally cheaper to book your room directly via email or phone. For business-class and chain hotels, or if you'd rather book online, reserve directly through the hotel's official website (not a booking website). For complicated requests, send an email. Almost all of my recommended hotels take reservations in English.

Here's what the hotelier wants to know:
- Type(s) of room(s) you want and number of guests
- Number of nights you'll stay
- Arrival and departure dates, written European-style as day/month/year (18/06/22 or 18 June 2022);
- Special requests (en suite bathroom, cheapest room, twin beds vs. double bed, quiet room)
- Applicable discounts (such as a Rick Steves discount, cash discount, or promotional rate)

Confirming a Reservation: Most places will request a credit-card number to hold your room. If the hotel's website doesn't have a secure form where you can enter the number directly, share this info via a phone call.

Canceling a Reservation: If you must cancel, it's courteous—and smart—to do so with as much notice as possible, especially for

Short-Term Rentals

A short-term rental—whether an apartment, house, or room in a local's home—is an increasingly popular alternative, especially if you plan to settle in one location for several nights. For stays longer than a few days, you can usually find a rental that's comparable to—and cheaper than—a hotel room with similar amenities. Plus, you'll get a behind-the-scenes peek into how locals live.

Many places require a minimum stay and have strict cancellation policies. And you're generally on your own: There's no reception desk, breakfast, or daily cleaning service.

Finding Accommodations: Websites such as Airbnb, FlipKey, Booking.com, and the HomeAway family of sites (HomeAway, VRBO, and VacationRentals) let you browse a wide range of properties. Alternatively, rental agencies such as InterhomeUSA.com and RentaVilla.com can provide a more personalized service (their curated listings are also more expensive).

Before you commit, be clear on the location. I like to virtually "explore" the neighborhood using Google Street View. Also consider the proximity to public transportation and how well con-

From: rick@ricksteves.com
Sent: Today
To: info@hotelcentral.com
Subject: Reservation request for 19-22 July

Dear Hotel Central,

I would like to stay at your hotel. Please let me know if you have a room available and the price for:
- 2 people
- Double bed and en suite bathroom in a quiet room
- Arriving 19 July, departing 22 July (3 nights)

Thank you!
Rick Steves

smaller family-run places. Cancellation policies can be strict; read the fine print before you book. Many discount deals require pre-payment and can be expensive to change or cancel.

Reconfirming a Reservation: Always call or email to reconfirm your room reservation a few days in advance. For B&Bs or very small hotels, I call again on my arrival day to tell my host what time to expect me (especially important if arriving late—after 17:00).

Phoning: For tips on calling hotels overseas, see page 424.

nected the property is with the rest of the city. Ask about amenities (elevator, laundry, Wi-Fi, parking, etc.). Reviews from previous guests can help identify trouble spots.

Think about the kind of experience you want: Just a key and an affordable bed...or a chance to get to know a local? Some hosts offer self-check-in and minimal interaction; others enjoy interacting with you. Read the description and reviews to help shape your decision.

Confirming and Paying: Many places require you to pay the entire balance before your trip, usually the listing site. Be wary of owners who want to take your transaction offline to avoid fees; this gives you no recourse if things go awry. Never agree to wire money (a key indicator of a fraudulent transaction).

Apartments or Houses: If you're staying in one place for several nights, it's worth considering an apartment or rental house (shorter stays aren't worth the hassle of arranging key pickup, buying groceries, etc.). Apartment or house rentals can be especially cost-effective for groups and families. European apartments, like hotel rooms, tend to be small by US standards. But they often come with laundry facilities and small, equipped kitchens, making it easier and cheaper to dine in.

Rooms in Private Homes: Renting a room in someone's home is a good option for those traveling alone, as you're more likely to find true single rooms—with just one single bed, and a price to match. These can range from air-mattress-in-living-room basic to plush-B&B-suite posh. While you can't expect your host to also be your tour guide—or even to provide you with much info—some are interested in getting to know the travelers who pass through their home.

Other Options: Swapping homes with a local works for people with an appealing place to offer (don't assume where you live is not interesting to Europeans). Good places to start are HomeExchange. com and LoveHomeSwap.com. To sleep for free, Couchsurfing. com is a vagabond's alternative to Airbnb. It lists millions of outgoing members, who host fellow "surfers" in their homes.

Hostels

A hostel *(Jugendherberge)* provides cheap beds in dorms where you sleep alongside strangers for about €25 per night. Travelers of any age are welcome if they don't mind dorm-style accommodations and meeting other travelers. Most hostels offer kitchen facilities, guest computers, Wi-Fi, and a self-service laundry. Hostels almost always provide bedding, but the towel's up to you (though you can usually rent one). Family and private rooms are often available.

Independent hostels tend to be easygoing, colorful, and informal (no membership required; www.hostelworld.com). You may pay slightly less by booking directly with the hostel. **Official hostels** are part of Hostelling International (HI) and share an online booking site (www.hihostels.com). HI hostels typically require that you be a member or else pay a bit more per night.

Eating

Germanic cuisine is heavy, hearty, and—by European standards—inexpensive. Each region has its specialties, which are often good values. Order house specials whenever possible. Though it's tasty, German food can get monotonous unless you look beyond the schnitzel and wurst. Fortunately, German chefs—especially in big cities—are increasingly adopting international influences, picking up previously unknown spices and ingredients to jazz up "Modern German" cuisine. Be adventurous.

For listings in this guidebook, I look for restaurants that are convenient to your hotel and sightseeing. When restaurant hunting, choose a spot filled with locals, not the place with the big neon

---

> ## Restaurant Code
>
> Eateries in this book are categorized according to the average cost of a typical main course. Drinks, desserts, and splurge items can raise the price considerably.
>
> | | |
> |---|---|
> | **$$$$** | **Splurge:** Most main courses over €20 |
> | **$$$** | **Pricier:** €15-20 |
> | **$$** | **Moderate:** €10-15 |
> | **$** | **Budget:** Under €10 |
>
> In Germany, a wurst stand or other takeout spot is **$**; a beer hall, *Biergarten,* or basic sit-down eatery is **$$**; a casual but more upscale restaurant is **$$$**; and a swanky splurge is **$$$$**.

---

signs boasting, "We Speak English and Accept Credit Cards." Venturing even a block or two off the main drag leads to higher-quality food for a better price.

RESTAURANT PRICING

I've categorized my recommended eateries based on the average price of a typical main course, indicated with a dollar-sign rating (see sidebar). Obviously, expensive specialties, fine wine, appetizers, and dessert can significantly increase your final bill.

The categories also indicate the personality of a place: **Budget** eateries include street food, takeaway, order-at-the-counter shops, basic cafeterias, and bakeries selling sandwiches. **Moderate** eateries are nice (but not fancy) sit-down restaurants, ideal for a straightforward, fill-the-tank meal. Most of my listings fall in this category—great for a taste of local cuisine at a reasonable price.

Pricier eateries are a notch up, with more attention paid to the setting, presentation, and (often inventive) cuisine. **Splurge** eateries are dress-up-for-a-special-occasion-swanky—typically with an elegant setting, polished service, and pricey and intricate cuisine.

BREAKFAST

Most Berlin hotels offer breakfast for an extra fee (it's generally not included in the base room price).

Expect sliced bread, rolls, pastries, cereal, yogurt (both plain and with fruit), eggs, cold cuts, cheese, and fruit. You'll always find coffee, tea, and some sort of *Saft* (juice). Along with orange, apple, and grapefruit, multivita-

min juice is popular. This sweet, smooth blend of various fruits is less acidic than a citrus juice. A bottle of mineral water is standing by to mix with any juice to turn it into a *Schorle* (spritzer).

For breakfast, most Germans prefer a sandwich with cold cuts and/or a bowl of *Müsli* (an oat cereal like granola, but less sweet), sometimes mixed with corn flakes. Instead of pouring milk over cereal, most Germans begin with a dollop of yogurt (or *Quark*—sweet curds that resemble yogurt), then sprinkle the cereal on top. If it's not sweet enough, drizzle on some *Honig* (honey). *Bircher Müsli* is a healthy mix of oats, nuts, yogurt, and fruit. To make a German-style sandwich for breakfast, layer *Aufschnitt* (cold cuts), *Schinken* (ham), *Streichwurst* (meat spread, most often *Leberwurst*—liver spread), and *Käse* (cheese) on a slice of bread or a roll.

If a buffet has eggs, they're most likely soft-boiled *(weichgekochte Eier)*. To eat it as the Germans do, set the egg in its stand, gently crack the shell around its perimeter and remove the top half, salt it, and eat it as if from a tiny bowl. Hard-boiled eggs *(hartgekochte Eier)* are often served with rémoulade (similar to tartar sauce). Occasionally a buffet will have *Rühreier* (scrambled eggs) or *Spiegeleier* (fried eggs—literally "mirror eggs"—typically sunny-side up).

In some hotels, a small garbage can is set on the table for you to dispose of trash as you eat.

LUNCH AND DINNER

German mealtimes align well with American stomachs; lunch is generally served from 12:00-14:00 and dinner from 18:00-21:00.

Traditional restaurants go by many names. For basic, stick-to-the-ribs meals—and plenty of beer—look for a beer hall *(Brauhaus)* or beer garden *(Biergarten)*. *Gasthaus, Gasthof, Gaststätte,* and *Gaststube* all loosely describe an informal, inn-type eatery. A *Kneipe* is a bar, and a *Keller* (or *Ratskeller*) is a restaurant or tavern located in a cellar. A *Weinstube* serves wine and usually traditional food as well.

Germans are health-conscious and quite passionate about choosing organic *(Bio)* products: *Bio* fruits and vegetables, and even *Bio* bread, ice cream, and schnitzel. You'll often see footnotes on restaurant menus marking which dishes have artificial ingredients. However, despite Germans' healthy ways, many starchy, high-fat, high-calorie traditional foods remain staples of the national diet.

(For a rundown of common German foods, see "Traditional German Fare," later.)

Most eateries have menus tacked onto their front doors, with an English menu inside. If you see a *Stammtisch* sign hanging over a table at a restaurant or pub, it means that it's reserved for regulars—don't sit here unless invited. Once you're seated, take your time—only a rude waiter will rush you. Good service is relaxed (slow to an American).

To wish others "Happy eating!" offer a cheery *"Guten Appetit!"* When you want the bill, say, *"Die Rechnung, bitte"* (dee REHKH-noong, BIT-teh).

Tipping: You only need to tip at restaurants that have table service. If you order your food at a counter, don't tip. At restaurants with wait staff, it's common to tip after a good meal by rounding up (roughly 10 percent). Rather than leaving coins behind on the table (considered slightly rude), Germans usually pay directly: When the server comes by with the bill, simply hand over paper money, stating the total you'd like to pay. For example, if paying for a €10 meal with a €20 bill, while handing your money to the server, say "Eleven, please" (or *"Elf, bitte"* if you've got your German numbers down). The server will keep a €1 tip and give you €9 in change.

Budget Tips

It's easy to eat a meal for €10 or less here. At lunchtime, locals grab a sandwich (around €2.50) and perhaps a pastry (€1-2) from one of the ubiquitous bakeries, which often have tables to sit at (but not table service). If there aren't any sandwiches on display at the bakery counter, ask to have one made for you.

Department-store cafeterias (usually on the top floor with a view) are common and handy, and they bridge the language barrier by letting you see your options. A *Schnellimbiss*—or simply *Imbiss*—is a small fast-food takeaway stand where you can get a bratwurst or other grilled sausage (usually less than €2, including a roll); for a rundown of common sausages, see the "Best of the Wurst," later.

All schnitzeled out? International restaurants provide a welcome break from Germanic fare. Italian, Turkish, and Asian food are generally a good value. A freshly baked pizza, a Turkish sandwich, or a rice or noodle dish will cost you €4-7, and can be packed up to enjoy on a park bench or in your room.

Stands and shops selling Turkish-style *döner kebab*—gyro-like, pita-wrapped rotisserie meat—are common (€4 at any time of day). Turkish cafés abound, selling not only the basic *döner kebab*, but also several variations, plus falafel (chickpea croquettes), "Turkish pizzas," and much more.

Some restaurants offer inexpensive €7-10 weekday hot-lunch specials that aren't listed on the regular menu (look for the *Tages-*

karte or *Tagesangebot,* or just ask—sometimes available at dinner, too). For smaller portions, order from the *kleine Hunger* (small hunger) section of the menu. Simple dishes of wurst with sauerkraut and bread tend to run €6-8.

TRADITIONAL GERMAN FARE

Here are some typical dishes you'll see at German eateries.

Specialties

Traditional German dishes tend to be meat-heavy. The classic dish is sausage—hundreds of varieties of bratwurst, *Weisswurst,* and other types of wurst are served with sauerkraut as an excuse for a vegetable (for a list of common types of wurst, see the "Best of the Wurst" section, later).

Many traditional eateries serve some kind of meat on the bone, such as pork knuckle (called *Schweinshaxe* or *Eisbein* on menus) or

shoulder, which has been boiled or roasted until tender. It goes down well with a big mug of beer. The fish and venison here are also good.

Another ubiquitous meat dish is schnitzel (a meat cutlet that's been pounded flat, breaded, and fried). Though traditionally made with veal, pork schnitzel is cheaper and more common.

You'll often see stuck on the beginning and end of menu items a form of the word *Braten* (which can mean "roasted" or "grilled" or "fried")—as in *Bratkartoffeln* (roasted potatoes), *Schweinebraten* (roasted pork), or *Bratwurst* (grilled sausage).

Here are a few other specialties—both regional and nationwide—to look for:

Aal Grün: Boiled eel served with *Spreewaldsauce* (parsley, dill, and cream sauce)

Buletten: Giant pan-fried meatball, sometimes flattened like a hamburger

Dampfnudeln: Steamed bread roll with various toppings (also available sweet)

Eisbein (or **Hachse, Haxe, Schweinshaxe**): Boiled ham hock

Flammkuchen (or **Dünnele**): German version of white pizza, on a thin, yeastless dough; the classic version is topped with bacon and onions

Geschnetzeltes: Strips of veal or chicken braised in a rich sauce and served with noodles

Kassler (or **Kasseler**): Salted, slightly smoked pork

Kohlrouladen: Cabbage rolls stuffed with minced meat

Königsberger Klopse (or *Sossklopse*): Meatball with capers and potatoes in a white sauce (a staple of eastern Germany)

Kümmelbraten: Crispy roast pork with caraway

Labskaus: Mushy mix of salted meat, potatoes, often beets, and
sometimes herring, onions, and sour cream

Leber Berliner Art: Pan-fried veal liver served with sautéed apple
rings and onions

Maultaschen ("mouth pockets"): Ravioli with various fillings, such
as veal, cheese, and spinach

Mett (or *Hackepeter*): Raw, minced pork spread onto a roll

Ratsherrentopf: Stew of roasted meat with potatoes

Rollmops: Pickled herring fillets wrapped around a filling of pickled cucumber or onion. A popular hangover cure.

Rostbrätel: Marinated and grilled pork neck

Rouladen (or *Rinderrouladen*): Strip of beef rolled up with bacon,
onion, and pickles, then braised

Sauerbraten: "Sour"-marinated and roasted cut of beef (sometimes
pork), typically served with red cabbage and potato dumplings

Saure Zipfel: Bratwurst cooked in vinegar and onions

Schäufele: Oven-roasted pork shoulder with gravy

Schlachtplatte (or *Schlachtschüssel*): "Butcher's plate"—usually
blood sausage, *Leberwurst,* and other meat over hot sauerkraut

Schnitzel Holstein: Schnitzel topped with a fried egg, capers, and
anchovies

Schweinebraten (or *Schweinsbraten*): Roasted pork with gravy

Senfeier: Hard-boiled eggs in mustard sauce served with potatoes
(classic eastern German dish)

Spargel: Big, white or green asparagus in season in May and June

Speckpfannkuchen: Large, savory crêpe with bacon

Stolle (or *Butterbrot*): Simple open-faced sandwich with butter and
one topping

Stolzer Heinrich: Grilled sausage in beer sauce (Berlin)

Best of the Wurst

Sausage (wurst) is a fast, tasty staple of the Germanic diet. Most
restaurants offer it (often as the cheapest thing on the menu), but
it's more commonly eaten at takeout fast-food stands (called *Würst-
chenbude*). Options go far beyond the hometown hot dog. Most are
pork-based. Generally, the darker the weenie, the spicier it is.

Sausages can be boiled or grilled. The generic term *Bratwurst*
(or *Rostbratwurst*) simply means "grilled sausage." *Brühwurst* means
boiled. *Kochwurst* describes sausage made of precooked ingredients,
then lightly steamed. While some types of wurst can be found all
over, others are unique to a particular area (as noted here).

When surveying your options at a sidewalk sausage stand or butcher *(Metzgerei)*, these terms may help:

Blutwurst (or *Blunzen*): Made from congealed blood. Variations include *Schwarzwurst, Rotwurst,* and *Beutelwurst.*

Bockwurst: Thick pork-and-veal sausage with a mild, grassy flavor and a toothsome, smoky casing

Bosna: Spicy sausage with onions and sometimes curry (Austrian)

Cervelat: Smoky, mild, chewy sausage that's butterflied at each end before grilling (mostly Swiss)

Currywurst: Grilled pork sausage (usually *Bockwurst*), often chopped into small pieces, with ketchup/curry sauce, served *mit* or *ohne Darm* (with or without skin; with skin tastes smokier)

Frankfurter: A skinny, pink, boiled sausage—the ancestor of our hot dog (also called *Wienerwurst, Wienerwürstchen,* or simply *Wiener*)

Jagdwurst: Baloney-like "hunter's sausage"—smoked pork with garlic and mustard

Käsekrainer: Boiled, with melted cheese inside (Austrian)

Knackwurst (or *Knockwurst*): Short, stubby, garlicky, beef or pork sausage with a casing that "cracks" *(knackt)* when you bite into it

Krakauer: Type of Polish sausage *(kiełbasa)*

Landjäger: Skinny, spicy, air-dried (almost withered and sometimes flattened, not round) salami. *Ahle Wurst* is similar.

Leberkäse: Finely ground corned beef, pork, bacon, and onions that's baked as a loaf (like a bologna sausage). *Leberkäsesemmel* is a pâté sandwich.

Leberwurst: Usually made from pig or calf livers and customarily served as a spread on open-face sandwiches, often with mustard or pickled cucumber

Mettwurst: Made of minced pork that's cured and smoked

Milzwurst: Made of pig spleen *(Milzstückchen)*

Saumagen: "Sow's stomach" stuffed with meat, vegetables, and spices

Teewurst: Air-dried, often smoked pork sausage similar to prosciutto, traditionally spread on bread and eaten at teatime (hence the name). It can also be grilled.

Thüringer: Long, skinny, peppery, and wedged into a much shorter roll. *Thüringer Rotwurst* is a blood-sausage variation.

Weisswurst: Boiled white sausage (peel off the casing before you eat it), served with sweet mustard and a pretzel (traditionally from Munich but served at any Bavarian-themed restaurant). If it's *frisch* (fresh), you're supposed to "eat it before the noon bell tolls."

Zwiebelmettwurst: Spicy, soft sausage made with raw pork and onions; usually spread on bread, it comes *fein* (smooth) or *grob* (chunky)

Accompaniments: Sauces and sides include *Senf* (mustard; ask for *süss*—sweet; or *scharf*—spicy), ketchup, curry-ketchup, or *Currysauce* (a tasty curry-infused ketchup), *Kraut* (sauerkraut), and sometimes horseradish (called *Meerrettich* in the north, *Kren* in the south and Austria).

At sausage stands, wurst usually comes with a roll (*Semmel*—not your typical hot-dog bun). The sausage might be inside the roll, or it may come on a plate with the roll to the side. You might be given the choice of a slice of bread *(Brot)*, a pretzel *(Brezel)*, or in restaurants, potato salad.

Starches

Besides bread *(Brot)* and potatoes (*Kartoffeln*; boiled, fried, or grilled), other typical starches include:

Kartoffelsalat: Potato salad

Knödel: Large dumplings, usually made from potatoes but also from wheat, sourdough, semolina, or even liver; baseball-size dumplings are called *Klöss*

Schupfnudeln: Stubby, diamond-shaped potato noodles

Spaetzle: Little noodles made from egg dough scraped through a wide-holed sieve; often served with melted cheese and fried onions as a standalone meal *(Käsespätzle)*

Salads

Germans make excellent salads; for a meal-sized one, order a *Salatteller*. Besides *grüner Salat* (mostly lettuce), you'll likely come across these options:

Bauernsalat: Greek salad, sometimes with sausage

Bohnensalat: Bean salad

Fleischsalat: Chopped cold cuts mixed with pickles and mayonnaise

Gemischter Salat (or *Bunter Salat*): A mixed salad of lettuce, fresh and (often) pickled veggies, and a tasty dressing

Gurkensalat: Cucumber salad—usually just cukes in vinegar

Nudelsalat: Pasta salad

Ochsenmaulsalat: "Ox mouth salad" with vinegar, onion, and herbs

Oliviersalat: Russian-style salad—potatoes, eggs, vegetables, and mayonnaise

Wurstsalat: Chopped sausage in onion and vinegar

Snacks

Pretzels *(Brezeln)*, either plain or buttered, make for an inexpensive snack. The brown crust comes from dunking them in water boiled with baking soda or lye.

Brotzeit ("bread time") is
the all-purpose word for a light
between-meals snack that's
served cold. *Brotzeit* involves
cold cuts, cheeses, breads, and
other cold snacks, such as salads
and some sausages. Other snack
items include:

Kartoffelkäse: "Potato cheese"
spread made of mashed po-
tatoes, onion, and sour cream (but no cheese)

Krautsalat: "Coleslaw," basically cold sauerkraut

Matjesfilet: Raw herring in yogurt

Obatzda: Pungent Bavarian cheese spread with paprika and onions

Schmalzbrot: Bread smeared with lard

Schnittlauchbrot: Bread with cream cheese and diced chives

Streichwurst: Meat spread; the most popular is *Leberwurst,* made
from liver

Sweets

Make sure to visit a bakery *(Bäckerei)* or pastry shop *(Konditorei)*
to browse the selection of fresh pastries *(Feingebäck)* and cakes
(Kuchen). Pastries can include the familiar *Apfelstrudel* and crois-
sant (sometimes called *Gipfel,* "peak"). Pastries often have a filling; these can include jam *(Marmelade* or *Konfitüre),* apple *(Apfel),*
cherry *(Kirsche),* raisins *(Rosinen),* nut *(Nuss),* almond *(Mandel),*
poppy seeds *(Mohn),* or the sweet cheese curds called *Quark.* Don't
mistake *Mohn* for cinnamon, which resembles *Mohn* but is far less
common in German desserts. Here are some other sweets you
might see:

Amerikaner: A flat, round doughnut with a thick layer of glaze
frosting on top

Berliner Pfannkuchen: A jelly-filled doughnut, known simply as a
"Berliner" elsewhere in Germany (so JFK was really saying, "I
am a jelly doughnut.")

Berliner Luft: An airy dessert made of cream, eggs, and gelatin,
and served with raspberry sauce

Rohrnudel: Roll-like sweet dumpling with raisins

Schnecken: "Snail"-shaped pastry roll with raisins and nuts

Gummi Bears from the German candy company Haribo are
everywhere and taste better here close to the source. Ice-cream
stores abound (often run by Italian immigrants). While you can
always get a cone to go (ask for *eine Kugel,* a scoop—literally "ball"),
many Germans sit down to enjoy their ice cream, ordering fancy
sundaes in big glass bowls.

BEVERAGES
Water, Juice, and Soft Drinks
At restaurants, waiters aren't exactly eager to bring you *Leitungs-wasser* (tap water), preferring that you buy *Mineralwasser* (*mit/ohne Gas*—with/without carbonation). Half-liter mineral-water bottles are available everywhere for about €1. (I refill my water bottle with tap water.)

Popular soft drinks include *Apfelschorle* (half apple juice, half sparkling water) and *Spezi* (cola and orange soda). Menus list drink sizes by the tenth of a liter, or deciliter (dl): 0.2 liters is a small glass, and 0.4 or 0.5 is a larger one. Buy juice at a grocery store in cheap liter boxes, then drink some and store the extra in your water bottle.

At stores, most bottled water and soft drinks require a deposit (*Pfand;* usually €0.15 or €0.25—listed in small print on the shelf's price label), which is refunded if you return the bottle for recycling. You can generally return bottles to any supermarket, provided the bottle is a type they sell. Some supermarkets have vending machine-like bottle-return stations (marked *Leergutrück-gabe* or *Leergutannahme*) that issue a coupon after you insert your bottles (redeem when you pay for your groceries). If you don't want to bother getting your deposit back but do care about recycling, set the bottle on top of or right next to any trash can, whether on the street or in your hotel room. Chances are someone will collect it for the extra cash.

Beer
The average German drinks 40 gallons of beer a year and has a tremendous variety to choose from. *Flaschenbier* is bottled, and *vom Fass* is on tap. A typical bottle size is 33 centiliters (cl; about 12 ounces), and beer from the tap comes in 30 cl or 50 cl pours (10 or 17 ounces). For more on Berlin's beer scene, see page 290.

Broadly speaking, most German beers fall into four main categories:

Helles Bier: Closest to American-style beer, this is the generic name for pale lager. Light-colored (but not "lite" as in low-calorie), a *helles Bier* is similar to a *Pilsner,* but with more malt. *Helles Bier* is usually served either in a straight glass (*Stange,* meaning "rod," which its shape resembles) or a mug. Unfiltered lager (like cask ale) is *Kellerbier* or *Zwickelbier.*

Dunkles Bier: This is a general term for dark beer. Munich-style *dunkles* is sweet and malty, while farther north it's drier and hoppier. Variations include *Schwarzbier* (a "black" lager with a chocolaty flavor), *Rauchbier* (with a "smoky" flavor, from Bamberg), and *Weihnachsbier* (or *Festbier*—a seasonal Christmas beer). *Dunkles Bier,* like *helles Bier,* is typically served in a straight glass or mug.

Weissbier or **Weizenbier:** "White" or "wheat" beer (better known in North America as Hefeweizen) is a yeasty, highly caloric beer. It is poured slowly to build a frothy head in a tall, rounded-top glass and served with a lemon wedge. Unfiltered *Weissbier,* especially common in the south, is cloudy (and usually called *Hefeweizen*). *Kristallweizen* is a clear, filtered, yeast-free wheat beer. *Roggenbier* is darker colored and made with rye.

Pilsner (a.k.a. **Pilsener** or simply **Pils**): This is a barley-based, bottom-fermented, flavorful, hoppy, light-colored beer. Particularly common in the north, a *Pilsner* is usually served in a tall, slender, tapered, and sometimes stemmed glass. If it takes a while for the beer to arrive, it's because they're waiting for the head to die down.

Other Beer Drinks: *Radler* (literally "bicyclist"—designed to be refreshing and not too intoxicating for a biker on a hot day) is half lager and half lemon soda. Wheat beer and lemon soda is *Russ* (or *Russ'n*). Cola-beer mixes are also common: *Diesel* (a.k.a. *Schmutziges* or *Krefelder*) is cola and lager, and *Colaweizen* is cola and wheat beer.

Nährbier ("Near Beer") is just that—low-alcohol lager. The closest thing to our "lite" beer is *leichtes Bier*—a low-calorie, low-alcohol wheat beer.

Nonalcoholic Beer: While virtually all nonalcoholic brews in the US are watery, bitter lagers, Germany produces some excellent alcohol-free white/wheat beers *(Weisses),* which have a somewhat sweeter flavor—very smooth drinking on a hot day. Teetotalers, or anyone who wants a refreshing beer at lunch without being tipsy all afternoon, can look for *"ohne Alkohol"* or *"alkoholfrei."* There's also the drink called *Malztrunk* (or *Malzbier*)—the sweet, malted beverage (resembling dark beer) that children quaff before they start drinking the real thing.

Wine

Though famous for its beer, Germany also has excellent wine. The best-known white wines are from the Rhine and Mosel, and there are some good reds (usually from the south), including *Dornfelder* (velvety, often oaky, sometimes sweet) and *Spätburgunder* (or *Blauburgunder;* German for "pinot noir").

Wein is commonly sold by the deciliter, with prices listed per 1 dl (sometimes written as 0.1 L on menus; 1 dl is about 3.5 ounces). You can order by the glass simply by asking for *ein Glas,* or to clarify that you don't want much, *eine Dezi* (one deciliter). For a mini-pitcher of wine, ask for *ein Viertel* (quarter-liter, about two glasses' worth). For a half-liter pitcher (about four glasses), request *ein Hal-*

ber. For white wine, ask for *Weisswein;* red wine is *Rotwein.* Order your wine *lieblich* (sweet), *halbtrocken* (medium), or *trocken* (dry). Many hotels serve the inexpensive *Sekt,* or German champagne, at breakfast.

Here are some of the white wines you may see:

Eiswein: Ultra-sweet dessert white made from frozen shriveled grapes

Gewürztraminer: Aromatic, intense, and "spicy"

Grauburgunder: German for "pinot gris"—a soft, full-bodied white

Liebfraumilch: Semisweet "beloved maiden's milk" blending Riesling with Silvaner and Müller-Thurgau

Müller-Thurgau: Light and flowery, best when young, smooth, and semisweet

Riesling: Fruity, fragrant, elegant

Silvaner (or *Grüner Silvaner*): Acidic, fruity white from Franconia, comes in jug-shaped bottle

Weinschorle: A spritzer of white wine pepped up with a little sparkling water

Staying Connected

One of the most common questions I hear from travelers is, "How can I stay connected in Europe?" The short answer is: more easily and affordably than you might think.

The simplest solution is to bring your own device— phone, tablet, or laptop—and use it just as you would at home (following the money-saving tips below, such as getting an international plan or connecting to free Wi-Fi whenever possible). Another option is to buy a European SIM card for your US mobile phone. Or you can use European landlines and computers to connect. More details are at RickSteves.com/phoning. For a very practical one-hour talk covering tech issues for travelers, see RickSteves.com/mobile-travel-skills.

USING YOUR PHONE IN EUROPE

Here are some budget tips and options.

Sign up for an international plan. To stay connected at a lower cost, sign up for an international service plan through your carrier. Most providers offer a simple bundle that includes calling, messaging, and data. Your normal plan may already include international coverage (T-Mobile's does).

Before your trip, research your provider's international rates. Activate the plan a day or two before you leave, then remember to cancel it when your trip's over.

Use free Wi-Fi whenever possible. Unless you have an unlimited-data plan, save most online tasks for Wi-Fi. Most ac-

Hurdling the Language Barrier

German—like English, Dutch, Swedish, and Norwegian—is a Germanic language, making it easier on most American ears than Romance languages (such as Italian and French). These tips will help you pronounce German words: The letter *w* is always pronounced as "v" (e.g., the word for "wonderful" is *wunderbar*, pronounced VOON-der-bar). The vowel combinations *ie* and *ei* are pronounced like the name

of the second letter—so *ie* sounds like a long *e* (as in *hier* and *Bier,* the German words for "here" and "beer"), while *ei* sounds like a long *i* (as in *nein* and *Stein,* the German words for "no" and "stone"). The vowel combination *au* is pronounced "ow" (as in *Frau*). The vowel combinations *eu* and *äu* are pronounced "oy" (as in *neu, Deutsch,* and *Bräu,* the words for "new," "German," and "brew"). To pronounce *ö* and *ü,* purse your lips when you say the vowel; the other vowel with an umlaut, *ä,* is pronounced the same as *e* in "men." (In written German, these can be depicted as the vowel followed by an *e*—*oe, ue,* and *ae,* respectively.) The letter Eszett (ß) represents *ss.* Written German capitalizes all nouns.

Though most young or well-educated Germans—especially those in the tourist trade and in big cities—speak at least some English, you'll get more smiles if you learn and use German pleasantries. Study the German survival phrases in the appendix. Give it your best shot. The locals will appreciate your efforts.

For more tips on hurdling the language barrier, consider the *Rick Steves German Phrase Book* (available at RickSteves. com).

commodations in Europe offer free Wi-Fi. Many cafés (including Starbucks and McDonald's) offer hotspots for customers; ask for the password when you buy something. You may also find Wi-Fi at TIs, city squares, major museums, public-transit hubs, airports, and aboard trains and buses.

Minimize the use of your cellular network. The best way to make sure you're not accidentally burning through data is to put your device in "airplane" mode (which also disables phone calls and texts) and connect to Wi-Fi networks as needed. When you need to get online but can't find Wi-Fi, simply turn on your cellular

Tips on Internet Security

Make sure that your device is running the latest versions of its operating system, security software, and apps. Next, ensure that your device and key programs (like email) are password protected. On the road, use only secure, password-protected Wi-Fi. Ask the hotel or café staff for the specific name of their network, and make sure you log on to that exact one.

If you must access your financial info online, use a banking app rather than accessing your account via a browser, and use a cellular connection, not Wi-Fi. Never log on to personal finance sites on a public computer. If you're very concerned, consider subscribing to a VPN (virtual private network).

network (or turn off airplane mode) just long enough for the task at hand.

Even with an international data plan, wait until you're on Wi-Fi to Skype, download apps, stream videos, or do other mega-byte-greedy tasks. Using a navigation app such as Google Maps over a cellular network can require lots of data, so download maps when you're on Wi-Fi, then use the app offline.

Limit automatic updates. By default, your device constantly checks for a data connection and updates app content. Check your device's menu for ways to turn this off, and change your email settings from "auto-retrieve" to "manual" (or from "push" to "fetch").

Use Wi-Fi calling and messaging apps. Skype, WhatsApp, FaceTime, and Google Hangouts are great for making free or low-cost calls or sending texts over Wi-Fi worldwide. Just log on to a Wi-Fi network, then connect with friends or family members who use the same service. If you buy credit in advance, with some services you can call or text anywhere for just pennies.

Buy a European SIM card. If you anticipate making a lot of local calls, need a local phone number, or your provider's international data rates are expensive, consider buying a SIM card in Europe to replace the one in your (unlocked) US phone or tablet. SIM cards are sold at department-store electronics counters, some newsstands, and vending machines (you may need to show your passport). If you need help setting it up, buy one at a mobile-phone shop. There are generally no roaming charges when using a European SIM card in other EU countries, but confirm when you buy.

WITHOUT A MOBILE PHONE

It's less convenient but possible to travel in Europe without a mobile device. You can make calls from your hotel and check email or get online using public computers.

Most **hotels** charge a fee for placing calls—ask for rates be-

How to Dial

Here's how to dial from anywhere in the US or Europe, using the phone number of one of my recommended Berlin hotels as an example (030 443 2990). If dialing internationally, drop the initial 0 from the number.

From a US Mobile Phone
Phone numbers in this book are presented exactly as you would dial them from a US mobile phone. For international access, press and hold the 0 key until you get a + sign, then dial the country code (49 for Germany) and phone number.

► To call the Berlin hotel from any location, dial +49 30 443 2990.

From a US Landline
Replace + with 011 (US/Canada international access code), then dial the country code (49 for Germany) and phone number.

► To call the Berlin hotel from your home landline, dial 011 49 30 443 2990.

From a European Landline
Replace + with 00 (Europe international access code), then dial the country code (49 for Germany, 1 for the US) and phone number.

► To call the Berlin hotel from a French landline, dial 00 49 30 443 2990.
► To call my US office from a German landline, dial 00 1 425 771 8303.

From One German Phone to Another
To place a domestic call (from a German landline or mobile), drop +49 from the phone number (including the initial 0).

► To call the Berlin hotel from Munich, dial 030 443 2990.

More Dialing Tips
Local Numbers: European phone numbers and area codes can vary in length and spacing, even within the same country. Mobile phones use separate prefixes (for instance, in Germany, mobile numbers begin with 015, 016, or 017). When a European phone number begins with 0, drop it when dialing internationally (except when calling Italy).

Toll and Toll-Free Calls: It's generally not possible to dial European toll or toll-free numbers from a US mobile or landline (although you can sometimes get through using Skype). Look for a direct-dial number instead.

Calling the US from a US Mobile Phone, While Abroad: Dial +1, area code, and number.

More Phoning Help: See HowToCallAbroad.com.

PRACTICALITIES

fore you dial. You can use a prepaid international phone card (usually available at newsstands, tobacco shops, and train stations) to call out from your hotel. Dial the toll-free access number, enter the card's PIN code, then dial the number. Even small hotels in Germany tend to have a direct-dial system, so callers can reach you without going through reception. Ask the staff for your room's specific telephone number.

Some hotels have **public computers** in their lobbies for guests to use; otherwise you may find them at public libraries (ask your hotelier or the TI for the nearest location). On a European keyboard, use the "Alt Gr" key to the right of the space bar to insert the extra symbol that appears on some keys. If you can't locate a special character (such as @), simply copy and paste it from a web page.

MAIL

You can mail one package per day to yourself worth up to $200 duty-free from Europe to the US (mark it "personal purchases"). If you're sending a gift to someone, mark it "unsolicited gift." For details, visit www.cbp.gov, select "Travel," and search for "Know Before You Go." The German postal service works fine, but for quick transatlantic delivery (in either direction), consider services such as DHL (www.dhl.com).

Transportation

If your trip will cover more of Germany than just Berlin, you may need to take a long-distance train or bus, rent a car, or fly. I give some specifics on trains, buses, rental cars, and flights here. For more detailed information on transportation throughout Europe, see RickSteves.com/transportation.

TRAINS

German trains—most operated by the **Deutsche Bahn** (DB, www. bahn.com), Germany's national railway—are speedy, comfortable, and nonsmoking. Though German trains are fairly punctual, very tight connections can be a gamble.

Once the obvious choice for long-distance travel within Germany, DB trains now face competition from buses offering ultra-low fares (described later) and green **FlixTrains** (www.flixtrain.com), operated by a private company that started with buses and now offers limited rail service between big cities in (mostly) northern Germany. Flix-Train tickets and schedules are independent from the DB system, and rail passes are not accepted.

If you have a rail pass, you can hop on any DB train without much forethought (though for a small fee, you can reserve a seat on a fast train). Without a rail pass, you can save a lot of money

Germany's Public Transportation

by understanding the difference between fast trains and cheaper "regional" trains. The following sections relate only to DB trains.

Types of Trains

The three levels of DB trains differ in price, speed, and comfort. **ICE** trains (white with red trim and streamlined noses) are the fastest, zipping from city to city in air-conditioned comfort, and costing proportionately more. Midlevel **IC** and **EC** trains are also white with red trim, but look older than the ICEs. **Regional trains** (mostly red and labeled RB, RE, IRE, or S on schedules) are slowest but cost much less. Milk-run S and RB trains stop at every station.

If you have a rail pass, take the fastest train available; rail-pass holders don't pay a supplement for the fast ICE trains. If you're buying point-to-point tickets, taking a slower train can save a lot of money. You also save with day-pass deals valid only on slower trains.

Schedules

Schedules change by season, weekday, and weekend. Verify train times listed in this book at www.bahn.com. This website also includes public transport in cities (buses, trams, and subways). The handy DB Navigator app is also a useful tool for schedules.

At staffed train stations, attendants will print out a step-by-step itinerary for you, free of charge. You can also produce an itinerary yourself by using the trackside machines marked *Fahrkarten* (usually silver, red, and blue). The touch-screen display gives you an English option; choose "Timetable Information," indicate your point of departure and destination, and then hit "Print" for a personalized schedule, including transfers and track numbers.

If you're changing trains en route and have a tight connection, note the numbers of the platforms (*Bahnsteig* or *Gleis*) where you will arrive and depart (listed on itineraries). This will save you precious time hunting for your connecting train.

To reach Germany's train information number, dial +49 180 699 6633 and ask for an English speaker.

Rail Passes

The single-country German Rail Pass can be a great value, often saving money while allowing you to hop on trains at your convenience (since most daytime routes in Germany, including fast ICE trains, do not require seat reservations). Rail passes are an even better deal if you're under 28 (you qualify for a youth pass) or traveling with a companion (you save with the "twin" rate). For only shorter hops, a rail pass probably isn't worth it, especially if you get discounts on point-to-point tickets and day passes (explained later).

Rail Pass or Point-to-Point Tickets?

Will you be better off buying a rail pass or point-to-point tickets? It pays to know your options and choose what's best for your itinerary.

Rail Passes

A German Rail Pass lets you travel by train in Germany for three to fifteen days (consecutively or not) within a one-month period. Discounted "Twin" rates are offered for two people traveling together. Germany is also covered (along with most of Europe) by the classic Eurail Global Pass.

Discounted rates are offered for youths (ages 12-27). Up to two kids (ages 4-11) can travel free with each adult-rate pass (including the German Twin pass, but not with Eurail senior rates for ages 60 and up). All passes offer a choice of first or second class for all ages.

While most rail passes are best purchased outside Europe (through travel agents or Rick Steves' Europe), the German Rail Pass is also sold at main train stations and airports in Germany. For more on rail passes, including current prices, visit RickSteves.com/rail.

Point-to-Point Tickets

If you're taking just a couple of train rides, buying individual point-to-point tickets may save you money over a pass. Use this map to add up approximate pay-as-you-go fares for your itinerary, and compare that to the price of a rail pass. Keep in mind that significant discounts on point-to-point tickets may be available with advance purchase.

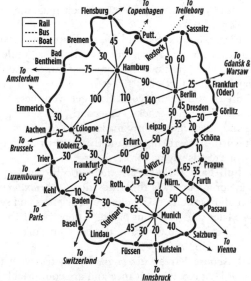

Map shows approximate costs, in US dollars, for one-way, second-class tickets on faster trains.

If you're traveling beyond Germany (and beyond the international bus and train coverage of the German Rail Pass), consider the Eurail Global Pass, covering most of Europe. If you buy separate passes for neighboring countries, note that you'll use a travel day on each when crossing the border.

Your rail pass covers certain extras, including travel on city S-Bahn systems (except in Berlin, where it's only good on S-Bahn lines between major train stations), German buses marked "Deutsche Bahn" or "DB" (run by the train company), and international express buses operated by Deutsche Bahn (covered by either a German Rail Pass or a pass for both countries of travel).

For more detailed advice on figuring out the smartest rail-pass options for your train trip, visit RickSteves.com/rail.

Point-to-Point Tickets

Ticket fares are shown in the "Rail Pass or Point-to-Point Tickets?" sidebar, and for some journeys, at www.bahn.com and via the DB Navigator app (though not for most trains outside of Germany). Deutsche Bahn can charge a wide variety of fares for the same journey, depending on the time of day, how far ahead you purchase the ticket, and other considerations. Know your options to get the best deal.

Kids: Kids ages 6-14 travel free with a parent or grandparent, but the ticket needs to list the number of children (unless purchased from a regional-train ticket machine). Kids under age 6 don't need tickets.

First Class vs. Second Class: First-class tickets usually cost 50 percent more than second-class tickets. While first-class cars are a bit more spacious and quieter than second class, the main advantage of a first-class ticket is the lower chance that the cars will fill up. Riding in second class gets you there at the same time, and with the same scenery. As second-class seating is still comfortable and quiet, most of my readers find the extra cost of first class isn't worth it. Germans tell me they never ride in first class unless someone else is paying for it.

Full-Fare Tickets *(Normalpreis):* The most you'll ever have to pay for a journey is the unrestricted *Normalpreis*. This full-fare ticket allows you to easily change your plans and switch to an earlier or later train, without paying a penalty. (If you buy a *Normalpreis* ticket for a slower train, though, you can't use it on a fast one without paying extra.)

Discount Fares *(Sparpreis):* If you reserve a ticket on a fast train at least a day in advance and are comfortable committing to specific departure times, you can usually save 25-75 percent over the *Normalpreis*. These tickets are more restrictive; you must take the train listed on the ticket (or pay a €19 fee to cancel at least one day ahead). Discounted fares go on sale nine months in advance and remain available until one day before departure, though the cheap seats often sell out earlier.

Savings on Slow Trains: You can always save money on point-to-point tickets if you're willing to skip Germany's high-speed trains (IC, EC, and ICE) and limit yourself to regional trains (most commonly labeled RB, RE, IRE, or S, but also a range of region-specific names). To limit your search to these slower, cheaper trains, select "only local transport" on the Deutsche Bahn website or at ticket machines.

Day Passes

You may save even more with two types of extremely popular day passes valid only on slow trains: the various Länder-Tickets and the Quer-durchs-Land-Ticket. They are most cost-effective for groups of two to five people, but single travelers can benefit from them, too.

With a **Länder-Ticket,** up to five people traveling together get unlimited travel in second class on regional trains for one day at a very cheap price (generally €23-26 for the first person plus €4-8 for each additional person). There are a few restrictions: A Länder-Ticket only covers travel within a certain Land (Germany's version of a US state, such as Brandenburg, where Berlin is), doesn't work for the fastest classes of trains (ICE, IC, EC), and doesn't cover travel on weekdays before 9:00. Still, Länder-Tickets offer big savings, don't require advance purchase, and are also valid on local transit. For example, a Brandenburg-Berlin-Ticket covers five people traveling between Berlin and Wittenberg or Berlin and Potsdam for €33.

The **Quer-durchs-Land-Ticket** works like a Länder-Ticket, but gives you the run of the whole country. It's valid on any regional train anywhere in Germany, but doesn't include city transit (first person-€44, each additional passenger-€8, maximum of 5 travelers, only valid weekdays after 9:00, but on a Saturday or Sunday it starts at midnight).

Buying Tickets

Online: You can buy train tickets online (www.bahn.com) and print them out, or have them sent to your phone as an eticket. If you print out your ticket, the conductor may also ask to see your passport. You can also book seat reservations (optional) with a rail pass for trips within Germany—start to buy a regular ticket, then check the box for "seat only (no ticket)." Another option is to use the DB Navigator app, which lets you buy tickets with your credit card—even for the same day of travel.

At the Station: Major German stations have a handy *Rei-*

sezentrum (travel center) where you can ask questions and buy tickets (with a €2 markup for the personal service). You can also buy tickets from machines, which come in three types.

The silver, red, and blue touch-screen machines (marked with the Deutsche Bahn logo and *Fahrkarten*, which means "tickets") are user-friendly. They sell both short- and long-distance train tickets, and print schedules for free. Touch the flag to switch to English (some rare screens are German-only). You can pay with bills, coins, or credit cards—but US credit cards may not work. There's one exception: Any trip that is entirely within the bounds of a regional transport network is considered local: Tickets can only be bought on the day of travel, and you must pay cash.

Each German city and region also has its own machines that sell only same-day tickets to nearby destinations (usually including Länder-Ticket day passes). In cities, these machines also sell local public transit tickets. At some smaller, unstaffed stations, these machines are the only ticket-buying option. You'll see the logo of the city or regional transport network on the machine. Increasingly, these machines are multilingual, with touch screens, and some even take American cards with a PIN (though others take only cash and German cards).

Some cities and regions still have older, silver ticket machines with smaller screens and plenty of buttons. To buy a train ticket from these machines, press the flag button until it gives you a screen in English. Then look for your destination on the long list of towns on the left side. If your destination isn't on the list (because it's too far away), you can buy the ticket on board (let the conductor know where you boarded so you won't have to pay the small markup for buying a ticket on the train). If your destination *is* on the list, note its four-digit code and enter it on the number pad. The machine defaults to a one-way *(Einfache)* second-class ticket, but you can alter that with the buttons below the keypad (press *Hin- und Rückfahrt* for a round-trip ticket, and *1./2. Klasse* for first class; also note the buttons for Länder-Ticket day passes and children's tickets). Feed the machine cash (small bills are OK, but it won't take credit cards), then collect your ticket and change. *Gut gemacht!* (Well done!)

On the Train: You can buy a ticket on board from the conductor for a long-distance journey by paying a small markup. But if you're riding a local (short distance) train, you're expected to board with a valid ticket...or you can get fined. Note that ticket checkers on local trains aren't necessarily in uniform.

Getting a Seat

As you board or exit a train, you'll usually have to push a button or flip a lever to open the door. Watch locals and imitate.

On the faster ICE, IC, and EC trains, it costs €4 extra per person to reserve a seat, which you can do at a station ticket desk, a touch-screen machine, or online (especially useful with a rail pass or a second-class ticket). If buying a first-class ticket on these trains, you can add a seat assignment for free at the time of purchase. German trains generally offer ample seating, but popular routes do fill up, especially on holiday weekends. If your itinerary is set, and you don't mind the small fee, seat reservations can be worth it for the peace of mind. They're especially smart for small groups and families (€8 reservation cap for families).

On ICE trains, families with small children can book special compartments called *Kleinkindabteil*, which have extra room for strollers and diaper changing, for the regular seat-reservation price.

With rare exceptions, there's no need to go through a US agent to make a seat reservation in advance of your trip; just do it online or at a German station. Reservations may be required on international trains and buses (specified in schedule). Slower regional trains don't even accept them.

If you have a seat reservation, while waiting for your train to arrive, note the departure time and *Wagen* (car) number and look along the train platform for the diagram *(Wagenstandanzeiger)* showing what sector of the platform the car will arrive at (usually A through F). Stand in that sector to avoid a last-minute dash to the right car or a long walk through the train to your seat. This is especially important for ICE trains, which are often divided into two unconnected parts.

If you're traveling without a reservation and are looking for an open seat, check the displays (or, in older trains, the slips of paper) that mark reserved seats. If you have a hard time finding an unreserved seat, take a closer look at the reservations—if you find a seat that's reserved for a leg of the journey that doesn't overlap with yours, you're free to take the seat.

In stations without elevators, you can take advantage of the luggage belts along the stairs to each platform. They start automatically when you put your bag on the bottom or top of the belt.

Bikes on Board

Your bike can travel with you for €5 per day on regional trains or €9 per trip on fast trains. Deutsche Bahn's helpful website even has a list of bike-rental shops that are in or near train stations. Rentals usually run about €10-15 a day, and some rental outfits offer easy "pick up here and drop off there" plans.

PRACTICALITIES

LONG-DISTANCE BUSES

While most American travelers still find the train to be the better option (mainly because rail passes make German train travel affordable and no-hassle), ultra-low-fare long-distance buses are worth considering.

While buses don't offer as extensive a network as trains, they do cover the most popular cities for travelers, often with a direct connection. The primary disadvantage to buses is a lack of travel flexibility: Buses are far less likely than trains to have a seat available for those who show up sans ticket (especially on either end of a weekend). And compared to trains, buses also offer fewer departures per day, though your options probably aren't too shabby on major routes served by multiple operators. Trains also beat buses in travel time and convenience, although often not by much.

Bus tickets are sold on the spot (on board and/or at kiosks at some bus terminals), but because the cheapest fares often sell out, it's best to book online as soon as you're sure of your plans (at a minimum, book a few days ahead to nab the best prices). The main bus operator is FlixBus (www.flixbus.de). Though not as comfortable as trains, their brightly colored buses are surprisingly well outfitted and make for a more pleasant ride than your average Greyhound trip. Most offer free Wi-Fi and on-board snack bars and WCs.

Bus terminals vary; you may find a true depot with ticket kiosks and overhead shelter, or just a stretch of street with a cluster of bus stops. Serious bus stations are labeled across Germany as "ZOB" (for *Zentraler Omnibusbahnhof*—central bus station). While most cities' bus terminals are usually a block or two from the train station, in some bigger cities (such as Munich and Berlin), bus travelers have to go a little farther afield to catch their ride.

TAXIS AND RIDE-BOOKING SERVICES

Most European taxis are reliable and cheap. In many cities, two people can travel short distances by cab for little more than the cost of bus or subway tickets. If you like ride-booking services such as Uber, their apps usually work in Europe just like they do in the US: Request a car on your mobile phone (connected to Wi-Fi or data), and the fare is automatically charged to your credit card. For more about taxis and ride-booking services in Berlin, see the Orientation to Berlin chapter.

FLIGHTS

To compare flights, begin with an online travel search engine: Kayak is the top site for flights to and within Europe, easy-to-use Google Flights has price alerts, and Skyscanner includes many inexpensive flights within Europe. To avoid unpleasant surprises, before you book be sure to read the small print about refunds, changes, and the costs for "extras" such as reserving a seat, checking a bag, or printing a boarding pass.

Flights to Europe: Start looking for international flights about four to six months before your trip, especially for peak-season travel. Depending on your itinerary, it can be efficient and no more expensive to fly into one city and out of another. If your flight requires a connection in Europe, see my hints on navigating Europe's top hub airports at RickSteves.com/hub-airports.

Flights within Europe: Flying between European cities has become surprisingly affordable. Before buying a long-distance train or bus ticket, first check the cost of a flight on one of Europe's airlines, whether a major carrier or a no-frills outfit like EasyJet or Ryanair. Others with strong presence in Germany are Eurowings, Condor, WizzAir, and TUIfly. Be aware that flying with a discount airline can have drawbacks, such as minimal customer service and time-consuming treks to secondary airports.

Flying to the US and Canada: Because security is extra tight for flights to the US, be sure to give yourself plenty of time at the airport (see www.tsa.gov for the latest rules).

Resources from Rick Steves

Begin Your Trip at RickSteves.com

My mobile-friendly **website** is *the* place to explore Europe in preparation for your trip. You'll find thousands of fun articles, videos, and radio interviews; a wealth of money-saving tips for planning your dream trip; travel news dispatches; a video library of travel talks; my travel blog; our latest guidebook updates (RickSteves.com/update); and the free Rick Steves Audio Europe app. You can also follow me on Facebook, Instagram, and Twitter.

Our **Travel Forum** is a well-groomed collection of message boards where our travel-savvy community answers questions and shares their personal travel experiences—and our well-traveled staff chimes in when they can be helpful (RickSteves.com/forums).

Our **online Travel Store** offers bags and accessories that I've designed to help you travel smarter and lighter. These include my popular carry-on bags (which I live out of four months a year), money belts, totes, toiletries kits, adapters, guidebooks, and planning maps (RickSteves.com/shop).

Our website can also help you find the perfect **rail pass** for your itinerary and your budget, with easy, one-stop shopping for rail passes, seat reservations, and point-to-point tickets (RickSteves.com/rail).

Rick Steves' Tours, Guidebooks, TV Shows, and More

Small Group Tours: Want to travel with greater efficiency and less stress? We offer more than 40 itineraries reaching the best destinations in this book...and beyond. Each year over 30,000 travelers join us on about 1,000 Rick Steves bus tours. You'll enjoy great guides and a fun bunch of travel partners (with small groups of 24 to 28 travelers). You'll find European adventures to fit every vacation length. For all the details, and to get our tour catalog, visit RickSteves.com/tours or call us at 425 608 4217.

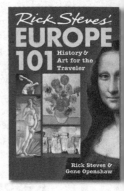

Books: This book is just one of many books in my series on European travel, which includes country and city guidebooks, Snapshots (excerpted chapters from bigger guides), Pocket guides (full-color little books on big cities), "Best Of" guidebooks (condensed, full-color country guides), and my budget-travel skills handbook, *Rick Steves Europe Through the Back Door.* A complete list of my titles—including phrase books, cruising guides, and travelogues on European art, history, and culture—appears near the end of this book.

TV Shows and Travel Talks: My public television series, *Rick Steves' Europe,* covers Europe from top to bottom with over 100 half-hour episodes—and we're working on new shows every year (watch full episodes at my website for free). In particular, two *Rick Steves' Europe* TV shows worth viewing are my *Berlin* episode and my one-hour special on *The Story of Fascism in Europe.* My free online video library, Rick Steves Classroom Europe, offers a searchable database of short video clips on European history, culture, and geography (Classroom.RickSteves.com). And to raise your travel I.Q., check out the video versions of our popular classes (covering most European countries as well as travel skills, packing smart, cruising, tech for travelers, European art, and travel as a political act—RickSteves.com/travel-talks).

Audio Tours on My Free App: I've produced dozens of free, self-guided audio tours of the top sights in Europe. For those tours and other audio content, get my free **Rick Steves Audio Europe app,** an extensive online library organized by destination. For more on my app, see page 22.

Radio: My weekly public radio show, *Travel with Rick Steves,* features interviews with travel experts from around the world. It airs on 400 public radio stations across the US. An archive of programs is available at RickSteves.com/radio.

Podcasts: You can enjoy my travel content via several free podcasts. The podcast version of my radio show brings you a weekly, hour-long travel conversation. My other podcasts include a weekly selection of video clips from my public television show, my audio tours of Europe's top sights, and live recordings of my travel classes (RickSteves.com/watch-read-listen/audio/podcasts).

PRACTICALITIES

APPENDIX

Holidays and Festivals

This list includes selected festivals in Berlin and Wittenberg, plus national holidays observed throughout Germany. Many sights and banks close on national holidays—keep this in mind when planning your itinerary. Before planning a trip around a festival, verify the dates with the festival website, Berlin's tourist office (www. visitberlin.de), or my "Upcoming Holidays and Festivals in Germany" web page (RickSteves.com/europe/germany/festivals).

Jan 1	New Year's Day
Jan 6	Epiphany (Heilige Drei Könige)
Feb	Berlinale (international film festival, www. berlinale.de)
Late Feb-early March	Fasching (March 3-9 in 2021, Feb 24-March 1 in 2022; carnival season—parties, parades leading up to Ash Wednesday)
April	Easter weekend (April 2-5 in 2021, April 15-18 in 2022; Good Friday-Easter Monday)
May 1	May Day (maypole dances, closures)
Late May	Ascension (May 13 in 2021, May 26 in 2022)

May or June	Carnival of Cultures (four-day street festival of international music and dance culminating in a parade through Kreuzberg's Blücherplatz on Pentecost Sunday, www.karneval.berlin)
May or June	Pentecost and Pentecost Monday (May 23-24 in 2021, June 5-6 in 2022)
Mid-June (second weekend)	Luther's Wedding festival, Wittenberg
July	Open Air Festival (six days of music on Gendarmenmarkt, www.classicopenair.de), Berlin
July-Aug	Concert Summer Season Berlin (free outdoor music Sun evenings at the English Garden in Tiergarten, https://konzertsommer.jimdo.com)
Early Aug (first weekend)	International Beer Festival, Berlin
Aug 15	Assumption (Mariä Himmelfahrt)
Sept	International Literature Festival (www.literaturfestival.com), Berlin
Late Sept-mid Oct	Berliner Oktoberfest (www.schaustellerverband-berlin.de)
Oct 3	German Unity Day (Tag der Deutschen Einheit); party along Unter den Linden, Berlin
Mid-Oct	Festival of Lights (landmark buildings artistically lit, www.festival-of-lights.de), Berlin
Oct 31	Reformation Day celebration, Wittenberg
Nov	Jazzfest Berlin (www.berlinerfestspiele.de)
Nov-Dec	Christmas Garden Berlin (light show in Botanical Gardens, http://christmas-garden.de)
Dec 6	St. Nikolaus Day
Dec 24	Christmas Eve (Heiliger Abend), when Germans celebrate Christmas
Dec 25	Christmas
Dec 31	New Year's Eve (Silvester, fireworks)

Books and Films

To learn more about Berlin past and present, check out a few of these books and films.

Nonfiction

A Woman in Berlin: Eight Weeks in the Conquered City (Anonymous, 2006). This translated diary of a young German woman is a frank recounting of the post-surrender occupation of Berlin by Russian forces.

Berlin Diary: The Journal of a Foreign Correspondent (William Shirer, 1941). Stationed in Berlin from 1934 until 1940, CBS radio broadcaster Shirer delivers a vivid and harrowing day-by-day account of the rise of Nazi Germany.

Berlin Now—The City After the Wall (Peter Schneider, 2014). A long-time resident and journalist explores aspects of Berlin since 1989, including the Stasi legacy, the debate about how to preserve sections of the Wall, the city's frenetic club scene, thorny urban planning issues, and the Brandenburg airport debacle.

Berlin—Portrait of a City Through the Centuries (Rory MacLean, 2014). MacLean's colorful look at this pivotal and resilient city focuses on the people (from Frederick the Great to JFK to David Bowie) who were instrumental to its narrative—and its unique soul.

Boys in the Boat (Daniel James Brown, 2013). The true story of the University of Washington men's rowing team that defied the odds to win gold at Hitler's 1936 Berlin Olympics.

Culture Shock! Germany (Richard Lord, 2008). Lord provides cultural insights on German customs and etiquette.

Here I Stand: A Life of Martin Luther (Roland Bainton, 1950). Bainton delivers an authoritative biography of the man who initiated the Reformation.

In the Garden of Beasts (Erik Larson, 2011). Larson captures Berlin during the rise of the Nazis, as seen through the eyes of a reserved US ambassador to Germany and his socialite daughter.

Martin Luther: A Life (Martin E. Marty, 2004). Marty offers a short, vivid biography of the irascible German reformer who transformed Western Christianity.

Stasiland: Stories from Behind the Berlin Wall (Anna Funder, 2002). Funder delivers a powerful account about the secrets of the Stasi and how it affected the citizens of East Germany.

The Spy Who Came in From the Cold (John LeCarre, 1963). This spy novel about a British intelligence operation in Cold War East Germany was later made into a movie.

When in Germany, Do as the Germans Do (Hyde Flippo, 2002). Want to fit in? This lighthearted and helpful guide details the dos and don'ts of being German.

Fiction

Berlin Noir (Philip Kerr, 1993). An ex-policeman-turned-detective struggles with secrets and crime in 1930s and '40s Berlin.

The Berlin Stories: The Last of Mr. Norris and Goodbye to Berlin (Christopher Isherwood, 1945). Composed of two novellas published in the 1930s, these stories capture the freewheeling early '30s Berlin and inspired the Broadway musical/motion picture *Cabaret*.

Winter (Len Deighton, 1987). Deighton's engrossing historical novel traces the lives of a German family from 1899 to 1945. The book also serves as a prequel to Deighton's masterful nine-part Cold War spy series, which kicks off with *Berlin Game* (1983).

Film

The Baader Meinhof Complex (2008). Lightly fictionalized account of terrorism committed by radicalized Germans in 1967, rocking the still-fragile German democracy.

Cabaret (1972). The multiple-Oscar-winning classic musical about 1930s Berlin, when Hitler and anti-Semitism was on the rise, and the only refuge was the cabaret.

The Counterfeiters (2007). This Oscar-winning film tells the story of Sachsenhausen Concentration Camp inmates forced to run a counterfeiting ring to undermine the British pound.

Downfall (2004). Bruno Ganz delivers a frightening performance as Hitler in this story of Der Führer's final days in his Berlin bunker.

Good Bye, Lenin! (2003). In this funny, poignant film, a son struggles to re-create a preunification Berlin for his ailing communist mother.

Hannah Arendt (2012). This biographical drama examines the life of the German-Jewish philosopher who reported on Adolf Eichmann's 1961 Nazi war crimes trial for the *New Yorker*.

The Lives of Others (2006). In this gripping, Oscar-winning drama, a member of East Germany's secret police becomes too close to those whose lives he surveils.

Valkyrie (2008). This historical thriller chronicling the July 20, 1944 attempt to assassinate Hitler includes scenes shot on location in Berlin's Bendlerblock, the nerve center of the failed coup and now a memorial to the resistance effort.

Wings of Desire (1987). Set in the former West Berlin, Wim Wenders' romantic fantasy tells the story of an angel who falls in love with a human. The story concludes in Wenders' 1993 sequel, *Faraway, So Close*.

Conversions and Climate

Numbers and Stumblers

- Europeans write a few of their numbers differently than we do. 1 = 1, 4 = 4, 7 = 7.
- In Europe, dates appear as day/month/year, so Christmas 2022 is 25/12/22.
- Commas are decimal points and decimals are commas. A dollar and a half is 1,50, one thousand is 1.000, and there are 5.280 feet in a mile.
- When counting with fingers, start with your thumb. If you hold up your first finger to request one item, you'll probably get two.
- What Americans call the second floor of a building is the first floor in Europe.
- On escalators and moving sidewalks, Europeans keep the left "lane" open for passing. Keep to the right.

Metric Conversions

A **kilogram** equals 1,000 grams (about 2.2 pounds). One hundred **grams** (a common unit at markets) is about a quarter-pound. One **liter** is about a quart, or almost four to a gallon.

A **kilometer** is six-tenths of a mile. To convert kilometers to miles, cut the kilometers in half and add back 10 percent of the original (120 km: 60 + 12 = 72 miles). One **meter** is 39 inches—just over a yard.

1 foot = 0.3 meter	1 square yard = 0.8 square meter
1 yard = 0.9 meter	1 square mile = 2.6 square kilometers
1 mile = 1.6 kilometers	1 ounce = 28 grams
1 centimeter = 0.4 inch	1 quart = 0.95 liter
1 meter = 39.4 inches	1 kilogram = 2.2 pounds
1 kilometer = 0.62 mile	32°F = 0°C

Clothing Sizes

When shopping for clothing, use these US-to-European comparisons as general guidelines (but note that no conversion is perfect).

Women: For pants and dresses, add 30 in Germany (US 10 = German 40). For blouses and sweaters, add 8 for most of Europe (US 32 = European 40). For shoes, add 30-31 (US 7 = European 37/38).

Men: For shirts, multiply by 2 and add about 8 (US 15 = European 38). For jackets and suits, add 10. For shoes, add 32-34.

Children: Clothing is sized by height—in centimeters (2.5

cm = 1 inch), so a US size 8 roughly equates to 132-140. For shoes up to size 13, add 16-18, and for sizes 1 and up, add 30-32.

Germany's Climate

First line, average daily high; second line, average daily low; third line, average days without rain. For more detailed weather statistics for destinations in this book (as well as the rest of the world), check Wunderground.com.

	J	F	M	A	M	J	J	A	S	O	N	D
Berlin												
	35°	37°	46°	56°	66°	72°	75°	74°	68°	56°	45°	38°
	26°	26°	31°	39°	47°	53°	57°	56°	50°	42°	36°	29°
	14	13	19	17	19	17	17	17	18	17	14	16

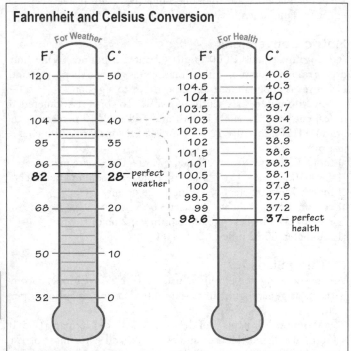

Fahrenheit and Celsius Conversion

Europe takes its temperature using the Celsius scale, while we opt for Fahrenheit. For a rough conversion from Celsius to Fahrenheit, double the number and add 30. For weather, remember that 28°C is 82°F—perfect. For health, 37°C is just right. At a launderette, 30°C is cold, 40°C is warm (usually the default setting), 60°C is hot, and 95°C is boiling. Your air-conditioner should be set at about 20°C.

Packing Checklist

Whether you're traveling for five days or five weeks, you won't need more than this. Pack light to enjoy the sweet freedom of true mobility.

Clothing

- ❏ 5 shirts: long- & short-sleeve
- ❏ 2 pairs pants (or skirts/capris)
- ❏ 1 pair shorts
- ❏ 5 pairs underwear & socks
- ❏ 1 pair walking shoes
- ❏ Sweater or warm layer
- ❏ Rainproof jacket with hood
- ❏ Tie, scarf, belt, and/or hat
- ❏ Swimsuit
- ❏ Sleepwear/loungewear

Money

- ❏ Debit card(s)
- ❏ Credit card(s)
- ❏ Hard cash (US $100-200)
- ❏ Money belt

Documents

- ❏ Passport
- ❏ Tickets & confirmations: flights, hotels, trains, rail pass, car rental, sight entries
- ❏ Driver's license
- ❏ Student ID, hostel card, etc.
- ❏ Photocopies of important documents
- ❏ Insurance details
- ❏ Guidebooks & maps

Toiletries Kit

- ❏ Basics: soap, shampoo, toothbrush, toothpaste, floss, deodorant, sunscreen, brush/comb, etc.
- ❏ Medicines & vitamins
- ❏ First-aid kit
- ❏ Glasses/contacts/sunglasses
- ❏ Sewing kit
- ❏ Packet of tissues (for WC)
- ❏ Earplugs

Electronics

- ❏ Mobile phone
- ❏ Camera & related gear
- ❏ Tablet/ebook reader/laptop
- ❏ Headphones/earbuds
- ❏ Chargers & batteries
- ❏ Phone car charger & mount (or GPS device)
- ❏ Plug adapters

Miscellaneous

- ❏ Daypack
- ❏ Sealable plastic baggies
- ❏ Laundry supplies: soap, laundry bag, clothesline, spot remover
- ❏ Small umbrella
- ❏ Travel alarm/watch
- ❏ Notepad & pen
- ❏ Journal

Optional Extras

- ❏ Second pair of shoes (flip-flops, sandals, tennis shoes, boots)
- ❏ Travel hairdryer
- ❏ Picnic supplies
- ❏ Water bottle
- ❏ Fold-up tote bag
- ❏ Small flashlight
- ❏ Mini binoculars
- ❏ Small towel or washcloth
- ❏ Inflatable pillow/neck rest
- ❏ Tiny lock
- ❏ Address list (to mail postcards)
- ❏ Extra passport photos

German Survival Phrases

In the phonetics, ī sounds like the long i in "light." Bolded syllables are stressed.

English	German	Pronunciation
Good day.	Guten Tag.	**goo**-tehn tahg
Do you speak English?	Sprechen Sie Englisch?	**shprehkh**-ehn zee **ehgn**-lish
Yes. / No.	Ja. / Nein.	yah / nīn
I (don't) understand.	Ich verstehe (nicht).	ikh fehr-**shtay**-heh (nikht)
Please.	Bitte.	**bit**-teh
Thank you.	Danke.	**dahng**-keh
I'm sorry.	Es tut mir leid.	ehs toot meer līt
Excuse me.	Entschuldigung.	ehnt-**shool**-dig-oong
(No) problem.	(Kein) Problem.	(kīn) proh-**blaym**
(Very) good.	(Sehr) gut.	(zehr) goot
Goodbye.	Auf Wiedersehen.	owf **vee**-der-zayn
one / two	eins / zwei	īns / tsvī
three / four	drei / vier	drī / feer
five / six	fünf / sechs	fewnf / zehkhs
seven / eight	sieben / acht	**zee**-behn / ahkht
nine / ten	neun / zehn	noyn / tsayn
How much is it?	Wieviel kostet das?	**vee**-feel **kohs**-teht dahs
Write it?	Schreiben?	**shrī**-behn
Is it free?	Ist es umsonst?	ist ehs oom-**zohnst**
Included?	Inklusive?	in-kloo-**zee**-veh
Where can I buy / find...?	Wo kann ich kaufen / finden...?	voh kahn ikh **kow**-fehn / **fin**-dehn
I'd like / We'd like...	Ich hätte gern / Wir hätten gern...	ikh **heh**-teh gehrn / veer **heh**-tehn gehrn
...a room.	...ein Zimmer.	īn **tsim**-mer
...a ticket to ____.	...eine Fahrkarte nach ____.	**ī**-neh **far**-kar-teh nahkh
Is it possible?	Ist es möglich?	ist ehs **mur**-glikh
Where is...?	Wo ist...?	voh ist
...the train station	...der Bahnhof	dehr **bahn**-hohf
...the bus station	...der Busbahnhof	dehr **boos**-bahn-hohf
...the tourist information office	...das Touristen-informations-büro	dahs too-**ris**-tehn-in-for-maht-see-**ohns**-bew-roh
...the toilet	...die Toilette	dee toh-**leh**-teh
men	Herren	**hehr**-rehn
women	Damen	**dah** mehn
left / right	links / rechts	links / rehkhts
straight	geradeaus	geh-**rah**-deh-**ows**
What time does this open / close?	Um wieviel Uhr wird hier geöffnet / geschlossen?	oom **vee**-feel oor veerd heer geh-**urf**-neht / geh-**shloh**-sehn
At what time?	Um wieviel Uhr?	oom **vee**-feel oor
Just a moment.	Moment.	moh-**mehnt**
now / soon / later	jetzt / bald / später	yehtst / bahld / **shpay**-ter
today / tomorrow	heute / morgen	**hoy**-teh / **mor**-gehn

In a German Restaurant

English	German	Pronunciation
I'd like / We'd like...	Ich hätte gern / Wir hätten gern...	ikh **heh**-teh gehrn / veer **heh**-tehn gehrn
...a reservation for...	...eine Reservierung für...	**ī**-neh reh-zer-**feer**-oong fewr
...a table for one / two.	...einen Tisch für eine Person / zwei Personen.	**ī**-nehn tish fewr **ī**-neh pehr-zohn / tsvī pehr-**zoh**-nehn
Non-smoking.	Nichtraucher.	**nikht**-rowkh-er
Is this seat free?	Ist hier frei?	ist heer frī
Menu (in English), please.	Speisekarte (auf Englisch), bitte.	**shpī**-zeh-kar-teh (owf **ehng**-lish) **bit**-teh
service (not) included	Trinkgeld (nicht) inklusive	**trink**-gehlt (nikht) in-kloo-**zee**-veh
cover charge	Eintritt	**īn**-trit
to go	zum Mitnehmen	tsoom **mit**-nay-mehn
with / without	mit / ohne	mit / **oh**-neh
and / or	und / oder	oont / **oh**-der
menu (of the day)	(Tages-) Karte	(**tah**-gehs-) **kar**-teh
set meal for tourists	Touristenmenü	too-**ris**-tehn-meh-**new**
specialty of the house	Spezialität des Hauses	**shpayt**-see-ah-lee-**tayt** dehs **how**-zehs
appetizers	Vorspeise	**for**-shpī-zeh
bread / cheese	Brot / Käse	broht / **kay**-zeh
sandwich	Sandwich	**zahnd**-vich
soup	Suppe	**zup**-peh
salad	Salat	zah-**laht**
meat	Fleisch	flīsh
poultry	Geflügel	geh-**flew**-gehl
fish	Fisch	fish
seafood	Meeresfrüchte	**meh**-rehs-**frewkh**-teh
fruit	Obst	ohpst
vegetables	Gemüse	geh-**mew**-zeh
dessert	Nachspeise	**nahkh**-shpī-zeh
mineral water	Mineralwasser	min-eh-**rahl**-vah-ser
tap water	Leitungswasser	**lī**-toongs-vah-ser
milk	Milch	milkh
(orange) juice	(Orangen-) Saft	(oh-**rahn**-zhehn-) zahft
coffee / tea	Kaffee / Tee	kah-**fay** / tay
wine	Wein	vīn
red / white	rot / weiss	roht / vīs
glass / bottle	Glas / Flasche	glahs / **flah**-sheh
beer	Bier	beer
Cheers!	Prost!	prohst
More. / Another.	Mehr. / Noch eins.	mehr / nohkh īns
The same.	Das gleiche.	dahs **glīkh**-eh
Bill, please.	Rechnung, bitte.	**rehkh**-noong **bit**-teh
tip	Trinkgeld	**trink**-gehlt
Delicious!	Lecker!	**lehk**-er

For more user-friendly German phrases, check out *Rick Steves German Phrase Book* or *Rick Steves French, Italian & German Phrase Book*.

INDEX

MAP INDEX

Explore Europe

At ricksteves.com you can browse through thousands of articles, videos, photos and radio interviews, plus find a wealth of money-saving travel tips for planning your dream trip. And with our mobile-friendly website, you can easily access all this great travel information anywhere you go.

TV Shows

Preview the places you'll visit by watching entire half-hour episodes of *Rick Steves' Europe* (choose from all 100 shows) on-demand, for free.

ricksteves.com

your travel dreams into affordable reality

Radio Interviews

Enjoy ready access to Rick's vast library of radio interviews covering travel tips and cultural insights that relate specifically to your Europe travel plans.

Travel Forums

Learn, ask, share! Our online community of savvy travelers is a great resource for first-time travelers to Europe, as well as seasoned pros.

Travel News

Subscribe to our free Travel News e-newsletter, and get monthly updates from Rick on what's happening in Europe.

Classroom Europe

Check out our free resource for educators with 400+ short video clips from the *Rick Steves' Europe* TV show.

Audio Europe™

Rick's Free Travel App

Get your FREE **Rick Steves Audio Europe**™ app to enjoy…

- Dozens of self-guided tours of Europe's top museums, sights and historic walks
- Hundreds of tracks filled with cultural insights and sightseeing tips from Rick's radio interviews
- All organized into handy geographic playlists
- For Apple and Android

With Rick whispering in your ear, Europe gets even better.

Find out more at ricksteves.com

Pack Light and Right

Gear up for your next adventure at ricksteves.com

Light Luggage

Pack light and right with Rick Steves' affordable, custom-designed rolling carry-on bags, backpacks, day packs and shoulder bags.

Accessories

From packing cubes to moneybelts and beyond, Rick has personally selected the travel goodies that will help your trip go smoother.

Experience maximum Europe

Save time and energy

This guidebook is your independent-travel toolkit. But for all it delivers, it's still up to you to devote the time and energy it takes to manage the preparation and logistics that are essential for a happy trip. If that's a hassle, there's a solution.

Rick Steves Tours

A Rick Steves tour takes you to Europe's most interesting places with great

great tours, too!

with minimum stress

guides and small groups. We follow Rick's favorite itineraries, ride in comfy buses, stay in family-run hotels, and bring you intimately close to the Europe you've traveled so far to see. Most importantly, we take away the logistical headaches so you can focus on the fun.

Join the fun

This year we'll take thousands of free-spirited travelers—nearly half of them repeat customers—along with us on 50 different itineraries, from Athens to Istanbul. Is a Rick Steves tour the right fit for your travel dreams?

Find out at ricksteves.com, where you can also check seat availability and sign up. Europe is best experienced with happy travel partners. We hope you can join us.

See our itineraries at ricksteves.com

A Guide for Every Trip

BEST OF GUIDES

Full-color guides in an easy-to-scan format. Focused on top sights and experiences in the most popular European destinations

Best of England
Best of Europe
Best of France
Best of Germany
Best of Ireland
Best of Italy
Best of Scotland
Best of Spain

COMPREHENSIVE GUIDES

City, country, and regional guides printed on Bible-thin paper. Packe with detailed coverage for a multi-week trip exploring iconic sights and venturing off the beaten path

Amsterdam & the Netherlands
Barcelona
Belgium: Bruges, Brussels,
   Antwerp & Ghent
Berlin
Budapest
Croatia & Slovenia
Eastern Europe
England
Florence & Tuscany
France
Germany
Great Britain
Greece: Athens & the Peloponnese
Iceland
Ireland
Istanbul
Italy
London
Paris
Portugal
Prague & the Czech Republic
Provence & the French Riviera
Rome
Scandinavia
Scotland
Sicily
Spain
Switzerland
Venice
Vienna, Salzburg & Tirol

HE BEST OF ROME

, Italy's capital, is studded with
n remnants and floodlit-fountain
es. From the Vatican to the Colos-
with crazy traffic in between, Rome
derful, huge, and exhausting. The
, the heat, and the weighty history

of the Eternal City where Caesars walked
can make tourists wilt. Recharge by taking siestas, gelato breaks, and after-dark
walks, strolling from one atmospheric
square to another in the refreshing evening air.

Pantheon—which
dome until the
2,000 years old
over 1,500).

Athens in the Vat-
es the humanistic

diators fought
ther, entertaining

Rick Steves books are available from your favorite bookseller
Many guides are available as ebooks.

POCKET GUIDES
Compact color guides for shorter trips

SNAPSHOT GUIDES
Focused single-destination coverage

CRUISE PORTS GUIDES
Reference for cruise ports of call

Complete your library with...

TRAVEL SKILLS & CULTURE
Study up on travel skills and gain insight on history and culture

PHRASE BOOKS & DICTIONARIES

PLANNING MAPS

Credits

RESEARCHER

For help with this edition, Rick relied on...

Robyn Stencil

Robyn's adventurous spirit sprouted from childhood explorations of the Pacific Northwest and the competitive sports circuit. After studying in Rome, she joined Rick Steves' Europe, where she's become devoted to Europe's friendly locals, lived-in cities, and vibrant cultures. When she's not researching, trapezing, climbing mountains, or running marathons, Robyn calls Everett, Washington, home and works as a tour product manager for Rick Steves' Europe.

ACKNOWLEDGEMENTS

Many Berliners—and others with a passion for Berlin—helped shape this book. *Vielen herzlichen Dank* to Gretchen Strauch, Lee Evans, Holger Zimmer, Carlos Meissner, Torben Brown, Maisie Hitchcock, Caroline Marburger, and Nick Gay for informing and inspiring us over many years of visits. And thank you to Risa Laib for her 25-plus years of dedication to the Rick Steves guidebook series.

PHOTO CREDITS

Front Cover: Aerial view of Berlin © golero, Getty Images

Back Cover: Dreamstime.com (left to right) Berlin street food © Frantic00; Reichstag © Roberto Nencini; outdoor cafe © Radio-kafka

Title Page: Couple at Brandenburg Gate © Dominic Arizona Bonuccelli

Alamy: 242 Peter Forsberg

Dreamstime: 218 (bottom) © Dragan Jovanovic; 231 (top) © Hansenn; 231 (bottom) © Richair; 290 © Diamant24; 319 © Boarding-1now

Public Domain via Wikimedia Commons: 70, 85, 114, 241, 251, 262, 263 (bottom), 355, 376, 379 (top), 382, 386 (top), 388

Additional Photography: Dominic Arizona Bonuccelli, Cameron Hewitt, David C. Hoerlein, Sandra Hundacker, Robyn Stencil, Rick Steves, Gretchen Strauch. Photos are used by permission and are the property of the original copyright owners.

Avalon Travel
Hachette Book Group
1700 Fourth Street
Berkeley, CA 94710

Printed in Canada by Friesens.
Third Edition. First printing January 2021.

ISBN 978-1-64171-302-3

For the latest on Rick's talks, guidebooks, tours, public television series, and public radio show, contact Rick Steves' Europe, 130 Fourth Avenue North, Edmonds, WA 98020, 425 771 8303, RickSteves.com, rick@ricksteves.com.

Rick Steves' Europe
Managing Editor: Jennifer Madison Davis
Assistant Managing Editor: Cathy Lu
Editors: Glenn Eriksen, Suzanne Kotz, Rosie Leutzinger, Jessica Shaw, Carrie Shepherd
Editorial & Production Assistant: Megan Simms
Contributors: Cameron Hewitt, Gene Openshaw
Researcher: Robyn Stencil
Research Assistance: Rich Earl
Graphic Content Director: Sandra Hundacker
Maps & Graphics: David C. Hoerlein, Lauren Mills, Mary Rostad
Digital Asset Coordinator: Orin Dubrow

Avalon Travel
Senior Editor and Series Manager: Madhu Prasher
Associate Managing Editors: Jamie Andrade, Sierra Machado
Indexer: Stephen Callahan
Production: Lisi Baldwin, Rue Flaherty, Jane Musser
Cover Design: Kimberly Glyder Design
Maps & Graphics: Kat Bennett, Mike Morgenfeld

COLOR MAPS

Berlin Overview • Central Berlin
• Berlin Public Transportation

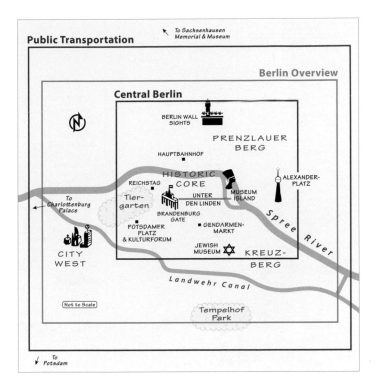

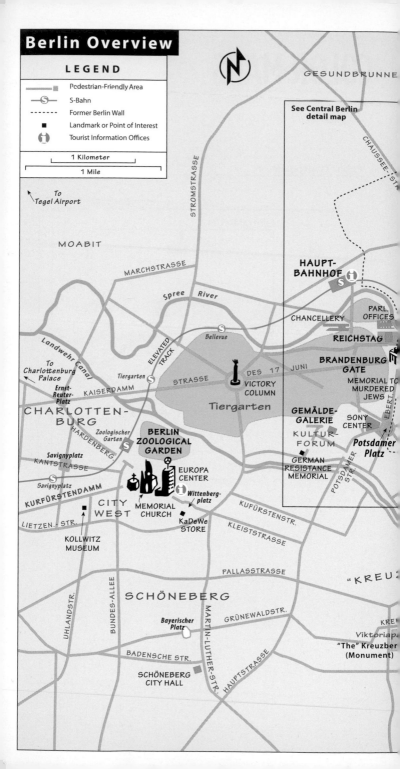

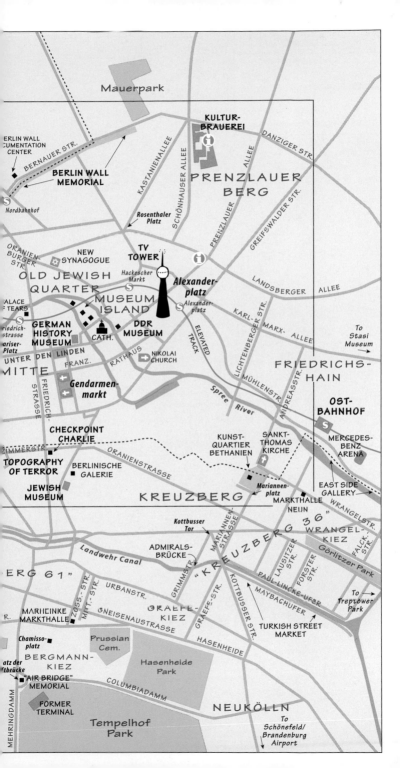

Mauerpark

KULTUR-
BRAUEREI

DANZIGER STR.

BERLIN WALL
~~CUMENTATION~~
CENTER

BERNAUER STR.

KASTANIENALLEE

SCHÖNHAUSER ALLEE

PRENZLAUER
ALLEE

PRENZLAUER
BERG

BERLIN WALL
MEMORIAL

Nordbahnhof

GREIFSWALDER STR.

Rosenthaler
Platz

LANDSBERGER ALLEE

ORANIEN-
BURGER
STR.

NEW
SYNAGOGUE

TV
TOWER

Hackescher
Markt

Alexander-
platz

OLD JEWISH
QUARTER

MUSEUM
ISLAND

Alexander-
platz

~~ALACE~~
~~F TEARS~~

DDR
MUSEUM

KARL- MARX- ALLEE

~~riedrich-~~
~~strasse~~

GERMAN
HISTORY
MUSEUM

CATH.

NIKOLAI
CHURCH

ELEVATED TRACK

LICHTENBERGER STR.

To
Stasi
Museum

~~ariser-~~
Platz

UNTER DEN LINDEN

FRANZ.

RATHAUS

FRIEDRICHS-
HAIN

MITTE

FRIEDRICH- STRASSE

Gendarmen-
markt

Spree

River

MÜHLENSTR.

ANDREASSTR.

OST-
BAHNHOF

CHECKPOINT
CHARLIE

ORANIENSTRASSE

KUNST-
QUARTIER
BETHANIEN

SANKT-
THOMAS
KIRCHE

MERCEDES-
BENZ
ARENA

ZIMMERSTR.

TOPOGRAPHY
OF TERROR

BERLINISCHE
GALERIE

Mariannen-
platz

EAST SIDE
GALLERY

JEWISH
MUSEUM

KREUZBERG

MARKTHALLE
NEUN

WRANGELSTR.

Kottbusser
Tor

MARIANNEN-
STRASSE

"KREUZBERG 36"

WRANGEL-
KIEZ

FALCK-
STR.

Landwehr Canal

ADMIRALS-
BRÜCKE

GRIMMSTR.

LAUSITZER
STR.

FORSTER
STR.

Görlitzer Park

~~ERG 61"~~

ZOSS-
STR.

MITT-
STR.

URBANSTR.

GRAEFE-
STR.

PAUL-LINCKE-UFER

KOTTBUSSER STR.

MAYBACHUFER

To
Treptower
Park

~~R.~~

MARHEINEKE
MARKTHALLE

GNEISENAUSTRASSE

GRAEFE-
KIEZ

TURKISH STREET
MARKET

Chamisso-
platz

BERGMANN-
KIEZ

Prussian
Cem.

HASENHEIDE

~~atz der~~
~~ftbrücke~~

"AIR BRIDGE"
MEMORIAL

Hasenheide
Park

NEUKÖLLN

MEHRINGDAMM

COLUMBIADAMM

FORMER
TERMINAL

Tempelhof
Park

To
Schönefeld/
Brandenburg
Airport

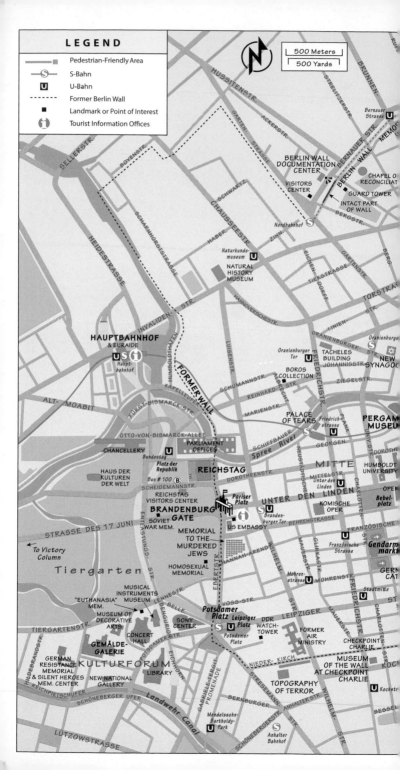

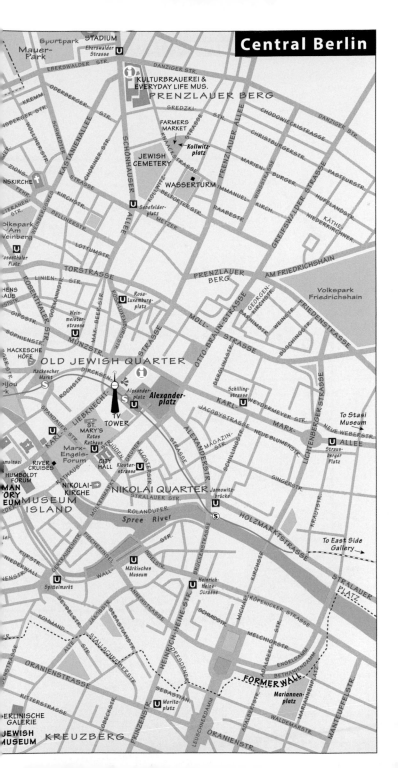

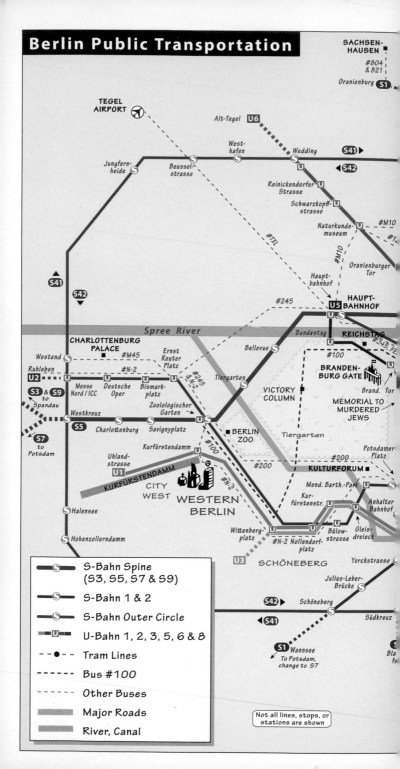

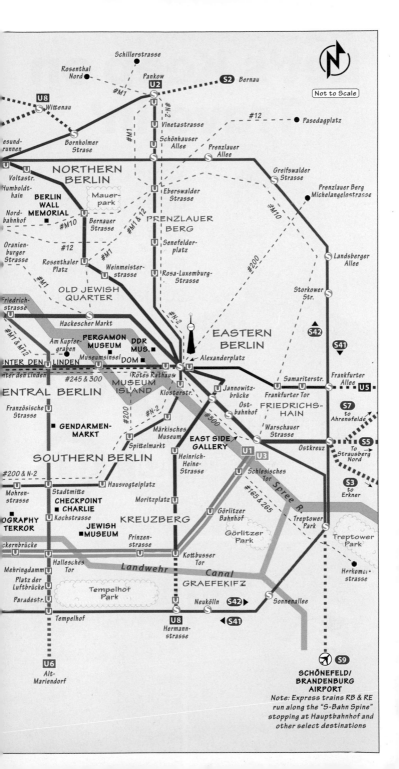

Let's Keep on Travelin'

Your trip doesn't need to end.

Follow Rick on social media!